KNOWLEDGE
& POLITICS

KNOWLEDGE
& POLITICS

Roberto Mangabeira Unger

THE FREE PRESS
A Division of Macmillan Publishing Co., Inc.
NEW YORK

Collier Macmillan Publishers
LONDON

The Free Press
A Division of Macmillan Publishing Co., Inc.
866 Third Avenue, New York, N.Y. 10022

Collier Macmillan Canada, Ltd.

First Free Press Paperback Edition 1976

Library of Congress Catalog Card Number: 74–15369

Printed in the United States of America

printing number

   3 4 5 6 7 8 9 10

Library of Congress Cataloging in Publication Data

Unger, Roberto Mangabeira.
  Knowledge and politics.

  Includes bibliographical references and index.
    1. Liberalism. 2. Knowledge, Theory of.
3. Political science--History. I. Title.
HM276.U53   320.5'1   74-15369
ISBN 0-02-932840-3
ISBN 0-02-932870-5 pbk.

I have written this essay as an act of hope. It points toward a kind of thought and society that does not yet and may never exist. Thus the work is a sketch rather than the finished expression of a doctrine. It cannot pretend to be the statement of a metaphysic or a discussion of concrete political problems. Instead, it seeks to accomplish a lesser though perhaps prior task: to help one understand the context of ideas and sentiments within which philosophy and politics must now be practiced.

CONTENTS

KNOWLEDGE
& POLITICS

INTRODUCTION

Partial and total criticism

In its ideas about itself and about society, as in all its other endeavors, the mind goes from mastery to enslavement. By an irresistible movement, which imitates the attraction death exercises over life, thought again and again uses the instruments of its own freedom to bind itself in chains. But whenever the mind breaks its chains, the liberty it wins is greater than the one it had lost, and the splendor of its triumph surpasses the wretchedness of its earlier subjection. Even its defeats strengthen it. Thus, everything in the history of thought happens as if it were meant to remind us that, though death lasts forever, it is always the same, whereas life, which is fleeting, is always something higher than it was before.

Mastery in thought is the mark of periods in which a novel set of ideas is introduced by men at a loss to solve particular problems in the different fields of knowledge. They have discovered that these problems are connected with one another. Then they find the source of their bafflement in premises that underlie the disciplines within whose boundaries they have been working. At last, they establish a new system of thought that sweeps away the difficulties they faced.

For a brief moment, the newly established theory throws a strong light on the connection among the principles that govern the several branches of knowledge and on the relationship of those principles to more general ideas about mind and society. But the emerging system of thought no sooner becomes a dominant one than it begins to fall into pieces that can no longer be put back together. Its formulation encourages a world of initiatives men would previously have thought impossible. New disciplines are brought into being, and things dismissed before as clear and simple are now treated as riddles that demand solutions. "Only a brief celebration of victory is allowed to truth between the two long periods during which it is condemned as paradoxical and disparaged as trivial."[1]

The new sciences continuously refine and reverse the different parts of the general theory, for its defects and limitations were hidden at the time of its birth. So extensive are the revisions and refinements that what was once a revolutionary event now comes to be seen as a classical tradition. The sciences are then believed to differ from one another in their problems and methods and to have a strictly historical tie to the system of thought out of which they once grew.

In each branch of learning, men have before them only those aspects of the classical system that seem to bear directly on their own concerns. These are the aspects they criticize and transform. They are not troubled by other parts of the system and, after a while, they are no longer aware of them. Nonetheless, if the classical theory is itself a unity, the problems it produces cannot be understood or solved separately. Because they attempt to remake part of the classical system without confirming and attacking it as a whole, the specialized sciences continue to accept tacitly many of the principles of that system while pretending to reject other postulates with which those principles are indissolubly connected. This is the main source of their vices and limitations.

There is thus a close relation between the two characteristics of the age of specialized sciences: the revision of classical ideas and the continuing reliance on them. The sciences are simply partial critiques of the classical theory. It is the partiality of their criticism, rather than the criticism itself, that both separates the sciences from each other and enslaves them to the theory from which they already imagine themselves free.

The completion of each of the partial critiques requires the total criticism of the classical system. Total criticism must begin with an effort to restore that system to light. Only through such a restoration can the fundamental riddles of the specialized sciences of society be solved.

Total criticism arises from the inability of partial critiques of a system of thought to achieve their objectives and from the desire to deal with the difficulties the partial critiques themselves produce. It was in just such a manner that the present work was conceived. Having turned my mind to some familiar matters of jurisprudence, I soon found that these were so closely tied to one another that the answer to any of them would be the answer to all. Then I discovered that the solutions generally offered to each of the problems fall into a small number of types, none adequate by itself, yet none capable of reconciliation with its contenders. Thus, the house of reason in which I was working proved to be a prison-house of paradox whose rooms did not connect and whose passageways led nowhere.

Two considerations began to suggest a way of breaking out of the prison-house. First, it became clear that the problems of legal theory, the immediate subject of my interest, are not only connected with each other, but are also strikingly analogous to the basic issues in many other social disciplines. Second, it seemed that the views that give rise to these problems and the theories used to deal with them are aspects of a single mode of thought. Though taken apart and refined, this style of thought has neither been refuted nor abandoned.

The premises of this vision of the world are few; they are tied together; and they are as powerful in their hold over the mind as they are unacknowledged and forgotten. They took their classic form in the seventeenth century. For reasons that will become clear, I resolved to call them the liberal doctrine, even though the area they include is both broader and narrower than the one occupied by what we now ordinarily take for liberalism. This system of ideas is indeed the guard that watches over the prison-house.

KNOWLEDGE AND POLITICS

Until the present time, few ideas were so widely shared among thinkers of the most diverse persuasions as the belief that the decisive question for political thought is, What can we know? This belief was accompanied by the doctrine that the manner in which we solve the problems of the theory of knowledge in turn depends on the way we answer questions in political thought. The theory of knowledge, according to this conception, is part of an inquiry into the psychological question, Why do we, as individuals, act as we do? It therefore bears on ethics, which asks, What ought we to do? Political theory is defined as the study of how men organize their societies and of how society should be organized. The branches of political theory are the disciplines that examine distinct aspects of society: law, economy, government. If the theory of knowledge is basic to political theory, it must also be crucial to these specialized areas of study. Conversely, if political theory has implications for the problems we confront in the theory of knowledge, those who are puzzled by the nature of knowledge will do well to seek whatever insights they can find among students of law, economy, and government.

Such a view of the relationship between knowledge and politics seems odd to us. The theory of knowledge, as it is now practiced, appears to devote itself to certain technical riddles notable for their remoteness from our concern with the understanding and the transformation of society. To imagine a continuum of accessible truth that bridges the distance from the study of knowledge to the understanding of individual conduct, from the understanding of individual conduct to the science of society, and from the science of society to the exercise of political choice, seems a reverie. On the contrary, it will be said, only confusion could result from the assumption that there is a relationship of reciprocal dependence between specific solutions to problems in the theory of knowledge and in the theory of society. Of these two views, I hold the ancient true and beneficial, and the present false and nefarious.

This claim may be justified in two ways. First, it will be seen that only this assumption allows us to reconstruct the dominant system of ideas I describe as the liberal doctrine. Through this reconstruction and the practice of total criticism, we might hope to cure the vices of the partial critiques of that system, which constitute the greater part of our available sciences of society. Second, much of the argument will be devoted to demonstrating the connections among the different elements of liberal theory. The understanding of the relationship between psychological and political ideas will therefore serve as the key that will allow us to escape from the prison-house, just as it was the chain with which the gates were long ago locked by the builders.

The practice of total criticism includes both a negative and a positive element: the reconstruction and critique of a mode of thought and the anticipation of an alternative doctrine. I turn first to the critical and then to the constructive features of the study. I shall begin by stating the general view that guides my critique of the liberal doctrine; then summarize the basic claims of the critical argument in the form of eleven theses; and finally discuss three kinds of difficulties raised by the critical inquiry.

THE CRITICAL ARGUMENT

The hypothesis from which the discussion starts is that the present state of our psychological and political ideas is similar in one fundamental respect to the situation of European social thought in the mid-seventeenth century. Then as now, partial critiques of a still dominant tradition could not be taken further without being changed into a total critique of that tradition.

Many movements, from the nominalism of Ockham to the political doctrines of Machiavelli and the epistemology of Descartes, had worked to subvert the foundations of classical metaphysics in its scholastic form. But it was in the work of Thomas Hobbes, of his contemporaries, and of his successors that the ancient political and psychological theories of the schools were first criticized as a whole. Only then did it become fully clear that theorists had not yet freed themselves from the medieval Aristotle; that the framework of thought within which they worked suffered from defects and carried consequences of which they were not previously aware; that the ideas about mind and about society which defined this kind of thought formed a single system; and that this body of doctrines turned on certain metaphysical principles. The attempt to come to terms with the implications of these insights produced a new system of ideas, the liberal doctrine, which rivaled and even surpassed in coherence and generality the tradition it displaced. The novel theory, at first the possession of a tiny band of thinkers, increasingly became the common property of broader social groups and the basis of the modern social sciences.

Now as then, a unified set of ideas has been refined and rejected piecemeal. Our approaches to social study are nothing but partial assaults on a mode of thought they have neither repudiated nor understood in its entirety. Again, however, a study of the main difficulties faced by these traditions shows the unbroken tyranny that the classical theory, in this case the liberal doctrine, exercises over the minds of those who believe they have extricated themselves from its clutches.

If this view of our predicament is correct, our initial efforts should be devoted to defining with as much precision as possible the ideas that determine and limit the possibilities of our thinking. Liberalism must be seen all of a piece, not just as a set of doctrines about the disposition of power and wealth, but as a metaphysical conception of the mind and society. Only then can its true nature be understood, and its secret empire overthrown.

The very first step is to reconstruct the design of the whole doctrine, and to understand the relationship of its different parts. Until we draw the map of the system, we shall misunderstand our own ideas by failing to apprehend their premises and implications. Moreover, we shall be condemned to accept incoherent views of whose incoherence we are unaware or to acquiesce in paradoxes we suppose inescapable when they are just the consequences of postulates on which we need not rely. Lastly, one who regards as disparate principles what are in fact different aspects of a single doctrine will be deluded into imagining it possible to dispose of one without rejecting all the others, or to accept one without conforming to the rest.

The claims of the critique may be summarized in the following eleven propositions. First, a large number of the views about knowledge, epistemology, human nature (psychology in the strict sense), and morals (ethics) that we share in our everyday experience and use in our social studies can be accounted for by a much smaller number of principles, premises, or postulates than are commonly thought necessary. I shall deal with these assumptions under the name of liberal psychology. Second, these principles of psychology (or of the theory of knowledge) depend upon one another. If any one of them is false, the others cannot be true, and the truth of any one implies the truth of the others. The sense of the interdependence is analogized to a relation of logical entailment. But the inadequacies of the analogy will be pointed out, as will the requirements of the effort to move beyond it. Third, these principles of psychology lead to an antinomy in our conception of the relation between reason and desire in the moral life, an antinomy that subverts the idea of personality with which moral beings cannot dispense. Liberal psychology justifies two kinds of conceptions of the self and of morals that are inconsistent with one another; cannot be reconciled on the basis of the premises from which they are derived; and are equally untenable. Fourth, the elucidation of our moral beliefs, of many of our political ideas, and especially of those most basic to the liberal doctrine can be reduced to a small number of postulates. Fifth, these postulates require each other in the same sense that the principles of psychology do. Sixth, liberal political theory, as the system of these principles, generates an antinomy in the conception of the relation between public rules and private ends. This antinomy in the liberal doctrine is fatal to its hope of solving the problems of freedom and public order as those problems are defined by the doctrine itself, and it leads to conflicting, irreconcilable, and equally unsatisfactory theories of society. Seventh, the principles of the psychology and of the political doctrine presuppose one another. Properly understood, they constitute a single body of thought. Eighth, this system of ideas is inadequate. It results in basic and insoluble paradoxes; its principles, considered in their interrelationships, are unsound as accounts of experience and as moral standards. Ninth, one can begin to imagine the rudiments of a better alternative to the liberal doctrine, but this alternative should not be mistaken for the liberal view set upside down. Tenth, a particular conception of the relationship between parts and wholes in knowledge and in society plays a central role in liberal thought, and must be revised in any superior theory of mind and politics. Eleventh, to solve the antinomies of liberal thought, replace its view of parts and wholes, and work toward a different system of psychological and political ideas, we must abandon the manner in which our modern schools conceive the relationship of universals to particulars.

THE PROBLEM OF RECOGNITION

Of the difficulties that attend total criticism three are forbidding enough to give all hope of success the appearance of pretense. If the progress of thought beyond its present state were not so closely bound to the ambitions of the moral sentiments to escape the dilemmas of their modern condition, the task would surely be given up at the outset as too stern in its demands and too uncertain in its promise. The first obstacle has to do with our capacity to acknowledge the view I criticize as one that in some sense is still our own. It may therefore be called the problem of recognition.

The liberal doctrine described in these pages was embraced with varying degrees of fidelity by many of the most revered modern philosophers. At the same time, through its impact on the traditions of psychology and social study, it became the dominant and central element in modern thought. This thesis must be qualified in a number of ways.

First, what I shall call liberalism is not tantamount to modernity. Much in modern thought is irreconcilable with liberal principles; the polemic against them dates back to the time of their original formulation. Thus, what the critical argument proposes is less an attack on the tradition of post-Scholastic philosophy as a whole than on a certain side of that tradition.

Second, there is no one thinker who accepts the liberal theory, in the form in which I present it, as a whole, or whose doctrines are completely defined by its tenets. If one looks at the writings of the philosophers most closely identified with the beliefs I examine, one finds a family of ideas rather than a unified system. There appears to be analogy instead of sameness. Hence, it might be objected that the view I discuss is a view nobody has ever held.

Third, the contemporary social sciences have moved further and further away from liberal ideas. Each discipline prides itself on its independence from the metaphysical prejudices of its forerunners.

None of these qualifications, however, refutes either the possibility or the importance of the critical endeavor. Though liberal theory is only an aspect of modern philosophy, it is an aspect distinguished by both the degree of its influence and the insights it conveys into the form of social life with which it was associated. All other tendencies have defined themselves by contrast to it; so it offers the vantage point from which to grasp the entire condition of modern thought.

We should also not be misled by differences among liberal thinkers. A critical account of past or present ideas must always be more than a mere description of what was said or believed. To grasp a way of thinking we have to understand the problems with which it is concerned and the methods it uses to solve them. The problems and the methods become in turn intelligible in the context of an experience of the world. Problems, methods, and experience constitute the "deep structure" of the thought.[2] This "deep structure" allows room for a variety of philosophical positions, depending on which part of the underlying experience is illuminated and which chain of problems pursued. But the number of these positions is limited, and their relationship to each other is determined by their place within the larger system. The search for the "deep structure" means total criticism.

But why should we look for this hidden framework of ideas and by what signs can we identify its existence? It allows us to comprehend an enormous range of philosophical problems and traditions with much greater simplicity than would otherwise be possible. The opportunities for thought available to us within a given vision of the world are laid bare, and their limits, premises, and interconnections become transparent. Hence, the discovery of the "deep structure" dispels confusion by determining the positions we are entitled to take simultaneously and by forbidding us to suppose we possess more than we have in fact acquired. Without that discovery, the critique of the metaphysical framework of our ideas about knowledge and politics would be reduced to an endless game of hide-and-go-seek. In the game the one who hides will change position each time the one who seeks draws near, and the chaser will be trapped in a hall of echoes in which the mocking voice of his quarry will seem to come from everywhere and nowhere.

Thus, disagreements among the liberal thinkers fall into perspective. When a novel mode of thought is established, its consequences and the interdependencies among its parts only gradually leave the shadows that surround the new movement of ideas. Many formulations contend, each governed by the seemingly unique speculative principles of its author. But each of them may be seen in retrospect as a different interpretation of the same underlying experience and as one of the few possible responses to the predicament the experience creates.

The predicament to which liberal thought responds was a central concern of Hobbes, Locke, Hume, and, to a lesser degree, Spinoza, Rousseau, and Kant. My references to them, however, are designed to illustrate rather than to prove their adherence to the doctrines that are the subject of the critique. In this sense, the critical argument remains hypothetical, the reconstruction of a system of thought that their writings partially exemplify rather than a study of the complexities and crosscurrents that mark the development of an intellectual tradition.

Consider now another aspect of the problem of recognition, the relation of the liberal doctrine to the different fields of social study as they exist today. After the mirror of critical argument has been held up, one may fail to see in it the state of our contemporary views of mind and of society. From this discrepancy, the inference might then be drawn that whatever pertinence the critical argument may have to the history of ideas, it is irrelevant to our present situation. Such an inference, however, again reveals a misunderstanding of the relationship between the original system and the era of partial criticism that must now be brought to a close.

Each specialized science of society, working on its own, has so enriched and revised the parts of the classical liberal theory with which it is most immediately connected as to destroy any appearance of continuing dependence on that theory. But because the deviations are partial, they must share the fate of all partial criticism: to remain enslaved by that from which it claims to be free.

Each science refuses to accept the premises of the liberal theory that bear most immediately on its chosen subject matter, while continuing to rely, unavowedly and unknowingly, on principles drawn from other branches of the system of liberalism. Thus, a social doctrine that purports to reject the political principles of the system may still make use of its psychological ideas. Alternatively, a psychological conception that repudiates the teachings of classical liberal philosophy about the mind may nevertheless tacitly embrace its political premises. Some of the political or psychological postulates may be cast out, yet others retained.

In all these cases, interdependent propositions are treated as if they could be accepted and rejected piecemeal. The result is that the specialized disciplines become in varying measures inadequate. Their inadequacy, however, is hidden by the illusion of their autonomy from one another and from commitments to any underlying system of thought. For example, Marx, Durkheim, and Weber attempted, in different ways, to construct a social theory opposed to the descriptive premises of liberal political doctrine. They did not, however, succeed in establishing a psychology that escaped the implications of the liberal distinction of reason and desire, and this failure in psychology runs as a poison through their political ideas. And if individual psychology lacks a satisfactory conception of the self and of the relation between self and others, this is because the psychologists have not dispensed with liberal beliefs about society, even when they have deviated from liberal ideas about reason and desire.

One who accepted the way I deal with the problem of recognition might still wonder why I call the political beliefs discussed here liberal. They are implied by conceptions of freedom and public order commonly identified with liberalism; they are at the root of a number of the more concrete doctrines thought to define the liberal position; and they underlie many of the arguments used to justify what we characterize as the liberal state. The psychology is described as liberal because its principles are interrelated with those of the liberal political doctrine.

According to a familiar view, liberal theory addresses the topic of the relationship between the individual and the state and, at a greater re-move, the problem of the distribution of wealth in society. My concern in this book, however, is with a set of issues that in the internal organiza-tion of the system of thought are more basic, general, and abstract than the problems of power and wealth usually considered the central pre-occupations of liberalism. Moreover, the relationship between the meta-physical system that is the subject of my inquiry and any set of positions on matters of political and economic organization is extraordinarily complex and obscure. It is possible to base a doctrine of limitation of state power upon the psychological and political principles I shall ex-amine. These principles have also been used, however, though perhaps not coherently or correctly, as a basis for radically different conclusions. (Compare Hobbes and J. S. Mill.) For this reason, a mode of thought that appears to diverge as radically from liberal ideas as Marx's social theory from Bentham's may nevertheless share the metaphysical postu-lates of the doctrine it attacks.

One of the insights to emerge from the present study is that the system of metaphysical ideas about the mind and society does indeed have consequences for the determination of the proper place of the individual in social life. The limits on the sorts of political and economic organization liberal doctrine will allow may be altogether broader than has been gen-erally supposed, but those limits exist. Because the limits are ample, we are entitled to criticize doctrines that purport to show the superiority of a particular plan of social and economic organization on the basis of premises that, with equal right, would allow for quite different plans. Because the limits nevertheless exist, we should be wary of views that attack the special political and economic solutions created within the cir-cumference of the liberal metaphysic without ever bringing the meta-physic fully to light, and therefore without ever being in a position to change it. As long as the unawareness of starting points persists, the cri-tique of the system of thought will never break the circle that arrests its progress.

If, despite all the factors which distinguish the set of ideas that are the subject of this essay from what we now ordinarily call liberalism, I persist in using the term liberal, it is not merely for want of a better word. The philosophers who laid the foundations upon which the better known forms of liberal theory were constructed saw those foundations as elements of a speculative account of the place of mind and of society in the world. They understood that this account is prior to more concrete ideas about the state and the individual, ideas in which a weaker vision sees the beginning and the end of political thought.

THE PROBLEM OF LANGUAGE

The problem of recognition refers to the difficulty of identifying the subject matter of total criticism with an intellectual situation one can acknowledge as one's own. The problem of language describes a predicament in the very formulation of the critique. In method as well as in substance, total criticism tries to stand outside the partial critiques and their hidden framework. It places itself in the perspective of a theoretical system that does not yet exist.

To construct we must criticize, but criticism cannot be clear and effective unless it anticipates what is to be built. To break this impasse, one must enter into the methods and conceptions of the classical system and still confer on them, in the course of argument, meanings they previously lacked. In this way, one language slowly becomes another. This strategy bears on the use of concepts in the critical argument, and it determines the method of the analysis.

One of the bases of my criticism of liberal psychology will be a study of its destructive implications for the idea of personality. Criticism of this kind presupposes the ability to define the correct idea of personality. In the light of such a definition, one can advance a different view of the relation between reason and desire and of the character of each.

To judge the contrast of rules and values in liberal political theory and the antinomy to which the contrast leads in our social and legal ideas, we must be able to understand their consequences for the conception of society. But how are we to achieve this understanding unless we are able to imagine an adequate view of the relation between self and others? Thus, the critique of liberal doctrine forces us to foreshadow the ideas of personality and society with which an alternative theory might be devised.

No aspect of the problem of language is more difficult and disturbing than this methodological one. The methods of proof and argument are part of the theory to be criticized. In what form then is total criticism to bring its suit, and by what law are its claims to be judged?

The aim of the critical analysis of liberal thought is to show, first,

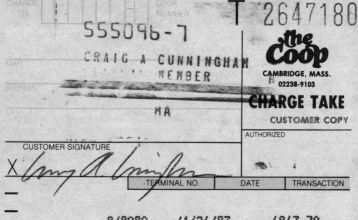

```
        8/8080    /1/26/83        6863 70
33TEXTBOOKS                       12.95
              SUBTOTAL            12.95
              SALES TAX  5%        .00
        5550967/00000000




        5550967/00000000


455        3 COOP CHG TL  12.95
```

COOP NO.	TYPE SALE	AMOUNT

CHARGE TAKE-WITH

that the principles informing liberalism are related to one another and, second, that they produce antinomies that cannot be resolved within the system itself. An antinomy is a contradiction among conclusions derived from the same or from equally plausible premises. It is resolved either by the proof that the contradiction of the conclusions is illusory or by the discovery that the premises are themselves contradictory. Consistent premises cannot be made to yield contradictory conclusions.

Should the antinomies of liberal thought prove to be indeed insoluble, would we not have to abandon the claim that liberal principles are interdependent? If we did, however, it would then no longer be clear in what sense the principles constituted a system, even though, as a contingent matter, they might coexist in certain minds. Thus, the objection to the partial critique of liberalism would be fatally weakened.

The fallacy in this argument lies in the passage from the denial that liberal principles strictly entail one another to the claim that they are altogether unrelated. Is it true that we must choose between a belief that propositions are reciprocally entailed and the view that they are unrelated? The answer to this question suggests a way to deal with the problem of language. Though the relationship among the principles of liberalism is not of a formal logical sort, it is important to begin by speaking in the familiar terms of logical consistency, entailment, and contradiction.

There is no conception more basic to the modern view of the world and to the liberal doctrine which expresses that view than the distinction between the order of ideas and the order of events. Events are linked to one another causally if they are linked at all. Ideas, considered as conceptual entities rather than as psychic events, are connected logically. Entailment and contradiction are the exemplary logical relationships.

The causal and logical schemata have a form, if *a*, then *b*, similar in everything save in this, that in the former the sequence has a temporal sense, whereas in the latter it has none. Thus, causal and logical explanation are both sequential, though only in causality is duration added to sequence, and they both establish relationships of necessity between the terms they join together.

Much of the history of modern philosophy can be understood as a series of attempts to elucidate the relationship between the order of ideas and the order of events. First, the order of events was reduced to that of ideas so that logic provided the key to all explanation (rationalism). Then the order of ideas was reduced to that of events so that causality served as the basis of a unified science of the world (empiricism). But finally an attempt was made to show the mediation and synthesis of the two orders of ideas and of events in the realm of consciousness and culture, and thereby to develop a mode of explanation neither logical nor causal (structural and dialectical theory).

The search for the third mode of explanation is keenest in social study. Simple causality seems inevitably to lead to reductionism in social theory, to the singling out of certain key factors as prior to others or as determinants of them. But circular causality, according to which all the elements of a system cause one another reciprocally, eviscerates sequence, a distinguishing attribute of causal explanation. On the other hand, to take the formal analysis of ideas and the operations of deductive logic as the apparatus of social theory is to fall into that unhistorical rationalism in which Marx detected the mortal vice of political economy.

The ideas of style, type, structure, and dialectic all have in common the intention of providing an alternative to logical analysis and causal explanation. Unlike the terms of a logical or of a causal relationship, elements in the style, the type, the structure, and the dialectical whole, though related, are not related to one another sequentially, for they cannot be laid out in a series. Nevertheless, like causal explanation, each of the schemes is used to describe historical phenomena, events that take place in time. Unlike the terms of the logical and the causal connections, the elements of a structure are not connected with one another by necessity. Their coexistence is ordered, but it is an order best described as one of adequacy, harmony, or appositeness.

The concept of style helps illustrate these points. The distinctive elements of a style in painting do not cause one another, nor are they logically entailed by each other. They cannot be ordered serially, for there is no feature that comes first. Nevertheless, the idea of a style describes a particular historical movement, placed in space and time. The different attributes of the style, as displayed in a work of art, are not necessary conclusions or effects of one another, but they stand in a relationship of appositeness. What precisely is the nature of this harmony, and by what standards do we establish and measure it?

To pose this question, for which no adequate answer has been found, is to recognize that the ideals of style, type, structure, and dialectic constitute only the names of a solution to the fundamental problem of method engendered by the disjunction of the order of ideas and the order of events. They are not the solution itself. If both the problem and the disjunction that produces it are themselves bound up with the fate of the liberal system, it will not be possible to go from the name of the solution to the solution until we have found an alternative to liberalism.

In the light of the preceding discussion, let me return to the issue of method in the argument as part of the problem of the language of total criticism. It cannot in fact be demonstrated that the different premises of the liberal doctrine follow from one another by a strict logical necessity, nor would such a demonstration be consistent with the discovery that these premises lead to contradictory conclusions. But it would be equally misleading to suppose that the liberal principles form no system at all.

There are two ways to deal with this quandary. One is to view the relationship among the principles as stylistic, typical, structural, or dialectical, and thus to embrace that third and yet undefined mode of explanation that stands beyond the boundaries of formal logic and causality. When we proceed in such a manner, however, we easily delude ourselves into thinking we are masters of a method that is in fact still little more than a mystery. In exchange for the meretricious expedients of the dialectic, we sacrifice the chaste and powerful weapons of logical analysis.

The willingness to make this sacrifice wantonly was the occasion of many of the better known partial critiques of liberal thought (e.g., Marxism, structuralism). The dismal consequence for the study of society has been whim masquerading as revolution, for what is it that the dialectic will not show? No wonder social theory stands discredited in the eyes of the friends of reason.

An alternative is to begin by analogizing the relationships among the doctrines of liberalism to logical entailments and the conflicts among them to logical contradictions, with an awareness that the analogy is a crutch to be cast off as soon as we start to walk. The objective is to work toward a situation in which the critique of liberalism will itself forge a method of interpretation more adequate than logical analysis, a result only to be achieved fully through the construction of a nonliberal system of thought. This procedure will require the introduction of certain plausible but contingent empirical assumptions at various points of the exposition and the abandonment of strict demonstration in favor of suggestive argument. These departures from a clearly accepted standard of proof will leave the weaknesses of the critique and its provisional character naked for all to see. Precisely since the relationship among the premises is not strictly logical, it is possible to imagine how the premises might be related and nevertheless lead to contradictory conclusions.

In method, then, as in substance, the only solution to the problem of language is the use of old words in new ways. By treating liberalism as a system of ideas, we prepare the way for a more complete account of it as a mode of consciousness and a type of social organization. By embracing provisionally traditional views of consistency, implication, and contradiction, we achieve some clarity in the definition of liberal thought. The need to deviate from logical analysis compels us to prefigure that other and more complete sort of explanation to which we have aspired, and which must constitute the cornerstone of another theory. If it were possible to summarize the tactic in a single counsel, that would be to imitate in bad faith the great Spinoza, rejecting his logical method as the necessary condition of speculative thought, but using it as a ruse by which to advance beyond our present state.[3]

THE PROBLEM OF HISTORY

The strategy of caution, which consists in dealing with liberalism as a system of ideas and in emulating the methods of logic, pays for its solidity by its narrowness. This mode of argument cannot fail to give the impression that the doctrines examined are an autonomous sphere; that they advance by their own internal dynamic; and that the problems they pose can be resolved by pure theory, just as they were produced by theory alone.

Surely this is an illusion. Suppose that many of the antinomies of liberal thought turned on a principle of subjectivity of values, according to which there are no standards by which an individual may justify some of his preferences except that their satisfaction serves to advance other preferences. It might appear that we could quickly dispose of the contradictions by just replacing the principle of subjectivity with another and perhaps opposite premise, that values are objective. This would mean that there are standards for the justification and criticism of choices other than our own preferences or the combined preferences of different individuals.

The objection to such a solution is that the premise of the subjectivity of value does not derive its force from the decision of a philosopher to accept it in his system. It describes a way men have in fact come to experience their moral life, and this experience will not be reversed by a philosopher's trick.

The belief that a substitution of premises can accomplish the task of total criticism is often associated with the view that theory is the master of history. Those who suffer from this misconception, rarely expressed but often accepted, imagine that if we thought with sufficient clarity and patience, life's problems would surrender their secrets to us. They dream that the progress of theory will resolve the contradictions in the sole sense in which they are capable of resolution, and the drama of history will be played out in the head of the thinker.

This view, however, need not be tolerated once it is understood that the treatment of liberalism as an autonomous order of concepts is only a principle of expository method and a stage toward the more complete and precise comprehension of the liberal doctrine. Each of the theoretical problems will be seen to correspond to a problem in life that only the transformation of experience through politics can truly resolve. It is precisely because the authority of speculative thought is so closely circumscribed that a major part of its efforts must be devoted in every age to the criticism of existing ideas, and that it cannot pretend to construct at one bound as much as it is capable of destroying.

When this is granted, however, total criticism meets with a final and most difficult embarrassment. The source of this difficulty is the attempt to reconcile the premise of the objectivity of truth with the principle of the historical relativity of ideas, an attempt that disinguishes modern social thought and must be reckoned the most remarkable foundation of its greatness. If the principles of the classical system are signs of an established form of social life, must total criticism not be dicounted as a futile exercise? Shall we not be forced to adopt the view that "the owl of Minerva spreads its wings only at the full of dusk,"[4] and that theory must therefore serve as the witness of history, waiting if it is modest, prophesying if it is rash, but denied the power to rebuild?

The answer to these questions is twofold. First, total criticism may anticipate in an abstract form a system it cannot yet make fully concrete. It may define the conditions under which the resolution of contradictions in thought would be capable of being actualized in society. For example, it might determine in what sense and by what general means the principle of subjectivity of values could be replaced, and the experience to which that principle corresponds transformed. Second, through its workings on our self-consciousness, the practice of total criticism itself may work toward the revision of the moral sentiments and the reorientation of politics. Thus, we are able to recognize theory as neither the master, nor the witness, but the accomplice of history.

THE POSITIVE PROGRAM

By its very nature, total criticism must invoke the elements of a system of thought that has not yet been formulated (the problem of language) and that cannot be completed within the sphere of pure theory (the problem of history). To understand and to evaluate the contradictions of liberal thought, it is necessary to measure the consequences of the contrast of reason and desire against an adequate notion of personality and the implications of the contrast of rules and values against a satisfactory conception of society.

Once we possess correct ideas of personality and society, we shall be able to begin the revision of the psychology and of the political theory of liberalism. The germs of these ideas are contained in the criticism of liberal thought.

The discussion of the problem of history has already suggested that it is a misunderstanding of the character of theory to suppose that a direct substitution of the premises can remedy the vices of liberal thought. Thus, for example, we arrive at absurd conclusions if we merely reverse liberal principles by identifying theory and fact, reason and desire, rules and values. We must try instead to define the historical conditions under which men would be entitled by their experience to accept a different view of the relations of reason and desire, rules and values, and therefore different ideas of personality and society. To execute such a plan, however, one needs to understand the experience with which liberal thought is associated and the nature of this association.

The theory of the welfare-corporate state

The first stage of the positive argument has a double aim: to grasp liberalism as a kind of social life rather than just as a system of concepts and to show how the transformation of this kind of life points the way to an alternative doctrine.

The liberal state is characterized by distinctive types of consciousness and of organization. Their connection to one another can only be understood in the light of a method that emerges from the criticism of the liberal doctrine, and is inconsistent with the premises of that doctrine. Theirs is a relationship of appositeness or common meaning, a relationship neither logical nor causal, which is foreign to the contrast of the order of ideas and the order of events.

The dominant consciousness in the liberal state includes a characteristic view of the relation between man as an agent or a thinker and the external world, between man and his fellows, and between man and his work or social place. With respect to the first, it emphasizes the subjection of nature to human will as the ideal of action and the choice of efficient means to given ends as the exemplary procedure of reason. With regard to the second, it underlines the separateness of person, the artificial character of society, and the ties of reciprocal need and hostility among individuals. As to the third, it focuses on the ambivalent value of work as both a manifestation and a surrender of personality.

These three aspects of consciousness express a more general view of the world, the religion of transcendence, which asserts the radical separation of God and man, heaven and earth, soul and body. But transcendence takes a secularized form in the liberal mentality. The consequences of secularization are so far-reaching that they ultimately imply a radical transformation of the dominant consciousness itself.

At this point, I turn to the liberal state as a mode of social organization. My purpose is to define two basic principles of order in liberal society, class and role or merit, and then to show how, though they begin by reinforcing each other, they end in conflict. Superimposed upon the antagonism of class and role, and associated with it, there is a second opposition. It is the struggle between the commitment to impersonal rules as the foundation of social order and the experience of personal dependence and domination, to which that commitment is in part a response, but which it does not manage to abolish.

Together, the two conflicts constitute a source of change in liberal society. Moreover, they make for a social order that corresponds to the dominant liberal consciousness according to the principle of appositeness or common meaning elaborated in the essay. It is part of my method to deny that either order or consciousness may in any sense be thought of as prior one to the other.

The study of liberalism as a form of social life concludes with a discussion of the bureaucracy as the characteristic institution that is the visible face of liberalism's hidden modes of consciousness and order.

The historical inquiry then turns to its second aim, the search for changes in social life that might serve as the basis, or as the inspiration, of a nonliberal doctrine of mind and of society. I distinguish an emerging welfare-corporate state from liberal society and go on to study its distinctive features of consciousness and organization.

The developing consciousness of the welfare-corporate state rejects the manipulative view of action in favor of the conception that things have a worth independent of their conformity to will, and the instrumental conception of knowledge in favor of a rationality of ends. It vindicates the claims of communities of shared purposes against the liberal conception of society as an association of independent and conflicting individuals. And it attacks the previous approach to the relation between the individual and his work either by repudiating the division of labor or by accepting the individual's place in the division of labor as an adequate expression of his personality.

These aspects of the emergent consciousness may be interpreted as specifications of two distinct general views. In one sense, they represent the reassertion of an earlier ideal of immanence, which in its religious form as pantheism affirms the unity of God and the world, and in its secular mode denies the contrast of the ideal and actuality. At the same time, however, this consciousness seems to contain the elements of a possible reconciliation of immanence and transcendence.

My next concern is the social organization of the welfare-corporate state. A distinct type of social order results from the transformation of the class structure through the workings of the principle of role and from the continuing tension between the search for impersonality in the exercise of power and the experience of personal dependence. A central feature of the new mode of social order is the conflict between the playing of roles and participation in communities of shared ends as two principles of order in society. But the emphasis on community, like the reaffirmation of the ideal of immanence to which it corresponds, has a two-faced significance. It may mean either a reversion to closed or hierarchical community life or the beginnings of a mode of association that somehow does justice to the goods of both autonomy and community. After suggesting how socialist societies already present us with a vision of the basic problems and features of the welfare-corporate state, I bring the historical investigation to an end.

Insofar as they foreshadow a possible union of transcendence and immanence in consciousness and of autonomy and community in social organization, the welfare-corporate and the socialist state change the experience of which the liberal doctrine is both a part and a metaphysical representation. Thus, they allow us to move beyond that doctrine. But the historical investigation by itself fails either to define adequately what the new theory might be or to justify the ideals it would vindicate. To accomplish these ends, I pass to another part of the argument.

The theory of the self

The second stage of the positive doctrine is a theory of the self. It aims to define what a union of transcendence and immanence, autonomy and community, would mean; to justify it; and to show in what sense it would resolve the antinomies of liberal thought.

The revision of liberal views about reason and desire, and rules and values, demands adequate ideas of personality and society. Each of these two ideas is the reverse side of the other; both presuppose a conception of what human beings are and should become, an idea and an ideal of the self. Such a conception can elucidate and guide us beyond the form of social life that arises from the transformation of the liberal state.

Through a critical reflection on some of our commonplace moral ideas and on the history of types of social order and consciousness, I go on to outline certain attributes of the self. These attributes are meant to be at once descriptions of human nature as it has developed in history and standards for judging the good. Thus, the critique of the liberal division of facts and values is complemented and completed by the discovery that an understanding of the character of our humanity cuts across the division.

First, I focus on the features of the self that determine its relation to nature. Then I turn to the connection of the self with other individuals. Lastly, I discuss the relationship within personality between the abstract and the concrete self, between man as a universal being, who has the potential many-sidedness of the species, and man as a particular being, who can only make use in his own life of a tiny fraction of the talents of the race.

Implicit in each of these relations is an ideal, which liberalism never succeeded in stamping out and whose force was acknowledged even by many of the liberal philosophers. It is the view that the conscious self should be, and in a sense always is, related to nature, to others, and to its own concrete life and station, yet, in another sense, remains independent from them. The ideal of the relation between self and nature I call natural harmony, that of the relation between self and others sympathy, and that of the relation between the abstract and the concrete self concrete universality. These ideals provide, respectively, a way of dealing with the problems of theory and fact, rules and values, and reason and desire in liberal thought.

The foundation of natural harmony, sympathy, and concrete universality is a more general view of the place of the self in the world. It is the joining together of a mode of union and a mode of separation between self and the world, whether the world appears as nature, as the others, or as one's own determinate life and work. To achieve this ideal is the good. The mode of union between self and world is represented in religion as the ideal of immanence, in politics as community, and in metaphysics as the denial of the independence of the universal and the particular or, more concretely, of the distinctions between reason and desire and rules and values. The mode of separation between self and world is expressed in religion as the ideal of transcendence, in politics as autonomy, and in metaphysics as the contrast of the universal and the particular, exemplified by the dualisms of liberal thought. Consequently, the doctrine of the self serves as the standpoint from which to establish the meaning and the merits of the historical forms of social life at the same time as it develops the conceptions of mind and of society intimated by the attack on liberal theory.

We can understand the nature of the ideal because we have a real though imperfect knowledge of it through personal love, art, and religion. If we view these kinds of experiences without regard to their place in society, they seem to show us the manner in which it is possible for the conflicting modes of the self to be brought into harmony with one another and the antinomies of liberal thought overcome. Nevertheless, they represent the good in a merely abstract way, a way separated from everyday life and set up in opposition to it. Love, the artistic, and the sacred are defined by antithesis to egoism, the prosaic, and the profane. The extraordinary is contrasted with the everyday.

Because the abstract forms of the ideal are available, men are able to confer meaning on individual existence despite the fact that the everyday is surrendered to the division between self and world. But because the abstract manifestations of the ideal do not penetrate into ordinary existence, they are the signs in the individual life of a more complete realization of the good in the history of the species. An actualization of the ideal that broke through the logic of the everyday and the extraordinary would require, if it could be accomplished at all, the reformation of society.

The theory of organic groups

The third and final stage of my positive argument is the theory of organic groups. Its purpose is to define the political implications of the ideal of the self. It accomplishes this aim by showing in what sense and under what circumstances the contemporary state might be changed so that it would allow us to achieve the good more perfectly. Thus, the third stage of the positive argument closes the circle begun by the first. And it identifies the part of life at stake in the criticism of liberal thought and in the transformation of society of which that criticism is a part.

My initial step is to discuss the relationship among the sharing of values, the problem of power, and the nature of the good. I suggest how the resolution of the problems of domination and community in social life may proceed hand in hand. The community in which this resolution is accomplished is called the organic group. Its institutional features derive from the theory of the self, and the context from whose transformation it might emerge are the bureaucracies of the welfare-corporate and socialist states.

Even in its furthest development, the organic group is an incomplete manifestation of the ideal. There are necessary limits to our capacity to achieve in the world natural harmony, sympathy, and concrete universality. Alongside the imperfection of politics, there is an imperfection of understanding. Though our conception of thought becomes practical and evaluative, we can never fully bridge the gap between abstract and concrete knowledge, theory and prudence, science and art. That is why the doctrine of organic groups remains indeterminate. From its principles different conclusions may be derived for settings of choice, and among those conclusions theory by itself is powerless to arbitrate.

At the core of the imperfections of politics and of knowledge lie the very problems of the universal and the particular, transcendence and immanence, the self and the world, that are the different aspects of my central theme. The meaning of the impossibility of resolving these problems within history in a full and final manner is the concluding topic of the essay.

THEORY AND THE MORAL SENTIMENTS

The criticism of liberal thought foreshadows a nonliberal doctrine of mind and society, leads into it, and is elucidated by it. Both the criticism and the doctrine it makes possible have now been outlined. It would be rash, however, to launch into the argument without having understood the reasons why one should undertake it. Awareness of those reasons is the first step in the argument itself.

All theory begins and ends in the clarification of immediate experience. We see this most readily in the sciences of nature, whose hypotheses must ultimately be validated by their ability to explain what can be seen and touched even when they depart most radically from the common sense view of things. The appeal to experience is all the more inescapable in theories of mind and society because the view men have of themselves forms part of the reality for which such theories provide an account. This reflective experience is what I have called consciousness. Its different parts, insofar as they imply conceptions of what we might or should become, have been described as the moral sentiments.

The most basic moral sentiments define the ideal of our place in reality. By virtue of our humanity alone we desire to achieve an adequate formulation in thought and in society of the bond between the self and the world. To this bond, which must always remain the foremost object of our efforts, we give the name of 'meaning of life.'

There is a strange but recurring situation in which men come to see themselves as a field of battle between two warring armies of moral ideas and emotions. One army gives its allegiance to an ideal that current modes of thought reject; another serves the prevailing theoretical and political order, but cannot wholly subjugate the minds it occupies. In these moments, when the choice between despair and illusion seems unavoidable because the intellect cannot yet acknowledge what the moral imagination already demands, it is experience itself that cries out for the instruction of total criticism.

Such is the situation with which the lingering hegemony of the liberal doctrine confronts us. Because liberalism is a ruling consciousness as well as a metaphysical theory, it involves a particular organization of the moral sentiments, which reveals the consequences of failure to satisfy the ideal of the self. If we define the nature of that organization and trace its history, however briefly, we shall understand why and under what conditions the critique of liberalism must be undertaken. This task was begun for us by liberal thinkers themselves and continued by the classic social theorists. They described in many different ways the awareness of a radical separation between the self and nature, between the self and the others, between the self and its own roles and works.

Nature outside man appears as a fund of means capable of satisfying his cravings. It is a brute force that opposes the will and remains alien to its moral intentions.

In its relationship to others, the self experiences the weightlessness that is the reverse side of its fear of all social bonds as threats to individuality. Men begin by not recognizing the common humanity they share with persons far from them. Then even those who are close become foreign to them. Finally, through this unending disruption of community, they become strangers to themselves.

To acquire a coherent self, they must win the recognition of others. They gain it as a recompense for living up to the expectations that define the different roles of civil society. But these roles are external conventions. Though they may give the self the illusion of independent existence, they also deny it any true autonomy.

The struggle for recognition among individuals without selves is the moral counterpart to an experience men have of the relation of mind to world. The measure of knowledge is the capacity to persuade the others of the truth of one's beliefs rather than any direct apprehension of the essence of things. It is through the assent of the others that one is rescued from the opacity of the world, just as their approval is the sole cure of one's weightlessness in society.

Still another aspect of the classic account of the moral sentiments in modern society refers to the division between the person and his own social place, labors, or choices. This is the cleavage between the abstract and the concrete self. In the condition this rift creates, every work is seen as something foreign to the will that made it. Each course of life is identified as a sacrifice of the riches of one's potential humanity to one's need to become a determinate and finite being who suppresses some of his capacities so that others may develop.

Thus, men are torn between the dreams of youth and the meanness of maturity, between the abstract universality of refusing to assume a station and the pure particularity of adopting a social role. The power to infuse a work, pursued single-mindedly, with universal meaning, appears as the prerogative of genius.

These moral sentiments compose the conventional image of liberal man, the man surrounded by a void that separates him from nature, from others, and from his own efforts. Alone, he is nothing; he must secure the approval of his fellows in order to become something. But he cannot become anything without taking a place in the universal pantomime that consumes the entire life of society.[5] In that pantomime each applauds the others as if the clamor of their applause for one another could silence the intimations of their approaching death. Only in the private enjoyments of love, art, and religion does one find respite, for they recall to his mind the image of that wholeness and perfection of being to which he has never ceased secretly to aspire.

The present situation of the moral sentiments can no more be understood in terms of these familiar ideas than can the political condition of the welfare-corporate state be identified with that of its liberal predecessor. Two seemingly opposite paths have lead us to a novel moral predicament. It is within and against this predicament that the critique of liberal thought must be carried out.

The first is the way of disintegration. Its characteristics are the falling apart of different elements of the self, and revulsion against the external world, especially against the social world. Disintegration is the defining experience of the culture of modernism. It is the fate of the dejected, the defeated, and the damned, who have never shared the consciousness of which the liberal doctrine is a philosophical expression.

The second path leads to the sentiment of resignation. Resignation is a despairing submission to a social order whose claims are inwardly despised. It is the governing idea and emotion of the peculiar Stoicism in which the bureaucratic and professional classes of the welfare-corporate state so deeply participate. We should not suppose that these two modes of the moral intelligence, disintegration and resignation, oppose and preclude one another. On the contrary, only when we become aware of their complementarity do we begin to understand their true nature.

First, each of the two sentiments is, in a sense, the truth of the other and brings to the fore what is hidden as a secret in its counterpart. The modern Stoic is not at peace with the order he has accepted and sanctified, and hates the yoke to which he has submitted. On the other hand, all the sound and fury of disintegration ends in the forced peace of resignation, for there is no alternative to living within society as it exists except to transform it, and this the sentiment of disintegration despairs of doing.

Second, the estranged and the resigned share a common view of the relation of thought to life. They both believe that there is a public realm of factual and technical discourse and an intimate world of feeling. Within the cage of private emotion all religion, art, and personal love is arrested, and from it all rational thought is banished. The narrow conception of reason as a faculty addressed to the public rather than to the private life, to means rather than to ends, to facts rather than to values, to form rather than to substance, is necessarily accompanied by the cult of an inward religiosity, aesthetic, and morality that thought cannot touch, nor language describe. The self is split in two, each half finding the other first incomprehensible, then mad. Thus, the subversion of the standards of sanity and madness is a consequence of the progress of these sentiments.

Third, an even larger number of persons come to experience disintegration and resignation at the same time. It is a part of the situation of the bureaucratic and professional classes, upon which the welfare-corporate state depends so much, to undergo both trials at once. In their professional training, they must share the education once reserved for the literati. For that reason, they are subject to the burden of self-awareness which the ideals of high culture, even in their most vulgar forms, impose, and from which the descent into disintegration is easy if not inevitable. Yet the members of this class cannot even pretend to a posture of estrangement. Whether they will or not, they must resign themselves to a position in the state as it is. So the struggle of the sentiments comes to be fought out within individuals as well as among groups.

The ascendancy of resignation and disintegration is a disaster in the history of the moral life, but also an occasion to hope for its revision and progress. It is a disaster because it creates a condition in which the conscious self is neither united with the world nor independent from it. Disintegration is a parody of transcendence, as resignation makes a mockery of immanence.

Parody and mockery though they be, they contain the image of the reconciliation of the two modes of the self, that of separation from the world and that of union with it. Disintegration and resignation undermine everything upon which meaning in individual life depends, for they are both forms of despair. Yet they pose in the simplest and most complete terms the problem of the self, which the liberal doctrine and the liberal state are incapable of resolving.

There is a moving hand behind the critique of liberal thought. It is the desire to escape from the condition of the moral sentiments I have described into that state of simultaneous union and division of self and world in which all resignation becomes immanence and all disintegration transcendence.

That we are capable of experiencing the circumstances of our moral life as being in this way incomplete is a sign to us that, for all its power, the liberal doctrine is not powerful enough to subjugate the full range of our feelings and ideas. On the contrary, it lives in the presence of designs with which it can never make peace. But these opposing tendencies are speechless. The doctrine they reject, and in whose categories we still think, so divides the realms of reason and emotion that what occurs in the second is imagined to have no bearing on the concerns of the first, for a wish is not an understanding. A theory that repudiates the liberal distinction of reason and desire will give back to these emotions their voice, and the critique that is its forerunner will celebrate an alliance with them to make hope a form of knowledge.

Speculative thought is hostile by its very nature to resignation and disintegration. To examine our most simple ideas systematically is to assert the claims of unity against disintegration and of the mind's authority over the world against resignation to the world's dark order. Hence, philosophy is revolutionary even when it appears conservative, and thought is the denial of fate even when it seems to be its defense. No one who has heard a whispered intimation of the power and greatness of theory will ever surrender to despair, nor will he doubt that this sound of thought will one day awaken the stones themselves.

1

LIBERAL PSYCHOLOGY

INTRODUCTION

The aim of this chapter is to study critically some basic aspects
of liberal psychology. As I use it, the concept of psychology
means both more and less than what it now commonly describes. It leaves
out the empirical or scientific study of what determines human conduct,
though not the metaphysical ideas on which much of that study still
relies. On the other hand, psychology includes both ethics and the theory
of knowledge. Ideas about why, as individuals, we act as we do, what we
ought to do, and what we can know are intimately and explicitly connected with one another in the philosophical tradition of liberalism.
They are bound together by the central issue of the relation of the individual mind to personality and to the world as a whole. All go to the
questions, What makes us persons and what follows from the fact that
we are persons? Psychology is the theory of personality.

The chapter begins with a sketch of the conception of nature and
science in the context of which liberal doctrines of mind and of society
developed. This picture of physical nature, and of the place of the
human mind in it, was the one adopted by the seventeenth century

European thinkers who founded the liberal doctrine. Though contemporary advances in the natural sciences have changed, or even wholly transformed, our cosmology, the impact of these changes on ideas about personality and society has remained small. Thus, the traditional view of nature continues to furnish much of the material with which liberal theory is made. The modern idea of nature leads to an antinomy in the understanding of the relation between the mind and the world. This antinomy will turn out to have something in common with the main problems of liberal psychology and political theory.

I then turn to the unreflective view of mind liberal psychology vindicates and refines. In considering that view, I summarize some aspects of a conception of personality which influences our everyday ideas about knowledge and human nature, as well as the social sciences.

The next step of the discussion is to show that this unreflective view can be reduced to three principles or postulates. The three principles are not meant to be exhaustive, and the propositions they advance might be formulated differently. The first is the separation of understanding and desire. The second states that desires are arbitrary. The third holds that knowledge is acquired by the combination of elementary sensations and ideas; rephrased as a metaphor, it states that in the acquisition of knowledge a whole is simply the sum of its parts. The three psychological postulates are linked in a way analogous to logical entailment, with the qualifications mentioned earlier.

The latter part of the chapter discusses how the principles of liberal psychology produce an antinomy in the conception of the link between reason and desire, the fundamental elements of personality in liberal doctrine. The antinomy forces us to choose between two moralities, a morality of reason and a morality of desire. Though both moralities are incapable of sustaining an adequate moral doctrine, neither can be reconciled with the other within the limits imposed by liberal psychology. I examine the nature, and emphasize the significance, of the antinomy of reason and desire by showing how it subverts the idea of personality. The argument concludes with a discussion of the idea of role as an attempt to resolve the paradoxes of liberal psychology.

In this chapter, as in the succeeding ones, my purpose will be to think as simply as I can about the problems I discuss. In our age, philosophy has won some triumphs because a few men have managed to think with unusual simplicity. If only one could think even more simply, it might be possible to move still further ahead.

THE ANTINOMY OF THEORY AND FACT

Imagine the world as a field of space and a continuum of time that are the scene of facts or objects-events. An object exists through time as a succession of events. The world constituted by space, time, and objects-events has the following characteristics. There are an indefinite number of objects-events. Events succeed one another constantly and objects collide with each other in certain ways. The occurrence of a set of events will be followed by the occurrence of another set. The regularities that exist or that we suppose exist among events are different from the events themselves, or from the objects whose temporal aspect those events represent. A causal law of nature is distinct from the phenomena it joins together. Regularities are general; objects-events particular. Objects-events exist independently of our perception of what they are or of what they should be. Either we assume that everything that happens in nature happens necessarily, or we say that we do not know why things happen. The latter conception, however, implies unintelligible chance, which is also a kind of necessity. So, in either case, the field of objects-events is given to us as a necessity. We call this necessity experience.

It is possible to divide the world in an indefinite number of ways. No one way of dividing it describes what the world is really like. That is because things lack intelligible essences. Something has an intelligible essence if it has a feature, capable of being apprehended, by virtue of which it belongs to one category of things rather than to another category. According to such a view, a stone is different from a plant because it has a quality of stoneness, if you like, which we can grasp immediately. Some say that the essence can be understood directly as an abstract category, quite apart from concrete things that exemplify it. Others claim that it can only be inferred or induced from its particular instances. On the latter view, we learn to distinguish the quality of stoneness by looking at particular stones.

Many, though not all, of the metaphysical systems of ancient and medieval Europe accepted the view of knowledge whose keynote is the idea that all things in nature have intelligible essences. Hence they taught that the mind can understand what the world is really like. Now this doctrine is truly a master principle, for its friends have drawn from it conclusions about language, morals, and politics. They have reasoned that because everything has an essence, everything can be classified under the word which names its category. And the supporters of the doctrine of intelligible essences have gone on to hold that the standards of right and wrong must also have essences which thought can comprehend. Plato's ethics and Aquinas' theory of natural law exemplify this line of argument.[1]

The modern conception of nature and of the relation of thought to nature that I am describing rejects the doctrine of intelligible essences. It denies the existence of a chain of essences or essential qualities that we could either infer from particular things in the world or perceive face to face in their abstract forms. And it therefore insists that there are numberless ways in which objects and events in the world might be classified.[2]

We cannot decide in the abstract whether a given classification is justified. The only standard is whether the classification serves the particular purpose we had in mind when we made it. Every language describes the world completely, though in its own way. On the modern view of nature, there is no basis for saying that one language portrays reality more accurately than another, for the only measure of the 'truth' of language is its power to advance the ends of the communities of men who speak it. The theories of science are partial languages because they classify things in the world. Their claims to acceptance must therefore rest on their ability to contribute to particular ends, like the prediction or control of events, rather than on their fidelity to a true world of essences.[3]

This simple idea, the denial of intelligible essences, leaves no stone of the preliberal metaphysic standing. Its consequences for our moral and political views are as far-reaching as they are paradoxical. And among its implications is a riddle about how theories relate to facts. However familiar the puzzle may be, its meaning will continue to elude us until we are able to understand its place in the system of liberal thought.

According to the view of science and of nature I have sketched, facts can be perceived solely through the categories with which the mind orders experience. We are accustomed to think of this as a principle of Kant's philosophy,[4] but it follows directly from the beliefs outlined in the preceding section.

If there are no intelligible essences, there is no predetermined classification of the world. We can distinguish among objects-events only by reference to a standard of distinction implicit in a theory. It is the theory that determines what is to count as a fact and how facts are to be distinguished from one another. In other words, a fact becomes what it is for us because of the way we categorize it. How we classify it depends on the categories available to us in the language we speak, or in the theory we use, and on our ability to replenish the fund of categories at our disposal. In whatever way we view the play of tradition and conscious purpose in the manipulation of the categories, there is no direct appeal to reality, for reality is put together by the mind.

Yet we also believe that the history of science is progressive and that ultimately one can make a rational choice among conflicting theories about the world. Some theories describe the world more accurately than others. This belief is just as firmly grounded in the traditional conception of nature as the principle that insists we can never step outside the categories of a particular language or theory to see the world naked. Its basis is the proposition that things are what they are no matter what we think they are or ought to be. How can we sustain confidence in the possibility of an ultimate comparison of theory and fact unless we are willing to qualify the principle that the world of facts is constructed by the mind according to its purposes? The conception that there is a realm of things, independent of the mind, and capable at some point of being perceived as it truly is, seems necessary to the notion of science. Yet this conception also appears to rely on the doctrine of intelligible essences or of plain facts, assumed to be inconsistent with the modern idea of science.[5]

In its simplest form, the antinomy of theory and fact is the conflict of the two preceding ideas: the mediation of all facts through theory and the possibility of an independent comparison of theory with fact. Each of the principles seems plausible in its formulation and absurd in its consequences. They contradict one another, but to qualify either of them would seem to require a drastic revision of the view of nature and thought from which both are drawn. Here is a conundrum that appears to imply the incoherence of our idea of science, indeed of knowledge in general.

Why then are we not struck by the incoherence? Why are we not more frequently disturbed by the antinomy of theory and fact? Perhaps the reason for our misguided assurance is that the theories with which we work are always partial theories. They are not, like languages, descriptions of the whole world. Consequently, it always seems possible to stand apart from the particular theory we are considering. We forget that when we do this we are stepping into another theory rather than into the realm of plain facts.

Or again, when faced with a choice between two radically different theoretical systems—for example, Newtonian and quantum mechanics—we hold on to standards of justification like the power of the competing theories to predict events or to control them. Such standards seem to be above the war of hypotheses. But that too is an illusion. We must still interpret the results of whatever experiments we perform and justify the methods of proof we have chosen. If there are no intelligible essences, the facts of the test experiment may mean different things in different theoretical languages. And the methods of proof will have to be defended by their relation to purposes we have, whether they be our interests in power over nature, in simplicity of explanation, or in the corroboration of religious belief. Assume for the moment that in the moral doctrine that develops the implications of the denial of intelligible essences such interests are taken to be arbitrary, and you will see that the antinomy of theory and fact remains unsolved. The apparent solutions simply carry the riddle to a higher level of abstraction. The more general the theory, the clearer the inadequacy of the solution becomes.

It was Kant's great merit to propose an entirely different solution, one that rejects the terms of the problem. It tries to cut the Gordion knot by imagining that there are certain universal categories of the mind, besides the categories distinctive to particular theories and languages. Thus, though we can never see facts naked, we can see them through the lens of a universal language, the categories of understanding. This universality is the only kind of objectivity open to us. It serves both as the surrogate for the doctrine of intelligible essences and as the seat from which an impartial judgment can be passed on the claims of conflicting theories and methods.[6]

Kant's alleged solution to the antinomy of theory and fact is analogous to and connected with a major attempt to solve the antinomies of liberal psychology and political theory, which I shall call structuralism. A criticism of Kant's proposal will therefore be postponed to the time when I take up the structuralist doctrine. What I want to emphasize for the moment is the light the Kantian doctrine throws, even if the doctrine should prove false, on the meaning of the antinomy of theory and fact and on the whole modern conception of mind and nature.

In the natural sciences knowledge progresses by becoming steadily more abstract, general, and formal. The substance of things, the rich and particular appearance with which they strike us, is relegated to art and common sense. Scientific knowledge achieves perfection only at the cost of partiality. Though empirical science may be able to explain better and better why we have the particular impressions of the world that we do, and to explain this precisely because science has become more formal, it can never fully describe what the senses see. It cannot replace their kind of knowledge. On the contrary, science must constantly go from substance to form, and from the particular to the universal.

Even as it looks for ever more simple and unified explanations, science moves forward by accepting a plurality of theories at different levels of abstraction. Thus, at any given moment, what one science considers significant in a phenomenon may be dismissed by another as accidental and thereby removed to the level of irrelevant substance. Physics may have little to say about the anatomy of horses, but even zoology will be incapable of accounting for everything that is peculiar to an individual horse. The ineffability of the individual is the necessary consequence of the modern view of science. To attribute the limitation simply to a stage in the development of scientific knowledge is to misunderstand the way science develops.[7]

The genius of Kant's answer to the question of theory and fact lies in its acknowledgment of the separation of the universal and the particular as the fate of modern thought. The Kantian categories of the understanding are universal because they are formal, that is to say empty.

The true source of the antinomy of theory and fact is the radical separation of form and substance, of the universal and the particular, for that separation is the basis of the difference between general ideas or theories, which are formal and universal, and the understanding or intuition of individual events, which is substantive and particular. Only when this distinction has been established does the problem of theory and fact arise.

A different conception of the relation of the universal and the particular would not produce the antinomy of theory and fact. Take, for example, our understanding of geometrical truths. As Euclidean geometers, we know both perfectly and completely because the subject matter of our thought is pure form without substance and pure universality without particularity. Each particular example of a circle is fully defined by the geometrical idea of a circle. Nothing can be known about any particular circle, except the dimension of its radius, that is not part of the knowledge of the theorem of its construction.[8] Such a geometry knows nothing of the issue of classification of particulars under general categories, and therefore it need never face the antinomy of theory and fact.

The view that it is necessary to attain universality through abstraction from particularity rather than through the direct elucidation of the particular, as we do in art, is the core of the antinomy of theory and fact. It will also be a touchstone for the understanding .of the contradictions of liberal thought.

The antinomy of theory and fact can be rephrased and summarized in a more familiar way. Thinking and language depend on the use of categories. We must classify to think and to speak. But we have no assurance that anything in the world corresponds to the categories we use. Our ideas about science and nature seem to imply we believe both that our classifications can be true or false and that the question of their truth or falsehood is unanswerable or illusory.

THE UNREFLECTIVE VIEW OF MIND

Of what does knowledge consist? How do we acquire it? These are among the first questions psychology addresses. One way to begin dealing with them is to determine what knowledge is *not.* Will or desire is an activity of our conscious life that we ordinarily distinguish from understanding. The most elementary aspect of our everyday psychology is therefore the distinction between the mind that understands or knows and the will that desires. (I shall use the terms mind, understanding and knowledge, or will and desire, interchangeably.) Understanding and desire are distinct though not wholly independent. Together, they constitute the self.

The mind is comparable to a machine. That it understands objects-events (facts) means the following. First, it can join together objective characteristics of facts with characteristics facts appear to have because of the structure of the mind. When these two sorts of attributes are summed up, facts become sensations. Sensations are the basis of all knowledge about the world of objects-events. Second, the mind machine can combine and recombine facts (or rather sensations) in an indefinite number of ways. It can see different objects-events as if they were a single fact, or it can split them up until perhaps it reaches the indivisible. Third, all sensations that are combined can be analyzed back again into the elementary sensations with which they were made and into the facts to which the elementary sensations correspond. Fourth, sensations do not change by being combined with other sensations. Combination and analysis, the two operations of the mind, produce nothing new in the world of facts, a world oblivious to the workings of the intellect. Fifth, there is a kind of knowledge, which mathematics and logic exemplify, whose subject matter is not the combination or analysis of sensations. It consists of the understanding of relationships among entities that exist outside the world of facts. Such entities are called ideas. (The same name, however, is also given to combinations of sensations by the mind machine.)[9]

The mind is in a peculiar predicament. It knows things as they appear to it through sensation rather than as they really are. Perfect certainty, therefore, can only be achieved in the study of those things we may know without sensation, like the truths of logic and mathematics. The understanding of the natural world advances toward the sole certain knowledge it can hope for when it analogizes relationships among facts to relationships among ideas. Because mathematical physics carries furthest the analogy of the order of events to the order of ideas, it is the most accomplished of the sciences.

One might take this description as a crude image of the view of knowledge developed by Hobbes and Locke, and now familiar to us. It could stand as well for Kant's theory of knowledge if it were revised as follows. First, there is no distinction between the transformation of facts into sensations and the processes of analysis and combination. The content of sensations is determined by the same operations of analysis and combination that allow the mind machine to reconstruct complex sequences of events in the field. Second, there are a limited number of possible forms of analysis and combination. They have peculiar characteristics, which we can attribute to the apparatus of the mind.[10]

The description of this conception of knowledge, however, is incomplete until we understand what impels the mind machine to its operations of analysis and combination. Or, to rephrase the question, What is the relation between understanding and desire? The answer is concisely given by Hobbes and repeated in a thousand different ways by all the disciplines that sprung from the new science he helped create: "For the Thoughts are to the Desires, as Scouts, and Spies, to range abroad, and find the way to the things desired: All Stedinesse of the mind's motion, and all quickness of the same, proceeding from thence."[11] The mind is moved by desire, the active element of the self.

To pursue the metaphor of the mind as a machine, suppose desire is its mover. Desire is both blind and hungry. It needs the help of the machine to execute its designs, to teach it the most effective means by which to reach its goals. By using his machine, with its two-staged operation, the mover can see facts in the world and grasp which sets of events will produce which other sets. The knowledge gained allows the mover to defend himself from the events or objects that threaten him, and to turn benign occurrences to his own advantage.

The simplest and most common explanation of what leads desire to prefer one course of action to another is that it seeks pleasure and avoids pain. Desire is subject to the same forces that act upon facts in the field. The relation of the mind to desire is one of subjection. When understanding focuses on desire and tries to comprehend the causes that lead desire to seek one end rather than another, it does so under the impulse of desire itself. Thus, whatever its own causal background, desire determines the uses to which intellect is put.

THE PRINCIPLE OF REASON AND DESIRE

By calling the preceding sketch the unreflective view of mind, I meant to underline its commonplace character. It is the stuff of many of our everyday beliefs. In a more elaborate, though not fundamentally changed form, it would describe the premises on which much of our contemporary philosophy and social science is built. This conception of mind is not the only possible one. Men have held very different beliefs in the past. The unreflective view is in fact just a vulgarized version of the philosophical doctrine I call liberal psychology.

Hence, the next step in the argument should come as no surprise. The unreflective view of mind can be reduced to three postulates, which will count as the principles of liberal psychology. They are implicit in the outline of the unreflective view. But they might also be inferred independently from the theoretical systems of the classic liberal thinkers or from the hypotheses of the modern social sciences. These three principles imply one another. In judging the sense of their reciprocal implication, bear in mind the argument of the Introduction.

Because it is one of my aims to show that all the principles of liberal psychology are connected with the postulates of political theory, the psychological principles are stated in a way as free from obvious political assumptions as possible. In this manner, I hope to avoid the objection that by describing psychology in an unnecessarily political form I have smuggled in a conclusion I set out to demonstrate. Therefore, the argument must be more intricate than it might otherwise be, but no caution can be too great in the discussion of such important matters.

The first principle of liberal psychology states that the self consists of understanding and desire, that the two are distinct from one another, and that desire is the moving, active, or primary part of the self. The mind machine, by itself, wants nothing; desire, unaided by understanding, can see nothing. This might be called the principle of reason and desire.[12]

Reason or understanding is the faculty by which the self determines what the world is like. The terms understanding and knowledge also describe the pictures of things in the world produced by the use of reason. Desire or will is the faculty by which the self determines the objects of its appetites and aversions. The appetites themselves are also called desires. A choice is a decision about which of several courses of action to pursue, when some of the courses of action are more capable of satisfying a desire than others. An inclination is a predisposition toward certain kinds of desires and toward things or situations capable of satisfying those desires.

There are several ways to develop the principle of reason and desire so that we may more easily be able to recognize it as our own. Things are not simply what we think they are or ought to be; they are what they are. Our choices are choices we make. We may be able to show why it is that we choose one course of action rather than another, but, with reservations I shall soon state, we do not suppose that the choice of a goal is the same as the acknowledgment of a fact. Indeed, the distinction between reason and will is simply the converse of the separation of facts from goals, ends, or values.

So far I have treated the principle of reason and desire as a function of the differences in the characteristic activities in which the understanding and the will engage, or of the objects to which each is directed.[13] Consider now the principle of reason and desire from the standpoint of the positions reason and will occupy in relation to one another within the unreflective view of mind. Understanding is a tool of desire. The former must serve the appetites of the latter. When the mind hunts for knowledge it may seem to run on its own motion. But the search for truth is only a device to satisfy the desires all the more effectively, to arrive by a shorter route at a goal the will has already chosen. Even the increase of knowledge is an end that, like all other ends, must first be desired in order to command the obedience of the understanding.[14]

The principle of reason and desire can be stated in frankly political form, and it is in this form rather than in the preceding ones that we find it more often expressed among the classic thinkers of liberalism. What distinguishes men from one another is not that they understand the world differently, but that they desire different things even when they share the same understanding of the world. There is only one world of facts and only one form of understanding, fundamentally alike in everyone. A man may know more or less about the world, but whenever two men know something truly what they know is the same thing.[15] The basis of their individual identities cannot be simply their relative degree of ignorance. It must be the choices they make, the ends they choose. The realm of desires comes much closer to being a democracy than does the republic of letters, as the discussion of the second principle of liberal psychology should make clear.

In whichever way the principle of reason and desire is developed, there is no mistaking its currency in the history of the dominant intellectual tradition of the modern West or its importance to the manner in which we experience personality. For at least three hundred years the division of thought and feeling has been the starting point of ideas about human nature. Stated forcefully by the inventors of the liberal doctrine, it has ever since been the beneficiary of a thousand revisions and the target of a thousand attacks. Neither the attacks nor the revisions, however, have done away with the original teaching. All moderns are disciples of Rousseau in that they view the bridging of the gap between reason and sentiment as the foremost problem of the moral life. But it is a problem that continues unsolved. The fury visited on the classic liberal thinkers has not been enough to create an image of the self that truly dispenses with the principle of reason and desire.

The Freudian conception of the psyche and the Marxist contrast of science and ideology represent, despite their accompanying refinements, two latter-day versions of the principle of reason and desire. Freud is no less anxious than Hobbes to portray the blind and self-sustaining power of the desires. He does not leave in doubt either their relative autonomy from the understanding or their mastery over it. And for Marx it is precisely the masking of interest as knowledge that constitutes the distinctive feature of ideology and denies it the quality of science. The presentation of interests as knowledge is a distortion; it confuses two things that are different in nature. Interest is the prey of the will, but knowledge the prize of reason.

When we consider how utterly enslaved to the principle of reason and desire are these two revolutionary movements of modern social thought, we should expect to have difficulty comprehending, much less accepting, an altogether different view. Plato's conception of a science of ideals, in the practice of which knowledge and desire become one, is so alien to our ways of thinking that every attempt to emulate it dissolves in mysticism, or ends in an arbitrary cataloguing of abstract 'values.'

The unfamiliar spirit that animates this preliberal denial of the principle of reason and desire is the conception that what ought to be and what is are not wholly different. In this conception, the ideal does not stand above the world, but is part of it. Values are facts because they have a mode of existence outside the minds of individuals who acknowledge them. And facts themselves, correctly understood, are in a sense already what they ought to become. More concisely put, the intelligible essence of each thing in the world is its ideal. So, for example, according to this view, there is a universally valid ideal of perfected human life. We call this ideal humanity because it distinguishes man from all other kinds of beings. It is his intelligible essence.[16]

Wherever liberal psychology prevails, the distinction between describing things in the world and evaluating them will be accepted as the premise of all clear thought. Because classical metaphysics disregards that distinction, we can no longer speak its language. Yet there is at least one familiar way of thinking to which the distinction cannot be applied, the beliefs of religion. Indeed, the view that the understanding of what we ought to do is part of a comprehension of what the world is really like is a well-recognized characteristic of religious ideas.[17] Between liberal psychology and religion there can be no lasting peace, but at most an illusion of mutual tolerance. From the standpoint of the liberal psychologist, religion must be treated as a creature of desire, just as magic can be described as a forerunner of reason.

I have stated the principle of reason and desire, and indicated some ways in which it might be reformulated. But why does it exercise power over us? I cannot answer this question until I have made my picture of liberal psychology more concrete by introducing a second principle.

THE PRINCIPLE OF ARBITRARY DESIRE

The second principle of liberal psychology is an extension of the first. It states that desires are arbitrary from the perspective of the understanding. This is the principle of arbitrary desire.

Let me first explain what I mean by calling desires arbitrary. We cannot derive a justification for choices we make simply from an understanding of facts. Even if we understood how all things are necessarily what they are, we would still have to choose among alternative courses of action, and all our science would be powerless to justify our choices. Desire, then, is arbitrary in the sense that we cannot determine what to want, or rather we cannot defend our determinations, solely by enlarging our comprehension of facts. Again, choice is not reducible to understanding, because, over time and in the life of the same person, different choices are consistent with the same understanding of the world. Conversely, a person whose view of the world changes over time will not necessarily change his ends. The arbitrariness of the desires consists in the impossibility of using reason to justify their content.[18] In liberal psychology, there are two main types of qualifications to this initial formulation of the principle of arbitrary desire. A discussion of each will help make the principle clearer.

A first qualification is that the desires themselves are capable of being objects of the understanding. Reason can turn back on them and treat them as facts, with causes and effects, like all other facts.[19] That is what scientific psychology tries to do. But, for the understanding, desires can never be just facts, set over against the self in the external world. They are also what make us individual persons. Because desires are an element of the self, they will always have a double aspect for the understanding. On the one hand, they are psychic events, to be explained causally. On the other hand, they are experienced as possessed of an element of pure contingency, which causal explanation can never fully penetrate.

The contingency of our choices and inclinations has, in turn, two characteristics, of which the second depends on the first. The choices must be acts we might not have committed; the inclinations, tendencies we might not have fostered. This is called free will. The second characteristic of the contingency of desires is that reason alone cannot defend or attack them. It has nothing to say about whether they are right or wrong, with the reservation of a point made below. Unless there were free will, however, the problem of criticizing and justifying desires would never arise; it would be absurd.

The idea that desires can be viewed as either determined facts or contingent choices, depending on whether we want to explain conduct or to criticize and to justify it, is a sore point in liberal psychology. Here also Kant proposed a solution whose virtue was to show that no solution was possible, unless the terms of the problem were redefined. Think of man, he said, as if he were a citizen of two kingdoms, a natural realm of causal determination and a moral realm of freedom. We assume he is the former because we want to explain the world, and that he is the latter because we want to justify conduct. But the relation between the two assumptions, desire as determined fact and as arbitrary choice, remains forever a mystery. Though Kant claimed that a moral law rather than the caprice of the will would take the place of natural determination in the moral realm, he was forced to leave the connection of the two laws in darkness.[20]

Because desires can be treated as facts or as ends, though never as both at the same time, classic liberal psychology turns into two distinct disciplines, empirical psychology and ethics. The scientific psychologist imagines that his concerns are of a different order from those of the moralist. He is interested in desires as events to be explained rather than as bases for criticism and justification. The moralist, in turn, supposes that his inquiries are beyond the pale of 'science.' So the very way in which the psychologist and the moralist define the scope of their respective disciplines obscures the system of thought from which those disciplines arose and upon whose premises they continue to rely.

The second qualification to the principle of arbitrary desire is the subsidiary role reason can play in the justification and criticism of choice. It is the distinctive concern of the understanding to discover the most effective means for reaching the goals the will has chosen.

This instrumental use of knowledge involves reason in the process by which ends are defined and ordered, but it does not change the fundamental character of the relation between understanding and desire. Reason may tell us that if we want *a*, which we like, we must also accept *b*, which we dislike, because *b* cannot be separated from *a*. Or it may advise us that we cannot have *a* and *b*, both of which we desire, at the same time, because they are inconsistent with one another. Finally, it may teach us how to organize the satisfaction of our desires over time, depriving ourselves of some things now in order to reap all the more richly later.[21]

But when all is said and done, reason cannot command us to choose a course of action simply because it is worthy of being chosen, nor can it prohibit us from settling on some new aim for our activities. Its industry in the service of desire is indispensable, but limited. The limit is the line that divides the elucidation of relations among desires from the decision about what in the end to choose. The scope of the principle of arbitrary desire should now be clear. But what precisely is its relation to the principle of reason and desire?

If reason is the universal and desire the particular element in man, both the exaltation of the former and the denial of the latter will undermine individuality. The ideal of single-minded service to reason will lead to a recognition of the illusory character of individuality and the undivided oneness of the world (Spinoza). When philosophy points the way to the extinction of all desire as the path of wisdom that alone can free us from illusion and suffering, it also takes away the basis of individual identity (Schopenhauer). From the standpoint of liberal psychology, rationalism and mysticism are the twin enemies of the separateness of persons.

Together, the principle of reason and desire and the principle of arbitrary desire stand at the center of a system of beliefs whose surface I have just begun to scratch. In order to suggest something of the weight these principles carry, I shall discuss their connection with a series of dichotomies that run through many of our ideas.

The opposition of means and ends as a fundamental category of moral discourse presupposes the contrast between objective knowledge and arbitrary desire. Everything in the world is potentially an object of appetite or aversion. But whatever an individual does not seek or fear as an end is important to him only as a possible means. The choice of the means to an end is an activity of the understanding and, as such, objective. The choice of the ends themselves is the work of desire and therefore arbitrary. We do reject certain courses of action because they are wrong rather than simply because they are inefficient. But the reason for this is that whenever we act we always have a host of goals other than the one to which the activity of the moment is directed, and we do not allow all our ends to be sacrificed to the achievement of an immediate objective. Nevertheless, the priorities among conflicting ends must be settled by the will.

The dualism of form and substance is also linked with the principle of reason and desire, though the influence of that dualism extends far beyond the frontiers of psychology. Understanding contributes to the organization of our goals by clarifying their interrelations, but it never ultimately determines their substance. Reason is as formal in the performance of its moral responsibilities as it is in the development of scientific truth. The substance of our goals is the object of arbitrary will, just as the substance of natural phenomena is left by science to the realm of our everyday sense impressions.[22]

The dichotomy of the public and the private life is still another corollary of the separation of understanding and desire. It offers a perspective from which we can look back on all the preceding dualisms. Since men are made up of the two different elements of reason and will, they move in two worlds only precariously bound together. When reasoning, they belong to a public world because knowledge, to the extent it is true, does not vary among persons. When desiring, however, men are private beings because they can never offer others more than a partial justification for their goals in the public language of thought. Means and form, as objects of reason, are public; ends and substance, as concerns of desire, are private.

There is one final dichotomy that, though associated with the categories just discussed, has a unique and disquieting place in liberal psychology. It is the division of technique and theory. By technique I mean knowledge interested in things as objects of formal manipulation or as means to ends. In this sense, technical knowledge includes both science and what we define more narrowly as technological or instrumental choice, the application of science to the advancement of whatever goals we have set. The liberal psychologist would have us believe that technique exhausts the powers of reason. Because reason is technical, means and forms are its only possible objects, and public life its proper setting.

But now suppose a different view of the duties of reason. Imagine that the intellect presumes to elucidate the ends as well as the means of conduct, that it does not rest satisfied with purely formal generality of statement, and that it drags into the arena of public debate matters usually confined to the private life. When it acts in this way, the mind is engaged in what one might call theory by contrast to technique.

As long as philosophy is theory, it cannot fade away into the technical disciplines that grow out of it. All revolutions in our general ideas about mind and society are accomplished by theory. Yet the liberal revolution, though made by theorists, attacked the conception of theory itself. It did this by carving life into categories within which theory had no place.

The attempt to think theoretically is therefore by its very nature a defiance of the strictures of liberal psychology. Theory disrespects the dichotomies that separate means from ends, form from substance, and public from private life. Hence, it will come as no surprise to discover later on that speculative thought cannot accept the contrast of reason and desire with which all the earlier dualisms are connected. To develop an adequate conception of personality, we must cross the line that protects description from evaluation, and reestablish at a higher level the unity of fact and value the liberal thinkers tried to destroy.

THE PRINCIPLE OF ANALYSIS

The first two principles of liberal psychology are addressed to personality as a whole. The third goes more directly to knowledge. It states that there is nothing in any piece of knowledge that cannot be analyzed back into the elementary sensations or ideas from which it was composed and then built up again from those sensations and ideas. It is the principle of analysis.

The principle of analysis acknowledges that sensations are different from facts, and ideas different from sensations. But it insists that all the operations of the mind by which we acquire knowledge fall into two categories. First, there is the joining together of discrete sensations and ideas into more complex and general ideas. Second, there is the breaking down of these complex ideas into their building blocks. The former is combination, juxtaposition, or aggregation; the latter analysis. The procedures of analysis and combination exhaust the ways in which we can gain knowledge of either the natural world or of the formal truths of mathematics and logic.[23]

Suppose we consider any aspect of our knowledge a whole whose parts are the sensations or ideas with which it is made. The principle of analysis may then be rephrased as the proposition that in the acquisition of knowledge the whole is the sum of its parts. The virtue of this apparent tautology is to evoke the possibility of a quite different conception of the process through which we learn about the world.

According to this alternative view, which one might call the principle of synthesis, it is impossible to account for the content of any complex piece of knowledge by simply adding up the more elementary sensations or concepts with which it was fabricated. On the contrary, the information a more complex level of knowledge provides introduces something genuinely new in comparison to what was known before. This is the notion the metaphor of the whole as something different from the sum of its parts is meant to describe. Many movements in modern social thought, like Gestalt psychology and structural anthropology, have rejected the principle of analysis in favor of the principle of synthesis, but because they have continued to rely on the other psychological and political premises of liberalism, all suffer from the vices of partial criticism.[24]

A familiar conception of the nature of mathematical and logical truths, that whatever is in our conclusions must already have been in our premises, even though not in our awareness, illustrates the principle of analysis. The claim that we have to understand the organization of particular sensations and concepts before being able to assign identity or meaning to the particulars exemplifies the principle of synthesis.

The spirit that unifies the liberal theory of knowledge is confidence in the primacy of the simple. The world is made of simple things. Our ability to understand it depends on our success in going from the simple to the more complex and then returning again from the latter to the former. Like Antaeus, we regain strength by touching the earth. The complex, on the contrary, is always derivative and contrived. Hence, simplicity is associated with naturalness and concreteness; complexity with abstraction and artificiality.[25]

In the history of liberal theories of mind, trust in the priority of the simple has never been a thesis easy to maintain. Its fundamental weakness is its dependence on the doctrine of intelligible essences. How else are we to justify the claim that simple facts have an identity of their own before they are placed within the framework of a definite theory? To accept the doctrine of intelligible essences would be to abandon the modern view of science and to open the gates to theories of objective value or natural law. To these theories, however, liberalism must be unrelentingly opposed, for they disregard its most basic moral and political premises.

The social implications of the principle of analysis are of two orders: its influence on the kinds of beliefs men consider themselves entitled to have and its relation to the way society is organized.

The analytical view of knowledge completes the dismemberment of the classical conception of theory that the first two principles began. Its general consequence is to demoralize all attempts to construct conceptual systems before the patient investigation of particulars, for it is in these particulars rather than in the system which pretends to describe them that reality lies. Consequently, the principle of analysis furnishes a priceless defense of the specialization of the sciences and of the limitation of all criticism of liberal thought to partial criticism.

It also turns us away from any attempt to understand our social situation as a whole, a whole that could never be elucidated by the study of parts alone. Awareness of the character of our historical position must therefore be restricted to the analysis of particular historical events. All other studies of society will be disparaged as charlatanism, pretending to do that which the liberal notion of mind says cannot be done. Because the social world cannot be understood as a whole, it is also impossible to imagine how it might be changed as a whole. The principle of analysis is the eternal enemy of revolution.

Nowhere is the inherent conservatism of the liberal view of mind more striking than in its strange consequence for the study of liberalism itself. The axiom of analysis stands opposed to any attempt to pass, in the discussion of liberal thought, from partial to total criticism. It always points toward the study of individual problems by denying that there is any whole in the tradition of liberalism except a collection of particular ideas entertained at different times. The emperor of Japan, separated by a screen from his groveling subjects, could not have hoped for a better hiding place than the one this view of knowledge gives to the liberal doctrine.

The principle of analysis may owe much of its appeal to a particular form of social order, to whose perpetuation it in turn contributes: the situation in which each man's social existence is divided into a diversity of roles. Every role calls for the exercise of special skills and the satisfaction of special expectations. There is no social position that brings together in the performance of a single activity the different aspects of social life, thereby making it possible to survey the social order in its entirety. When all interests are viewed as either private and subjective themselves or as combinations of subjective and private interests, no activity can be seen as the expression of a universal interest whose realization demands a universal knowledge of society. A fract d social existence can only produce a fractured knowledge of the soc l order. The principle of analysis is therefore the natural limit to its self-consciousness.

The three postulates discussed are the simplest elements of liberal psychology and the basis of much of our thinking about morals and human nature. The nature of the relation between the principle of reason and desire and the principle of arbitrary desire has already been suggested. It will be more surprising to discover that these two principles imply and are implied by the analytical view of mind. I am unable, however, to elucidate the character of this interdependence right away, for the understanding of my argument requires a grasp of the doctrines of liberal political theory, to be discussed in the next chapter.

THE MORALITIES OF REASON AND DESIRE

My criticism of liberal psychology moves forward in three steps. First, I distinguish two basic types of moral theory to which liberal psychology gives rise. Then, I show how both these theories are caught in a paradox, the antinomy of reason and desire. Finally, I examine the destructive effect of the two moralities on the conception of personality. The antinomy of reason and desire, which is the central theme of the argument, lies at the heart of the history of moral ideas in the modern West just as the antinomy of theory and fact is the axis of the evolution of views about science and nature.

Our beliefs about standards of conduct invariably depend on our view of personality. Because liberal psychology singles out two ultimate elements in the self, it has two main kinds of answers to the moral question: the morality of desire and the morality of reason. Though these are names none of the classic liberal philosophers ever adopted, they describe the main alternative solutions to the common moral problems all of them have faced. The relation of the ethical speculations of the great philosophers to these elementary types of moral thought is like that of the style of the greatest writers to ordinary language, a language kept alive and perfected in the prose of the artist.

The morality of desire defines the good as the satisfaction of desire, the reaching of the goals to which our appetites and aversions incline us. Contentment is the imaginary state in which all desire is satisfied. The task of ethics on this view is to teach us how to organize life so that we shall approach contentment. We call this continual progress happiness.[26]

As part of their endeavor for happiness, men select the desires that should be satisfied first, because of their greater intensity or because their satisfaction is a condition of the satisfaction of other desires.

According to the morality of reason, reason establishes the standards of right conduct. This is a strange idea from the start. The tradition of classical metaphysics previous to the invention of the liberal doctrine laid great store by the conception of practical reason. Just as there is a theoretical reason that distinguishes the true from the false, so there is a practical reason that separates the good from the bad.[27] The idea of practical reason took a long time to be abandoned by the moderns, but it is certainly incompatible with the premises of liberal psychology.

By definition, the understanding does not evaluate; it describes. If it is to be the source of moral standards, it has to forbid certain courses of conduct because they are wrong, not just because they are inexpedient or inconsistent with one another. How then can the liberal psychologist build a morality of reason?

Recall the political formulation of the principle of reason and desire. Men differ by what they desire, but they are capable of knowing the world in the same way. Particular desires felt by the individual are arbitrary from the standpoint of the understanding. The only morality reason could establish would therefore have to be one that bound men independently of their individual, capricious ends. Indeed, it would be an indispensable characteristic of such universal standards of rational morality not to favor the goals of any single individual just because it is he who happens to want them. Hence, the morality of reason could not be devoted to the promotion of any substantive end except the end of freedom, whose unique status will be discussed later.

The main point made by the moralist of reason is that there are certain rules we must accept in order to be able to move beyond the assertion of naked desire to the practice of judging right and wrong. Unless we made such judgments, we would have no way to justify before others or before ourselves the satisfaction of any of our desires. Consequently, we would have to surrender all that is implied in the notion of a moral man, a man who, because he is able to argue about rights and wrongs, can evaluate experience as well as undergo it. When reason states universal rules, it is not really pretending to be a legislator of the good; it is only telling us what principles we would have to accept in order to engage in moral criticism. But reason alone cannot persuade us of the importance of being able to justify our own or others' claims.

Kant's ethical theory is the purest example of the morality of reason. Its categorical imperative, "act according to a maxim you might will to be a universal law," illustrates in the most general form what a rule in such a morality would be like, or rather the constitutional standard to which all its propositions would have to conform. So also Kant's conception of will (*Wille*) is that of a desire that has submitted completely to the formal prescriptions of universal reason.[28]

Notice that both ethics differ in their conceptions of the role of moral theory, as well as in the way they solve the moral problem. For the moralist of desire there is just a tenuous and elusive line between descriptive psychology and ethics. For him, the contingent desires individuals have are the only material out of which moral standards can be made, and therefore all moral thinking must begin with an understanding of the passions to which men are subject as desiring animals. The moralist of reason thinks differently. He draws a sharp distinction between the universal rules of conduct and the contingent appetites of individuals, and confines his attention to the former.

Again, the morality of desire is an ethic of goals, concerned with the satisfaction of particular desires. But the morality of reason is an ethic of rules, the universal principles that constrain the pursuit of any of our ends. Thus, the former is said to assert the priority of the good over the right, and the latter the priority of the right over the good.

The two moralities correspond roughly to two traditions in the history of modern ethics. The first tradition began with Hobbes' conception of value as a reflex of appetite, changed into the search for a logic of the moral sentiments associated with the Scottish moralists, and returned with Bentham to the cruder idea of utility. The second tradition started to take form with the seventeenth century rationalists but became well defined only in the writings of Kant and his disciples.

THE ANTINOMY OF REASON AND DESIRE

Neither the morality of desire nor the morality of reason withstand closer inspection. Each is inadequate, and needs to be qualified by the other. Yet no synthesis of the two seems possible within liberal psychology.

A first objection to the morality of desire is that it is incapable of passing from the description to the evaluation of conduct and, therefore, of laying down any standards of justification. Desires, it has been assumed, are random with respect to any given understanding of the world. We are not entitled to assume that there exists an order among our choices and inclinations, an order reason might discover or impose on the will. A pattern among an individual's desires would only be possible if he were able to ask what the system of his ends committed him to in a particular case.

True, liberal psychology allows reason a subsidiary role in planning the satisfaction of the appetites, but that is not enough to ensure the possibility of an order. Though the understanding can clarify the relations of the desires to one another, it cannot legislate any sort of hierarchy for them. And though it can inquire into the implications of a novel end, it cannot determine whether that end ought to be accepted or rejected. There is no rational barrier to the proliferation of new goals, for in the final analysis all aims are equally capricious.

Because the morality of desire provides no standards for preferring some desires to others, it fails to serve as a basis for the justification or criticism of choice. Another way to say this is that it recognizes the moral impotence of reason in liberal psychology and draws from it the conclusion of absolute moral scepticism. An appeal to the relative intensities of competing desires as a criterion of choice carries the problem to another level. It is dubious that such measurements of intensity can be made and unclear why they should be made. Moreover, the strength with which one 'feels' a want may depend in part on a judgment of its worth.

The morality of desire must therefore be condemned as an ethic that is no ethic at all, only an inadequate descriptive psychology. Its main flaw as a basis for the description of how choices are made is its failure to account for how in fact we praise and blame and for how our practices of moral judgment are connected with the development of our appetites and aversions. From whatever way we approach the problem, the conclusion is always the same. The liberal psychologist cannot jump over the wall between description and evaluation he himself has built.

The first objection to the morality of desire has to do with its ability to serve as a moral doctrine. The second is addressed to the inadequacy of the kind of life toward which it points. This latter argument is a transition to my later discussion of the significance of the antinomy of reason and desire for the idea of personality.

The morality of desire is paradoxical. It canonizes contentment as the good, and defines contentment as the satisfaction of desire. But contentment cannot be achieved so long as we lack criteria with which to judge and to order our ends. Once a desire is satisfied, another must come to take its place, for according to liberal psychology we are striving beings who covet as long as we live. There is no reason to think that the number of dissatisfied desires diminishes over time.[29]

It is here that the moral importance of the principle of analysis becomes clear. If it is impossible in the acquisition of knowledge to see a whole as different from the sum of its parts, it will also be impossible for the self to understand its own moral vocation as distinct from the sum of its particular desires. Left without a basis upon which to exclude new desires, it is condemned to dissatisfaction and discontentment.

The succession of desires by mere aggregation, from which the morality of desire offers no escape, resembles the idea of infinity as a never-ending series of numbers. The sequence of particular numbers or desires is always incomplete; it never becomes more than a linear series.[30] This point is borne out by hedonism, the doctrine that pleasure, and especially pleasure of the senses, is the good. Hedonism is a common, though by no means the only, example of the morality of desire. Its paradox is the paradox of that morality. Pleasure consists in the satisfaction of present appetite, but because of the relentless succession of wants there will always be a present desire that remains unfulfilled. Therefore, the pursuit of pleasure as an ethical principle is forever condemned to remain a step short of its destination.[31]

The morality of reason is as untenable as its rival. Again, my first objection is directed at the capacity of the morality of reason to serve as the foundation for moral judgments of any kind, and my second argument is concerned with the inadequacy of the way the moralist of reason conceives the moral life. These two criticisms constitute the dilemma of the morality of reason. That morality must be either workable and incoherent or coherent and unworkable, but it cannot be coherent and workable at the same time. It will always say either too much to be coherent or too little to be workable.

Coherence demands that the universal principles of the morality of reason be, like the golden rule, neutral toward the purposes of specific individuals. Given the postulate of arbitrary desire, there is no basis on which to prefer some ends to others. But as long as this formal neutrality is strictly maintained, the standards it produces will be, like the golden rule itself, empty shells. Until the shells are filled up by more concrete principles, they are capable of accommodating almost any pattern of conduct and incapable of determining precisely what is commanded or prohibited in particular situations of choice. Do unto others as we would have them do unto us, but what is it that we ought to want them to do unto us?

As soon as we try to make the rules more concrete, however, we run into trouble. The decision about what kinds of benefits to seek from the others, or which commands and prohibitions to cast in the form of universal laws, forces us to descend to the level of conflicting individual goals whose relative worth reason lacks authority to judge.[32]

Suppose that it were possible to make the rules of reason determinate. The subordination of the desires to purely rational rules would mean the immolation of what liberal psychology defines as the striving and individual part of the self.[33] The morality of reason deals with men in a domain in which they are identical to one another. If, however, the rules of reason were indeterminate enough to allow for the pursuit of different individual goals, the problems of the morality of desire would reappear.

Having considered the main objections to the two kinds of moral theory the liberal doctrine of mind supports, I can now state precisely in what the antinomy of reason and desire consists. Two equally untenable and mutually contradictory moral doctrines seem to follow from the postulates of liberal psychology. If the morality of desire fails to provide guidance, abandoning us to our random and changing appetites, the morality of reason disregards or suppresses our existence as subjective beings with individual ends. The former prohibits us from bringing our striving to a conclusion; the other does not allow us to strive at all. One never concludes; the other never begins.

To establish the possibility of an order among our desires, we must appeal to reason. But within the limits of liberal psychology, reason cannot evaluate anything. To give content to the formal principles reason establishes, one has to abandon the posture of neutrality among the desires of the individual and among the desires of different individuals. Yet it was precisely to avoid the need to choose among equally arbitrary desires that we attempted to construct a morality of reason. On the one hand, there is no way to justify the prescriptive role reason would have to perform in order to cure the defects of the morality of desire. On the other hand, there is no basis for the ordering of concrete wants that a tenable morality of reason would require. The root of the problem is the separation made by the liberal doctrine between understanding and evaluation. As long as that separation persists, the Hobson's choice with which the two moralities present us is inescapable.

The antinomy of reason and desire is more than a philosopher's conundrum; it is a fate that falls with terrible force upon those whose moral experience the principles of liberal psychology describe. Its mark on everyday life is the unacceptability, indeed the incomprehensibility, of the two halves of the self to each other. For reason, when it sets itself up as moral judge, the appetites are blind forces of nature at loose within the self. They must be controlled and if necessary suppressed. For the will, the moral commands of reason are despotic laws that sacrifice life to duty. Each part of the self is condemned to war against the other.

THE IDEA OF PERSONALITY

The next stage of my critique of liberal psychology is an examination of the implications of the antinomy of reason and desire for the idea of personality or self. My thesis will be that the psychological principles of liberalism make it impossible to formulate an adequate conception of personality. In one sense, the argument will expand on the points underlined by my discussion of the antinomy of reason and desire, but, in another, it will foreshadow the theory of the self developed in Chapter Five.

The first thing to do is to outline the elements of a minimal idea of personality, an idea implicit in our everyday practices and judgments. The major defense of this concept of self is the absurdity of the consequences to which its rejection would lead. When we speak of someone as a person there are at least four simple notions we have in mind.

First, the person must have a continuing identity over time. If he had no such temporal continuity, he could not be held accountable for his actions, nor entitled to his deserts. Moral judgments would be meaningless. Moreover, the experience of consciousness itself, because it is an experience of existence in time, would be an insoluble riddle.

Second, the self must share a common humanity with others. It must be able to recognize other persons as like beings capable, thanks to their likeness, of binding themselves to it by systems of rights and duties. If no such system of entitlements were possible, the individual would never have a basis on which to defend his own choices, or to criticize those of his fellows. Nor could he, in the absence of this shared humanity, account for the relation between his sense of self-identity and the recognition others bestow on him, or for the dependence of his consciousness on the social medium of language and culture.

Third, a person must be able to change his ends over time, as well as to acknowledge the continuity of his existence. Otherwise, we could not make sense of the experience of innovation in the life of individuals and in the history of the species. The liberal psychologist would add, in his language, that to deny that our ends change over time is to discount the will, the seat of activity in the self.

Fourth, the person must be a unique individual despite his membership in a species of like beings. The experience of standing apart from others is the most fundamental condition of selfhood. Without such individual identity the self would have no bounds, and nothing could be said about it. The precise character of the separation between the self and others need not trouble us for the moment.

The qualities of personality I have enumerated seem to be agreed upon tacitly even when they are not remarked. There is no thinker who has not accepted them in one form or another, and this is as true of the philosophers of liberalism as of the defenders of opposing traditions of thought. Yet neither the morality of desire nor the morality of reason can do justice to the notion of the self that contains the four elements. This is a serious objection, for personality is the honor of our moral being and the pride of life.

The morality of desire destroys the basis for understanding the continuity and shared humanity of the self. Consider first the problem of temporal unity. As previously shown, it is a necessary consequence of the morality of desire not to permit the creation of an order among our purposes either at a single moment, or, with better reason, over time. The identity of the self is defined by the ends it holds. If over time these ends are truly arbitrary and do not form a system reason can grasp, there will be no rational connection among the selves that exist at different moments.

Within the limits of liberal psychology, it is an insufficient warrant for the continuity of the self that a sequence of desires be felt by an individual with the same body. The liberal psychologist cannot conceive of the relation between self and body as an unanalyzable whole or as a whole that differs from the sum of its parts without his violating the principle of analysis. For him to base the temporal unity of the person on the survival of the body would be like claiming to have established that different photographs belong to a single film because they are run on the same machine.[34]

The question is precisely, How do we know that the same *person* is in the body before us at different moments? We can be certain of this only if we are able to grasp the continuity of his striving, a continuity the sequence of arbitrary desires does nothing to prove. It follows that the self must appear to the moralist of desire as a series of discontinuous persons, hence no person at all, just like a film that told no story, because each of the pictures was a story of its own.[35]

A second consequence of the morality of desire is to undermine the conception of a shared humanity. Translated into the language of liberal psychology, a shared humanity would mean that there are certain ends men necessarily have in common. But to the liberal psychologist any convergence of preferences is an accident without moral significance. To be sure, one might demonstrate as a causal matter that the circumstances of human life operate to impose a core of universally shared goals on all human beings. But these common necessities could never be given a distinctively moral significance without the intervention of some independent principle.

The implications of the morality of reason for the idea of personality are exactly symmetrical to those of the morality of desire. The latter denies the continuity and the humanity of the self; the former negates its capacity for moral innovation and its individual identity.

The defining characteristic of principles of rational morality is to bind us regardless of our desires at a given time. They are principles that apply to us simply because we are rational and striving beings, not because our striving is directed to one objective rather than to another. As formal, indeterminate laws, the principles of reason disregard our changing desires. As concrete commands, they suppress them.

The second consequence of the morality of reason is to erode the basis of the individuality of the self. Its confessed aim is to found an ethic upon the universal element in man. It will not and cannot suit the principles it legislates to the goals of specific individuals. Again, it must either pass over individuality in silence or actively demand its dissolution.

My analysis of the bearing of the two liberal moralities on the conception of personality states in abstract and summary form a moral experience with which all moderns are familiar in the measure of their modernity. Just as liberal theory is unable to account for the possibility of selfhood, life in modern, liberal society continually denies us the possession of coherent personality. The dissolution of the temporal unity of the self, the loss of its ability to acknowledge the quality of universal humanity, accompany its despair of moral innovation and its surrender of the sense of individual identity.

Thus, the conclusions the philosopher infers from opposing moral doctrines are experienced simultaneously by the living person. The everyday predicament of men in modern society repeats the lesson theory has already taught us. The moralities of reason and of desire may be contrasting poles, but they are poles of the same spectrum, the complementary parts of a single moral situation. That situation leaves its mark on every aspect of life and thought from the abnormalities of the mind to its highest achievements.

As the most general malady of the psyche, schizophrenia dramatically illustrates the dissolution of the four elements of personality described. The schizophrenic is unable to keep an awareness of his continuity as a person and of the humanity in which he participates. At the same time, however, he is locked into a condition of being he feels incapable of changing, and deprived of any clear conception of his individual identity. Schizophrenia brings to light the hidden truth of the moral condition liberal psychology describes.[36]

Even the most ambitious endeavors of the speculative intellect carry the mark of the liberal doctrine. All our fundamental ways of thinking distinguish between a universal, formal, or rational and a particular, substantive, or appetitive aspect of their subject matters. The Kantian moralist contrasts the universal laws of the rational will with the particular strivings of concrete individuals.[37] The classical political economist separates the ideal profit maximizer of his hypothetical theory from the concrete trader with a specific set of inclinations and resources. The modern positivist lawyer draws a line between the abstract 'legal person,' who is a subject of rights and duties, and the determinate individual, who uses his legal entitlements to promote particular interests with which the jurist is not concerned.[38]

In all these cases, an ideal and abstract humanity is opposed to a real and concrete one. Like the morality of reason, political economy and positivist jurisprudence speak to men only at that level at which the differences among persons disappear. The study of the individual interests and goals of the economic actor or the legal person is relegated to some other discipline, like sociology or psychology, only to be in turn abandoned by those sciences in favor of a search for the universal structures of society and mind.

There is a remarkable parallel between this recurring contrast of an abstract and a concrete humanity and the view of science outlined at the beginning of the chapter. The equivalent to the formal rules of the legal order are the universal rules of logic, just as the logical reasoner echoes the 'legal person.' We distinguish the legal validity of an act or the logical validity of a conclusion from the rightness of the goals toward which the act is addressed, or from the truth of the thesis the conclusion sets forth. The counterpoint of abstract and concrete humanity, which the moralities of reason and desire enshrine, is a special case of the more general distinction between form and substance in thought, between the universal and the particular.

ROLES AND PERSONALITY

The omnipresence of the categories of liberal psychology would remain a mystery if it depended exclusively on the influence of a philosophical tradition. In fact, however, the metaphysical principles draw their power from association with a dominant form of social organization. The political form of the opposition of formal reason to arbitrary desire is the contrast between public and private existence. In our public mode of being we speak the common language of reason, and live under the laws of the state, the constraints of the market, and the customs of the different social bodies to which we belong. In our private incarnation, however, we are at the mercy of our own sense impressions and desires.

The discomfort of life is a consequence of the relentless battle these two aspects of life must wage against one another, each longing for peace with its enemy, yet unable to achieve it. In its public existence, the self is threatened by the loss of its individual identity and of mastery of its own future. Its private existence is marred by the fear that it inhabits a world of illusion, because its opinions and impressions are not shared by others and a world of helpless discontentment, because it is chained to the wheel of unsatisfied desire. To overcome the sense of illusion, it must be able to persuade others that its views of the world are not mad. To deal with the dissolving effect the lack of a finite and coherent system of ends has on its sense of identity, it must secure the approval of others.

Thus, the self flees constantly from the public to the private life, only to be compelled in the interests of its survival as a private person to deal publicly with others. Thrown back and forth between two fates, it cannot accept either as a resting place. Public organization strikes the private self as a preordained fact in whose making it had no part. Private interest, on the other hand, has, for the public self, the appearance of enslavement to blind instinct and ambition.

The conflict between the public and the private self, which we undergo as a moral experience, has its roots in a social situation. The distinguishing mark of that situation is the barrier between the individual and the impersonal, remote institutions of the state. It is only through the multitude of private associations with which all modern states have surrounded themselves and through the family that the antagonism inside the person is kept within manageable bounds.[39]

If the evolution of liberal society into what I shall later describe as the welfare-corporate and the socialist state is accompanied by the simultaneous publicization of private bodies and the privatization of public ones, and thus by the fading away of the separation of individual and state, one may ask why the conflict between public and private self does not tend to disappear. To answer this question, one must first understand in what sense such social institutions respond to the problem of personality. Then it will become apparent why the solution they offer is illusory.

Groups and associations seem to guarantee the unity of the self by providing a person with a social place, which, for the moment, might be loosely called a role. The role is a position in the division of labor. The role occupants are expected to undertake particular tasks for which they are suited by their special skills or talents. As industrial workers or civil servants, fathers or children, men occupy roles in the different associations of which they are members. The position of citizen in the state is too diffuse in the responsibilities it implies to be a role in the sense defined here.

Organization by role is to be distinguished from organization in which places are assigned according to standards other than recognized skill and talent, like hereditary succession. Each role helps its occupants picture the continuity of their lives and the ties of common humanity that bind them to their fellows. In exchange for doing what is expected of you, you will be rewarded by other men's opinion that the things you do at different times are connected with one another rationally, that is to say, in a way they can understand. This is just what you need to take the place of the coherent and limited system of ends you lack. It is just what you need to feel safe in the possession of a continuous self. Then again the role is always a recurring position; many men are in it besides yourself. You will naturally come to have interests and inclinations in common with them. It will not take you long to recognize that in many respects you are like the others.

At the same time that it underlines the temporal unity and the common humanity of the self, the public side of life, the role seems to respect life's private aspect, the instability of desires and the individuality of the person. A role may be severe in exacting obedience to the expectations it imposes, but it touches only a limited part of life. As long as you do what is expected of you in the various places you occupy, there will still be many things left over for you to decide on your own. You can change your orientations over time, and pursue objectives of your choice without sacrificing the benefits of conformity.

Alas, you have cried victory too soon. The apparent guarantee of your safety will be the final cause of your degradation. The self whose continuity your obedience ensures is not your own, but merely the mask you are compelled to wear in order to win the approval you crave. The others save you from being nothing, but they do not allow you to become yourself. The common humanity your roles let you discover is not what you truly have in common with all men; it is just the shifting interests and prejudices you may share with persons thrown into a position like your own. The freedom to be unstable in your desires and to pursue the goals you choose, after you have rendered tribute to Caesar, simply confronts you once again with the paradoxes of the morality of desire from which you were trying to escape.

In the role, the public and the private aspect of the self are kept apart. The rules and expectations that govern one's public conduct function as a half-empty cup into which different desires can be poured. The union of the public and the private self is never brought about. The more the external conventions of role are accepted, the less does the private self exist. But the more freedom one achieves from the constraints of these conventions, the less he finds support for his sense of the temporal unity and social character of the self. Instead of a solution, we are given a dilemma.

The horns of the dilemma are the occasions for the two main moral sentiments of men in a system of roles. To the extent they sacrifice the private self to the public one, they surrender their individual identities. When they try to cast off convention and to follow their own course without definite roles, they undergo the disintegration of the unity of self. To suffer at the same time from resignation and disintegration has become the ordinary circumstance of the moral life.

2

LIBERAL POLITICAL THEORY

INTRODUCTION

My discussion of liberal political doctrine will proceed along the same lines as the preceding study of liberal psychology. I start by describing some elements of the unreflective view of society that occupy a central place in our everyday thinking as well as in the specialized branches of social study. The next step will be to state more rigorously three principles implied in the unreflective view. The first postulate contrasts rules and values; the second affirms that values are subjective; the third holds that the characteristics of a group are reducible to the qualities of its individual members. These principles lie at the core of the classic political theory of liberalism. They account for how and why liberalism defines order and freedom as the master problems of politics.

The statement of these problems will open the way to the criticism of the liberal theory of society. I shall argue that liberal political thought cannot answer the very questions it defines as fundamental. Then, I shall look for the cause of this failure in an inability to arrive at a coherent understanding of the relations between rules and values in social life. Without such an understanding, however, no adequate view of society is possible. Finally, I shall discuss the idea of shared values as an attempt to solve the riddles of political thought, an attempt that foreshadows the transformation of the doctrine it tries to preserve.

THE UNREFLECTIVE VIEW OF SOCIETY[1]

Recall my description in Chapter One of the mind as a machine. The individual is made up of reason and will. Will directs reason, but does not control the content of knowledge. Society is the plurality of individuals with understanding and desire.

As desiring beings, men are blind creatures of appetite. Nevertheless, with the important qualification suggested by the antinomy of theory and fact, they are capable of an objective understanding of the world. Different men, each by the use of his own mind, can come ever closer to the same truth about reality. On the other hand, the things men want, and therefore the purposes they make their minds serve, are infinitely diverse.

Amidst this abundance of ends, there are some goals almost everyone pursues. Men want comfort and honor, and avoid the opposite of these. Above all, they try to keep life, for desire wants to be satisfied, not annihilated. Comfort is the satisfaction of material wants by material things. Honor is the satisfaction of the wish to be the object of other men's obedience or admiration. Accordingly, there are two kinds of honor: power and glory.

Power is the capacity to command, to subordinate the wills of others to one's own will. Glory is the winning of admiration, the applause with which one is favored. The tranquil exercise of power, which men call authority, depends either on the acknowledgment of the glory of the powerholder or on the limitation of power by impersonal laws. The laws make possible power without glory. Glory may be a source of power, and power of glory, but not all powerful men are glorious, nor all glorious men powerful. Freedom is the condition in which a person is not under the control of an alien will, or is only under the control of a will limited by impersonal laws in whose making, according to those who are democrats as well as liberals, he must participate. The love of freedom is part of the avoidance of enslavement to another, which is the opposite of power. The weakening of the want of comfort and honor is called holiness when its cause is the love for God and madness when it has a different cause.

A society of individuals who seek to achieve their particular objectives and to satisfy their needs for comfort and honor must be characterized by mutual hostility and mutual dependence. Both hostility and dependence are based on the nature of human ends and on the scarcity of means to satisfy them.

The first source of hostility, given the scarcity of material resources, is the desire for comfort. There are not enough of the goods people want in order to be comfortable. They must therefore scramble. Scrambling is all the more inevitable because men want not just to have, but to have more than their fellows. Only by fighting to get more can they be assured of keeping what they already possess. The reason for this is that the control of things is a tool of power.

Power is the second cause of antagonism in society. The power of some is the powerlessness of others. The more one man's desire for power is satisfied, the more will his fellows' wish for it remain frustrated. The fight for power must be as unceasing as the struggle for things.

Glory too stimulates hostility, for it shines by contrast to insignificance of person. There is not enough time to admire everyone, and then, if everyone were equally famous, fame would lose its meaning. The race for glory is as exacting and brutal as the battle for comfort and power, though it is usually more ceremonious.

The same goals that make men enemies also make them indispensable allies. To satisfy their hunger for comfort, they depend on each other's labor. In a sense, the necessary reliance on other people's work is a consequence of the scarcity of time. No man has enough time to satisfy his desire for material things through his own efforts, for death comes soon. Hence, individuals must find ways to buy and sell one another's time. There must be a labor market and the institution of contract for services.

The control of labor is the most direct form of power, and the wish for power is the second source of cooperation, just as it is the second cause of personal rivalry. By definition, power requires obedience, and obedience, if it is to last, must be given as well as taken. Men cannot foresee what would happen to them in a free-for-all fight for power. But if they collaborate to establish a polity under law, they can be assured that each will have a chance to exercise some modest form of power or, at least, that no one will be completely deprived of freedom.

Finally, human interdependence is a consequence of the general love for glory. Aside from the recognition he gains from his fellows, a person has no coherent self, for his ends do not form a stable system, and the different parts of his being are at war with one another. He is defined by others. Thus, individuals must join together to give one another a self and, by their mutual admiration, to console as much as possible their fear of death.

Though everyone cannot be admired in the same measure, we can, by establishing a well organized society, make sure that no one need be completely defeated in his wish for glory. By performing social roles according to expectation, men can secure the modicum of approval necessary to lend a semblance of coherence to their persons.

We may insist that in our polity all be entitled to a measure of recognition simply because they are humans. Kant called this kind of recognition respect. Respect and approval for the performance of one's role moderate the hostility the struggle for glory produces in the same way that law tempers the battle for power through its guarantees of freedom. While there are freedom and respect, the loss of power and glory will never be an unmitigated disaster.

The wants of comfort and honor, together with the circumstance of scarcity, which is implied in them, make reciprocal antagonism and reciprocal need the everlasting conditions of society. To promote their interests in hostility and collaboration, men are constantly making alliances by forming groups. But these groups are always precarious. Left to themselves, they would last only as long as the common convenience that brought them into being. The two fundamental problems of politics, order and freedom, are the consequences of the conditions of mutual antagonism and need, and of the drives that underlie those conditions.

The first task of society is to place the restraints on mutual antagonism necessary to satisfy mutual need. The struggle for comfort, power, and glory can be moderated so that everyone may be assured that he will not be threatened by the worst of discomfort, enslavement, and disrespect, or by violent death. But how is the control of hostility to be achieved? This is the problem of order.

As soon as men seek to place limits on their antagonism, they confront a second difficulty. For each person, the good is the satisfaction of his own desires; no other good exists. Freedom, to rephrase the earlier definition, is the power to choose arbitrarily the ends and means of one's striving. In principle, nothing makes one man's goals worthier of success than another's. Yet it seems that whatever restraints are established to ensure order will benefit the purposes of some individuals more than those of their fellows. Any such preference would be arbitrary, in the sense that it could not be justified. How then can order be instituted in such a way that no one's liberty is unjustifiably preferred or downgraded and that everyone has the largest amount of liberty compatible with the absence of such arbitrariness? This is the problem of freedom.

The common solution to the problems of order and freedom is the making and applying of impersonal rules or laws.

THE PRINCIPLE OF RULES AND VALUES

The distinction between rules and values, as the two basic elements of social order, is the first principle of liberal political thought. It may be called simply the principle of rules and values. It articulates the conception, embraced by the unreflective view of society, that the eternal hostility of men to one another requires that order and freedom be maintained by government under law.

To explain what is meant by the principle of rules and values and to work out its implications, I begin by defining the concepts of value and of rule. Then I discuss how the relationship between rules and values is conceived. Lastly, I suggest ways in which the idea of a society governed by law ties together several seemingly unrelated aspects of liberal thought.

Value and rule

Value is the social face of desire. It refers to an end of action or to a want when the emphasis is on relations among persons. In contrast, the term desire is used when the discussion concerns the relation within an individual between the setting of goals and the understanding of facts. End, objective, goal, and will are generic concepts that cover both usages.

The satisfaction of an individual's wants is his good. Assuredly, through lack of understanding, men may fail to appreciate that a single-minded insistence on the pursuit of a particular objective may prejudice the attainment of other goals. Moreover, they may also distinguish between what they think is right or proper and what they want. In this sense, the concept of value is ambiguous as between want or interest and standard or ideal. Nevertheless, as the discussion of liberal psychology has already suggested and the study of liberal political thought will confirm, the second sense of value ultimately collapses into the first. The sole measure of good that remains is the wants of an individual or some combination of the wants of different individuals revealed by the choices they make. The good has no existence outside the will.[2]

The need for rules arises from the undying enmity and the demands of collaboration that mark social life. Because there are no conceptions of the good that stand above the conflict and impose limits on it, artificial limits must be created. Otherwise, the natural hostility men have for one another will run its course relentlessly to the prejudice of their interdependence.

Self-interest, the generalized search for comfort and glory, and any sharing of common values will all be insufficient to keep the peace. It is in the individual's self-interest to benefit from a system of laws established by others but not to obey or establish that system himself. As long as most persons are not robbers, robbery can be a profitable business.[3] Furthermore, though everyone has similar interests in comfort and glory, they are interests that, because of the scarcity of their objects, throw men against one another as much as they bring men together. Finally, every other sharing of values is bound to be both precarious and morally indifferent. It is precarious because the individual will is the true and only seat of value, forever changing direction as the dangers and opportunities of the struggle for comfort and glory shift. The sharing of values is also without ethical significance. We are not entitled to pass from the fact that we happen to agree upon our ends to the claim that someone else ought to agree to them, or at least should do nothing to stop us from attaining them.

Peace must therefore be established by rules. By its significance to society, by its origin, and by its form, a rule differs from a value. A good way to develop the point is to make the concept of rule used in liberal political thought more precise. One can do this by distinguishing different kinds of rules with respect to their uses in social life and then by focusing on the type of rule with which liberal political doctrine is most directly concerned.

Rules are general and they bear on conduct. Beyond this, however, little can be said before we have distinguished three sorts of rules: constitutive, technical or instrumental, and prescriptive.[4]

Constitutive rules define a form of conduct in such a way that the distinction between the rule and the ruled activity disappears. It has been said that the rules of games and the rules of logic are of this sort. The moves of a game and thus the game as a whole are defined by its rules. The laws of identity and contradiction determine a particular mode of discourse.[5]

Technical or instrumental rules are guides for the choice of the most effective means to an end. They take the form, do *x* if you want *y*. They simply state a generalization about what means are most likely on the whole to produce the desired result. In any given situation, one may find a more efficient means than the one indicated by the rule.[6]

Prescriptive rules are imperatives that state what some category of persons may do, ought to do, or ought not to do. Accordingly, they are permissions, general commands, and prohibitions. Prescriptive rules differ from constitutive rules because they are clearly distinguishable from the conduct they govern and from instrumental rules because they are not hypothetical.

The rules to which the first principle of liberal political doctrine refers must be prescriptive. The war of men against one another lacks the voluntary or unthinking stability of conduct presupposed by constitutive rules. Moreover, the same antagonism precludes the constant and general agreement about ends that would be necessary for instrumental rules to serve effectively as a basis for the ordering of social relations.

The prescriptive rules established by government are usually called laws. Many laws, to be sure, lend themselves easily to being viewed as instrumental or constitutive rules.[7] Indeed, it is possible to see the whole legal order as either instrumental or constitutive; the implications of these alternative possibilities will be mentioned later. Nevertheless, for the moment it is enough to remember that for a powerful if not dominant strain in liberal political thought laws are above all prescriptive rules.

They place limits on the pursuit of private ends, thereby ensuring that natural egoism will not turn into a free-for-all in which everyone and everything is endangered. They also facilitate mutual collaboration. The two tasks are connected because a peaceful social order in which we know what to expect from others is a condition for the accomplishment of any of our goals. More specifically, it is the job of the laws to guarantee the supreme goods of social life, order, and freedom.

Positivism and natural right

The two basic manners in which the political doctrine of liberalism defines the opposition of rules and values correspond to two ideas about the source of the laws and to two conceptions of how freedom and order may be established. To establish order and freedom the laws must be impersonal. They must embody more than the values of an individual or of a group. Rules whose source is the interest of a single person or class of persons destroy the good of freedom because, by definition, they constitute a dominion of some wills over the wills of others. Furthermore, they leave order without any support except the terror by which it is imposed, for the oppressed will not love the laws.

There are other ways to avoid the dictatorship of private interest. One way is to imagine that public rules are made by a will that stands above the contending private wills and somehow represents them. Hobbes' sovereign monarch and Hegel's bureaucratic class and king exemplify this notion of a political deity.[8] The political deity's circumstances supposedly allow it to understand and to promote the common interests men have in the control of hostility and in the furtherance of collaboration.

According to this view, which one might call in an ample sense positivism or absolutism, the problem of determining *in general* the best way to guarantee coordination and to limit antagonism is insoluble. This may be either because there are no solid standards for choosing the best solution or because the complexity of the task exceeds the powers of the mind. The right laws will therefore be whatever rules are chosen by the sovereign, whose condition allegedly places him beyond the contention of individual wants.

The absolutist view leads to a kind of legislative agnosticism that makes it impossible to define when the laws are impersonal other than by the standard of their origin. Moreover, the sovereign, the government, or the class in whose impartiality the positivist conception trusts are always in danger of sinking into the very battle of private interests from which they claim to escape. Indeed, given the impossibility of rising above individual choice as a measure of the good, this disaster seems unavoidable.

For these reasons, there arises within liberal thought a second family of attempts to define the relationship between rules and values. It consists in trying to formulate standards or procedures that will establish in a general fashion which laws are impersonal and therefore capable of securing order and freedom in society. The more familiar liberal theories of legislation fall into this category.

Among such views, there is one that calls for separate and immediate treatment because of its direct bearing on the relationship between rules and values. It starts from the premise that the circumstances of reciprocal hostility and need, and the universal interest in comfort and glory, carry implications of their own for how society ought to be arranged. Intelligence can spell out the implications and then take them as a basis for impersonal legislation. Thus, the solution to problems of order and freedom preexists the making of the laws and can be used as a standard with which to judge them. It is this preexisting solution that settles the entitlements of individuals; rights precede rules. Here you have the core of the modern theory of natural right, under whose star the liberal state was born.[9]

There is in most statements of the natural rights conception an ambiguity that obscures a fatal dilemma. If we treat the rights as somehow derived from the circumstances of social life, we are forced to explain how evaluative standards can be inferred from facts. If, on the contrary, we present the rights as simply prudent means to achieve agreed-upon ends, like peace and prosperity, we have to explain how we go about judging divergence from these ends and what happens when, in a particular case, the purpose seems to be better served by disrespecting the right.[10] These and other consequences of such an attempt to view the law as a system of instrumental rules are discussed at greater length later on.

Despite their divergence, the positivist and natural right interpretations of the principle of rules and values have in common the insistence that it is on the whole better for men to live under laws than to be without them. The two doctrines agree that the absence of coercively enforced public rules would deny us the blessings of collaboration and security in the search for comfort and glory. The point can be put in an altogether more inclusive form. Whenever we want something, we must also want not to have it kept away from us or taken away once it is already ours. When we want to carry out a course of action, we must also want not to be stopped by others from executing it.

To will intelligently and consequentially is to will that others respect our objectives. We wish to be entitled to the objects of our choices. Entitlements, however, are possible only when there is a system of general rules that limits the wants of each man in comparison to those of his fellows so that each may be safe in the enjoyment of what is his. In short, will implies the will to be entitled, which in turn implies the acceptance of a system of rules either to distribute or to confirm and enforce the entitlements. With similar arguments, some have even suggested that a legal order is entailed by the very concept of a society of men with conflicting values.[11]

At a still more basic level, positivism and natural rights theory may be viewed as expressions in political thought of opposing yet complementary views of the dualism of the universal and the particular. In Chapter One, I pointed out that this dualism is the common ground of the antinomies of theory and fact and of reason and desire. In this chapter, it will reappear as the basis of an antinomy of rules and values.

To the positivist, society has no inherent order of its own. He sees rules as the impositions of a will, even though of an enlightened one, on the chaos of social life. The universal laws are simply conventions which set the boundaries among particular interests so that these interests will not destroy each other.

The natural rights theorist, on the contrary, claims to discover an intrinsic order in social relations, an order it is his purpose to make explicit and to develop. For him the universals that describe this order—rights, rules, and institutional categories—have an existence and a worth quite independent of the particular interests that may take advantage of them. Thus, the natural rights thinker treats the system of private law concepts of contract and property or the doctrine of separation of powers in public law as if they had an autonomous logic that survived in all their transmutations.

Though they differ in the priorities they assign to the universal and the particular, positivism and natural rights doctrine are at one in accepting a radical distinction between universals and particulars and in identifying the former with the abstract and the latter with the concrete. The significance of this assumption for the entire system of liberal thought will gradually become clear.

The legal mentality

To explain the principle of rules and values, I have defined its constituent terms and suggested how the liberal doctrine conceives their relationship to each other. Now I shall complete my study of the principle by describing some of its links to a more general view of social life.

The society evoked and described by the first postulate of liberal political thought is a society governed by law. Only a system of prescriptive rules with the characteristics of law can resolve the problems of order and freedom. These characteristics are already implicit in the preceding discussion of what prescriptive rules have to be like to satisfy the requirement of impersonality. For liberal political thought, the laws must be general, uniform, public, and capable of coercive enforcement.

Because the laws are general, it is possible to state what sorts of acts are commanded, prohibited, or permitted to categories of persons before specific problems of choice under the laws arise. The generality of the laws makes it possible for them to be impersonal either because they may represent some ideal outcome of conflicting private interests or because they somehow abstract altogether from considerations of private interest.

To be meaningful, generality requires uniformity of application. Some decisions under the rules may be attacked as mistaken, and others defended as correct. Entitlements or rights are interests of individuals protected by uniformly applied laws.

If they are impersonal, the laws must also be public. They are the rules established by a particular institution, the government or the state. The state is viewed either as above the antagonism of private values or as the framework within which those interests are represented and reconciled. Only such an institution can hope to frame laws that do more than embody a factional interest.

Hence, a clear line is drawn between the state and other social groups, and between the laws of the former and the rules of the latter. But the distinction is always breaking down. The government takes on the characteristics of a private body because private interests are the only interests that exist in the situation of which it is a part. Thus, the state is like the gods on Olympus, who were banished from the earth and endowed with superhuman powers, but condemned to undergo the passions of mortals.

Lastly, the laws must on the whole be capable of coercive enforcement. Failure to achieve one's goals has an automatic sanction. In psychology, the sanction is described as discontentment; in political thought, as the loss of comfort and glory. If, however, the laws, by virtue of their very impersonality, fail to live up completely to the interests of any person, obedience to the public rules cannot be spontaneously protected by self-interest. A sufficiently stiff punishment, however, will make it in the interest of all to obey them by outweighing the advantages that might be gained from disobedience.

Generality, uniformity, publicity, and coercion are therefore the distinguishing attributes of impersonal laws. Each of them is connected with a deeper set of presuppositions about thought or society. The relationship of the attributes of law to their assumptions, and of the assumptions to one another, is neither logical nor causal, but is of a kind described later as a relationship of common meaning. These foundations of the idea of law are aspects of the peculiar legal mentality that animates liberal political thought.

Generality is associated with the political ideal of formal equality and with the moral ideal of universalism. Formal equality means that as citizens of the state and legal persons men are viewed and treated by the law as fundamentally equal. Social circumstances must therefore be clearly distinguished from legal-political status. By disregarding or accepting the inequality of the former in order to emphasize all the more intensely the equality of the latter, we commit ourselves to general laws. To equalize men's social circumstances with respect to even a few of the divergences among those circumstances, we would have to treat each man or each group differently and thus to move away from the attribute of generality. The language of formal equality is a language of rights as abstract opportunities to enjoy certain advantages rather than a language of the concrete and actual experience of social life.[12]

The ethical analogue to formal equality is universalism. It is the belief that moral judgment, like political order, is primarily a matter of rights and duties. The rights and duties are established by principles whose formulation becomes more general and therefore more perfect the less their applicability turns on who and where one is. The morality of reason is a classic form of the universalist ethic.

Formal equality and moral universalism both include the conception of universals and particulars encountered before. The legal person or the moral agent are constructed, as abstract and formal universals, out of individual lives, and then treated as if they were real and independent beings. Particular interests, experiences, or circumstances are viewed as a contingent substance of the forms, or as concrete examples of the abstract propositions. Thus, one can define a right independently of the interests an individual may use it to promote.

The basis of uniformity is the formal conception of reason. Reason cannot establish the ends of action, nor does it suffice to determine the concrete implications of general values on which we may happen to agree. That is why rules are so important in the first place. Nevertheless, if the laws are to be uniformly applied, we need a technique of rule application. This technique must rely on the powers that reason possesses because it is a machine for analysis and combination: the capacity to deduce conclusions from premises and the ability to choose efficient means to accepted ends. Consequently, the major liberal theories of adjudication view the task of applying law either as one of making deductions from the rules or as one of choosing the best means to advance the ends the rules themselves are designed to foster.

The public character of law has its immediate ground in the distinction between state and society and in the more inclusive dichotomy of public and private life. The state appears in a double light, as the providential alternative to the blindness of private cupidity and as the supreme weapon of some men in their self-interested struggle against others. The separation of the public and the private alternates with the destruction of the latter by the former. In either event, the conflict between the two is never resolved.

The assumption of the belief that the laws must be capable of coercive enforcement is the artificial view of society. According to this view, even though society may have an implicit order, as the natural rights theorist claims, it is not a self-regulating or self-enforcing one. Because individuals and individual interests are the primary elements of social life, and because thy are locked in a perpetual struggle with one another, social order must be established by acts of will and protected against the ravages of self-interest.

The ideas that there is no natural community of common ends and that group life is a creature of will help explain the importance of rules and of their coercive enforcement. But the same factors may also account for the fascination of terror, the systematic use of violence unlimited by law, as a device of social organization. The less one's ability to rely on participation in common ends, the greater the importance of force as a bond among individuals. Punishment and fear take the place of community.

Moreover, when they view everything in the social world as a creation of the will, men come to believe there is nothing in society a will sufficiently violent cannot preserve or destroy. Thus, legalism and terrorism, the commitment to rules and the seduction of violence, are rival brothers, but brothers nonetheless.[13]

The legal mentality described in the preceding pages is no mere invention of philosophers. It is a way of thinking about social life, a mode of consciousness that is bound together with both a doctrine and an experience of social life. For the present, let me continue to focus on the doctrine. As the argument moves forward, I shall come back to the consciousness and examine the experience.

THE PRINCIPLE OF SUBJECTIVE VALUE

There is an aspect of the principle of rules and values so important that it deserves to be distinguished and developed in its own right. It is the proposition that all values are individual and subjective, the principle of subjective value. My discussion of this principle will proceed in three steps. First, I shall explain what I mean by individuality and subjectivity and contrast the conception of individual and subjective value with an alternative view. Then, I shall examine the relation of the principle to other aspects of liberal political theory. The last step of the argument will show how the idea of subjective value serves as the connecting link between the repudiation of intelligible essences and the central political problems of lawmaking and law application.

Ends are viewed by liberal theory as individual in the sense that they are always the objectives of particular individuals. By contrast, values are called communal when they are understood as the aims of groups, and of individuals only to the extent that the individuals are members of those groups. The political doctrine of liberalism does not acknowledge communal values. To recognize their existence, it would be necessary to begin with a vision of the basic circumstances of social life that took groups rather than individuals as the intelligible and primary units of social life. The individuality of values is the very basis of personal identity in liberal thought, a basis the communal conception of value destroys.

Values are subjective in the sense that they are determined by choice. Subjectivity emphasizes that an end is an end simply because someone holds it, whereas individuality means that there must always be a particular person whose end it is. The opposing conception is the idea of objective value, a major theme of the philosophy of the ancients. Objective values are standards and goals of conduct that exist independently of human choice. Men may embrace or reject objective values, but they cannot establish or undo their authority.

From the start, liberal political thought has been in revolt against the conception of objective value.[14] If we were able to perceive such values, they would become the true foundation of the social order. Public rules would be relegated to a subsidiary role, as devices for the specification of the objective standards, when those standards were imprecise, or for their enforcement, when they were disobeyed. The problems of order and freedom would be cast in a different light if we could think of these norms of conduct as ends whose fulfillment would bring our worthiest capacities to their richest development rather than as constraints imposed by an external will. Even the premises of liberal psychology would be affected by an objective theory of value. Ends would be at least as intelligible as facts. They would be things that exist in the world, like triangles, if not like tables. The distinction between the objective understanding of facts and the arbitrary choice of goals would therefore collapse.

For all these reasons, the teachings of liberalism must be, and almost always have been, uncompromisingly hostile to the classic idea of objective good. The theoretical antagonism is accompanied and in part inspired by a historical process, the progressive disintegration of the system of fixed social classes or estates in postfeudal European societies. It is only in the context of a well-defined hierarchy for the distribution of wealth and power that the objective values of the earlier philosophy seemed precise in their implications. As a result of the dissolution of that hierarchical order and of the expansion of the market economy, concepts like 'just price' in exchange and distribution according to 'virtue' lost their meaning.

Granted that the doctrine of objective value is incompatible with the premises of liberalism and that its political implications are unclear, might it nevertheless be true? For the present, I shall be content to suggest some preliminary reasons why I think it is false, but the main argument will have to wait. The criticism of the rival doctrine of subjective value will be developed in the course of this chapter.

First, the theory of objective value presupposes that the mind can grasp and establish moral essences or goods. But this has never been shown, and the conception of reason on which it rests has been discredited in nonmoral areas of thought.

Second, the doctrine denies any significance to choice other than the passive acceptance or rejection of independent truths. Our experience of moral judgment, however, seems to be one of at least contributing to shape the ends we pursue. A conception that puts this fact aside disregards the significance of choice as an expression of personality.

Third, the inability of the theory of objective value to determine how we should act in particular situations is no remediable mishap. To make the doctrine plausible in the absence of divinely revealed moral truth, its proponents rely on references to moral opinions shared by men of many different ages and societies. The more concrete the allusions to this allegedly timeless moral agreement, the less convincing they become. Therefore, to make their case the proponents of objective value must restrict themselves to a few abstract ideals whose vagueness allows almost any interpretation.

There is a conception of the place of values in society that does not at first seem to fit into the categories of the individual and the communal, the subjective and the objective, but that nevertheless plays an overpowering role in our everyday views, in the modern social sciences, and in classical liberal thought itself. It is the idea that the more or less stable sharing of values among persons is a fundamental fact about society. Theories like Hutcheson's doctrine of benevolence or Hume's doctrine of sympathy foreshadowed this idea by emphasizing the extent to which the unity of human nature allows men to enter into each other's sentiments. However, as long as the sharing of ends is conceived simply as a convergence of individual preferences, with no change of other postulates of liberal thought, it does not truly qualify the principle that values are individual and subjective.

On the other hand, each convergence of preferences remains a precarious alliance of interests. The source of value continues to be the individual will, given the derivative and artificial character of groups according to the principle of individualism I later describe. Hence, the individuality of values persists despite the possibility of varying degrees of consensus at different moments.

On the other hand, reliance on combinations of interests as a mechanism of social order is consistent with the premise that these interests are significant only because they happen to be agreed upon. Democracy may require that the shared ends of the majority be imposed on a minority that does not share them. The liberal theorist, however, will be careful to point out that the duty of a minority to obey laws that advance the goals of a majority must be founded on the minority's rationally self-interested consent. The rules or the procedures for rulemaking are in the minority's enlightened self-interest even when they operate prejudicially in particular cases (Locke). Or perhaps the will to obey the laws is implied in all the more concrete desires one has, when those desires are clearly understood (Kant). In no way, then, does the idea of sharing of values, as it appears in liberal thought, disrespect the subjectivity of values.

We have seen that the principle of subjective value is closely linked with the liberal conception of rules as the basis of order and freedom in society and with the psychological distinction of reason and desire, description and evaluation. But to understand the principle fully we must return to the problem of intelligible essences. The temporary retreat to a level of even greater generality and abstraction will enable us to see how the postulate of subjective value bears on much more concrete issues of political and legal theory.

The doctrine that there are no intelligible essences is the ultimate basis of the principle of subjective value. The theory of intelligible essences states that there are a limited number of classes of things in the world, that each thing has characteristics that determine the class to which it belongs, and that these characteristics can be known directly by the mind.

Were we to make any concessions to the doctrine of intelligible essences in our view of natural facts, there seems to be no way we could keep the doctrine from penetrating into the sphere of language, conduct, and values. This is an obvious conclusion in a philosophy that denies the separation of values from facts. For such a philosophy our notions of right and wrong, good and bad, have to be taken as interpretations of objective standards of value just as our capacity to distinguish tables from chairs is a consequence of our ability to perceive the respective essences of each.

But even a doctrine like the liberal one that contrasts facts and values cannot ultimately uphold the ontological distinction between them. Values may be experienced as subjective, and desires as arbitrary, but there is still an important sense in which they are facts like all other facts. The arbitrariness of desires and the subjectivity of values have to do with the significance of ends as bases for the criticism or justification of conduct. The fundamental point remains: precisely because ends are denied an objective existence, they must be conceived as psychic events going on in the heads of particular men. If events in general had intelligible essences, so would these psychic events. The battle against objective values would be lost. Thus, to maintain the principle of subjective value, we must reject the doctrine of intelligible essences completely.

Not only did the classic liberal thinkers recognize the truth of this conclusion, but they devoted a large part of their efforts to dealing with its many troublesome implications.[15]

Now, however, a difficulty arises. If there are no intelligible essences, how do we go about classifying facts and situations, especially social facts and social situations? Because facts have no intrinsic identity, everything depends on the names we give them. The conventions of naming rather than any perceived quality of 'tableness' will determine whether an object is to count as a table. In the same way, convention rather than nature will dictate whether a particular bargain is to be treated as a contract.

It is not surprising, then, that language should become an obsession of the liberal thinker, for he worships it as the demiurge of the world. But the real sovereigns that stand behind the demiurge are the interests that lead men to classify things as they do. He who has the power to decide what a thing will be called has the power to decide what it is. This is as true of persons as of things. There cannot be patricians and plebeians unless we are able to distinguish the two groups. To distinguish them is to name them because there is no essential quality that determines who is patrician; who plebeian.[16]

Properly understood, the system of public rules is itself a language. Every rule is addressed to a category of persons and acts, and marks its addressees off from others. To mark off is to name. To apply the rules to particular cases is to subsume individual persons and acts under the general names of which the rules consist. Hence, the theory of law is a special branch of the general theory of naming.

At last, I can state the great political problem toward which I have been winding my way. The resort to a set of public rules as the foundation of order and freedom is a consequence of the subjective conception of value. The subjective conception of value in turn presupposes the abandonment of the doctrine of intelligible essences. In the absence of intelligible essences, however, there are no obvious criteria for defining general categories of acts and persons when we make the rules. (The making of rules is legislation.) Nor are there clear standards by which to classify the particular instances under rules when we come to the stage of applying the rules we have made. (The application of rules is adjudication.)

All the fundamental issues of modern political and legal theory have to do with the need to supply standards of legislation and adjudication when intelligible essences, and therefore objective values, are rejected. Each attempt to provide guides for the making and application of the laws seems to undermine the system of thought it was meant to support.

THE PRINCIPLE OF INDIVIDUALISM

The interplay of rules and values in society, described by the first two principles of liberal political thought, does not exhaust the basic features of the unreflective view described at the beginning of the chapter. There is still the problem of the relation of individuals to groups. Thus, the need for a third principle: a group is simply a collection of individuals; in other words, the attributes of a group are the sum of the attributes of its individual members. It is the principle of individualism, or simply individualism.[17]

If we take the group as the whole and the members as parts, the principle of individualism affirms that the whole is just the sum of its parts. In this sense, it is formally analogous to the principle of analysis, which states that all complex knowledge (the whole) can be analyzed back into the elementary ideas or sensations (the parts) with which it was built. This formal analogy will later turn out to be the outward sign of a profound connection.

The vision the principle of individualism expresses can be described in several ways. In one sense, it is the view that society is artificial: groups are products of the will and interests of individuals. For the individual, the group is characteristically a means to the satisfaction of ends he could not achieve except through membership. Because the interests of their members are unstable, groups themselves are precarious associations, constantly destroyed and reborn in different forms. The central problem of the theory of groups will therefore be defined as the study of the interests that keep men faithful to their associations.

In another sense, the conception advanced by the principle of individualism is the idea that personality is independent of history. The genesis and disintegration of groups occurs against the background of an abiding unity of human nature, for groups are less real and fundamental than the individuals who compose them.

When I say that the group is viewed as a collection of individuals, or that all the attributes of the group can be explained as a combination of the attributes of its members, I have both a methodological and a moral idea in mind. The methodological idea is that by summing up all we know about the individual members taken separately we can find out all there is to know about the group. But what is summed up in this operation? Clearly, we must count in the addition characteristics the individuals have because they are members of the group. Otherwise, the principle of individualism would be trivial and without importance for our ideas about society. But once these characteristics are included and their causes elucidated, there is nothing more about the group left to explain. If group behavior is governed by scientific laws, these laws derive from the more general laws that govern individual conduct. Psychology is more basic than sociology.[18]

The moral side of individualism follows as a result of its methodological aspect. The group must never be viewed as a source of values in its own right. Within the group there will be a greater or lesser degree of sharing of values. But this sharing will be contingent and subjective, in the way described in the preceding section. Typically, there will be no single set of shared ends, but only varying coalitions of interests among particular members. Suppose we admit the possibility of values held by the group as an entity, and by individuals only partially and insofar as they are absorbed into the group. The consequence would be that an important feature of group life could not be either described or explained through a study of its members. The postulate of individualism is meant to avoid this.

Individualism is so deeply rooted in our thought that it is hard to understand. A great part of the difficulty lies in imagining a different principle that might help define it by contrast. Yet such a polar view has been a staple of social thought in the West since the Romantic movement and the birth of sociology as a discipline. It is the principle of collectivism, exemplified by romantic, organicist conceptions of the group. These conceptions view the group as an entity with independent existence irreducible to the lives of its members, with group values that stand apart from the individual and subjective ends of its membership, even with its own 'personality.' Collectivism is one of the most influential partial critiques of the liberal doctrine.

The antagonism between the liberal and the collectivist view of the relation of individuals to groups is illustrated by their divergent conceptions of the state. For liberal thinkers the state is an artifact of the laws; indeed, for some it is the legal order itself. Rules, procedures, and sanctions are what hold the state together. The state has a vicarious existence; its true life is the life of its citizens. For the organicist, however, the core of the state is the 'nation.' The unity of the nation is based on the tradition of collective values to which countless individuals have contributed as streams flowing into a great sea. The sea does not evaporate because the streams run dry. If we could correct the metaphor to say that the streams begin as well as end in the sea, we would have the beginnings of an image of the collectivist theory of the state. The activities of the citizens must be inspired by the 'spirit' of the nation; their values derived from its. The core of the collectivist view is the idea of the spontaneity of social bonds and of their priority over individual striving.[19]

Individualism and the first two postulates of liberal political theory depend on each other. Groups are artificial because all values are individual and subjective. If the group had an autonomous existence and were a source of value in its own right, we could no longer maintain that all ends were individual. If we went further, with some of the collectivists, and claimed an objective moral worth for the values of the community or the nation, we would also have to abandon the idea of subjectivity. Finally, the liberal doctrine of groups is connected with the principle of rules and values. Because community is always precarious and depends on the convergence of private interests, fixed rules are needed as the guarantees of peaceful and free association.

ORDER, FREEDOM, AND LAW: THE PROBLEM OF LEGISLATION

There can be no coherent, adequate doctrine of legislation or adjudication on liberal premises. When viewed together, as a set of related answers to questions of rulemaking and rule application, liberal political and legal doctrines are like a spider's web with a hole. If one pushes over a thread of the web to cover the hole, another hole opens up someplace else. In the end, one may conclude that something is wrong with the spider.

The issues of legislation and adjudication, in the very broad sense in which they are defined here, lie at the heart of liberal political thought. Society, as it appears to the liberal, is held together by rules. Rules are the main devices for establishing order and freedom. The major part of modern political philosophy is the theory of legislation, and the core of modern jurisprudence the theory of adjudication. The most effective critique of liberal political doctrine would therefore be one which showed that theories tied to the political premises of liberalism fail to account for the possibility of order and freedom. The focus on the making and application of state law in the following pages is simply a way to approach the more general issue of rules through what, for liberal political thought, is its most crucial aspect.

The problems of order and freedom collapse into each other. If one knew to what standards the laws would have to conform so as not to prefer arbitrarily one man's advantage to another's (freedom), one would also be able to determine how best to restrain antagonism in society in the interest of collaboration (order). Put in different words, to be effective as a means of order, the laws must deserve and win the allegiance of the citizenry, and to do that they must be capable of being justified. The justification of the laws would consist in showing that the restraints put on men's struggle for comfort, power, and glory are fair because no man's freedom is set without reason above another's and each man is allowed the maximum freedom compatible with the prohibition of arbitrary preference. A study of the theory of legislation can therefore rest content with an inquiry into the foundations of freedom.

Freedom may be defined positively or negatively in liberal thought. Positively, it is the power to pursue one's goals without human interference. Negatively, it is the condition in which one does not have to submit to someone else's will. The positive and the negative definition are interchangeable, given the qualification attached to the former, 'without human interference.'

They can both be stated in a strong as well as in a weak form. According to the strong interpretation, a man is free to the extent no one else stands in the way of his goals or dictates his conduct. According to the weak variant, a person is free as long as any human interference with his objectives is governed by impersonal laws or commanded by an impersonal agency, the sovereign or state.

The weak form does not do justice to the scope of the liberal conception of freedom, for freedom may be equally distributed, and each man still have less of it than he might. Moreover, in its effort to justify the public rules, liberal political thought is irresistibly drawn toward democracy, which requires that the individual participate, however indirectly, in the making of the laws and in the management of the state. Nonetheless, the weaker formulation has the advantage of drawing attention to the issue of impersonality, equality, or uniformity of the laws as a necessary though insufficient condition of a regime of freedom. Part of the task of a theory of legislation is to define what that condition means.

There are three main ways in which modern political philosophy conceives of the establishment of freedom through legislation. The first two are variations on liberal political premises; the third is a halfhearted attempt to escape from those premises. I cannot present in this essay a detailed criticism of each of the doctrines, nor need I, for the criticisms, taken individually, are well known. The important thing is to be able to see them in the context of their interrelations and of the assumptions they share with the doctrines they attack.

The first type of solution to the problem of freedom attempts to derive the laws solely from the idea of freedom itself. Consequently, it denies that legislation has to choose among competing individual and subjective values, and to give preference to some over others. This is the formal theory of freedom. It is illustrated by the political and legal doctrines of Kant and by the kinds of legal positivism that grew directly out of the Kantian tradition.[20]

The theory of formal freedom suffers from the same dilemma as the morality of reason, of which it is the political equivalent. Take Kant's universal principle of right, "Every action is right that in itself or in its maxim is such that freedom of the will of each can coexist together with the freedom of the will of everyone according to a universal law." When this proposition is left in its abstract form, it seems impossible to derive from it definite conclusions about what precisely the laws should command, prohibit, or permit. If we interpret freedom according to universal laws to mean equal freedom and even add the qualification 'maximum freedom' we are still in the dark on what to legislate. Which of the indefinite number of things men want to do should be allowed and which forbidden? But, as soon as we try to reach the level of concrete regulation of conduct, we are forced to prefer some values to others. This, however, is just what the formal theory of freedom was meant to avoid. Given the principle of subjective value, any such preference would be inherently incapable of justification. Like the morality of reason, the formal doctrine of freedom has to choose between being unworkable and being incoherent.

The second main response to the question of freedom in liberal thought is the claim that there exists some procedure for lawmaking on the basis of the combination of private ends, to which procedure all individuals might subscribe in self-interest. Self-interest means the intelligent understanding of what we need in order to achieve our own individual and subjective goals. To the extent that such a method for legislation is available, there will be no contradiction between the premise of the subjectivity of ends and the existence of laws that command, prohibit, or permit particular forms of conduct.

This doctrine, the substantive theory of freedom, has three main forms. According to the first, the method directly determines the aggregation of interests to be protected by the state and, therefore, the content of the laws. Classical utilitarianism is an example of this view.[21] According to the second form, we subscribe in self-interest to procedures for making laws and settling disputes rather than to a concrete plan of social organization. The doctrine of the social contract, as formulated by Locke and Rousseau, represents this position.[22] The utilitarian and social contract versions of the substantive theory of freedom can be collapsed into a third. It appeals to the conception of an ideal system of procedures for lawmaking that all men might accept in self-interest and the operation of which can be shown to lead to certain specific conclusions about the distribution of wealth and power. The work of J. Rawls, the American moralist, illustrates this view.[23]

The main deficiencies of the substantive doctrine of freedom turn out to be similar to those of the formal doctrine. The substantive theory of freedom breaks down because it does not succeed in finding a neutral way to combine individual, subjective values.

In the utilitarian variant of the theory, the problem is to find a standpoint outside the subjective purposes of individuals from which to decide which combination of those values should be favored by the laws. Which of the infinite number of ends will be added up and what weight will be given to each? Such a neutral, Archimedean point, however, would be precisely the objective good whose nonexistence drove us into the attempt to devise a liberal doctrine of legislation.

Similarly, the social contract version of the substantive theory of freedom presupposes the possibility of finding a procedure for lawmaking to which any man, no matter what his values, would have reason to agree. The more indeterminate the procedure in specifying particular laws, the less would anyone have reason to object to it. But, then, the problem of legislation would simply be postponed. On the other hand, the more concrete the procedure, the less would it be likely to benefit equally everyone's wants.

Take, for example, a constitutional representative democracy. Some of its laws will be part of the constitutional framework. Others will be the results of decisions made by authorized persons within the framework.

The first category of laws already prefers some values, but with what justification? The second class of laws has a content validated though not required by the constitution. To justify them one must resort to some independent principle such as majority rule. The reason for having such and such tax laws, for example, is simply that they are the laws the majority wants. But why should all men have equal reason to favor majority rule? Surely some expect to find more allies than others in the pursuit of their objectives. That majority rule is not a principle of self-evident wisdom is shown by the fact that in a constitutional regime there are certain things the majority is not allowed to do.

The third subcategory of the substantive theory of freedom resembles the social contract doctrine because it proposes a procedure for law-making, and utilitarianism because it seeks to prove that this procedure would result in specific laws governing power and wealth. It tries to escape from the traps of both the social contract and utilitarian doctrines by imagining a hypothetical ideal situation in which men would be able to legislate without knowing their positions in society, and thus without knowing what their particular values as real individuals would be. The difficulty with this is analogous to the objections against the earlier types of the substantive theory of freedom. The less concreteness we allow to the persons in the ideal position, the less will they have standards by which to legislate specific laws, leaving the problem of legislation unsolved. But the more they become like actual human beings, with their own preferences, the more will they be forced to choose among individual, subjective values in the ideal situation itself.

Both the formal and the substantive theory of freedom are confronted and destroyed by the same dilemma, the impossibility of reconciling the needs for concreteness and for neutrality in the doctrine of legislation. The same premises that bring the liberal problem of freedom into being, the principle of subjective value and the related principles of rules and values, and of individualism, make the problem insoluble.[24]

The third solution to the conundrum of freedom denies the assumption upon which the conundrum rests, the subjectivity of values. It appeals to the idea of shared values as the basis for lawmaking. In each well-organized society there is a core of widely agreed upon purposes on which either lawmaking itself or the choice of procedures for lawmaking can be based. Laws or procedures with such a foundation are not arbitrary preferences for certain ends; they are the embodiment of the common ends. The shared values do more than serve as a source of legislation. They also work beyond the limits of formal rules as a fundamental tie among men. Though it played an important part in the works of political thinkers as diverse as Rousseau, J. S. Mill, and T. H. Green, the theory of shared values was best stated in classic social theory, particularly in the tradition that goes from Saint-Simon and Comte to Durkheim.[25]

The doctrine of shared values differs in kind from the formal and the substantive theory of freedom insofar as it seems to deny the individuality and perhaps even the subjectivity of values, premises on which the other doctrines founder. In my discussion of the principle of subjective value I have anticipated the idea of a sharing of values as a solution to the problem of freedom. I shall defer discussion of that idea until I have examined its role in the theory of adjudication.

The freedom the formal and the substantive theory are meant to protect is liberty to do whatever one wants. Kant, von Humboldt, J. S. Mill, and the English Neo-Hegelians remind us that a second idea of freedom has come to occupy an important though insecure place in liberal thought. This is the view of freedom as the development of the capacities, powers, or talents men possess. The task of the state, and the standard of legislation, is to choose the social arrangements most conducive to the flourishing of these capacities.[26]

If this doctrine were to be given any degree of precision—which it never has—it would represent a break with the whole system of liberal thought as decisive as a theory of shared values that repudiated the ideas of individuality and subjectivity. It would be necessary for the legislator to select among the indefinite number of human talents those most deserving of protection, and to determine which are more readily left to the individual's own care. The lawmaker would have to make use of conceptions of value and of human nature very different from the ones handed down in the tradition of liberalism. The theory of the development of talents is, indeed, one of those partial critiques of the classical system that opens the way for total criticism and can only be completed through it.

THE ANTINOMY OF RULES AND VALUES: THE PROBLEM OF ADJUDICATION

It is no help to have a doctrine for the justification of rulemaking unless we also have one for the application of rules. Freedom requires general, impersonal, or neutral laws. The definition of neutrality and its reconciliation with the demands of concreteness are the central themes of the theory of legislation. Once we manage to formulate an adequate doctrine of lawmaking, we still have to be able to determine what it means to apply the laws to particular cases. (Whenever I use the terms rule or law without further qualification, I mean a prescriptive rather than an instrumental or constitutive rule.)

Unless we can justify one interpretation of the rules over another, the claim of legislative generality will quite rightly be rejected as a sham. The theory of adjudication is therefore a continuation of the theory of legislation. Its main question is, By what standards, or in what manner, can the laws be applied without violating the requirements of freedom? If the law applier cannot justify his decisions, because they appear to rest on his own individual and subjective values, liberty will suffer. Those to whom the law is applied will have surrendered their freedom to the judge, the person authorized to apply the rules.[27]

The scope of this section is broader than the theory of adjudication itself. To understand the nature of adjudication one must distinguish two different ways of ordering human relations. One way is to establish rules to govern general categories of acts and persons, and then to decide particular disputes among persons on the basis of the established rules. This is legal justice. The other way is to determine goals and then, quite independently of rules, to decide particular cases by a judgment of what decision is most likely to contribute to the predetermined goals, a judgment of instrumental rationality. This is substantive justice.

In the situation of legal justice, the laws are made against the background of the ends they are designed to promote, even if the sole permissible end is liberty itself. Only after the rules have been formulated do decisions 'under the rules' become possible. Hence, the possibility of some sort of distinction between legislation and adjudication is precisely what defines legal justice. The main task of the theory of adjudication is to say when a decision can truly be said to stand 'under a rule,' if the rule we have in mind is the law of the state, applied by a judge. Only decisions 'under a rule' are consistent with freedom; others constitute arbitrary exercises of judicial power.

Decisions made under rules must be capable of a kind of justification different from the justification for the rules themselves. The task of judging is distinct from that of lawmaking. Usually, the separation of functions will be accompanied and strengthened by a separation of powers: the person of the lawmaker will not be the same as the person of the law applier. To the extent power cannot be made impersonal, it can at least be dispersed. But the atomization of power is always a second best to its neutrality.

There are legal systems in which the line between legislation and adjudication is hazy from the start. This is especially true in a tradition of judge-made law like the Anglo-American common law. A system in which judges both make the law and apply it is not self-evidently inconsistent with a situation of legal justice as long as some screen can be interposed between reasons for having a rule and reasons for applying it to a particular case. But the question remains, What happens to legal justice when the screen becomes transparent? For the moment, it is enough to remark that systems of judge-made law are fated to be obsessed with the relation between legal and substantive justice.

In substantive justice each decision is justified because it is the one best calculated to advance some accepted objective. The relation between a particular decision and the objective is that of a means to an end. For example, given the goal of increasing national production, a certain bargain should be enforced because its performance will increase output.

The distinctive feature of substantive justice is the nonexistence of any line between legislation and adjudication. In the pure case of substantive justice, there is neither rulemaking nor rule applying, because rather than prescriptive rules there are only choices as to what should be accomplished and judgments of instrumental rationality about how to get it done. Technical or instrumental rules are at home in a regime of substantive justice. They are maxims of efficiency, subject to constant revision in the light of new knowledge and changed circumstances. Instrumental rules differ from prescriptive rules precisely by their provisional character. It is impossible to base fixed entitlements and duties on them. The enforcement of your bargain in the situation of substantive justice will depend on whether at the hour of decision enforcement would be beneficial or harmful to the aims we have set for ourselves. For this and other reasons, to be examined later, the laws in a regime of legal justice cannot be conceived as instrumental rules.

The contrast between the regimes of legal and substantive justice might therefore be restated more simply as a difference between decision by prescriptive rules and decision by instrumental rules. Still more light may be cast on the distinction by the remark that legal justice is the political counterpart to the morality of reason and substantive justice the political equivalent of the morality of desire. Like the morality of reason, formal justice uses rules as an immediate standard of justification. Like the morality of desire, substantive justice uses ends.

Here is a brief example of the difference between the two situations, drawn deliberately to include ambiguities that further discussion will explore. Take the case of the administrator of an industry, charged by the government with the task of producing a certain number of tons of steel. There are two different ways in which the government can direct the manager's conduct. On the one hand, it may lay down rules that prescribe the sources from which supplies are to be taken, and what techniques of manufacture are to be used. Moreover, it may treat these rules as binding quite independently of whether the manager's compliance with them will result in the desired tonnage of output. Alternatively, the government may simply fix the production quota, and direct the manager to choose the most efficient means for reaching it. It may go on to point out guidelines of production that have been found efficient in the past. But the manager, under this second regime, will only be justified in following the guidelines if he fails to discover a more effective procedure, or if the costs of looking for one would outweigh the advantages of abiding by the accustomed routines. If you extend this comparison of two ways of treating the manager to include two ways of dealing with the bargains he strikes with other managers, you will have an image of the contrast between legal and substantive justice.[28]

The central thesis of this section is that neither the regime of formal nor that of substantive justice is able to solve the problem of freedom. Nevertheless, formal and substantive justice cannot be reconciled. Thus, there is no coherent solution to the problem of adjudication as it is defined by liberal thought; we cannot dispose of the difficulties with which that problem confronts liberal political doctrine by embracing either substantive or formal justice. A system of laws or rules (legal justice) can neither dispense with a consideration of values in the process of adjudication, nor be made consistent with such a consideration. Moreover, judgments about how to further general values in particular situations (substantive justice) can neither do without rules, nor be made compatible with them. This is the antinomy of rules and values.

The antinomy of rules and values is the political analogue to the psychological antinomy of reason and desire. The two antinomies involve the same sorts of arguments, and have a common source. Because the antinomy of rules and values stands at the core of modern jurisprudence, any treatment of it has to deal with the main types of modern legal theory, and with well-known objections to each of them. My purpose is not to add to these objections or to examine them in detail, but to grasp and to criticize the situation of legal theory as a whole. To this end, I begin by considering the regime of legal justice, or the theory of adjudication, and I then turn to the situation of substantive justice.

The simplest and most familiar account of legal justice goes in the literature of jurisprudence under the name of formalism. At different times it has been embraced by proponents of legislative theories as diverse as the formal and substantive doctrines of freedom, by Kantians and by Benthamites. In its strictest version, the formalist theory of adjudication states that the legal system will dictate a single, correct solution in every case. It is as if it were possible to deduce correct judgments from the laws by an automatic process. The regime of legal justice can therefore be established through a technique of adjudication that can disregard the 'policies' or 'purposes' of the law.[29]

Those who dismiss formalism as a naïve illusion, mistaken in its claims and pernicious in its effect, do not know what they are in for. Their contempt is shallower than the doctrine they ridicule, for they fail to understand what the classic liberal thinkers saw earlier: the destruction of formalism brings in its wake the ruin of all other liberal doctrines of adjudication. The first step toward understanding this is to discover that the argument against formalism rests on a basis altogether broader than has been thought necessary. Once this broader basis is described, it will become clear that the formalist position is incoherent because it is inconsistent with the premises of liberal political theory, which it also presupposes.

The formalist believes that words usually have clear meanings. He adopts, in one mode or another, Augustine's view of language as a series of names that point to things.[30] If, to recall Puffendorf's example, the law prohibits the spilling of blood in the streets, it is clear that it refers to fighting, not to the emergency assistance given by a surgeon.[31] Rules consist of strings of names, the words that describe the categories of persons and acts to which the rules apply. To the extent that words have plain meanings, it will be clear to what fact situations they apply. The judge who applies the laws to the persons and acts they denote is, by definition, applying the laws uniformly. He exercises no arbitrary power. Formalism is indeed the simplest of the alleged solutions to the problem of adjudication.

The view of rules and therefore of naming implicit in the formalist thesis depends on the preliberal conception of intelligible essences. To subsume situations under rules, and things under words, the mind must be able to perceive the essential qualities that mark each fact or situation as a member of a particular category. As soon as it is necessary to engage in a discussion of purpose to determine whether the surgeon's emergency assistance falls in the class of acts prohibited by the law, formalism has been abandoned.

The sole possible alternative to the belief in intelligible essences as a basis of formalism would be the notion that in the great majority of cases common values and common understandings of the world fostered by a shared mode of social life will make perfectly clear to what category something belongs. Social practice will take the place of both intelligible essences and explicit consideration of purpose. I shall leave this thesis for later discussion because it is a variant of the more general idea of shared values as a solution to the problems of legislation and adjudication.

The basic objection to formalism is that the doctrine of intelligible essences, whose truth the formalist's confidence in plain meanings assumes, is incompatible with the view of social life to whose consequences it responds. The aim of theories of legislation and adjudication in liberal thought is precisely to show how freedom is possible despite the individuality and subjectivity of values. If objective values were available to us, if we knew the true good with certainty, and understood all its implications and requirements perfectly, we would not need a method of impartial adjudication. With qualifications to be mentioned in good time, we would content ourselves with a regime of substantive justice, in which rules were unnecessary. The problem of adjudication, as presented in modern jurisprudence, is therefore inextricably linked with the conception that values are subjective and individual.

It was shown earlier that the principle of subjective value, which formalist theories of adjudication take for granted, cannot go together with the doctrine of intelligible essences. On the contrary, the idea of subjective value is an integral part of a view of the world for which there are no natural distinctions among things, nor any hierarchy of essences that might serve as the basis for drawing up general categories of facts and classifying particulars under those categories.

This is the modern or conventionalist idea of nature and science. For the conventionalist, there are an infinite number of possible ways of dividing the world up and of classifying particular things under general words. Classification must always be justified by some interest or purpose it serves. Hence, there are in principle no 'plain meanings.'

The rightness of punishing Puffendorf's surgeon under the law that prohibits shedding blood in the streets depends on whether we assume that the purpose of the law is to preserve public tranquility or to avoid dirtying the cobblestones. It is only because one of the purposes compared in this extreme example strikes us as absurd that the problem of purpose does not rise to consciousness. But it is always there, controlling the subsumption of facts under names, and of situations under words.

The chief vice of formalism is its dependence on a view of language that cannot be reconciled with the modern ideas of science, nature, and language that formalists themselves take for granted. Formalism is a doctrine of adjudication that relies on two sets of premises, premises about language and premises about value, that contradict one another. It is therefore an incoherent theory, a fallacy that results from a blindness to the unity of liberal psychology and liberal political theory.

The history of modern jurisprudence may be characterized as a continuing attempt to find an adequate alternative to formalism as a basis for legal justice. If the true nature of the formalist fallacy had been understood, the attempt might have been less enthusiastically undertaken. For the very considerations that defeat formalism vitiate the main doctrine of adjudication that has taken its place, the purposive theory.[32]

The purposive theory states that to apply the laws correctly and uniformly, the judge must consider the purposes or policies the laws serve. Thus, the decision not to punish the surgeon turns on the determination that the objective of the law is to guarantee safety in the streets and that this objective would be more hindered than helped by the punishment of the surgeon. The purposes or policies are the ends; the laws themselves are the means.

Whatever values or combinations of values are accepted by the theory of legislation as adequate justifications of the laws will also be used as standards for distinguishing good interpretations from bad ones. Thus, the same value of public safety that justifies the law determines who ought to be punished under its provisions. Lawmaker and law applier are viewed as participants in a collaborative endeavor. The judge uses his judicial power to promote the legislator's aims or aims the judge has reason to attribute to the laws he is applying. The purposive theorist does not hesitate to accept the modern, conventionalist view of language and thought, and to scorn the formalist's trust in plain meanings.[33]

The purposive theory leaves the regime of legal justice hanging in the air. Notice first that the purposive doctrine needs some way of defining the values, policies, or purposes that are to guide the judge's work.

In general, a rule will be thought to serve many purposes. Moreover, a judge deals with a whole system of rules, from which he must select the rule appropriate to the case before him. When he applies one of these rules to the case, he must weigh the policy of the rule he is choosing against the policies of all other rules he might have applied to the case with a different result. Thus, the purposive theory of adjudication requires not only a criterion for the definition of controlling policies, but also a method for balancing them off one against another. In the absence of a procedure for policy decision, the judge will inescapably impose his own subjective preferences, or someone else's, on the litigants.

But in fact no such method for the choice and arrangement of values exists, nor can it exist within liberal thought. Even devices like majority rule or the market, used to deal with the problem of freedom at the legislative level, are of little help in adjudication. Adjudication presupposes the separation of functions; the judge cannot pretend to base his decision directly on the 'political' forces that the market or the electoral process pit against one another. He must be the master of some independent mechanism for the combination and weighing of policies. For this mechanism to be created, however, the principle of subjective value would have to be abandoned and, together with it, all the related postulates of liberal political thought that set the stage for the problem of adjudication.

The characteristic predicament of the modern lawyer is to argue constantly about policy, as if rational choice among competing values were possible, yet to remain faithful to the idea that values are subjective and to the political doctrine of which that idea is a part. The purposive doctrine of adjudication is simply the theoretical statement of this everyday contradiction. I leave for study in the next section the possibility that this contradiction might be resolved by shared beliefs and values on which the judge could draw.

A second major objection to the purposive doctrine is the impossibility of reconciling the prescriptive view of rules with the implications of judgments of purpose or policy. For the purposive theory, the decision about when to apply a given rule to a case depends on the responses to a prior question, Will the ends of this law and of the legal order as a whole best be served by its application to the case? The interpretation of the law turns on a calculus of instrumental rationality. It may not be necessary to discuss policy explicitly in most cases, but only because the purposes of the law and their implications seem so clear that they dispense conscious scrutiny. To a stranger who pressed us on our interpretation of a particular law, we would ultimately have to give a purposive defense of the interpretation. Judgments of instrumental rationality, which define the most effective means to the end or purpose, always have the last say about the classification of acts and persons under the rules.

A judgment of instrumental rationality, however, cannot pretend to have any generality or stability. It is always possible to discover a more efficient means, either because circumstances have changed or because knowledge has improved. Thus, the only kind of rule consistent with the standpoint of means and ends is an instrumental rule. If the scope of every rule has to be determined in the end by a judgment of instrumental rationality, the whole law is reduced to a body of instrumental rules. The consequences for a regime of legal justice are fatal.

First, it is no longer sensible in such a situation to speak of fixed entitlements and duties. If the policy of the law of contract is to promote national wealth, and if the scope of the rules of contract law has to be determined by the analysis of purpose, a bargain that harms the objective more than it helps it will not be considered an enforceable contract. We would be neither under an obligation to keep promises as private citizens, nor justified in enforcing contractual arrangements as officials whenever a refusal to comply or to enforce was authorized by an appropriate judgment of instrumental rationality.

Another consequence of the purposive theory is to undermine the separation of functions and of powers. The judges will be called upon to engage in the same kinds of assessments of instrumental rationality that characterize legislation and administration. Moreover, the rules that allocate authority among different agencies of government will themselves have to be applied in the light of their policies. One can never exclude in principle the possibility that in a particular case the benefit done to the policies underlying the jurisdictional rules by disobeying those rules may outweigh the disadvantages, proximate or remote, of violating the rules. In such a case the apparent usurpation will be permitted, indeed commanded.

These disastrous implications of the purposive theory of adjudication for legal justice cannot be avoided by a flat insistence that certain rules should be immune to interpretation, or that the judge not be allowed to rearrange the allocation of powers in the light of his understanding of the underlying policies of the allocation. That would be a retreat to formalism. The critique of formalism has shown that purposive interpretation is inescapable. Now, however, it turns out that it is also destructive of the very foundations of legal justice.

The problem of purposive adjudication is the chief preoccupation of every system of judge-made law. When the cases that make the law are the same ones that apply it, and the influence of views about what the law should be on views about what it is are constantly before one's eyes, the distinction between legislation and adjudication hangs by a slender thread. If the thread is only as strong as the purposive theory, it will break.

My discussion of the formal and purposive theories of adjudication was meant to show that a coherent theory of adjudication or of legal justice is not possible on the premises of liberal thought. Yet those premises are what make the distinction between lawmaking and the application of law possible and necessary. It remains to consider briefly whether the problem of freedom can be solved by a regime of substantive justice that, unlike both the formalist and purposive theories of legal justice, does not pretend to be committed to rules at all.

The first prerequisite of substantive justice is a set of values so firmly established that they can be taken for granted when decisions about individual cases are made. Particular choices may then be viewed either as means to the accepted values conceived as ends, or as ways of giving concreteness or substance to the formal or abstract values. For example, a decision not to enforce bargains between husband and wife may be considered either as means to the end of marital trust, or as a specification of the general value of marital trust. In the first case, the method of substantive justice is one of instrumental rationality; in the second case, it is a method of practical or prudential reason, which mediates between the abstract and the concrete. Because such an idea of practical reason is unknown to liberal thought and inconsistent with its premises, my discussion will be confined to the form of substantive justice that relies on instrumental rationality.

Regimes of substantive justice are not unknown. They are characteristic of many tribal societies, of certain kinds of theocratic states, and, in a sense, of the internal organization of the family even in modern, industrial societies. But there is no place for substantive justice in liberal thought.

To begin with, the principles of subjective value and of individualism preclude the possibility of any stable set of common ends. Moreover, the values or goals taken for granted are always indeterminate. They still leave us to determine the means we should prefer to further the ends we have chosen, or what substantive content we should give an abstract value. Thus, one cannot base a social order on judgments about how to advance given goals without relying on rules that establish what counts as an available means, and what does not. These boundary rules can do their job only if they function prescriptively rather than instrumentally.

Take the earlier example of the factory manager charged with a production quota under a regime of substantive justice. The state tells him to come up with the quota by the most efficient means available. But is he to kidnap workers from neighboring industries to increase his own labor force, or to prod workers on until they collapse of exhaustion? The legal system defines certain kinds of acts as crimes or administrative infractions, and these the manager may not choose as means to his ends.

The area of free play surrendered to instrumental rationality may vary enormously, but in any ordered social situation there must be boundary conditions set by prescriptive rules whose scope is not in turn subject to the calculus of instrumental rationality. Unless such fixed points of support are available, we shall lack a common understanding of what constitutes a possible means to the predetermined end. There will be no shared standard for evaluating decisions, and the regime of substantive justice will break down. However, once prescriptive rules are introduced to rescue substantive justice, we are back with all the difficulties of legal justice and of the theory of adjudication, difficulties from which substantive justice seemed to promise an escape. Because the prescriptive rules that establish the boundary conditions must be interpreted, we are again caught in the quicksand of the theory of adjudication.

Order based on rules and order based on values, the regimes of legal and of substantive justice, the theory of adjudication and the theory of instrumental rationality, are equally inadequate. To operate a system of rules we have to appeal to considerations of purpose that end up dissolving what we meant by a system of rules in the first place.

An especially important conclusion is that no coherent theory of adjudication is possible within liberal political thought. This means that even if the liberal doctrine of politics could establish an adequate theory of legislation, it would be unable to solve its own central problems of order and freedom. What a nonliberal theory of adjudication might look like we can hardly say, for our very notions of the making and applying of law have been shaped by liberal principles.

Throughout this section I have discussed the antinomy of rules and values strictly as a problem of ideas, without regard to the light the jurisprudential analysis might throw on the actual workings of society and the legal order. This is in line with the method of my critique, which is to take liberalism as a system of concepts or ideas. Nevertheless, a brief reference to the historical significance of the antinomy of rules and values may make the theoretical argument easier to grasp. The precise sense of the relation between problems of political theory and problems of politics will be taken up in Chapter Four.

In the modern Western welfare-corporate states, the purposive theory has come to be the dominant view of adjudication. At the same time, courts and administrative agencies in these countries are faced to an increasing extent with the task of administering open-ended standards, like the standard of unconscionability in the principle that unconscionable contracts should not be enforced, and with rules that have the character of an economic program, like the American antitrust laws. In these situations, the courts and agencies are caught between two roles with conflicting demands: the role of the traditional formalist judge, who asks what the correct interpretation of rules of law is, and the role of the calculator of efficiencies, who seeks to determine what course of action will most effectively serve a given goal, such as the maintenance of a competitive market.

The same duality, in less dramatic form, influences the entire legal system, producing an unstable oscillation between generalizing rules and *ad hoc* decisions. This instability is the outward sign of the internal contradiction between legal justice and instrumental rationality. For the courts and administrative agencies of the welfare-corporate state, conformity to rules is the restraint on power that guarantees freedom. An act that cannot be justified as a correct interpretation of the rules is an arbitrary or unjustified exercise of power, a form of domination.[34] Without a solution to the problem of value, the problem of domination cannot be solved.

The struggle between rule and purpose, freedom and efficiency, in the legal system of the welfare-corporate state suggests practical counterparts to the theoretical difficulties of legal justice. The internal evolution of law and politics in fully planned socialist societies illustrates the contradictions of a regime of substantive justice. In an ideal planning situation, the fundamental tie among units of production and other social groups should be loyalty to common objectives. In every situation of choice, one would ask which decision in the instant case would do the most to advance our common objectives rather than what the rules command. The use of fixed rules would be limited to circumstances in which it would be inefficient to engage in a calculus of means and ends. Nonetheless, these socialist societies are characterized by a relentless expansion of the use of rules, an expansion factors of efficiency seem inadequate to explain.[35]

The study of substantive justice suggests an alternative hypothesis. In the absence of widespread and concrete sharings of perceptions and values, like those of a tribal society, instrumental rationality is not enough to keep a social organization together; hence the need for rules and more rules as boundary conditions of the calculus of efficiencies. Without either the restraining rules of the liberal state or the background of common purpose that may animate an army in combat, orders given by officials in the management hierarchy to their inferiors will seem an exercise of personal domination to be resisted or sabotaged at every stage. Thus, the 'legalization' of socialist societies can be taken as an example of the instability of a regime of substantive justice. The consequence of that instability is to reintroduce into the socialist state the tensions that plague regimes of legal justice.

The historical analogies to the theoretical discussion suggest that the social experience to which the antinomy of rules and values corresponds is a peculiar relationship between the way values are conceived in society and the way power is controlled. If values are experienced as subjective, power unrestrained by law will be feared as an exercise of personal domination. Yet, because the interpretation of rules must be governed by judgments of value, as the refutation of formalism demonstrates, the problem of lawless power and hence of domination reappears within the very citadel of legal justice. Once again, it seems that to solve the problem of domination effectively one would have to possess an alternative to the principle of subjective value. What would such an alternative look like?

THE SHARING OF VALUES

Of all the devices used to deal with the difficulties of liberal political theory, there is one that surpasses the others in the richness of its implications. It is the view that order and freedom can be achieved because in every society men share a core of common beliefs and values. The thesis is of interest here as a metaphysical doctrine about the conditions of order and freedom instead of as a description of society.

At its most modest, it is a commentary on the possibilities of understanding. Men who participate in a common form of social life have a similar experience. It might be said that this allows them to comprehend each other and to assign conventional meanings to words and hence to rules, independently of the ends they hold.[36] Thus, individuals who disagree about the good might nevertheless be able to agree about how fact situations ought to be distinguished and rules applied. Formalism would be saved as a doctrine of plain meanings based upon a social situation rather than as a theory of self-evident meanings founded on intelligible essences. More generally, the critic might point out that my discussion of liberal political thought is marred by a pervasive confusion of the capacity to grasp what another person means with the state of entertaining the same ends he does.

There are two answers to this objection. First, the focus of my argument is an issue of justification rather than one of understanding. If individuals can know the meanings of laws, but are unable to accept the values that inform the rules, the problems of order and freedom will not have been solved. Second, there are limits to the autonomy of understanding from moral consensus, limits that will become clear as we study the merger of knowledge and evaluation in consciousness. Up to a point, we can grasp the operation of a system of rules without acquiescing in the values of the community. But the more repugnant or foreign the moral beliefs are to us, the harder will it become to enter into the vision of the world with which those beliefs are connected. Thus, it is necessary to pass from the notion of conventional meanings to the more ambitious idea of shared values.

Shared values might be the basis for a regime of substantive justice: every decision would be judged according to its capacity to promote the common ends. Similarly, the shared values would be the neutral source of the policy judgments which purposive theories of adjudication must bring into play.

Most remarkable of all, the idea of shared values might even make it possible to recast the formalist theory of adjudication in a version much more powerful than the familiar one, and free from the need to rely on the doctrine of intelligible essences. The modern, conventionalist view of language teaches that every distinction among facts must be justified by an interest. We prefer those classifications of things most useful in furthering our purposes. If we suppose that in any community certain ends are broadly shared, men will tend to classify things in the same manner without ever having to consider purposes explicitly. For example, the value of life may be so universally respected and preferred to that of cleanliness of the cobblestones that it would never occur to anyone to suggest that the surgeon should be punished under the law that prohibits bloodletting in the streets.

In most cases, rules will have plain meanings not because men believe in intelligible essences, but because their common interests lead them to categorize the world, and to subsume facts under the categories, in similar ways. Rules and the acts by which they are applied to particular situations can then be viewed as the working out of a common vision of the world, based on agreed-upon values. The convergence of values might in turn be explained, though it could not be justified, as the product of a particular form of social organization. As a possible solution to the problems of legislation and adjudication, this view is a special case of the more general idea of the sharing of values and beliefs in society.

There are two distinct ways to conceive of a sharing of values. On one view, it is a coincidence of individual preferences, which, even when combined, retain the characteristics of individuality and subjectivity. On another view, it refers to group values that are neither individual nor subjective. If we start from the premises of liberal political thought, we must treat every sharing of values as a precarious alliance of ends that simply reveals the subjective preferences of the allies. There is no reason in such a system of thought to expect that these convergences of interest will be stable, nor to bestow upon them an authority any greater than that of the individual choices that produced them. In these circumstances, the sharing of values will not be able to resolve the problems of the theories of legislation and adjudication. It will not constitute the stable, authoritative Archimedean point from which the laws can be assessed and on which criteria of naming can be based.

To achieve a different result, we would have to abandon the system of liberal political thought, and the ideas about knowledge and human nature connected with it. Only by rejecting the principles of subjective value and of individualism could we allow for the possibility of communal values. And only by repudiating the distinction between fact and value, could we go from the mere description of these communal values to their use as standards of evaluation.

It would be a dangerous illusion indeed to suppose that a mere revision of our philosophical ideas could suffice to accomplish the objective of giving force to the idea of shared values. The seriousness of the political premises of liberalism is a consequence of the accuracy with which they describe a form of social experience that theory alone cannot abolish. It is the experience of the precariousness and contingency of all shared values in society. This experience arises from the sense that shared values reflect the prejudices and interests of dominant groups rather than a common perception of the good. Thus, individuality remains an assertion of the private will against the conventions and traditions of the public life.

Two things are necessary for the conception of shared values to solve the problems of freedom and order, a theoretical advance and a political event.

The theoretical advance consists in the development of a system of thought that would enable us to deny the contrast of description and evaluation by taking the ends men share in their groups as indications of the good or right. The intuitive idea from which one might start is that a man's choices express his nature; that common choices maintained over time and capable of winning ever greater adherence reflect a common human nature; and that the flourishing of human nature is the true basis of moral and political judgment. The criticism and development of this idea is an objective of my theory of the self.

The political event would be the transformation of the conditions of social life, particularly the circumstances of domination, that produce the experience of the contingency and arbitrariness of values. In the preceding section, it was suggested that, as long as the principle of subjective value is maintained, the making and application of laws will depend on choices that cannot be justified and therefore have to be perceived as pure domination exercised by some men over others. Now, however, it appears that to escape from the premise of subjective value one must already have changed the reality of domination. The purpose of the theory of organic groups is to examine the conditions under which this vicious circle might be broken.

3

THE UNITY OF
LIBERAL THOUGHT

INTRODUCTION

I now conclude my critique of liberal thought. My aim is to show
    the unity of the psychological and political ideas of liberalism,
and to trace the source of its unity back to conceptions still more fundamental than the ones discussed in the earlier chapters. In this way, I lay
the groundwork for an attempt to move beyond total criticism to a revision of our ideas.

The chapter has two parts. The first part is a digression on method
in the study of society. An aim of this digression is to clarify the sense
in which the principles of liberal thought are interdependent and to show
the limits and uses of a critique that approaches liberalism as a system
of concepts. Another purpose is to suggest a view of the general characteristics of social phenomena as a background against which the interrelations and the inadequacies of liberal ideas can be more clearly seen.

In the light of the methodological discussion, the second part of the
chapter examines what makes liberal thought a unity and how its reconstruction might be undertaken. I begin by examining the relations

between the first two postulates of liberal psychology and the first two postulates of liberal political theory. The principles of reason and desire and of arbitrary desire are reciprocally connected with the principles of rules and values and of subjective value.

I then turn to the relationship between the psychological principle of analysis and the political principle of individualism. The analytical view of knowledge and the individualist conception of society are twins. They are the methodological foundations of all liberal, and hence of much of modern, thought, yet we have forgotten how close to one another they are. Though many of the most important movements of social thought since the seventeenth century are concerned with the reformulation of these two ideas, none of those movements has escaped the limitations of partial criticism. All have either misunderstood the link between analysis and individualism, or have failed to grasp the connection of each to the rest of liberal doctrine.

The principles of analysis and individualism have in common a view of wholes as equal to the sum of their parts that I call the·idea of aggregation. The contrasting principles of synthesis and collectivism see every whole in knowledge and in society as something different from the sum of its parts, a conception I name the idea of totality. After having established the interdependence of ideas about mind and about society in liberalism, I discuss the most important manner in which the moderns have attempted to reform liberal theory, the replacement of aggregation by totality as the dominant scheme of thought. The argument goes on to examine two ways, described as structuralism and realism, to refine liberal thought through the development of the idea of totality. Yet even the most far-reaching and profound forms of partial criticisms of classic liberal theory fall short of their goal. The problem of parts and wholes in knowledge and in society cannot be dealt with successfully apart from the other aspects of psychology and political theory.

To carry the criticism of liberal thought to a higher level of generality and abstraction and to find the exit structuralism and realism fail to provide, we need to reexamine the antinomies of liberal theory. The antinomies of theory and fact, reason and desire, rules and values are the central problems around which all other issues revolve. It is a remarkable fact that those antinomies arise out of an identical conception of the way universals (theory, reason, and rules) are related to particulars (fact, desire, and values).

At the moment at which we take the last step in the reconstruction and criticism of liberal thought, the formulation of the problem of the universal and the particular, we also come to the turning point of the entire inquiry. Where do we go from the completed critique? By imagining a different conception of the relation of the universal to the particular and hence of theory to fact, reason to desire, and rules to values, we can stand the liberal doctrine on its head. We can construct a system of thought that is in every respect the opposite of liberalism. It will become apparent, however, that such a system would be as inadequate as liberal theory itself and create difficulties which, though of a different sort, would be just as serious as the ones they replaced. How can a better basis for thought be found? The last section of the chapter deals with this question.

THE UNITY OF LIBERAL THOUGHT AND THE PROBLEM OF METHOD

In the course of total criticism there is a moment of severest difficulty, when the demands of the endeavor strain the powers of the mind and put its determination to the test. It is the time when the system of thought that is being criticized can already be surveyed as a whole, but the grounds of its unity remain unclear. Once those grounds are discovered, deeper understanding can make for greater simplicity in argument.

The single most important obstacle to the discovery of the roots of unity in liberal doctrine is the tendency to treat the theories of mind and of society as two completely distinct fields of inquiry. Even the most extensive partial criticisms often fail because of their inability to see what the authors of the classic liberal doctrine themselves acutely understood, that the principles of psychology and political theory are so closely connected that no one who divides them can advance far in philosophy.

The principles defined in the first two chapters are not the only ones with which liberal thought might be described. Many other postulates could be formulated to describe aspects of the system that were not discussed, and even the principles I did study might surely have been phrased in different ways. Still, I claim two virtues for my account. First, it takes seriously the modern prejudice that knowledge and society present fundamentally distinct problems to philosophical speculation. The unity of the problems cannot be taken for granted; it must be shown. That is the reason for the effort to state psychological and political ideas independently of one another. Second, the very arrangement of the propositions already draws attention to their interdependencies without disregarding their separateness.

But now the question raised in the Introduction as part of the problem of language must be taken up again. What holds the different elements within psychology and political theory together, and then connects each of the two with the other?

Because I am treating liberal thought as a system of theoretical concepts and propositions, I employ the method of formal logic and describe the links among the principles as relations of logical entailment. Yet, in every case, the proof of the reciprocal dependency lacks the perfection of an argument in logic. Added assumptions have to be introduced, analogies of form put in the place of indispensable conditions, or probable consequences substituted for necessary conclusions. It is tempting in such circumstances to recall Aristotle's warning that we should not insist on greater precision than the nature of the subject matter warrants.[1] But, in truth, the problem is less in the subject matter than in the inadequacy of the methods available to us, methods produced by the very mode of thought against which I would now direct them.

To study liberalism with the procedures of formal logic is to study it at the level of ideas, just as to examine causally the growth and influence of liberal views and institutions would be to view liberalism at the level of facts or events. The division of the world into an order of ideas and an order of events, with their corresponding methods of logical analysis and causal explanation, must not be accepted as the eternal fate of thought. Between the order of ideas and the order of events, there is a third realm, the order of consciousness, mind, culture or social life, for the understanding of which neither the logical nor the causal method is adequate. Instead, it calls for a method of appositeness or symbolic interpretation, which I shall soon describe.

Because partial criticism deals always with isolated elements of a single system, it is easily led to view its subject matter as a pure set of concepts, abstracted from their historical setting and appropriate for logical analysis. Total criticism, moved by the ambition to see the whole, avoids less easily the issue of the relation between thought and existence. Only the understanding of this relation fully elucidates the unity of the doctrine criticism attacks and the conditions under which the doctrine may be transformed. Every general way of thinking that dominates the ideas of an age has to be understood as a phenomenon of consciousness rather than just as a theory.

What does it mean to speak of a realm of consciousness, and what methods are needed to study it? Let me begin by suggesting three characteristics that distinguish the realm of consciousness from the orders of ideas and of events.

First, in the field of consciousness there is always a correlation between a form of social existence and a way of reflecting about mind, society, and nature itself. In this sphere, one cannot speak of a structure of ideas and of a pattern of events as independent worlds. For each characteristic of the organization of society there is a counterpart in the way men conceive the social world. Every social practice and institution is mediated through the categories of the mind, so that the manner in which people understand a social arrangement is an inseparable aspect of the arrangement itself. Hence, we never fully understand a phenomenon of consciousness, such as a religious ritual, a work of art, or an act of compliance with law, unless we can view it at the same time as a way in which men comprehend the world and organize their relations to one another. To grasp what a phenomenon of consciousness signifies as a form of reflection, one must be able to describe the place it occupies in social relations. To understand it as a social practice, a work, or an act, one has to describe what the participants, the workers, or the agents think about it. The reciprocal link between outward existence and inner reflection is called meaning. Unless it takes meaning into account, a method of social study misses what is peculiarly social about its subject matter.[2]

The reflection that occurs within the sphere of consciousness is not to be mistaken for logical analysis or causal explanation. Undoubtedly, it is possible to develop logical theories in the order of ideas, or causal ones in the order of events. These theories can be judged according to accepted standards of consistency and verification; they need not be interpreted by reference to a form of existence. But there is also a kind of knowledge that consists in the representation of a form of existence or of a social arrangement by those who participate in it. Such representations, which appear, for example, as religious or political doctrines, or as works of art, are typically unanalyzable wholes, a concept to be discussed in a later section of this chapter. We sense they are unities, though we cannot account for the oneness of their elements in either causal or logical terms.

The causal and the logical relation are sequential: *b* follows *a;* in one case within the dimension of time; in the other case, outside it. They are also necessary: given *a, b* must follow. Yet we often seem to believe that the elements of a work of art, or of a set of religious or political beliefs, hold together despite the fact that they cannot be ordered sequentially and that their coexistence is contingent rather than necessary. Their pattern is described in the language of modern social theory as one of structure, type, or style. It is a unity of harmony or of appositeness, and its basis is the common reference of the different elements of the whole to the form of existence they represent.[3]

A second feature of the realm of consciousness is that the reflective understanding men have of their social arrangements typically disrespects the dividing line between description and evaluation. This becomes more true the more encompassing the kind of reflection one has in mind. Thus, religious beliefs, grammatical understandings, and legal interpretations all share this characteristic. One's view on what is true of the world as a whole, or on how the language is in fact spoken, or on how the law on a given point stands cannot be cleanly separated from one's conception of the good, or of how the language should be spoken, or of how the disputed point of law ought to be resolved. The perception of fact and the choice of values are joined together at the deepest levels of consciousness.

The third distinctive feature of the realm of mind is ambiguity of meaning. The symbols of consciousness always have a double reference or a twofold determinant of meaning. On the one hand, every work or act has the meaning bestowed on it by the intention of the maker or agent. In this sense, to interpret it is to determine what he meant. On the other hand, the work can have a meaning fixed by the purposes or interests of some observer, perhaps from a distant culture or a later time, who is utterly ignorant of the intentions of the maker.

In this second sense, to interpret the work is to establish what it can mean to this third person, who looks in, as it were, from the outside. The artist who paints a painting may have a conception of its meaning that we can only understand in the context of his existence and of the existence of his society. And yet the same painting may have a wholly different significance to one who comes upon it many centuries later. This other significance will also be a product of the contribution the painting can make to the observer's own self-reflection, against the background of the particular circumstances of his existence.

All this is simple and familiar enough. But when we compare the third characteristic of the realm of consciousness, ambiguity of meaning, with the first two, the relation between reflection and existence, and the convergence of fact and value, a remarkable difficulty emerges. It is a difficulty that lies at the center of many great problems of method in social thought. I have said that to understand fully a practice or work, to comprehend it in its distinctively social sense, one must take account of what the practice meant to its original performers or the work to its creators. This initial meaning always has a moral as well as a descriptive aspect; the vision expressed in the art work reflects both an understanding and an ideal, and the more perfect the work, the greater the unity of the two. The problem faced by the observer remote in space or time is that he must approach the work from the standpoint of the conditions of his own existence and of his own ideas about those conditions. He is not the maker of the work; his perspective on it differs from the maker's; and yet he must somehow incorporate the latter's perspective into his own to reach a complete comprehension of the artifact. He must solve the ambiguity of meaning. How can he do so unless he establishes a community of understandings and of values with the maker whose work he interprets or with the agent whose act he observes?

Going over the three features of the realm of mind, one can see that each of them calls for a particular quality on the part of the method used to study social phenomena. And each of these qualities presupposes a solution to one of the antinomies of liberal thought.

The first characteristic of the realm of social life demands a method that can interpret existence from the standpoint of reflection and reflection from the perspective of existence. Such a procedure will not respect the distinction between the order of ideas and of events, nor will it be satisfied with the logical and causal explanations that correspond to them. But the distinction between the order of ideas and the order of events is the very heart of the modern view of science and nature and the source of the antinomy of theory and fact.

The beliefs that characterize the realm of consciousness tend to mesh description and evaluation. The interpretation of the phenomena of consciousness must therefore incorporate a pretheoretical experience of the world that is foreign to the contrast between fact and value. To know how to do this, however, one must have set aside the distinction between the understanding of facts and the choice of ends, a dualism that lies at the core of the antinomy of reason and desire.

Finally, the method of social study must be able to deal with the ambiguity of meaning—the double reference to the intention of the agent and the intention of the observer—that all phenomena of consciousness imply. The complete resolution of this difficulty would seem to require that between agent and observer there be a community of understandings and values. But the conception of such a community is surely inconsistent with the idea that men are bound together by rules and kept apart by their individual and subjective ends, the very idea from which the antinomy of rules and values springs.

A method with the three preceding characteristics is no mere fantasy. On the contrary, it is precisely the traditional procedure of the disciplines that stood in the mainstream of the classical humanistic culture of the West: theology, grammar, and legal doctrine. Only the ascendancy of liberal thought, and of the view of science that accompanies it, has almost managed to stamp out our appreciation of the distinctive form of knowledge those disciplines embody. Surely Francis Bacon was right when he remarked that "what in some things is considered a secret has in others a manifest and well-known nature, which will never be recognized as long as the experiments and thoughts of men are engaged on the former only."[4] A brief contrast of grammar, theology, and legal doctrine with modern empirical science will throw further light on the problem of method in social study.

Phenomena of consciousness have been subjected to two distinct types of inquiry. One is represented by what I shall call the dogmatic, interpretive, or symbolic disciplines, of which grammar, theology, and legal doctrine, including the reasonings of lawyers and judges about the interpretation of law, are examples. The other type of understanding is the aim of the empirical sciences we call linguistics, the sociology of religion, and the sociology of law. In every important respect, the standpoint of the first group of disciplines differs from that of the second. The common attempt to run the two groups together without really changing the characteristics of either betrays a misunderstanding of both. Moreover, it will be seen that the dogmatic disciplines peculiarly exemplify each of the qualities of adequate method in social study I described earlier.

To begin with, every grammar, theology, and legal doctrine addresses a particular language, or religion, or legal order, and is an integral part of it. By this I mean that in none of the dogmatic disciplines is there a clear distinction between the object accounted for and the account itself. On the one hand, the grammar, the theology, or the legal doctrine participates in the evolution of the language, the religion, or the law, helping define its shape and determine its directions. On the other hand, the categories of the grammarian, the doctrines of the theologian, or the reasonings of lawyers and judges are drawn from the very tradition they expound and develop. Lastly, because of the intimate relationship between the account and its object, every claim in a dogmatic discipline is an elaboration of some point of view already present in the community with which the discipline is associated. Thus, the ancient humanistic arts seem to satisfy the first requirement of method in the realm of consciousness, the incorporation of pretheoretical experience into theory itself.

Compare with this the approach of linguistics, or of the sociology of religion or of law, when they adopt the modern view of science sketched at the beginning of Chapter One. They want to become the science of language, of religion, or of law in general, rather than the doctrines of a particular language, religion, or legal order.[5] As empirical sciences, they treat views about language, religion, and law prevalent in specific societies as part of what has to be explained instead of as part of the explanation. The greater the independence a science achieves from the pretheoretical views of any one group, the more universal and objective it supposedly becomes.

Another characteristic of the dogmatic disciplines is their indifference to the contrast of description and evaluation. In this respect, they fulfill the second requirement of method in social study: a grammatical rule is both descriptive and prescriptive. It describes how a language is in fact spoken. But it also implies a selection of standard usages, and it serves as a basis for the criticism and justification of particular acts of speech. A theology both states a view of the world and defines an ideal of the good. It accepts and develops the unity of fact and value that is a hallmark of religious beliefs. So too the critique of the formalist theory of adjudication has already shown that every understanding of how the law stands on a given point depends on a conception of its purposes, on a view of what the law ought to accomplish. The empirical sciences of language, religion, and law, for their part, pride themselves on the strictness with which they hold the line between understanding and evaluation.

The interpretive disciplines must also deal with the ambiguity of meaning peculiar to the phenomena of consciousness. Every act of speech, or religious ritual and belief, or rule of law has a meaning or a purpose given to it by the intention of the original speaker, holy man, or lawmaker. Yet this meaning must always be rediscovered by an interpreter, who has his own purposes and his own form of existence. What then guarantees that interpreted and interpreter can communicate? The resolution of the ambiguity of meaning is possible to the extent that interpreter and interpreted participate in the same community or tradition of shared beliefs, beliefs that are both understandings and values. Thus, for example, the judge defines the purpose of the laws he applies by a combination of his view of the intentions of legislators or earlier judges and his sense of the demands of his own social situation at the time the case is decided. This combination can be achieved only because the judge is able to see himself as a collaborator of the lawmakers who preceded him, and as one whose ideas and values are not starkly at variance with theirs. Similarly, the philologist, faced with a text from an earlier age, can interpret it symbolically if he is able to bear in mind the literary tradition that leads back from his own perspective to the author's.

The difficulty of interpretation in the dogmatic disciplines comes from the fact that the community of intentions is never perfect and that it is always threatening to fall apart. Thus, the ambiguity of meaning cannot be resolved completely or with finality. In the empirical sciences, however, no attempt is made to base understanding on the intentions of speakers, holy men, or legislators and judges. Speech acts, religious objects or events, and rules of law are treated as facts. And a fact is just a fact, rather than a symbol to be measured against underlying purposes.[6]

There is a wonderful symmetry in the contrast between empirical sciences and dogmatic doctrines. The former distinguish clearly the dimension of their subject matter from the dimension of the theory with which they describe it. But they treat the subject matter itself as a one-dimensional thing that does not need to be set against the background of intentions or values. The latter, however, place their subject matter and their account in a single, continuous dimension. Yet they distinguish within the subject matter the two aspects of outward symbol and inward intent or value. The second gives the first its meaning.

If it is true that the method used by the dogmatic disciplines is the one most adequate to the realm of consciousness, why has it been driven from the center of social study to its periphery? The reason is that the empire of the liberal doctrine, and of the modern conception of science, has undermined the premises that would make the symbolic method intelligible. The opposition of the order of ideas and the order of events results in the impossibility of seeing the link between reflection and existence in its true light. It forces method to choose between the logical analysis of concepts and the causal explanation of facts, neither of which is suitable to the interpretation of symbols. The psychological contrast of description and evaluation dissolves the vantage point from which the two-faced, factual and moral aspect of the phenomena of consciousness can be elucidated. The political principles of subjective value and individualism destroy the foundations of the community of intentions between interpreter and interpreted.

Of all these factors it is the last that may exercise the most decisive influence on the attempt to force social study into the mold of a causal science of events. The humanistic disciplines always presuppose the existence of a particular community or tradition of shared understandings and values. They belong to that community or tradition. To use the symbolic method one seems forced to surrender the qualities of objectivity and universality, the very ideals to which modern science is most devoted.

The history of modern social theory is a history of the attempt to combine the attributes of the humanistic interpretation of symbols with the objectivity and universality of the empirical sciences of nature. Thus, for example, the crucial problem of the ambiguity of meaning was sometimes dealt with by recognizing that acts derive their meaning from the intent or purpose of the actor, and by defining this intention in an ideal or hypothetical manner as an intention all agents would have. This is what political economy did when it hypothesized the aim of maximizing profit as the purpose of economic transactions.[7]

Another device was to postulate that behind the particular communities of value and belief there are universal tendencies or categories of the mind at work. By tracing the phenomena of consciousness back to these constant though hidden tendencies of the mind, the symbolic method can be made objective and universal. This was the solution adopted by the proponents of what might be described as the metaphysic of the unconscious. It is the view of the thinkers who from Kant to Freud, Lévi-Strauss, and Chomsky tried to build a science of man on the conception of a universal mental apparatus with inherent predispositions.

Finally, there were those like Vico, Hegel, and Marx who looked for the answer in a metaphysic of history. They imagined that in the study of society both the interpreters and the interpreted are afloat on the same stream of history, a stream that moves relentlessly toward an end for whose achievement all men, willy nilly, collaborate. The teleology of history establishes a community of intentions between the observers and the observed at any moment in time. One must proceed as if history itself had its purposes, and the intentions of men in acting as they do were their fragmentary signs, just as the many-colored beams of light refracted through a prism flow from a common source.

These are the main types of attempts to formulate a method of social study by uniting the supposed universality and objectivity of empirical science with the powers of the ancient humanistic interpretation of symbols. Looking back on these efforts as a whole, one is struck by how partial and devious they are in the solutions they offer. Though they try to deal with the problem of ambiguity of meaning, the tasks of clarifying the interrelation of fact and value, and of defining a realm of consciousness between the order of ideas and the order of events, remain unaccomplished. Still more disturbing is the impression that even with regard to the issue of double intentionality each of the alleged solutions mentioned is, to speak baldly, a trick. In its various forms the trick consists in replacing real intentions of interpreters and interpreted with hypothetical or ideal intentions, whether they be attributed to the common mental apparatus of mankind, to history, or simply to explanatory convenience.

Is it not clear by now that the partiality and deviousness of the doctrines are consequences of their tendency to treat the problem of method as if it were separable from the critique of the substantive premises of liberal thought? The satisfaction of each of the requirements of an appropriate method for the study of the phenomena of consciousness would require the solution of the antinomies of liberal doctrine. To the extent a complete resolution of those antinomies depends on changes in the life of society, such changes are also conditions of a settlement of the controversy about method. For example, the reconciliation of the humanistic acknowledgment of the ambiguity of meaning with the ideal of universality in science might depend on the actual spreading of communities of shared ends.

It may be helpful to sketch the metaphysical premises of my argument. Liberalism may be approached as a system of logically related concepts or as a form of social life. To grasp the relationship between these two approaches, one must distinguish among the different senses in which something can exist.

There are three modes of being: one of events, one of social life (which for some purposes can be called more narrowly a field of consciousness, mind, or culture), and one of ideas. These modes might be described respectively as the kingdoms of nature, culture, and ideal truth. To each type of being, there corresponds a method: causality to the first; appositeness or symbolic interpretation to the second; and logic to the third.

The realm of social life has two aspects—belief and external conduct—each of which acquires meaning in the context of the other. The most general form of belief is a system of culture; the most comprehensive form of conduct, a pattern of social organization.

Everything in nonhuman nature must belong to the order of events. Thus, unless it is treated as a symbol for some human concern, it is subject solely to causal explanation.

Human behavior participates in both the mode of events and in that of social life. Thus, any act can be explained as a natural phenomenon by empirical science, or it can be interpreted as the counterpart to some kind of belief.

Ideas exist in all three senses of existence, and they are therefore subject to each of the methods of knowledge according to the aspect of their being on which one chooses to focus. Thus, an idea may be viewed as simply a psychic event. Like all other events, it has causes and effects that can be established by science. Ideas may also be understood as beliefs that are wedded to human conduct in a manner the interpretive method alone can properly define. Lastly, ideas are the content of thought: the concepts or propositions by which something is predicated of something else or the objective validity or invalidity, truth or falsehood, of the predication itself. It is exclusively at this level that one can attribute a distinct mode of being to ideas.

The outcome of this discussion is the outline of a stratified ontology that justifies a diversity of methods and relates each type of understanding to a special kind of being. There are various ways this ontology might be dismantled; each leads to a vice of thought. The effort to assimilate the existence of social life to that of ideas produces rationalism and idealism in social study. The attempt to deny altogether the independence of the sphere of events results in metaphysical rationalism and idealism. The willingness to collapse the realm of social life into that of events represents behaviorism in social science. The tendency to disregard the independence of the order of ideas is the mark of metaphysical empiricism.

Some of the most intractable problems of philosophy have to do with the relationship among these three modes of being. Thus, we are still baffled by the fact that the laws of nature seem to be written in the language of mathematics, and the reason for our puzzlement is that we do not understand the connection between the modes of ideas and of events. Similarly, we wonder how symbolic interpretation can be harmonized with logic and causality, for the precise relationship of social life to the realms of events and of ideas escapes us.

These are riddles to which I have no answer. Nevertheless, if we were to await their definitive solution, we might continue forever unable to think coherently about man and society. Therefore, one must look for partial and provisional solutions. At the end of this chapter, I shall advance a view of universals and particulars, one of whose implications is to suggest a way in which the abstract universals that inhabit the order of ideas can be embodied in the concrete particulars that are said to constitute the order of events. And in the remainder of the book this doctrine of universals and particulars will be used to relate social life to the other two kinds of existence. The lesson of the argument will be that there is a profound correspondence among the internal structures of the three modes of being, though one whose source remains hidden to us. For the moment, let us focus on how the issue of this correspondence affects one who would engage in the total criticism of a dominant tradition of thought.

It follows from my thesis about being and its modes that beliefs can be causally explained, symbolically interpreted, and logically analyzed. The second kind of understanding is the only one that might be called specifically human or social since it applies exclusively to man, whereas the others have a wider scope. There are two limits to this distinctively human understanding of human activity.

On the one hand, in some aspects of life, behavior oversteps belief. These are the situations in which men produce consequences they did not intend or in which they are moved by determinants of which they are unaware. To the extent this occurs, conduct can be causally explained, but it cannot be symbolically interpreted.

Another constraint on the interpretive method is that a set of beliefs develops in accordance with accepted criteria of truth and falsehood, validity and invalidity, that may not be directly related to any one type of social organization. To the extent we are interested either in the logical consistency of a system of ideas or in the truth of its representations, the issue of the connection of those ideas with conduct must be relegated to an inferior place. But this subordination becomes harder to effectuate when one deals with beliefs about man and society. For, as I argued earlier, the truth of such beliefs is never entirely separable from their fidelity to men's conscious experience of social life.

The methodological and metaphysical ideas formulated in this section can help elucidate the aims and limitations of my criticism of liberal thought. Liberalism is a philosophical system. But it is also a type of consciousness that represents and prescribes a kind of social existence. As a philosophy, it belongs primarily to the order of ideas. As a sort of consciousness, it participates in the life of society. Like any view that has shaped a whole era in the history of thought, it overruns the boundaries of the realm of ideas and lays roots in an entire form of culture and social organization.

Because it is a "deep structure" of thought, placed at the intersection of two modes of being, liberalism resists a purely logical analysis. The relationship among its parts is tighter than logical consistency though looser than mutual entailment. The fundamental incoherences of liberal thought are not quite contradictions. Its unity evokes a meaningful whole rather than a logical system, and its tensions represent conflicting trends in culture and society rather than logical contradictions. Hence, the liberal doctrine must ultimately be viewed with an interpretive method that can establish its relationship to social life instead of harping solely on its internal constitution.

With what dismay then do we discover that the unresolved antinomies of liberal philosophy, and the social circumstances associated with them, are what stop us from arriving at a satisfactory interpretive method for the study of liberalism. We cannot replace the system of thought until we have understood it, and we cannot understand it until we have already replaced it.

Surrounded on all sides, my tactic, a recourse of despair, is to retreat the better to advance. I shall continue to deal with liberalism as if it were just a system of concepts, to approximate, as much as possible, the reconstruction of its unity to the showing of logical consistency and the criticism of its vices to the proof of logical contradiction. But gradually, in the very process of reconstruction and critique, the elements of an alternative method will emerge, to be carried forward by the positive part of my argument. As we study the relationship between liberal psychology and liberal political theory, the failings of the liberal treatment of the realm of culture will slowly become clearer, and a superior conception will begin to appear.

Let anyone disheartened by this procedure remember Neurath's remark that the philosopher's task may be compared to that of a mariner who must rebuild his raft on the open sea.[8] How much more true is this in those periods of total criticism when the raft is caught in a storm and the repairs are as urgent as they are difficult and dangerous.

ARBITRARY DESIRE AND SUBJECTIVE VALUE

It is not hard to perceive the reciprocal interdependence of the psychological principles of reason and desire and arbitrary desire, on the one hand, and the political principles of rules and values and subjective value, on the other hand. Indeed, the classic liberal thinkers often failed to draw the distinction at all, and, from the outset, treated the problems the two sets of principles describe as a unit. That the relationship, however, cannot be dismissed as entirely self-evident is shown by the course of latter-day thought, which has often disregarded or misunderstood it. The main issue involved is the connection between the place individual ends occupy in the self and their position in society. I shall continue to use the term desire when emphasizing the former, the term value when calling attention to the latter, and other analogous terms generically.

A primitive though useful statement of the link is that the separation of desire from understanding is what makes the drawing of a radical distinction between rules and values necessary and, conversely, that the line between impersonal rules and individual, subjective value requires that understanding and desire be treated as wholly separate faculties. Necessity here should be taken in the quasi-logical sense invoked at the end of the preceding section. Now let us see how this preliminary notion can be developed.

First, consider the dependence of the political postulates on the psychological ones. Liberal psychology admits that desires, as psychic events, can be causally explained. But no operation of the mind can establish what one ought to want.

Suppose this were not so. If the understanding were capable of perceiving or establishing the ends of conduct, the basic conditions of social life would bear little resemblance to the liberal image of society. Values would be objective rather than subjective. Their validity would preexist anyone's adherence to them. Even if no one recognized them for what they were, they might still retain their authority as repositories of the right or the good. Moreover, they would tend over time to be communal rather than individual. Men with a similar mental apparatus would in principle be capable of arriving at, and therefore of holding, the same sets of ends. Finally, rules would no longer be the preeminent social bonds. Theirs would be a subsidiary role: to systematize, to specify, or if necessary to enforce the objective and communal ends grasped by the mind. Alternatively, a regime of legal justice might be unnecessary, and rules would have a still more modest place, constituting what I described earlier as boundary conditions of a regime of substantive justice.

The contrast of individual and subjective to communal and objective value need not exhaust the possibilities. Indeed, I shall later argue that there is a conception of shared value, different from the one to which liberals resort when in trouble, which should be preferred to these alternatives. Nevertheless, in the absence of an account of this third conception, an account I cannot yet provide, the argument does indicate that any falling away from the simple antithesis of description and evaluation would have consequences for our political ideas. To the extent we deviate from the premise that reason is blind in the world of ends, the conditions of order and freedom in society change.

We may turn the matter the other way around and consider the dependence of the psychological principles on the political ones. Suppose that the distinction between objective rules and individual, subjective values no longer held good. Imagine, furthermore, that the laws were viewed as the spelling out of standards of right or good which did not arise out of any combination of individual ends and, unlike the traditional liberal conception of freedom, were concrete, substantive guides for conduct.

In fact, there are two familiar versions of this notion in the history of modern thought. Each of them is a major partial criticism of liberal doctrine, and each left its mark on the ideas of the classical liberal thinkers themselves. One is the view, favored by some of the modern rationalist theories of natural law or natural right, that reason is capable of inferring what is good from an inquiry into the circumstances of social life. In this sense, there are objective values. The other is the collectivist idea, accepted by romantics and organicists, that there are communal values.

As soon as we depart from liberal political doctrine in either of these ways, we have to make wide-ranging adjustments in our psychology. If there are objective values, it is not true that reason is merely the tool of desire: ends can be rationally constructed, or rationally discovered, and the separation of fact and value breaks down. If there are communal values, represented in the laws, desires are no longer arbitrary in relation to the understanding. The moral question about what ought to be done need no longer be abandoned to unjustifiable choice; it can be answered by a study of the traditions or institutions of a nation, a class, or a group. Hence, the collectivist view implies that one can pass from the description of facts to the evaluation of choices without a break.

The interdependence of the first two principles of liberal psychology and political theory may be summarized as follows. The idea that the moral life is opaque to the mind is the reverse side of the conception that men are lost in society without natural guides and that they must be led about by threats and tied down by rules.

ANALYSIS AND INDIVIDUALISM

The psychological principle of analysis states that all knowledge can be analyzed back into the elementary sensations or ideas out of which it was composed, and then built up again from those elements. According to the political principle of individualism, the attributes of a group are simply a collection of the qualities of its individual members, including those which arise from the interaction among them. Consequently, there are no communal values.

It has already been noted that the principles of analysis and individualism, despite the apparent disparity of the problems to which they refer, have an identical form: the idea that the whole is just the sum of its parts. Conversely, the principles of synthesis and collectivism, which are the respective opposites of the axioms of analysis and individualism, claim that the whole differs from the sum of its parts.

Reciprocal ties underlie these formal analogies. The crucial step in understanding the link between analysis and individualism is to appreciate the implications each of them has for what was described before as the realm of mind. The clearer the connection between the two ideas becomes, the better shall we see the inadequacy of both.

Let us begin by considering the dependence of individualism on analysis, and then turn to the reliance of the latter on the former. If we are to maintain the individualist thesis, it is indispensable that we be able to decompose every aspect of group life into a feature of the lives of individual persons. More precisely, it must not be possible to point to facts about the group that no amount of study of its individual members, or even of their effects on one another, would be enough to explain. Otherwise, the reduction of group characteristics to individual ones would be incomplete.

The less a phenomenon of consciousness is capable of being understood by the method of analysis, the more difficult it is to effect the kind of reduction of the phenomenon to individual belief and conduct that the principle of individualism requires. Take, for example, the problem of style and stylistic period in art. Suppose the Baroque style in the history of European art could be adequately described as a collection of specific kinds of brushstrokes, techniques of musical composition, and modes of literary narrative. The concept of the Baroque would be simply a useful category for the classification of these particular methods of artistic expression, considered similar to one another for certain purposes. Such a concept would be what the schoolmen called a nominal universal; its only properties would be those of the finite set of elements that defined it exhaustively.[9] The invention and employment of the brushstrokes, forms of composition, or narrative techniques, might then be traced to the work of particular individual artists and to their influences on each other.

But there is another view of the character of the Baroque style, according to which the style would be a real universal. It would have a spirit or sense that could only be manifest in specific works of art and modes of expression, but that was never completely defined by any set of them. The more we studied the examples of the style, the better we would understand its spirit. The study, however, would be fruitful only if one already had in mind a conception of the animus of the style, the image of reality and of man that unified its manifestations. Far from being unfamiliar, this notion of style has had a brilliant though stormy career since the mid-nineteenth century.[10]

The argument for the dependence of individualism on analysis can be generalized against the background of my discussion of the realm of consciousness. The validity of the individualist thesis turns on the way one views the forms of reflection and of existence that characterize social groups. Phenomena of consciousness, like language, religion, or economic behavior, can be treated as the creations of distinct individuals interacting with each other only if they can be satisfactorily broken up into units sufficiently small and separate to be the products of individual efforts. In the absence of such an analytic procedure, the phenomena of consciousness must be recognized as distinctively social, irreducible to individual life.

The same considerations argue for the converse dependence of the principle of analysis on the principle of individualism. As soon as we admit that phenomena of consciousness are real rather than nominal universals, the principle of analysis is crippled. We are faced with beliefs that cannot be divided up into simple elements, and hence cannot be treated as compositions of such elements. The analytic image of the building made up of bricks that might be used to build a very different house becomes inappropriate.

The irreducibility of the phenomena of consciousness is recognized by the principle of collectivism, which rejects the individualistic thesis. It asserts that it is impossible to formulate a satisfactory account of these phenomena by looking for their constituents and origins in the minds of individuals. The basis of this impossibility is that the meaning of the whole cannot be established, and its history cannot be explained, by any possible hypothesis about the interaction of simpler elements. Consequently, the political principle of collectivism implies the psychological principle of synthesis, just as the opposite principles of individualism and of analysis depend on one another.

There is no *a priori* proof of the superiority of collectivism and synthesis to individualism and analysis in the study of social life. The vindication of the premises lies in the insights they make possible. I shall be content to refer back to my discussion of the role the principles of analysis and individualism play in producing the antinomies of liberal thought, and of the embarrassments they cause the student of society.

The most serious difficulty that confronts the principles of collectivism and synthesis is to explain the genesis of the unanalyzable wholes they postulate. Who are the authors of these wholes, if not individuals? Must we conceive of them as entities that preexist the minds they influence and pass through history as comets appointed to their courses? The antiliberal thesis need not accept the dilemma of the individual authorship or the suprahistorical reality of the wholes. It can answer that the most important makers of the wholes are not individuals, but groups: classes, factions, and nations.[11] Leaving for later discussion the ambiguities of this thesis, let me use it as the starting point for a final remark on the relation of individualism and analysis.

It is precisely when we break up the wholes of social life into infinitesimal parts that we tend to lose sight of their historical character. For example, the market organization of economic life, at the level of social existence, may be correlated, at the level of reflection, with an acceptance of the individualist view of the relation of persons to groups. Because the economy is viewed as the product of countless separable though interdependent individual decisions, its laws appear necessary. They are not created by individuals; so they must not have been created at all. Similarly, when language is analyzed into the innumerable speech acts that exemplify it, and its history is explained as the history of the reciprocal influence of these acts on one another, language takes on the appearance of something that was never made. It assumes the form of a force of nature that moves by its own dynamic. In both these cases, the principles of analysis and individualism operate together to cast society in the image of a nature whose evolution is beyond human choice. By disregarding the unity of social wholes and by forgetting that the main subjects of history are collective subjects, they present the given circumstances of social life as an inhuman necessity.

We are now in a position to understand the relationship between the analytic conception of mind and the other postulates of liberal psychology. Because it sets aside the holistic character of the phenomena of consciousness, the principle of analysis makes it possible to avoid coming to terms with the merger of understanding and evaluation in the realm of consciousness. The analyst fragments forms of social consciousness into individual beliefs, and then he divides these beliefs into supposedly distinct ideas, some descriptive, others normative. In this way, he can give a semblance of plausibility to the notion that statements about what the world is like and views about what it ought to be are altogether different things.

The Enlightenment and Romantic thinkers who developed the modern idea of imagination were well aware of the relationship of the analytic approach to the contrast of reason and desire. For they saw imagination as a faculty that unites thought and feeling at the same time that it makes men attentive to the organic wholeness of complex beings. At the hands of modern historicism, this view of the imagination was to turn into one of the major partial critiques of liberal thought.

Parts and Wholes

The principles of analysis and of individualism create serious obstacles for an adequate understanding of mind and science. It is therefore hardly surprising that much of the effort of modern social thought has been devoted to breaking out of the limitations those principles create and to fashioning a method that respects the integrity of social wholes.

Now that the interdependency of the postulates of liberal thought has been established, one can see the manner in which the analytic and individualist ideas can be overthrown. The main purpose of my discussion is to show how the attempt to deal with problems of parts and wholes separately from the other problems of liberal thought fails. In this way, I offer added confirmation of the unity of liberal doctrine, reassert the inadequacy of partial criticism, and prepare the way for a discussion of the relation among the antinomies of liberalism as the final stage of my critique.

I have shown that the view of the whole as the sum of its parts, which analysis and individualism share, is the sign of a reciprocal dependence; the two principles are the reverse side of each other. One can therefore carry the statement of principles to a higher level of generality, and say that both analysis and individualism are formulations of the idea that the whole is the sum of its parts. One might call this notion the principle of aggregation because it conceives every whole as a conventionally defined aggregate and as a nominal universal. Conversely, synthesis and collectivism can be reduced to the more abstract thesis that the whole differs from the sum of its parts. This may be described as the principle of totality because the whole is treated as an indivisible unit and as a real universal.[12]

There is no single tendency in the history of modern social thought more remarkable in its persistence or more far-reaching in its influence than the struggle to formulate a plausible version of the idea of totality. Sometimes the emphasis is on the synthetic or psychological aspect, and sometimes on the collectivist or political one, but, explicitly or not, both aspects are always at stake. Here are some well-known examples.

The Gestalt psychologists claim that perception is the perception of meaningful wholes. Only after these wholes have been recognized do particular elements within them acquire a meaning.[13] Chomsky and his followers deny that linguistics can be built on the analysis of elementary particles of meaning. They call attention to the fact that the speakers of every language are able to construct an infinite number of formally correct and meaningful sentences. Language must therefore be a unity, rooted in universal mental categories and irreducible to specific acts of speech.[14] Lévi-Strauss constructs an anthropology whose central concern is the elucidation of the interrelated structures of exchange or communication that preexist, organize, and give meaning to the interaction of individuals and groups.[15] An earlier and deeper thinker, Karl Marx, had already developed a theory whose most important insight, according to some of his disciples, is that every society is a totality that will never be understood until the entire framework of its internal order has been grasped.

The initial difficulty in interpreting these claims is to define what exactly is meant by the difference between the whole and its parts, or, in other words, how the relation between wholes and parts is to be understood when the principle of totality is accepted. At first, the notion that the whole differs from the sum of its parts might seem trivial or paradoxical, trivial if all it means is that two things together are not the same as two things apart, and paradoxical if the parts are by definition the things that make up the whole.[16] But there is neither triviality nor paradox in the idea that some entities have characteristics which no known type of combination of simpler entities would be enough to explain.

At this point, however, a second problem arises in the interpretation of totality. If the parts become something different and unitary in the whole, what entitles us to continue speaking about them as parts whose sum can still be contrasted with the whole? The answer is that under the principle of totality the concept of part means something different from what it means under the principle of aggregation. For the latter, the part is a real and separable being, with its own independent meaning. For the principle of totality, however, a part is just the whole viewed from a certain place. No single standpoint is sufficient in itself to exhaust the meaning of the whole, yet each is connected without discontinuity to all the other standpoints. Hence, we speak of parts only as a convenience of expression. For example, if as Marxists we consider the social order from the perspective of the productive forces, or of the relations of production, or of the ideological superstructure, our attention may emphasize different aspects of society, but the more perfect our understanding, the less do our insights into society change with the shift of perspective. Perhaps the most extreme formulation of the idea is Leibniz' view of the world as a whole completely mirrored in each of its parts.[17]

It is as if one moved about freely on a plain with an unmoving horizon. No matter what the position from which one looked out on the plain, the sight to be seen would be the same and the eye would travel to the furthest limits of the horizon on every side. But because of the weakness of vision, things would appear larger or smaller depending on their distance from us.

With these clarifications in mind, I turn to the two main interpretations of the principle of totality, with the aim of showing how the recognition of their defects allows a still deeper grasp of the unity of liberal thought.

According to one version of the principle of totality, the difference between the whole and the sum of its parts is strictly a convention of method. In other words, it is sometimes useful to regard certain phenomena as unanalyzable wholes, but we are not entitled to assume that these wholes correspond to anything in the world of fact. Thus, what for some purposes is regarded as a totality may be treated for other purposes as an aggregation in which the whole does equal the sum of its parts. This view of the principle of totality is usually called structuralism. Of the examples I gave earlier, Gestalt psychology, Chomsky's linguistics, and Lévi-Strauss' anthropology may all be considered structuralist in the sense defined.

If, in the structuralist manner, one combines the claim that the whole differs from the sum of its parts with the idea that wholes are conventions of method, the result is to deny that there is a real historical process by which the parts are transformed through their inclusion into the whole. The totality has no real history although it may have a hypothetical genesis. It is postulated by the theorist to help him explain things better; it does not emerge from a contingent sequence of events. One can use such a method to infer what must have taken place, and then to compare one's conclusions with the facts, but one cannot use it to describe what actually took place.

The structuralist version of the principle of totality is a development of one of the two sides of the modern idea of science described in Chapter One. Its starting point is the assumption that facts are entirely defined by theoretical categories because intelligible essences do not exist. Given the absence of intelligible essences, and the conventional character of thought and language, wholes may be treated as unanalyzable constructs, but they cannot be regarded as things in the world. All the vices of structuralism are consequences of its conventionalist premise.

First, the structuralist is caught in the antinomy of theory and fact. Though he denies that his wholes are anything more than mental constructs, he also believes that some constructs are better than others and that the history of his science is progressive. How is he to reconcile the two sets of beliefs?

Second, because he does not treat the genesis of the whole as a real historical process, the structuralist cannot explain how the phenomena of consciousness he studies came about. He is in the position of a man who knows the geometrical theorem for the construction of a hexagon, but is at a loss to say how and why human beings ever actually draw hexagonal figures. His typical recourse is to postulate, as a *deus ex machina,* a mental capacity for the perception of the geometrical theorem, a capacity which tends to express itself in drawings![18]

Yet it seems common in the development of phenomena of consciousness, whether as forms of existence or as forms of reflection, that two interacting elements combine to form a third, whose characteristics are irreducible to those of its constituents. The conventionalist cast of structuralism, however, condemns it to disregard or to distort the historical character of social phenomena and to lose itself in a logic of suprahistorical categories and capacities of the mind.

A third objection to the structuralist formulation of the idea of totality is that by treating wholes as conventions of method it is led to separate the problem of parts and wholes in knowledge from the other themes of liberal thought. The structuralist accepts a lopsided version of the principle of totality, and he leaves the other principles of liberalism untouched. Structuralism emphasizes the synthetic and downgrades the collectivist aspect of totality, by treating the problem of wholes as a problem about knowledge or at most about the knowledge of society, but not about society itself. Moreover, the structuralist characteristically respects the distinction between understanding and evaluation in his view of his own science. It will, therefore, be no surprise if in his approach to the political aspects of totality, he continues to treat prescriptive rules as a basis of social order, thus perpetuating the political theory of liberalism.

The conventionalist interpretation of totality, which builds a wall between theory and the world, reinforces, and is strengthened by, the tacit acceptance of all liberal ideas except the principle of analysis itself. But if the view of the preceding sections of this chapter is correct, one cannot validly reject the analytic principle without repudiating the entire system of liberal thought. The failure to understand that the idea of structure is only one incident in a larger map of psychological and political theory is one aspect of structuralism's chief sin.

A fourth remark about structuralism cannot yet be an objection, but it will grow into one as my positive argument unfolds. By recognizing, however inadequately, the principle of totality, structuralism represents an advance over the liberal doctrine. There is another sense, however, in which it is a step back from liberalism. Because he embraces a frankly conventionalist view of social study and denies that his wholes exist in the world of fact, the structuralist does not believe that his doctrines can serve as a basis of choice. He severs the link between the theory of mind and society, on the one hand, and political deliberation, on the other, a link liberalism had never completely destroyed. He reduces social study to a technique for the combination and recombination of concepts.[19] For him, thought can never really seize the social order as a whole and determine the conditions of its transformation.

Another way to state the same point is that by viewing social phenomena such as language and economic exchange as if they were expressions of universal categories of mind the structuralist produces the same political effect achieved by the pure liberal who dissolves all wholes into infinitesimal particulars. In the latter case, the infinitude of interactions among speakers or traders makes it seem that language or economy evolve by a force beyond human control, as parts of nature. In the former case, the universality of the categories they express lends to linguistic or economic organization the appearance of standing above history and therefore beyond politics. The structuralist view of totality illustrates the abiding alliance of skepticism and conservatism in political thought.[20]

There is a second interpretation of the principle of totality that has left its mark on modern thought, and of which Marx's social theory is the most finished example. It was foreshadowed by Spinoza and developed by Hegel. I shall call it realism. The basic element in the realist view is the notion that the unanalyzable wholes are real things in the world of fact. With respect to society, this means that the wholes are historical. Hence, the incorporation of parts into new wholes is an actual process that occurs in history. In this sense, the relation of parts and wholes is dynamic. For example, the interplay of certain productive techniques with a particular type of social organization results in a society that differs both in its organization and in its technology from the earlier one. The development of wholes will only cause a modification of the constituent parts if the emergence is an actual temporal process rather than just a logical one.

The virtues and defects of realism derive from its attempt to move beyond the separation of the order of ideas and the order of events by implying that unanalyzable wholes in social reality and in social theory are different sides of the same phenomena. Realism is not just the symmetrical opposite of structuralism. It does more than emphasize the nonconventionalist side of the modern idea of science, the possibility of measuring theory against pretheoretical experience. One could not justify a belief in the possibility of pretheoretical experience without accepting the doctrine of intelligible essences. That doctrine, however, affirms that everything has an unchanging essence; it cannot be made consistent with the dynamic relation of parts and wholes the realist wants to elucidate.

Realism is an attempt to dispense altogether with the separation of the order of ideas and the order of events. For this reason, it is the most profound and daring of all the partial criticisms of liberal thought. Nevertheless, realism is open to attacks that could only be repulsed if the realist had solved the antinomy of theory and fact and the antinomies connected with it. This, however, the realists have not done, as the following difficulties with their position indicate.

First, what is one to make of the realist conception of truth? It is not enough to say that the unanalyzable wholes to which theory refers represent actual historical phenomena. The theorist must still have criteria to choose among conflicting possible interpretations of the phenomena. The problem of choice in the construction of theory cannot be solved by an appeal to the idea of representation. The issue is precisely to determine which representation of the phenomena is correct or what representation means.

Second, if the parts are actually changing in the course of the emergence of the whole, what entitles us to identify them as the same entities at different moments?

Third, if the categories of thought are historically relative, what reason is there to see in the realist method itself anything more than the illusion or the need of an age? Does not the assertion of the historical relativity of all ideas force us to fall back on the repudiated structuralist claim that the unanalyzable wholes are simply conventional?

Fourth, the realist method seems to confuse two distinct notions:

the idea of a change in social life itself, a change that necessarily takes place in time, and the idea of a purely theoretical or logical ordering of concepts, which has no temporal dimension. It is like confusing the act of drawing a hexagonal figure with the idea of the geometrical construction of a hexagon.

If we take the last point first, we may see both how the realist would respond to all the objections and where his answer would fall short. We must determine what would be necessary for a satisfactory response to be possible.

The fourth objection, like the preceding ones, stems from our puzzlement about the relationship between theory and historical experience. When one draws a distinction between the order of ideas and the order of events, there is always a point at which one has to ask, What is the relation of the internal logic of the concepts with which we explain the events to the actual relationships among events? With regard to any proposition the theorist will have to put to himself two sets of questions.

First, he will ask what follows from a given thesis. Is it consistent, as a proposition, with the other propositions of his theoretical explanation? If not, how should he reformulate his views? Having answered this question, he is faced with a second one.

What is the relationship between the operation by which one goes from one proposition to another in the internal logic of his theoretical propositions (*a* entails *b*, etc.) and the way in which he describes the interconnection of historical events? In other words, if we imagine history as one system and the theory of society as another, what is the relation of the way in which the elements of the former are connected with one another to the manner in which the components of the latter are linked together? There can be no answer to this second question within the confines of our present mode of thought, precisely because in that mode all relations must fall into one of two categories: either they are relations among ideas or they are relations among events. The very same puzzle appears in a different guise as one of the basic problems of the philosophies of nature and of mathematics. What is the connection between the functional and the causal statement of the natural laws? Or, in different words, why is mathematics applicable to the world?

The realist might answer the accusation that he confuses the logical ordering of concepts with the historical sequence of events by pointing out that it is precisely his purpose to abandon the standpoint from which the distinction between the orders of ideas and of events is drawn. He can then go on to deal with the other objections to his position in the same way.

He insists that his categories are meant to be actual representations of historical events and of their interrelations. We protest that the difficulty lies precisely in deciding what constitutes a correct representation. He replies that in his thought ideas are not representations of events at all. They are, as Spinoza argued, another "attribute" of the events themselves.

We object that if the parts change in the course of their incorporation into wholes we have no way of identifying them at different moments as the same and therefore no way of knowing that they change. The realist responds that the problem of identification does not arise, because our ideas are immediate expressions of events.

Nevertheless, these defenses of the realist interpretation of the principle of totality presuppose the possibility of a synthesis of the order of ideas and the order of events without describing its precise nature or showing how it is to be achieved. The fact remains that we can choose among different conceptions of the same phenomenon. Therefore, it is not enough to postulate that ideas and events are different "attributes" of the same things (Spinoza), that ideas are actualized in the world (Hegel), or that existence determines consciousness (Marx). All these doctrines avoid confronting the antinomy of theory and fact; they do not solve it.

The discussion of realism leads to a disquieting conclusion. The distinction of the order of events and of the order of ideas, of causal explanation and logical analysis, is an inevitable corollary of the separation of the mind from the world, or of the subject from its objects. The antinomy of theory and fact cannot be resolved by the mere suppression of the distinction. But there is more to the story.

The formulation of a satisfactory method of thought about mind and society requires the recognition of the pecularities of what I described earlier as the realm of consciousness. In this realm, the principle of totality holds. We need to state the principle of totality in a way that will describe the correspondence between reflection and existence in the sphere of consciousness and be free of the vices of structuralism. To achieve this goal we must be able to clarify the relationship of the order of ideas to the order of events, for it is between them that the realm of consciousness is located.

Realism is the most incisive of all the partial criticisms of liberal thought, the one that goes furthest toward undermining liberalism and suggesting the premises of an alternative system of thought. Yet even this most subversive of doctrines is foiled in its revolutionary intentions by its failure to resolve the antinomy of theory and fact, the antinomy that presents the issue of the order of ideas and the order of events.

The last step in my critique of liberalism will be to look beyond the antinomy of theory and fact to the issue that overshadows all the antinomies of liberal thought and binds them together.

THE UNIVERSAL AND THE PARTICULAR

The antinomies of theory and fact, reason and desire, and rules and values are the fundamental problems of liberal doctrine. The last two represent the main difficulties faced, respectively, by liberal psychology and liberal political thought. The first is the riddle posed by the modern idea of science and nature. Liberal psychology and political theory constitute a single system of thought. They are united to the modern idea of science and nature by a common allegiance to the notion that there are no intelligible essences.

It should be clear that liberal thought might be consistent with a different view of science and nature, for the view I have described is not necessarily the only interpretation of what the inexistence of intelligible essences implies. Nevertheless, it is the interpretation that came to prevail. We may therefore treat the antinomy of theory and fact as part of the same system of thought from which the antinomies of reason and desire, and rules and values, also derive.

In each of these antinomies a distinction is drawn between a universal element and a particular one.[21] Thus, in the antinomy produced by the modern idea of science and nature, theory is the universal and fact the particular. In the psychological antinomy, reason is the universal and desire the particular. In the political antinomy, rules are the universal and values the particular. In all three cases, the universal stands apart from the particular, does not vary as the latter varies, and never fully determines the content of the particular. Let me illustrate these points.

The more perfect a theory becomes, the larger the number of facts to which it applies. The theory, if it is true, does not change in formulation as the facts change; on the contrary, the measure of its power is its ability to hold good in the face of transformations of the facts to which it is addressed. Finally, because theory advances through increasing abstraction, it does not describe or explain all the features the phenomena it studies present to common sense impression. To be sure, one may imagine that a completely unified science would be able to account for all there is to know about an individual horse through the general laws of physics. But, at that hypothetical point, it is less that universal theory would have fully determined particular facts than that the very notion of the particularity of things would have become meaningless.

In liberal psychology, the moralities of desire and of reason converge in denying that reason varies with particular desires. By rejecting the possibility of any passage from description to evaluation, the morality of desire confines reason to the task of gaining knowledge necessary to the fulfillment of one's ends, whatever they happen to be. All men can approach an identical objective understanding of the world despite the individuality of their goals. On the other hand, a coherent rational morality, to the extent it is possible, must be based on rules whose validity is independent of the individual's desires.

In liberal political theory, rules must be impersonal in the sense that neither their making nor their application is determined by individual and subjective rules. At most, they will be made and applied according to a combination of values that must not itself be individual and subjective. Only thus can a regime of legal justice subsist.

The concept of the universal at work in these areas of thought is that of an unchanging abstract form, separated from a variable concrete substance. The antinomies of liberal thought all have their being in the fact that it is both necessary and impossible to assert the separation of the form and the substance, of the abstract and the concrete.

In the antinomy of theory and fact, fact, the particular or substantive element, must be independent from theory, the universal or formal one. It is part of what we mean by a theory that at some point it be capable of comparison with facts. Unless facts can be independently defined and understood, unless we have pretheoretical experience, no such comparison can be made. At the same time, however, facts can only be classified, defined, and explained in the language of a specific theory; hence the need both to affirm and to deny the separation of the universal and the particular, form and substance.

The same result is implied in the antinomy of reason and desire. According to the morality of desire, reason can clarify the relationship among ends, but it cannot ultimately tell us which ends to hold. There must be a complete separation of the will, which makes choices, and of reason, which produces objective knowledge. Yet, unless there are general standards for choosing among desires, the morality of desire cannot respond to the question it set out to answer, What should one do? Conversely, a coherent morality of reason depends on the statement of purely formal precepts of conduct that hold, whatever our ends happen to be. Nevertheless, it is only by preferring certain ends to others that we are able to make the standards of rational morality concrete enough to function as criteria of choice. One way or the other, the universal both must be and cannot be separated from the particular.

According to the political antinomy, rules and values must be treated as independent of one another. The former are impersonal or objective; the latter, individual and subjective. In the regime of substantive justice, which is the political counterpart of the morality of desire, we judge all things as means to our ends and dispense with rules, or treat all rules as instrumental. However, without noninstrumental rules to determine what counts as a permissible means, substantive justice is inconceivable. In the regime of legal justice, the political equivalent of the morality of reason, the results of legislation and adjudication cannot be justified simply by their usefulness to individual and subjective values. Above all, there must be a neutral method of adjudication that allows one to apply the rules regardless of considerations of value or purpose. Such a method is necessary for two reasons: the individuality and subjectivity of all purposes, and the contradiction between the requirements of rule following and those of instrumental rationality. The discussion of the formalist theory of adjudication showed that this method cannot exist. Legal justice and substantive justice, judgment according to rules and according to values, the universal and the particular in politics, both must be and cannot be separated.

The relation of parts and wholes described by the principle of aggregation is still another variant on the conception of universals and particulars that underlies the antinomies of liberal thought. As a universal, the whole becomes more abstract and formal the greater the number or the range of parts or particulars it subsumes. If the whole is complex knowledge, this means that theory progresses by flattening out the substance or concreteness of particular facts. If the whole is a social group, it means that group unity is preserved and understood only insofar as variations among members are disregarded.

By reason of the contrast of the universal and the particular that underlies the antinomies of liberal thought and the liberal conception of parts and wholes, two processes recur constantly in all areas of thought. One is the evisceration of particulars; the other, the reification of universals.

The evisceration of particulars consists in treating particulars as fungible examples of some abstract quality. To be sure, the particulars as parts are recognized as more concrete and therefore more real than the universals as wholes. That much is implied by the principle of aggregation. Nevertheless, as the concreteness of the particulars increases, so does their individuality. Therefore, it becomes impossible to think or to speak about them in general categories; hence, given the nature of thought and language, impossible to think or speak of them at all. That much is implied by the antinomy of theory and fact.

The way out is to treat particulars as if they were cases of an abstract or formal entity that did not really exist in the world. In the course of this mysterious transposition, the particulars begin to lose their substance, their concreteness, and, thus, their individuality. The particularity in which their being consists is eviscerated. Particularity dissolves in just this way when a man is treated as an example of a legal person, or when different ends are conflated into a general concept of interest, or when an event is subsumed under an explanatory law; one then stops thinking about what makes the person, the end, or the event different from others.

No sooner does the evisceration of particulars begin than a complementary process sets in, the reification of universals.[22] The abstract qualities take on a life of their own because they are the sole possible objects of thought and language. Despite the acknowledgment that universals are abstractions or conventions, everyone talks and acts as if they were real things, indeed the only real things in the world. Consequences are drawn for thought and for conduct from the nature of legal personality, of economic interests, or of the class of events explained by a scientific law, although it is supposedly only for the sake of expedience that we treat them as if they had a nature.

From the evisceration of particulars and the reification of universals there ensues a spectacle that would be strange if it were not too familiar to be noticeable. Though it is the particulars that are supposed to have concrete reality, it is to the universals that thought and action are addressed. The ghosts sing and dance on the stage while the real persons sit dumbly in the pit below. The observer may be forgiven for wondering who is alive and who dead.

All the fundamental issues of modern philosophy are variations on the three antinomies and on the problem of parts and wholes. And all are the expressions of the more fundamental problem of the universal and the particular. The universal as form and the particular as substance must be separate from one another if we are to make sense of our scientific, moral, and political ideas. But in each instance their separation seems impossible to uphold. Whenever we begin by thinking of them as independent from one another, we end by recognizing their interdependence. Whenever we start by conceiving of them as interdependent, we are forced to the conclusion that they must be independent.

It is little help to suggest that the ideas of unity and separation of the universal and the particular should be reconciled on the ground that each contains an element of truth. The problem is precisely that the system of our thought is so constituted that no reconciliation can be found, because none is possible without a reconstruction of our premises. The antinomies have never been resolved, nor will they ever until we find a way out of the prison-house of liberal thought. The figure on page 138 summarizes the scheme of the antinomies in their relation to the principles of liberalism and to the contrast of the universal and the particular.

FROM CRITIQUE TO CONSTRUCTION

The unity of universals and particulars

The task of moving beyond the total criticism of liberal theory to an alternative doctrine is forced upon us by the need to deal with the overarching issue of the universal and the particular. One way to solve the problem of the universal and the particular, and thus the antinomies of liberal thought, would be simply to deny its terms. Instead of assuming the separation of the universal and the particular, we would

FIGURE 1
The Antinomies of Liberal Thought

Nature and science
(There are no intelligible essences; language is conventional; etc.)

Liberal psychology
1. principle of reason and desire
2. principle of arbitrary desire
3. principle of analysis

└──→ principle of aggregation

Liberal political and legal theory
1. principle of rules and values
2. principle of subjective value
3. principle of individualism

The antinomies follow from the preceding premises and are connected with the distinctions between means and ends, form and substance, public and private life, technique and theory.

The antinomy of theory (ideas) and fact (events) subverts the conception of knowledge.

a_1 The identity of facts is defined by theories.

a_2 It is part of what we mean by a fact that it be distinguishable from a theory that explains it.

b_1 Theories exist only as arrangements of facts.

b_2 It is part of what we mean by a theory that it be distinguishable from the facts for which it accounts.

The antinomy of reason and desire subverts the conception of personality.

a_1 The morality of desire is only adequate when structured by rules of reason.

a_2 The morality of desire is inconsistent with the attribution of any normative significance to reason.

b_1 The morality of reason is only adequate when given content by substantive desires.

b_2 The morality of reason is inconsistent with the attribution of any normative significance to desire.

The antinomy of rules and values subverts the conception of society.

a_1 The practice of choosing means to ends (instrumental rationality) requires following prescriptive rules (adjudication).

a_2 Instrumental rationality is inconsistent with adjudication.

b_1 Adjudication requires judgments of instrumental rationality.

b_2 Adjudication is inconsistent with instrumental rationality.

The general form of the antinomies

(a_1) The particular (facts, desires, values) exists only through the universal (theory, reason, rules),

(a_2) but must be separate from it.

(b_1) The universal exists only through the particular,

(b_2) but must be separate from it.

start off from the premise of their identity. Thus, in a single move, we might stand liberal thought on its head in the hope of escaping from its internal contradictions.

In one sense, the unity of the universal and the particular might mean the identification of the very universals and particulars that liberal thought contrasts: theory or ideas and facts or events, reason and desire, rules and values. This antiliberal doctrine would accept Spinoza's view that ideas and events are different "attributes" of the same things. In psychology, it would represent the conception of a personality so constituted that all its desires coincided spontaneously with the universal commands of rational morality. Kant's idea of the "holy will," which does not have to sacrifice inclination to duty, because it is always naturally inclined to the right, exemplifies this position.[23] In political theory, the identification of universal and particular would point to a society in which standards of conduct were so completely internalized as the ends individuals pursued that the distinction between public rules and private values would become meaningless. Many ideals of social harmony, like the doctrine of Plato's Republic or Confucius' well-ordered state, come close to such a view.

In another sense, to unify the universal and the particular might mean to repudiate any distinction between universality and particularity, no matter what its form.

If the union of the universal and the particular is interpreted as a flat negation of the dichotomies of liberal thought, it leads to absurd descriptive and undesirable prescriptive results, and it reveals a misunderstanding of the relation between theory and history. When taken more broadly as a rejection of the very contrast of universality and particularity, it seems to disregard some ineradicable features of human life and thought.

In each case, the outright denial of the differences that liberalism turns into oppositions would fail to account for some crucial aspect of our experience of what the world is like, or of our intentions as moral beings. The identification of ideas with events makes it impossible to comprehend how we could ever have false ideas or formulate criteria for choice among competing theories. It disregards the separation of mind and world. The unification of understanding and desire as a basis for a theory of knowledge contradicts the notion that the world might be different from what we think it ought to be, thus leading to the sanctification of actuality. As the basis for an ethic, it describes a situation in which there would be no critical standpoint from which one's present desires could be evaluated, for they would have become by definition the good. The tension between reason and desire, though the source of discontent and disintegration, seems to be also the foundation of a critical moral consciousness. Finally, as a descriptive matter, the identification of rules and values undermines our capacity to understand the individuality of persons. As an ideal, it destroys any support for the belief that individuality ought to be protected.

Thus, the identification of the universal and the particular leads to insuperable difficulties in explaining aspects of experience as fundamental as the possibility of error and of evil, and the separateness of persons. Moreover, it forgets the necessity of choice in thought, in morals, and in politics, and the worth that the need to choose gives us. So it would seem that what we are looking for is not the denial of the separation of the universal and the particular, but rather a different conception of their relationship to one another. Instead of the liberal doctrine upside down, we need the synthesis of liberalism with its opposite.

The unacceptability of a pure antiliberal doctrine can be traced back to a misunderstanding of the relationship between theory and history. The premises of liberal thought describe a form of social existence and social consciousness. The separation of the universal and the particular, and the continual conflict between them, correspond to experiences we have as moral and political beings. The inability to arrive at a different understanding of the connection between rules and values, and reason and desire, is only part of this broader historical situation. Indeed, unless the antinomies of liberal thought revealed something profound about the way we live our lives, we would not be interested either in comprehending or in resolving the antinomies.

If the principles of liberalism draw their power and importance from the fact that they illuminate a historical situation, it is an illusion to suppose that the problems they produce can be solved by a mere replacement of postulates. We have to understand the features of existence and of consciousness the theoretical antinomies describe; to find out whether the historical situation itself already contains possible solutions; and to look for a theory that might contribute to these solutions. In this process theory plays a double role. It elucidates possibilities already present, and by the very act of elucidation it opens up possibilities not there before. Superficially, the notion of resolving the antinomies by simply formulating a doctrine in which they would not exist may appear to be a defense of speculation. In truth, however, it makes theory autonomous only by reducing it to frivolous impotence, for it severs the link between the progress of thought and the transformation of society.

The antiliberal doctrine is therefore unacceptable as a solution to the problems of liberal thought. We have to find out how to overcome in both theory and experience the opposition of ideas and events, reason and desire, rule and value, without denying their separation. We need a way to make the universal and the particular at once the same and different.

From the outset, however, it should be clear that this search does not involve a rejection of the concepts of universality and particularity, nor is it inconsistent with a recognition that there may be central aspects of existence in which the antagonism of the universal and the particular is unavoidable. Thus, we must learn to distinguish the liberal antinomies, products of a transitory form of thought and of life, from more basic and ineradicable conflicts between universality and particularity that arise in morals, knowledge, and politics. These conflicts represent the outer limits of our ability to escape tragedy in life.

Take morals. There are three main types of moral conduct. The first is a morality of consequences. We judge our acts by their results because we care about others and about the world. The second is a morality of principles. We cannot judge by consequences alone, because we grasp only dimly the effects of our actions and because it may be easier to determine the rightness of principles than the goodness of concrete outcomes. A man who acted solely according to a calculus of the benefits and harms he might produce would be indecisive if he were lucid, for no one can see until the end of time to measure the good and evil he will have ultimately brought about. Thus, the predicament of moral conduct is similar to that of a game of skill, which is made possible by the fact that the players can know some of the consequences of their moves, but cannot know all of them. The moralities of consequences and of principles are both universalist ethics: they support judgments that cut across space and time and apply uniformly to all persons or to general categories of persons.

But there is a third kind of moral conduct, the ethic of sympathy, which resists the claims of universalism. It is the ethic of sympathy, the expression of love, that leads the shepherd to place the safety of the stray lamb above the welfare of the flock. It values the present and immediate person more than the future or distant one, and it breaks all moral rules in behalf of the loved one. Such an act always seems irrational, for our very conception of rationality has become identical to the idea of following rules. Because all human love is a particular relationship among particular persons, it must rebel against the universalizing tendencies of consequentialist or rule-bound ethics.

The suppression of any of the three moralities would pervert the moral life by disregarding a basic feature of human existence. Nevertheless, the forms of moral conduct conflict with each other, and their conflict becomes especially acute in the rivalry between the universalist and the particularist ethics.

The antagonism of the particular and the universal in morals is most clearly exemplified by the confrontation between love and law or justice, if the latter are narrowly defined as matters of rules. When love hurls itself against justice under law, two results emerge. From the side of love, there is mercy, which acknowledges the bonds of reciprocity but loosens them through forgiveness. Mercy is what love turns into when it meets justice, as community is what love becomes when it touches society and reciprocity. From the side of law, the encounter of love and justice produces the idea of a right to the satisfaction of one's needs in public law, the theory of excuses in criminal law, and the idea of equity in private law. But whereas mercy is simply an ornament and a perfection of love, need, excuses, and equity undermine the rule of law. They favor the individualization of decisions in view of the person and his unique circumstances. Thus, whenever the battle between love and justice is joined through the workings of mercy, love is the stronger warrior that overpowers its rival in the struggle for mastery of the moral life.

In the realms of knowledge and of politics, the demands of the universal and of the particular are opposed just as fiercely as in ethics. In knowledge, there is the separation between the abstract understanding or judgment of universals, which is theory, and the concrete intuition and choice of particulars, which is prudence. In politics, there is the contest between the claims of intimate and of universal community. Both the cognitive and the political issue will be taken up at a later stage of the argument.

The interplay of universals and particulars

Despite the unending conflict of universality and particularity in some aspects of experience, other aspects embody a quite different relationship between the universal and the particular. This alternative, of whose true nature we have only the faintest awareness, might show us how to move ahead. The universal must exist as a particular, just as a person is inseparable from his body. There is no formal universality, no circumstance in which the universal can be abstracted from its particular form. It always exists in a concrete way.

Yet no single particular incarnation of the universal exhausts its meaning or its possible modes of existence. Thus, there is no one state of a person's body that at any given time, or over the course of his life, reveals all the sides of his identity. The body may change and still we say the person remains the same, in some ways though not in others, and that the different bodily conditions are his conditions.

In this conception, the universal and the particular are equally real though they represent different kinds of reality. The universal is neither abstract and formal, nor capable of being identified with a single concrete and substantive particular. Instead, it is an entity whose universality consists precisely in the open set of concrete and substantive determinations in which it can appear. Once again, it is the universality of a person in relation to the states of his body or of an organism to its different conditions rather than that of a number to the category under which it may be subsumed.[24]

This is a difficult view of the universal and the particular to understand because of its foreignness to our settled habits of thought. Moreover, if my argument about theory and history is correct, we should not expect to understand it fully all at once. Consider, however, aspects of our moral, artistic, and religious experience that exemplify this view.

We are often conscious of the fact that attempts to reduce our moral beliefs to abstract, universal principles fail. Characteristically, such principles lead either to paradox or to absurd results. The moralities of reason and of desire in liberal psychology illustrate the problem. The source of the difficulty is the acceptance of the modern conception of the universal, the standard of right conduct, as a pure form that can be separated from the particular, the contexts in which choices have to be made. Thus, we try to impose order on our moral ideas with the same type of abstract reason adopted by the sciences of nature.

The ancients, however, recognized that moral standards are casuistic. They cannot be stated adequately in abstraction from the very concrete situations to which they apply. That is what the classic metaphysicians meant by speaking of ethics as the domain of practical reason. Moral learning is the study and remembrance of what it was right to do in individual cases; hence, the use of the parable and of the paradigmatic anecdote. In this sense, the universal cannot be separated from its particular embodiment. At the same time, the lesson contained in the individual case goes beyond the case itself. Other cases can be analogized to it by virtue of our capacity to perceive in the model event a general lesson that cannot be reduced to an abstract rule. The universal is never exhausted in any one of its particulars.

In the plastic or narrative work of art, universality of meaning is often achieved not through abstraction from the particularity of individual things but by the very richness with which this particularity is represented. The work fails either when it lacks a general significance or when it stands for general ideas and ideals not fully expressed in the work itself but left in a formal, abstract state. In the first case, art becomes frivolous; in the second, didactic. But in the great work of art men are able to recognize that something is being shown that has a broad and therefore lasting significance and illuminates hidden features of many situations. This something, the universal, cannot be reduced to abstract propositions. It is embodied in expressions. Nevertheless, the universal is not wholly confined to those expressions; it can be rediscovered elsewhere.

At the center of the Christian religion, there is a similar view of the relation between the universal and the particular. The dogmas of the Incarnation and the resurrection of the body bear simultaneously on the problems of the divine and the human, the person and the body, and the universal and the particular, for these three problems are connected with one another. According to the doctrine of the Incarnation, through the birth of Christ, God became man without relinquishing His divinity. God is the infinite, that is to say, the universal being; man the finite, that is to say, the particular one. According to the doctrine of the resurrection of the body, men will be purged of everything finite and contingent in the world to come, yet they will continue to exist as individual beings, with their individual bodies. The mind is unable to understand how it is possible for God to confine Himself within the limits of humanity or for His creature to shake off the signs of its finitude. Thus, traditional Christian theology has usually held that the Incarnation and the resurrection of the body are mysteries faith can comprehend but reason cannot grasp.

The image of the universal and the particular represented in these moral, artistic, and religious doctrines is the very one we must now continue to look for in history.

4

THE THEORY OF THE
WELFARE-CORPORATE STATE

INTRODUCTION

The argument developed up to now has two main limitations. First, it is mainly critical rather than constructive. Second, as criticism it suffers from a narrowness of view, for it treats the liberal doctrine as a set of interlocking conceptions whose relationship to society is disregarded. The study of the internal structure of the theory has been pursued at the cost of an awareness of theory's social significance. Yet there is much in liberal thought that so unhistorical an interpretation fails to clarify. It is the aim of this chapter to remedy the second of these deficiencies and to lay the groundwork for dealing with the first.

The liberal doctrine is the representation of a certain type of social life in the language of speculative thought. It derives a large part of its unity and richness from its association with that form of life. Thus, to complete the program of total criticism there is the need to understand the nature of the association.

But the historical inquiry will also serve a second, more important purpose, suggested by my earlier remarks about the relation of theory to history. We have reached an impasse in the quest for an alternative to liberal thought. The attempt to turn liberalism upside down, to formulate a doctrine that is its symmetrical opposite, leads to absurd conclusions because it misconceives the link between philosophy and social experience.

Liberal thought commands our interest and our assent because its principles describe much of the way we think and live. Liberalism represents this experience by expressing its meaning. (Representation is the expression of meaning.) My thesis is that this underlying mode of social life has been changing in ways that both require a reconstruction of philosophical premises and guide us toward that reconstruction.

But in what sense would a different experience of thought and of society demand new metaphysical postulates? New conceptions may be needed when what metaphysics describes, to the extent that metaphysics is descriptive, changes. It would be a problem of novelty in the subject matter of philosophy. Alternatively, changed circumstances may just put us in a better position to grasp timeless truth about mind and society. The argument I am about to develop rejects both these views. It starts off from another postulate, which must be justified by the kinds of insights into society and self it makes possible.

The truth about knowledge and politics, says the principle, is both made and discovered in history. It is made because whatever one age regards as most fundamental to the nature of mind and of society, another is able to unmask as peculiar to a transitory historical situation. Total criticism arrives on the heels of such an unmasking. Nonetheless, the truth about knowledge and politics is in a certain sense eternal. Each basic change in psychological and political experience permits men to see their established system of thought as a special case of a more complete doctrine in which previous partial insights are at once preserved and revised.

The reason why earlier conceptions can be retained is that, even in the midst of the most striking changes, mind and society always bear the mark of certain ideal characteristics or characteristic ideals of the human species. There are times when these characteristics develop to a more complete point than the one they had reached up until then so that they can be understood more deeply and clearly. Thus, fundamental revisions in social thought typically begin with attempts to seize what is peculiar to the historical circumstances in which they are carried out. The theoretical advance prompted by this seizure is never automatic or passive. And whenever accomplished, it modifies the condition it set out to describe and to judge, uncovering hidden possibilities, deepening the awareness of the ideal, and serving as a weapon in the struggle for its actualization.

The same principle of method that explains why the transformation of social life requires the replacement of metaphysical ideas also suggests how the philosophic study of history can act as a guide. At a minimum, history can draw attention to alternatives the existing theoretical vocabulary either disregards or confuses. It should be clear from the outset, however, that history cannot in the end justify a choice of metaphysical doctrines, especially when the doctrines involve moral as well as descriptive judgments. Indeed, the very idea of the moral significance of historical changes must be independently established.

The chapter starts with a distinction between consciousness and order as two aspects of social life. It goes on to the description of two types of society that overlap in time, the liberal and the welfare-corporate state. In liberal society there is a dominant social consciousness, held together by a secularized ideal of transcendence; a social order marked by a certain relationship between class and role; and a characteristic institution, the bureaucracy. As liberal society changes into the welfare-corporate and socialist state, a mode of consciousness appears that expresses an ideal of immanence, and the major conflict within the social order becomes the opposition between class or role and emerging kinds of hierarchical or egalitarian community. The new experience suggests a new basis for thought.

SOCIAL CONSCIOUSNESS AND SOCIAL ORDER

Every type of social life can be viewed from two complementary perspectives, as a form of consciousness and as a mode of order. Both consciousness and order belong to the realm of mind. The distinction between them restates the correspondence of reflection and existence.

Each form of social consciousness is connected with a distinctive kind of social order. The two together constitute a form of social life, a state, or a society. The form of social life is not an abstract category that may be exemplified at any moment of history; it is the relationship among the elements of a particular social situation. Such a relationship is governed by the principle of totality. From this, several consequences follow, each of which will be illustrated in the present chapter.

The types of social consciousness and social order cannot be dissolved into their constituent elements without a crucial loss of understanding. When the totality represented by a form of social life is viewed historically, one sees that the elements out of which the whole was originally developed changed with its emergence. Another pertinent implication of the principle of totality is the inadequacy of any attempt to reduce a mode of social consciousness to the beliefs of individual minds, individually considered, or a kind of social order to the behavior of individual agents. Finally, the types of consciousness and order have a unity that is not one of logical or causal necessity and therefore cannot be accounted for by logical analysis or causal explanation. One may say that certain features make others more probable, but such quasi-causal language is simply a first approximation to the truth.

The unity of the whole is one of appositeness or aptness. This means that it is a unity of meaning, based on the fact that each form of consciousness, with its related type of social organization, represents a way of being of the self. The metaphysical description of these ways of being and of their roots in the theory of human nature is the main objective of the next chapter. Now let us see how some of the preceeding points help define the general character of social consciousness and social order.

The concept of social consciousness refers to a widely shared way of conceiving society and its relation to nature and to individuals. It embraces the most general conceptions and ideals about social life. These views need not be explicitly entertained as doctrines, but they are implied by more particular beliefs. The forebears of the idea of social consciousness were the notions of the spirit or mentality of an age, and one of its analogues is the conception of style in art history.

Social consciousness has the characteristics set out in my earlier discussion of the realm of mind. Thus, it is always connected with a type of existence or social order in a way to be defined later. It disrespects the contrast of fact and value, for it is placed, like a horizon, at a level at which the distinction between understandings and ideals vanishes. And it poses the issue of ambiguity of meaning: the relationship between the significance of the dominant conception of mind and society to those who entertain it and its meaning for those who, without adhering to it, want to understand it.

Other characteristics of social consciousness result from the principle of totality. Two of these characteristics are particularly important:

the unitary and the social nature of consciousness. A type of social consciousness is indeed a whole that can be stated with greater or lesser power in an indefinite number of ways. Once one has established its central vision or unifying principle, it is possible to discover in it new aspects without changing one's basic view of its character. In the same way, the finding of novel examples of an artistic style may enrich, yet not fundamentally transform, the definition of the style.

The mentality or mode of social consciousness exists only insofar as it is displayed in the beliefs of individuals. But no state of individual beliefs can be identified with a type of social consciousness. An individual can embrace only a small fraction of the wealth of understandings and ideals associated with a mentality. And in every individual there will be a conflict among different kinds of consciousness. Moreover, he may hold theories and accept moral ideals that do not fit into any one kind.

It nevertheless remains true that in every social situation there may be a dominant social consciousness. What makes it dominant is not the favor it receives from the majority of the population, or even from the most powerful groups in the society. Instead, a mentality achieves dominance because, among the many different sets of beliefs that compete for attention, it becomes actualized in the main forms of social order.

Thus, a dominant consciousness has to satisfy two distinct criteria. First, it must have the general attributes of consciousness, the most basic of which is to be an active mental experience. Sometimes, this experience will be common to many groups in the society. At other times, it will be quite restricted. Second, there must be a dominant form of social order that arranges individuals and groups similarly to the ways in which the type of consciousness pictures their relations. This is the sense in which one can speak of a tie of appositeness or common meaning between consciousness and order.

Alongside the dominant mentality, various deviant kinds of consciousness may exist. Each kind, whether dominant or deviant, is shared by many individual minds. Yet some of the roots of a dominant consciousness can be modest. Beliefs that at one moment are hidden in the heads of a few thinkers may at another become a ruling vision of society. Indeed, every great moral and political doctrine draws much of its power from its ability to foreshadow a form of social consciousness and then to contribute to its emergence and to participate in its history.

That we are still without a satisfactory conception of social consciousness is a consequence of the vices of partial criticism of liberal doctrine. Whereas the theory of society continues to be primarily an account of social organization, the theory of consciousness remains for the most part a study of the individual psyche. The category of social consciousness falls between the two stools.

Order—that is, organization—is the second aspect of social life. It is the external, observable form of society. When social relations are viewed from the standpoint of the beliefs that infuse them, I use the term conciousness. When they are studied as facts 'in themselves' that exist outside of the minds of their participants with a reality of their own, I refer to order. It is a real question whether, given the nature of the correspondence between reflection and existence, any distinction of order and consciousness makes sense at all. Nevertheless, the distinction is important because, as we shall see, the correspondence of reflection and existence is always imperfect and capable of breaking down.

In what sense, then, may one speak of a form of social order and of its relationship to consciousness? The method whose uses this chapter will illustrate begins with the principle that the forms of social order represent certain understandings and ideals of society less directly than, but just as truly as, theories or mentalities.[1] In any social situation, a few basic schemes of social relations are repeated with relative constancy in all realms of social life, from the briefest encounters of two persons to the struggle among groups in the society as a whole. Each of these schemes actualizes an ideal of social organization and arranges the elements of social relations according to a limited number of general principles. The ideal of hierarchic community, for example, is actualized by the principles of kinship and of estates.

Every principle of social order, then, is a hypothetical rule for the disposition of individuals and groups in social life. It can be viewed as the actualization of a general conception of social life. In this sense, it has a meaning. Thus, one can connect and compare it with different kinds of social consciousness according to the principle of appositeness or common meaning.

Of the many schemes of social relations that coexist in each historical circumstance, one will usually be supreme. The dominant mode of social order will tend to actualize the same conceptions of personality and of society represented by the prevalent form of social consciousness. The tie of common meaning between a dominant consciousness and a dominant order is the basis for the definition of a type of social life.

THE LIBERAL STATE

The first form of social life to consider is the liberal state, the society of which the liberal doctrine is the theoretical representation. I begin with a view of the liberal state as simple and commonplace as I can make it, with the intention of deepening and revising the conception as the argument moves forward.

The liberal state is the society established by the decisive social and cultural changes of the seventeenth century that culminated in the French and the industrial revolution.[2] It is a category that describes with greater or lesser fidelity the characteristics of many Western and assimilated societies until the emergence of the welfare-corporate and the socialist state. There are two main elements in the traditional definition of this form of social life. One has to do with the character of economic organization; the other with the relationship between society and the state as government.

The liberal state is an industrial and capitalist society. Its distinctive mode of economic activity is industrial production for mass consumption. Its characteristic type of economic organization is the private ownership of property.

With respect to its social and political organization, liberal society is defined by the dissolution of the postfeudal, aristocratic system of estates or fixed social ranks and by the consequent distinction between political status and social circumstance. Social position no longer defines political status. All persons in principle achieve formal equality as citizens and as legal persons; they acquire similar political and civic duties and entitlements. But a relatively broad range of inequities in social and economic circumstances is tolerated, and treated as a matter different from legal-political equality. The reach of politics is restricted by more or less explicit constitutional measures that replace the implicit 'fundamental law' of feudal and postfeudal societies. There is a range of private life, economic and moral, into which government may not intrude. And finally, political organization tends to be democratic as well as constitutional. Power is exercised through electoral representation.

The partisans of the analytic view of knowledge and of the antinomian conception of history are quick to point out that in this potpourri of platitudes there is never more than half truth and rarely more than the random conjunction of things as often found apart as together. If, however, we take this picture solely as a signpost that draws our attention in certain directions, we may be able to move on to a better conception of the liberal state.

SOCIAL CONSCIOUSNESS IN THE LIBERAL STATE

One might start with the hypothesis that there is in fact a dominant consciousness in the liberal state. This mentality has never monopolized the beliefs of the most powerful groups in any national society, much less those of the population as a whole. What lends it extraordinary interest is the peculiar intimacy of its relationship to the social organization of the liberal state, as well as to the premises of liberal thought. Because of this relationship, the dominant consciousness tends to occupy an even larger place in the imagination of the ruling elites and eventually in the minds of their subordinates. But the working classes often begin with a different, even antagonistic view of society.[3] It is part of the hypothesis that one can find a fundamental unity of perspectives among the varieties of national culture under liberalism.

These are empirical claims. They can in principle be tested against the particulars of historical experience. Instead of discussing the problem of verification here, I offer the account as a suggestive framework for the reexamination of the theoretical issues that are the focus of my concern.

Instrumentalism

One aspect of the dominant consciousness has to do with the relation between man as a thinker and agent and the world as a whole. A second goes to the relationship among individuals and groups. Still a third describes the conception of the place the individual's job and social position occupy in his life.

The first aspect of the dominant consciousness appears as a type of conduct, the manipulative posture toward the world, and as a form of thought, instrumental rationality. Thought and conduct together constitute instrumentalism.

The manipulative posture toward the world takes the form of a denial of the immutability of nature and of society. It is the tendency to regard and to treat both the phenomena of nature and the arrangements of society as if they were in their entirety proper objects of human will. The degree to which nature and society can be adapted to conscious purposes is limited at any given moment. But there is nothing either necessary or good in such limitations.

In an ideal situation, whatever happened in the natural and social worlds would be responsive to the ends chosen by the right moral and political procedures. This ideal can be gradually approached even if it can never be fully reached. Man stands before nature and society as the grand manipulator. Everything in the external world has been or might one day be transformed by his work. This capacity to change the world in the image of his intentions is the defiance of fate.

In the dominant social consciousness, the manipulative relationship to nature is so closely connected with the image of society that the two can be treated for many purposes as a unity. The belief in a stable organization of social ranks, estates, or classes coexists according to the principle of appositeness with the conception that many of the phenomena of nature are sacred and therefore must be respected by man. For such a consciousness, the interlocking harmonies of nature and of society display the irresistibility and the sanctity of a world design. That is why one speaks of a natural order in society and conceives of nature on the model of the perceived social order.[4]

The dominant consciousness of the liberal state, however, sees social ranks as relative and social arrangements as transitory. There is a view that every aspect of social life must eventually be justified as the means to the furtherance of accepted social ends. No group is inherently legitimated to exercise power. The ideas of the relativity of ranks and of the transitoriness of customs may, despite their hold, be violently contradicted by the objective circumstances of society. For the moment, however, it is enough to understand that the conception of the social order as a creature of will is connected by appositeness to the notion that nothing in nature is necessarily or morally foreordained. Even birth, death, and the physical forms of human life may be changed in conformity to willed objectives.

The same relationship to the world that is expressed in conduct as manipulation reappears in thought as instrumental rationality. The characteristic operation of mind is the choice of means to the attainment of given ends. Reason works in the neutral realm of means; the choice of ends is beyond its reach.[5] The distinction between means and ends parallels that of facts and values.

There are a number of difficulties in defining the conception of instrumental rationality, difficulties already encountered in the discussion of substantive justice. At the root of these difficulties is the problem of the reciprocal dependence of judgments according to rules and judgments according to values, purposes, or ends. What is a means in one context may be an end for another. There must be criteria to distinguish the category of things that may count as means. Moreover, instrumental rationality as a device for the organization of knowledge or of society requires a procedure for the definition of the ends for whose benefit the means are to be chosen. Yet it is precisely because reason cannot choose ends that instrumental rationality is accepted as the characteristic mode of thinking. The dominant consciousness deals with these problems by supplementing instrumental rationality with the formal conception of reason, and with the notions of prescriptive rules and shared values.

Formal reason is the cognitive complement to instrumental rationality. It is a kind of thought that does not directly depend on the choice of ends, and therefore need not run into the embarrassments the need for such choice creates. It is the realm of pure knowledge in which theory means contemplation even though it may be put to practical use. Formal reason produces understanding through the perception of what is universal in a set of particulars rather than through the choice of means or the advancement of ends.

The political complement to instrumental rationality is the system of prescriptive rules that sets the boundaries of the categories of permissible means and ends. (Sometimes formal reason is itself enlisted in the making of the rules, as in the formal theories of freedom.) Alternatively, one trusts in a core of common values to define the ends of choice and thus to make instrumental rationality workable.

In the liberal state the price or planning systems are viewed as institutional supports of instrumental rationality, just as technology and social policy are treated as expressions of the manipulative posture toward nature and society. But this does not mean either that the price and planning systems are required by instrumental rationality as procedures of social choice or that they in fact fulfill the ideal of instrumental reason.

The manipulative relationship to the world and instrumental rationality are the reverse sides of each other. The former translates into conduct what the latter grasps as thought. Instrumentalism is achieved through instrumental reasoning. And to treat reason as the discovery of means is to view its objects as objects of manipulation.

Individualism

A second aspect of the dominant consciousness is its view of the relationship among persons. The core of this view is the vision of society as an association of radically separate individuals who are fated to struggle against one another even when their antagonism is tempered by reciprocal forbearance and collaboration. This side of the dominant consciousness can be called individualism.[6] Liberal political thought is its theoretical interpretation.

Individualism recognizes the reality of the social bond, but it treats that bond as both precarious and threatening to individuality. It is precarious because of the fragility of every sharing of values and the impossibility of administering a system of rules in the absence of shared ends. It is threatening because the greater the sharing of ends the more is the substance of individuality eviscerated.

There are many different ways to define the manner in which the dominant consciousness represents the relationship of indviduals to one another. In one sense, it is the experience of the mysterious coexistence in each person of a universal and a particular humanity. When they view one another as objects of science or as means to the satisfaction of each other's ends, men are able to treat each other as alike. They separate out what remains as universal in the midst of their particularity. Then there are times when, suddenly thrown back on themselves and released for a moment from the cares of instrumental choice or scientific observation, they appear to one another as complete strangers among whom only silence would be truthful. The sentiments of identity and strangeness, of the universal and the particular in personality, are equally fundamental and forever at war in the dominant consciousness.

Another way to describe the individualist conception of the social bond is to point out its view of the ambiguous relationship each man has to his fellows. Liberal political thought holds that mutual need and mutual hostility have the same sources. The corresponding experience of social consciousness is the counterpoint between the impulse to seek the company of others and fear of the danger association poses for individuality.

Alone, a man is deprived of the supports of individuality. Without the social productions of culture, he cannot develop his characteristic human capacities. Without the recognition of his personality by others, he cannot arrive at a definition of his own identity. But in the company of others, he must conform to their expectations in order to be understood and to be recognized. This submission undermines his uniqueness. Thus, men are in the position of Schopenhauer's porcupines, who huddle together to protect themselves from the cold, but who, when they come together, wound one another with their spines.[7]

Social place

A third facet of the dominant social consciousness has to do with the way in which the individual conceives of his relation to his own work and to his place in society. It addresses aspects of social life with which both liberal psychology and liberal political doctrine deal, the relation between role and personality and between personality and society. For the moment, I shall use the concepts of social place and role synonymously to describe the ways the individual fits into the division of labor. And the division of labor refers broadly to the differentiation of forms of individual life as well as to the allocation of jobs.[8]

Everyone must have a job; he must play specific roles. There is more to this than the need to earn one's keep. The performance of a role is the means through which capacities are developed and recognition gained. It is what lends unity and continuity to the self.

In another sense, however, every social position is experienced as something more or less external to the substance of individual personality; not, like the body, as a part of it. It is a fate to which one must surrender, or a trophy one can win, but, above all, in either case it is a mask one wears. By living in society, men eventually become their masks. Thus, the social order transforms into a reality the Stoic metaphor of the world as a stage on which each man plays his part.[9]

Notice, then, that there are two competing strands in the view of the individual's relation to his social place. Neither must be forgotten. One is the acceptance of one's work and social place as a necessity and a good. The other is the experience of every social place as a burden and as an assault on individual identity. The brunt of the assault lies, on the one hand, in the constraint on the fullness with which individuality can be expressed and, on the other hand, in the need to submit to the pretenses of social conventions that disguise or destroy impulse and that lack moral authority. A man both is and is not his social position, and one part of him condemns what the other craves. Thus, the same themes encountered in the discussion of individualism reappear under a different form.

There are several common pitfalls to avoid in the description of the way the dominant consciousness represents work and social position. One error is the notion that the prevalent mentality in the liberal state does not go beyond the fatalistic acceptance of role, whereas critical social thought, in its deeper wisdom, grasps the evils and dangers of resignation. On the contrary, insofar as thinkers such as Rousseau and the young Marx were able to provide a powerful account of this aspect of the dominant consciousness, it is precisely because they drew on ordinary awareness, carrying insights already present in everyday life to a higher level of clarity and abstraction. Another mistake is to suppose that only some groups in the society, such as manual workers, are affected by the conception of social place I have described. The ambivalent relationship to work and role runs through the entire social order, and it may fall with the heaviest weight on precisely the most powerful and wealthy groups in the society.

The ideal of transcendence

The different aspects of the dominant consciousness are bound together by the principle of aptness or common meaning because they express in particular ways a more general view of the world, the idea or ideal of transcendence. In its primary theological form, transcendence may be described as the distinction between God and the world, between the divine and the human, or between the soul and the body.[10]

The religious conception of reality is the basic level of social consciousness in several senses. Religion represents the most general expression of the beliefs that nourish and unify the several branches of a type of social consciousness. It exhibits the characteristics of social consciousness in their purest and most complete form. And it is always involved, more or less directly, in every change of social ideals and beliefs. Thus, the religious consciousness deals with the whole of experience.[11]

As a mode of reflection about the world, it is inseparable from a way of life in the world. Neither the type of reflection nor the way of life can be comprehended apart from each other. The contrast of understanding and evaluation is foreign to the religious consciousness, for its beliefs about the world are simultaneously descriptions and ideals. No clear distinction can be drawn between religiosity and other aspects of social consciousness. Certainly the notion of a distinct god, or divine element, or sacred realm characterizes only some forms of religion. So I return to the initial point: religion is simply the most general dimension of social consciousness, the horizon at which all its perspectives meet.

Transcendence is a manifestation of the religious consciousness. It has a history; its most important roots lie in the Near Eastern salvation religions that fashioned the conception that the world was created by a deity who stands above it. One should remember, however, that there are many parallel lines of development, like the elaboration in pre-Socratic Greek theology of the idea of a biological generation of the world by a unitary god.[12] Transcendence comes into its own with the belief in the existence of a supramundane God, a divine person whose attributes are incommensurable with those of the sensible world. When the deity is conceived of as an impersonal element rather than as a personal being, the line that separates the divine and the worldy becomes tenuous.

Three complementary beliefs are included within the conception of transcendence: a cosmogonic, a cosmological, and a personal one. The cosmogonic component is the idea of the divine creation of the world. The cosmological element is the distinction of the two worlds, heaven and earth, the latter subordinate to the former or contained within it. The personal element is the contrast of body and soul, by virtue of which the separation of the two worlds takes hold within the individual himself. Through his soul man participates in the higher world, which he remembers from a previous life, looks forward to in a future one, or dimly perceives in the midst of his present existence.

The opposite pole of the religious consciousness is immanence, the typical form of savage and ancient religion. In its pristine theological form the religion of immanence denies the distinction between God and the world. It has no cosmogony of the creation of the world by God, and therefore tends toward the view that the world is eternal and uncreated. Its cosmology refuses to accept the contrast of heaven and earth. Instead, it recognizes a set of sacred objectives or activities within the profane world. Sometimes it goes further and affirms the omnipresence of the divine in all aspects of reality. In its conception of personality, the religion of immanence replaces the theology of soul and body with an idea of the participation of the entire person in the God-head. Pantheism is its characteristic guise, and the philosophy of Spinoza its fullest metaphysical statement. Its defining characteristics are just the reverse of those of transcendence. It admits no creation of the world, but tends to conceive of the world as eternal. The divine appears as a particular set of natural and social phenomena, that is, the sacred, or as the world in its wholeness rather than as a supramundane reality. And, therefore, the soul participates in no higher order.[13]

The opposition of immanence and transcendence, though real, is never more than relative. The religions of immanence foreshadow the contrast of two worlds when they distinguish the sacred from the profane.[14] And even the most one-sided versions of transcendence concede something to the claims of immanence. For example, the theological traditions that emphasize the transcendent features of Christianity may still represent the divine presence in this world through dogmas like the Incarnation and Eucharist. Let us now see how the ideal of transcendence is involved in each of the aspects of the dominant consciousness, first as a historical cause, and then, above all, as a bond of common meaning according to the principle of appositeness.

The conception of nature and society as possible and proper objects of unlimited manipulation becomes available when the world is regarded as profane rather than as the embodiment of the sacred. Because the world no longer represents the divine, the particular forms it takes at any given time need not command reverence. The features of nature and of society are prized as means to the satisfaction of ends, or as ends in themselves if their perpetuation is an object of desire. But they are never worthy by virtue of their existence alone. Being implies no sanctity.[15]

The religion of transcendence also contributes in several ways to the development of individualism. Groups, or society as a whole, are not divine, nor is any part of social life sacred. Most religions of transcendence stop short of carrying the conception of the profanity of social life to the extreme. They may recognize that all human association has a supernatural significance and that the Church is a body that is sacred as well as profane. Nevertheless, it is their tendency to desanctify society that takes the larger place in consciousness.

At the same time, these religions assert the possibility of a direct and unique link of the individual soul with God. The more the religious consciousness embraces transcendence, the stronger is its inclination to play down the mediating role of social bodies like the Church in the individual's relationship to God. This is illustrated by the evolution of Protestant religiosity.[16]

To believe in the profanation of society and in the autonomy of the individual soul is to assert the priority of individual over group life and to pose the problem of how individuals with separate souls can communicate. Only the universal fatherhood of God allows men to collaborate and to speak to one another because it kindles within each soul the same spark of divine personality.

Finally, transcendence fosters the conception of work and social place characteristic of the dominant consciousness. "Made in the image of God," the individual contains within himself a universal or absolute element, which we call the soul. His being can never be played out or adequately expressed by any particular work he completes or place he occupies in society. Hence, he will fear every social position or task as a threat to the completeness of his being.

Nevertheless, the individual is not God. He is a particular and finite being. His particularity is most strikingly shown by his having a body, and his finitude by death. Because he is particular and finite, he must live in particular social positions and accomplish specific works. These works and positions give unity and determinate form to the person. Thus, the religiosity of transcendence is a source of the ambivalent relationship to work and social place in the dominant consciousness, just as it is a cause of instrumentalism and individualism.

Consider now two objections to the preceding treatment of the place of the ideal of transcendence in the dominant consciousness: one methodological, the other historical. First, it views transcendence from a causal standpoint, as a common cause of different aspects of social consciousness. But it does not move clearly enough beyond causal explanation to an account of the way transcendence serves as the principle of common meaning that unites different aspects of the dominant consciousness. Second, whatever role transcendence may have performed in the development of the dominant consciousness, one must still clarify the part it plays in liberal society. And the initial puzzle one confronts when one begins to do this is that the prevalent consciousness and the metaphysic associated with it have always been more or less secular. From the outset, they have been in revolt against the ancient claims of theology.

A fundamental characteristic of liberalism, as a type of social consciousness and as a doctrine, is its tendency to abandon the explicitly theological form of the religiosity of transcendence and to put in its place an implicitly theological conception. Agnosticism is the most obvious sign of what appears as the collapse of transcendence, but is in fact, at least in the short run, the secularization of transcendence. The distinction between heaven and earth is transformed into the contrasts of culture and nature, and state and society. The opposition of soul to body becomes that of reason to desire.

Nature and culture are conceived as discontinuous realms, incommensurable with one another. Culture is the realm of consciousness, of symbols, and of freedom. It is constructed through the control of nature outside man and within him. It stands for the triumph of intelligence over the blind and stupid resistance of natural things to human will. The better culture controls nature, the more do its transactions with the natural world come to resemble those of God with His creation.

Similarly, the state as the political association of citizens under impersonal rules is to society what God is to the world. When we view man as citizens who make, apply, and respect impersonal rules, and who are formally equal to one another, we abstract from their particular passions and values. We disregard everything that divides them against one another and makes them particular. Society, on the contrary, is the domain of conflict and particularity. It is the state that stands above society and imposes its order upon the disorder of social life, as God stands above the world and implants His laws upon it.[17]

There is a sense in which, within this consciousness, reason is to desire what the soul is to the body.[18] It is the universal element in mind, whereas desire is the particular. From the standpoint of the experience of choice, the mind is the realm of necessity; the will that of contingency. Yet because this secular reason is no longer thought to participate in a truly divine wisdom, its relationship to desire is sometimes made the inverse of that of the soul and body. Instead of commanding, it obeys. To this reversal I shall soon return.

The contrasts of culture and nature, state and society, reason and passion, have in common the division of a universal or an abstract and a particular or concrete humanity. We are now able to see that this dualism has a theological aspect. Liberalism secularizes yet partially preserves the meaning of the separation of two worlds in the transcendent religion. As a maker of culture, a citizen of the state, and a possessor of reason, man is like God, a universal being who knows and uses to his purposes the particulars of nature and of society. As a being in the realm of nature, who pursues his subjective values and is the slave of passion, man is like God's creatures, who can come to good only through unthinking or intelligent obedience to His plan for the creation.

The different aspects of the dominant consciousness specify this more general vision without departing from it. Instrumentalism expresses the ideal of the subordination of nature and society to human will, putting mankind in the place of God. Individualism draws out the implications of the conflict between the individual and the social element in personality, the former represented by society and by passion, the latter by the state and by reason. The same conflict of two worlds is restated as a struggle within the individual himself between the views of work and social place as the fulfillment and as the sacrifice of personality. One view satisfies the claims of universality or heaven; the other those of particularity or earth. Thus, once we have seized the spirit of secular transcendence, the noncausal and nonlogical bond of common meaning among the different aspects of the dominant mentality becomes clear.

Secular transcendence is by its very nature precarious and transitory. The concept itself smacks of paradox. In the religions of transcendence, heaven is truly another world, and one's relationship to it, however intimately associated with a secular life, does not make the earthly city divine. But when the divine is remade into culture, into the state, and into one of the elements of personality; when God becomes mankind; part of the secular world itself is sanctified. This sanctification is a step toward the inversion of the claims of transcendent religion. It is only another step to extend the deification of culture to nature, of the state to society, and of reason to desire, until the relationship of subordination between the elements of each of the dichotomies is turned upside down. Once the divine is recognized to inhere in the world, whatever is most 'natural' and least the subject to the will may seem most sacred. The secularization of transcendence leads back to immanence.

The breakdown and denial of a relationship to God means that men must try to get from one another what they had previously gotten from Him. Without an immortal soul, a supernatural vocation, or a God-given place in the world, they are at one another's mercy. Each man will be what society makes him because there is no suprasocial basis upon which the sense of self might be brought to rest. Above all, death becomes the great belittler, the condemnation to nothingness, from which each man can hide only through immersion in the cares of social life. If one described the sentiment of mortality as the premonition of the finality of death and the sentiment of society as the experience of the preeminence of social rules and roles over individual desires and values, then one might say that the sentiment of mortality is fuel to the sentiment of society. In this respect, it has the same effect as the need for recognition to ensure what one is and for assent to confirm what one knows.

How then can it be that the ruling liberal consciousness, which represents the religiosity of transcendence in secular garb, seems to lead inescapably to the total destruction of that religiosity? No question is more important to the understanding of the history of the modern mind. The liberal consciousness is an inherently contradictory transition between two stages of the religious consciousness, one in which transcendence is emphasized and another that reasserts in a changed form the earlier religiosity of immanence. Liberalism is the mode of consciousness that has secularized transcendence without yet undergoing the consequences, or understanding the implied meaning, of this secularization. It maintains an uneasy balance between the pure theological form of transcendence and the reaffirmation of immanent religion. This balance is the significance for consciousness of the characteristic secular dichotomies of liberal thought. What seems simple contradiction from the standpoint of logic makes sense when reexamined against this background.

Here is the clarification of a mystery in liberal thought that will always elude us as long as we insist on treating liberal theory as just a metaphysical doctrine and fail to study it also as a representation of social consciousness, whose unity does not lie in logical coherence alone. Those philosophers whom we usually regard as the deepest exponents of the liberal doctrine—Hobbes, Rousseau, and Kant—may have begun with the program of making the world safe for individuality, but they invariably concluded in one way or another with the defense of the state against the individual, of the species against its members, of universal or abstract against particular or concrete humanity. The would-be apology of individual freedom always seems to end in the ruthless sacrifice of autonomy to society. Why? It was genius rather than perversity that forced them to conclusions which so shocked their contemporaries. They grasped the long-term implications of the secularization of transcendence within liberalism and recognized claims a future age would uphold. When, at a later time and in apparent opposition to liberal thought, Hegel deifies the world, or Comte and Marx mankind, or Durkheim society, they are in fact working out the last steps of a theoretical change that had begun long before.

SOCIAL ORDER IN THE LIBERAL STATE

Principles of social order

A social order is a system of elements, each of which is defined by its relation to all the other elements. The elements are individuals and groups. Their position in the system is a social place. One type of social order is distinguished from another by its principle of order, the hypothetical idea or rule according to which the elements are arranged. To trace a social organization back to such a generative principle is like explaining the characteristic features of an artistic style as the working out of a more general conception of order. In both cases, the interrelations among the parts of the system obey the postulate of totality.

Every individual lives in a social situation in which one or a few types of social order are dominant. The generative principles of the types are one of the foremost determinants of the way the person defines his own identity, comes to view himself as a certain kind of person, and conceives of his place in society. The most familiar principles of social order are kinship, estate, class, and role. The last three will be of special interest to the study of the dominant type of social order in the liberal state.

The distinctive feature of the principle of estates is the union of social circumstance and political or legal status. Within the system of estates, every individual has a fixed social place that governs almost the entirety of his life in society: the kinds of things he is expected to do and to know, the goods he possesses, and the duties or entitlements he has. Membership in one's estate is usually determined by birth. And each estate has a legal definition, strong ties of internal solidarity, a limited set of permissible jobs open to its members, and a type of power or political representation that distinguish it from other estates. Both European feudal society and what is described as the postfeudal European *Ständestaat* or society of estates exemplify the principle.[19]

The principle of class might be defined by contrast to that of estates. It is a characteristic basis of order in modern capitalism. Its objective marks are the partial separation of social and economic circumstance from legal and political entitlement, and the preeminence of inherited and earned wealth as a determinant of social circumstance. All men are in principle formally equal as citizens and as legal persons. The power of an estate as a whole is inseparable from its wealth, but the impoverishment of an individual need not destroy his estate position, which is fixed forever at birth. An individual's membership in a class more nearly comes and goes with his property. The liberation of wealth is primarily a liberation of money; it is encouraged by the commercialization of wealth in the history of capitalism. Lastly, the principle of class has a subjective side. Class is a polemical concept; its history is the history of the rejection of the idea of a fixed social hierarchy, in which each social group has settled duties to obey or entitlements to govern. In this sense, it is a transition from estate to role.[20]

Role is the principle according to which social order is conceived and set up as a division of labor. Within the division of labor there are particular jobs; for the performance of each of them certain skills and talents are required. Each role embraces a limited and often small part of the life of the individual. Every individual occupies a plurality of roles, which he may view as entirely disparate and as connected in his life solely by the fact that it is he who occupies them. Birth operates in an indirect way by distributing unequally both natural talents and opportunities for the learning of skills. Nevertheless, merit—defined as the sum of past efforts, learned skills, and natural talents—is the established ideal of the division of labor under the principle of role. All other bases for the definition of social place are illegitimate from the perspective of that principle. Whereas class is from the outset a descriptive and a pejorative concept, role begins as an ideal.[21]

In many ways, kinship, estate, class, and role are stages along a single spectrum. They describe social situations in which individual identity is increasingly distinguished from group existence, or the self is evermore separated from others. They are also parts of a continuum in the sense that more often than not they succeed one another as dominant principles of social order in the sequence in which I have enumerated them. The reasons for this lie in a certain relationship between history and the self that I shall discuss in the next chapter.

A new principle of social order never completely displaces earlier ones. The previous principles are preserved alongside the emergent ones in a subsidiary position. Thus, in every situation we should expect to find a variety of forms of order, even when one of them is dominant.

Class and role

In the liberal state, kinship is subordinated; estates disintegrate; and the principles of class and role coexist. It is said that European liberal society comes into being with the replacement of estates by classes. But the fundamental circumstance of social order in the liberal state, the first spring of its movement and transformation, is the relative autonomy of the division of labor by role from the class structure of society.

There are, then, two dominant types of social organization in the liberal state, whose relationship to one another changes over time. One type is the determination of social place by class. The individual's experience of belonging to a class, into which he has usually been born, preexists the particular jobs he has in society. It determines his access to material consumption, power, and knowledge. And though it does not establish once and for all the kinds of roles he may perform, it puts some of them much closer to his reach than others.

At first sight, class and role simply reinforce each other. Because the division of labor is set against the background of class, class position heavily influences the allocation of jobs. Conversely, the existence of jobs with widely disparate degrees of access to power, wealth, and knowledge, strengthens the preexisting class system. The links between class and role, between social stratification and the division of labor, are so numerous that the two may appear indistinguishable.

Nevertheless, there is a fundamental opposition at work beneath the apparent convergence. The principle of role expresses the ideal of merit and the interest in 'efficiency,' both of which emphasize, independently of class, the capacity to do one's job. As a distinct type of social order, the division of labor by role has its own implacable dynamic, to which the next section will return.

It is best to view the competition between class and role temporally. At first, the assignment of jobs in the division of labor is mainly determined by the place each individual occupies in the existing class structure, and thus shaped by inherited wealth and opportunity. The system of roles is an offshoot of the class order.

Increasingly, however, the relationship between the principles may be reversed. It is the role achieved through recognized merit that gives access to consumption, power, and knowledge. If this tendency were to extend beyond its present state of development in even the most socialized of the Western democracies, the result would be a truncated principle of class surviving as a creature of the principle of role.[22] One could then continue to speak of class only in the novel sense that members of each category of role occupants would have similar sorts of advantages, interests, and ideals by virtue of holding the roles they did. Class would be more a consequence than a cause of role, for the determinant of role would be an independent standard of merit.

Such a situation requires something more than a decline in the importance of inherited wealth. It also presupposes that the roles of parents have little influence on those of their children. This in turn implies the possibility of distinguishing clearly between the inheritance of social opportunities and the hereditary transmission of natural talents.

Impersonal rules and personal dependence

The principles of kinship, estate, and class have in common a reliance on personal dependence and personal domination as devices of social organization. By this I mean that they accept a degree of subordination of the wills of some to the wills of others that is not mediated by prescriptive rules or impersonal laws.[23]

In its fullest development, the principle of role actualizes in society an ideal with two basic elements: one is a conception of power or freedom; another, a standard for determining the jobs of each individual. All power should be disciplined by prescriptive rules whose making and application have the characteristic of impersonality described in my account of liberal political thought. Every power relationship unbounded by such rules will be unjustified and therefore despotic. It will involve the loss of freedom, the experience of personal domination for some and of personal dependence for others. Domination is defined simply as unjustified power.

Impersonal rules, though a necessary condition for the justification of power, are not a sufficient one. There is still the need to determine who should exercise the power. With respect to government, this may be decided by electoral democracy. But what about the different degrees of control over others that attach to nongovernment, private roles? Unless the distribution of these jobs and of the power or powerlessness they involve can be justified, one is back in the nightmare of despotism.[24]

This is where the standard of merit appears. According to the social ideal implicit in the principle or role, jobs are assigned by merit rather than arbitrarily. Merit is conceived as the ability to get a job done, to perform a role. It therefore presupposes a background of common understandings of what different sorts of jobs are for. Acquired skill, past efforts, and natural talents all enter into the conception of merit, but it is the last that proves its most troublesome element.

The adoption of the standard of merit is commonly justified as a requirement of efficiency, the common interest, including the interest of the least advantaged, in accomplishing agreed-upon objectives. Sometimes, however, merit is flatly identified with moral desert; the meritorious 'deserve' the advantages they have and the power they exercise simply because of their abilities or accomplishments. The main idea in either case is that when power is restrained by impersonal rules and distributed on the basis of merit, social relations can be emptied of any element of personal dependence or domination, without it being necessary to establish the precise ends for which power ought to be exercised.

In a society completely governed by the principle of role, men interact as the possessors of particular skills and talents. Every individual occupies a multiplicity of roles that have no clear or stable relationship to one another. Each role embraces a limited part of his life and personality. The role organization of society facilitates an increasing technical control of nature and of social relations. This is the very picture of social life invoked by liberal political thought and by the dominant consciousness of the liberal state. It is in the artificial society, in which men are bound together by impersonal rules, that instrumentalism, individualism, and resignation to role are carried to their ultimate consequences.

But now one must ask whether there is in fact a complete unity of meaning between the dominant consciousness and the social order of the liberal state, a correspondence that seems implied by the movement of the latter toward the principle of role. To start with, there is the survival of class alongside role. The experience of class is by definition one of personal dependency and personal domination. Pervading as it does every aspect of social life, it stands as a permanent refutation of the ideal or organization by impersonal rules presupposed by the principle of role. But why are personal dependence and domination such ubiquitous experiences even in the face of the decline of class in the traditional sense? The contrast between the experience of personal dependence and the ideal of impersonal rules does more than parallel the conflict of class and role; it comes up within the organization of roles itself.

Consider the two aspects of the principle of role: the appeal to the standard of merit and the commitment to bring all of social life under the dominion of impersonal rules. One of the decisive elements of the conception of merit, alongside skill and effort, is natural talent. But the distribution of genetic endowments is absolutely capricious in the sense that it is not itself a reward for anything. It is incapable of justification. In the absence of special conditions, which I shall mention later, the exercise of power by some men over others on the basis of the natural allocation of talents must therefore come to be felt as a surrender by society to the arbitrariness of nature and as a submission by the dominated to the personal superiority of the dominant. The brute facts of natural advantage are made decisive to the distribution of power. The meritocratic conception always involves a personal ascendancy or a personal subordination.

Now turn to the other side of the principle of role, the ideal of organization by impersonal rules. The starting point of this ideal is the notion that every power relationship unbounded by impersonal rules violates freedom, and every sharing of values is fragile or coercive. That the program of organization by impersonal rules cannot be carried out is what the earlier discussion of the problems of legislation and adjudication was designed to show. Whether one thinks of the rules established by a government, by an office, or by a factory, rulemaker and rule applier alike must make choices that involve the sacrifice of some individual and subjective values to others: such choices are themselves individual and subjective. For this reason as well there is no escape under the principle of role from personal dependence and domination.[25]

Let me now summarize the conclusion of my discussion of social order in the liberal state up to this point. Superimposed on the conflict between class and role as types of social order, there is in liberal society a pervasive contrast between the experience of personal dependency or dominance and the ideal of organization by impersonal rules. These two tensions touch upon every aspect of life in the liberal state, and they work as agents of instability and movement in the history of the society.

Those who reduce the social order to class and those who claim the supersession of class by role are equally mistaken. What is most distinctive and central to the organization of the society will slip through their hands. Similarly, some take the ideal of impersonal rules at its word, underplaying the importance of personal dependency and domination, whereas others discount the ideal as a mere veil that hides the true character of the social order. The former confuse consciousness with actuality; the latter fail to see that the consciousness men have of their situation is part of the situation itself. The ideal of impersonal rules introduces into the social order a permanent source of subversion of all forms of hierarchical community. In all these mistaken views, a defect of method lies behind the failure of vision.

The bureaucracy

The liberal state has a characteristic type of institution that reflects its prevailing kinds of social order. The types of social order are the general ways of disposing of the relations among individuals and groups. They are the deep and hidden modes of social organization. Institutions are the particular organized groups to which individuals belong. They are the immediately visible face of social life. Several principles of social order will often be at work in an institution. But in any social situation there will be prevalent kinds of institutions, just as there are dominant principles of order. We learn about social order by studying institutional life, but we can only fully grasp the character of the latter after we have understood the former.

The master institution of the liberal state is the bureaucracy. By this I mean something both broader and narrower than what the term usually denotes. Consider some familiar elements of a narrower definition of bureaucracy.[26] First, the bureaucracy is committed to organization by impersonal rules, but these rules may be explicit or tacit. Second, a hierarchy of authority exists among the members of the institution; there is an expectation that power will be exercised within the guidelines provided by the rules. Third, individuals in the institution have roles; there are specific jobs to get done. These jobs are defined in a standardized way with reference to their objectives and to the skills and talents they require. From the standpoint of the institution, the most important thing about the individual is whether he has the abilities demanded by the role to which he is assigned.

To accept the three preceding features as an adequate portrayal of the bureaucratic institution would be to distort its nature, mistaking some of the expectations it generates for the actual form of life it makes possible. There is a fourth characteristic of the bureaucracy, just as central as the first three, yet opposed to them in its thrust. This fourth attribute is the pervasive experience of personal dependence and domination. The making and application of the institutional rules is correctly perceived to involve individual and subjective acts of will. The allocation of authority is recognized as a hierarchy of persons, in which some personal ideals and interests triumph over others, as well as a hierarchy of roles.[27]

The bureaucratic organization appears everywhere in the liberal state. It is the corporation, the factory enterprise, and the private association as much as the government service. Any member of such an organization is, in this sense, a bureaucrat.

To understand the place of the bureaucratic institution in the liberal state, one must look to the genesis of its qualities. Why the insistence on impersonal rules, on the formal hierarchy of authority, and on the meritocratic allocation of roles? The suggestion that efficiency requires them begs the question. One wants to know what makes them efficient and in relation to what ends their efficiency ought to be judged.

It is often pointed out that the historical origins of bureaucratic institutions, in the much narrower meaning in which the term is generally used, lay in developments that accompanied the emergence of the modern European nation-state. On the one hand, the breakup of the feudal and postfeudal forms of hierarchical community in which there were stable and authoritative sharings of values made it necessary to increase the place of rules in the ordering of social relations. On the other hand, the bureaucratic staffs, called into existence to serve the new monarchies, soon acquired power interests of their own. Systems of rules, a formal heirarchy of authority, and the institutionalization of merit standards may all have helped the central political powers to control the bureaucracy. Nevertheless, they also had the opposite effect of giving the bureaucracy ways to legitimize its own power as somehow neutral or above politics, and to resist both the encroachments of the chief political rulers and the demands of other social groups.[28] Whatever significance factors like these may have had in the initial development of bureaucratic institutions, they do not seem sufficient to explain how the bureaucracy, as I have defined it, comes to be the characteristic institution of the liberal state. Nor do they clarify the relationship between bureaucracies and the dominant forms of social order and social consciousness.

Like the liberal state itself, the bureaucracy exists in the context of the class organization of society. It is in the nature of class society to involve the exercise by some classes of a power over others that is ultimately perceived as domination by both the dominant and the dominated. Thus, power is left without justification. The bureaucratic institution seems to offer an escape from the constraints of class society. In place of the experience of personal dependence and domination, it promises to put the impersonality of rules and of roles. Any deviation from impersonality necessarily means a relapse into the subordination of some wills to others according to the principle of class. For this reason, the bureaucratic organization, with its devotion to rules, to the formal allocation of roles under rules, and to the ideal of merit, is reborn over and over as the providential alternative to the despotism of class. Everything happens as if the working out of the principle of class itself called into existence a type of social organization governed by the opposing principle of role. Yet the bureaucracy fails in the end to solve the internal conflicts of liberal society.[29]

First, the bureaucratic role is never a total social place; it embraces only a defined and limited part of its occupant. In his social life, outside the job, the bureaucrat continues to belong to a particular class. The class organization of society influences the ways jobs are in fact assigned and relationships experienced within the bureaucratic institution.

Second, both the making and the applying of rules in bureaucracies require policy judgments, choices among competing values. Given the character of all sharings of ends in liberal society, these judgments of policy throw the bureaucratic institution back into the arbitrary exercise of power from which that institution seemed an escape.

Lastly, consider once again the implications of the ideal of merit. Suppose that the institutional notion of the principle of role succeeds in subordinating the class system to the division of labor according to skill and talent, and thereby transforms the general conditions of social order and the nature of class. The new social 'classes' would then be largely those groups whose similar degrees of access to wealth, power, and knowledge were determined by their place within the division of labor.

The closer the assignment of jobs comes to the ideal of merit, the more decisive the influence of natural talents in determining social place. The hierarchy of talents, distributed by nature without regard to men's moral purposes, succeeds the accident of inherited wealth and opportunity. The lucky ones can then cash in on the favors of nature like prostitutes whose price depends on whether they are fat or slim. The exercise of power by the higher talents over the less gifted becomes simply another form of personal domination unless a moral standard can be found to justify and limit it.

It should now be clear that the bureaucratic institution cannot ultimately keep its promise of solving the problem of personal domination. Either it remains trapped in the mechanism of class, or it produces a new kind of dependency. The principle of role, institutionalized in the bureaucracy, may either succumb to the principle of class or triumph over it. But if the struggle between class and role is overcome, another fundamental dialectic of liberal society remains, the conflict between the ideal of impersonal rules and the experience of personal dependence.

Each bureaucratic organization is a miniature of the liberal state. Life in the bureaucracy is therefore characterized by the prevalence of moral sentiments that reflect the dominant consciousness. These sentiments reveal the implications of the liberal order for community and personality.

First, there is the sentiment of unreality. The social relationships of bureaucratic life are completely severed from the relationship each individual has to nature. There is no natural basis for the definition of personality or community. Consequently, social relationships themselves establish who one is. But one is different in each of the seemingly unrelated roles one occupies. Which is the real person among these several persons, or, if all of them are masks, where is the true face to be found?

Then there is the sentiment of isolation. Individuals know each other and interact as occupants of particular roles, who have well-defined skills and from whom the performance of definite tasks is expected. Only in the intimacy of family or friendship do they come close to knowing and treating one another as unitary and complete persons. But even this respite is limited because what men are and do in their public roles may be only dimly grasped in the private life of friendship and family.

To these affections one must add the sentiment of self-abasement. The performance of the bureaucratic role is carried out under a double constraint. It is an expression of a particular side of the personality to the exclusion if not to the prejudice of the other sides. And the interests the bureaucratic job serves are always partial and subjective. They are not universal or objective ideals, nor in the end are they likely to be mistaken for such ideals. Thus, it is difficult to recognize any lasting worth in the performance of one's roles. All of them will seem, and they will be, to a greater or lesser extent, a diminishment of what I shall describe as the attributes of the self.

Many subtle hypothesis have been fashioned to explain the changes and conflicts that characterize the history of bureaucratic institutions. Sometimes mysterious laws of economic growth, of technological renewal, or of the organization of power have been invoked. But perhaps the main explanation is much more simple. Men want to be human, and the bureaucracy does not satisfy their humanity.

THE WELFARE-CORPORATE STATE

The conflicts within its dominant types of social consciousness and order push the liberal state in the direction of the welfare-corporate state. Though not the only possible successor to the liberal state, as the existence of socialist societies shows, it is the prevailing tendency, at least in the Western social democracies.

The premise of the welfare-corporate state is the notion that contemporary capitalist society witnesses the advent of kinds of social consciousness and social organization foreign to the liberal state and incompatible with many of its salient traits. These emergent forms of consciousness and order do not, of course, appear all at once, nor is it possible to assign a precise date to their birth in any given society. Nevertheless, they present us with problems and perspectives that call for new concepts, and indeed demand a reconstruction of the entire theory of society.

Classic social theory, the theory that grew out of the sociology of the Restoration and reached its fullest development in the works of Marx, Durkheim, and Weber, was largely an attempt to understand the liberal state. Almost all its basic conceptions of man and society were fashioned in the course of this endeavor and shaped by the peculiar set of questions it involved. Thus, the effort to grasp the identity of the welfare-corporate state cannot be satisfied merely by the addition of new insights to classic social theory. It requires instead a transformation of the substance and methods of social study.

But there is also a deeper objection to classic social theory: its continuing reliance on more or less extensive elements of the liberal doctrine, and its corresponding failure to advance from the partial to the total criticism of the liberal tradition. The anxiousness to assume the posture of science and to separate sharply the empirical study of history from the discussion of metaphysical issues was both a sign and a cause of the failure. Total criticism laughs at this anxiousness, for it has discovered the unity of the issues of metaphysics and of those of the specialized sciences, as well as the need to resolve both sets of problems simultaneously if they are to be resolved at all.

The study of the welfare-corporate state should be carried out in the light of this discovery and contribute to the working out of its implications. The emergent state transforms the experience of social life of which the liberal doctrine is a theoretical representation. Hence, it calls for a nonliberal system of thought and contributes to the formulation of such a system.

The conception of a second stage of liberal capitalist society is a familiar one, though the true character of its identity remains elusive.[30] It is useful to recall, again as a preliminary orientation, some of the commonplace ways in which the successor to the classic liberal society is characterized.

First, it is a state in which the government assumes a widespread and overt responsibility for the distribution of economic and social advantages, as a complement or a limit to the market. That is what makes it a welfare state. The firm distinction between formal equality of political or legal status and almost unlimited substantive inequality of social circumstance is abandoned as a premise of social policy.

Second, it is a state in which bodies intermediate between the individual and the agencies of government—corporations, unions, associations—achieve an ever larger place in the life of the society. This makes it a corporate state. The history of liberal society is in part the history of the ongoing dissolution of all the communal organizations associated with the earlier society of estates. The principles of class and role contribute to the disengagement of the individual from these organizations and to his dependence on markets, bureaucratic institutions, and national governments.

In the welfare-corporate state, there is a double-edged process of privatization of public bodies and publicization of private ones. Private institutions assume more and more of the responsibilities previously committed to government, or, without undertaking its responsibilities, they begin to resemble its organization and to imitate its power. This development extends the consequences of the universalization of bureaucracy as an institutional form. At the same time, a wealth of public bodies come into being that are only perilously connected with one another and that are as close, in interest, outlook, or mode of organization, to 'private' institutions as they are to the traditional agencies of government. Together, the welfare and the corporatist tendency break down the distinction between the state and civil society.

Lastly, the welfare-corporate state is often characterized by the importance of a process for the transformation of nature, technology, and by the preeminence of a bureaucratic class, the class of professionals, technicians, and managers who direct the welfare activities of the government and administer the corporate organizations. Both developments have roots in the history of the liberal state. Technology is the instrument and external expression of the manipulative relationship to nature and to society. The bureaucratic class exemplifies the new kind of class that is more a creature than a master of the system of roles.

Looking back over this list of attributes of the welfare-corporate state, one is struck by the sense that none of them need constitute a fundamental rupture with liberal society. In one way or another, each of them already has an important place in that society. They fail to describe a form of social consciousness and social order that would establish the identity of the welfare-corporate state, and thereby allow one to understand its bearing on the problems of this essay. To such a description I must therefore now turn. But let it be remembered that the welfare-corporate state is less an accomplished reality than a project or a tendency at work in the transformation of liberal society.

SOCIAL CONSCIOUSNESS IN THE WELFARE-CORPORATE STATE

The welfare-corporate state appears with the emergence of a type of consciousness and of social order. There is perhaps no particular society in which the forms of consciousness and order I have in mind are already dominant. Yet the developments that may indicate their advent strike hardest at some of the most influential groups and activities. The discussion of this distinctive form of social life will again be offered as a speculative hypothesis. But it is a hypothesis that may illuminate much of what is most puzzling in the circumstance of the state and reveal the connection among many of its seemingly disparate features.

The dominant or distinctive consciousness of the welfare-corporate state is already foreshadowed, as a deviant mentality, within the liberal state itself. In its most extreme formulations, it is associated with the Romantic movement and with the forerunners and offshoots of Romanticism. The worship of nature, the invocation of hierarchic or egalitarian community, and the repudiation of the division of labor have all been turned by these trends against the dominant types of consciousness and order in the liberal state. Sometimes the rebellion has been staged in the name of the past, as in Romantic conservatism with its program for the restoration of preliberal kinds of hierarchical community. And sometimes the struggle has been fought in the name of the future by utopian or socialist defenders of egalitarian community.

As it becomes the typical mind set of an emergent society, both the content of this way of viewing social life and the groups among which it flourishes change. This social vision ceases to be the prerogative of isolated factions of revolutionaries or reactionaries. Instead, it begins to infiltrate the ranks of the professional or bureaucratic class and the technical workers, and to change in the course of the infiltration.[31]

The rejection of the dominant consciousness

First, there is the tendency to reject instrumentalism both as a relationship to nature and society and as a conception of reason. The reaction to instrumental rationality takes the form of a search for a rationality of ends and of a more or less explicit critique of the very distinction between means and ends. When it supervises the welfare activities of the state or administers the corporate bodies, the bureaucratic class in a democracy must be able to justify its choices of ends as well as of means. The determination of social policy, the assessment of technological developments, and even the application of rules require that conflicting ends be ordered. If decisions about ends cannot be justified, they inevitably take on the character of personal domination. Alongside the attempt to discover ways of reasoning about values, there is unease with the notion that any aspect of social life can be treated as simply a means whose worth should be measured against some independently defined objective. Instead, the conviction grows that everything has a positive or negative value of its own.

The emergent consciousness shows its antagonism to the manipulative posture toward society by its willingness to accept the implications of the notion that, as the circumstances of domination are overcome, the ideal order of different kinds of groups will develop spontaneously from their internal processes of interaction. Order should not be imposed from above; hence the interest in the decentralization and debureaucratization of institutional life.

Perhaps the most subtle and far-reaching aspect of the departures from instrumentalism in the developing mentality is the change in the understanding and the ideal of man's relationship to nature. In place of the view of nature as the plaything of human will, a fund of tools for the satisfaction of desires, there is the increasing interest in the preservation of the natural order and in the respect for the continuity between man and nature. Sometimes this interest proceeds to the point of the deification of nature and to the related reassertion of a mystical religiosity of union with the natural world.

In its treatment of individualism the tendency of this cast of mind is to deny the opposition of the particular and the universal, the individual and the social element of personality. Either the antagonism is dismissed as fictitious or, more intelligently, it is perceived as the consequence of a particular set of social relations. The task then becomes to define and to establish a type of social order in which this opposition would not hold.

The interest in the problems of solidarity and especially in the idea of communities of shared purpose is one of the principal manifestations of this aspect of consciousness in the welfare-corporate state. As part of the attempt to deal with the conflict between the experience of personal dependence and the ideal of impersonal rules, the search for nonhierarchical communities of shared ends ceases to be a utopian concern of marginal groups; it becomes a factor in the internal politics of bureaucratic institutions. The welfare activity of government may be turned into an instrument for the subversion of the circumstances of class domination that make the problem of community insoluble. And the corporate bodies are the bureaucratic organizations whose internal conflicts bring the issue of community to the center of politics.

Finally, the emergent consciousness rebels against the conception of work and social place that characterizes the dominant culture of the liberal state. It no longer acquiesces in the inevitability of the conflict between the need to accept a definite social place and the desire to express in social life the many-sidedness of personality. Thus, it may oppose the established forms of the division of labor, demanding that job or role be organized so as to be a representation rather than a denial of the unity and range of the self. When, for example, technical workers turn against the assembly line, it is this aspect of consciousness that may be at stake.

The antagonism to the liberal contrast of the worker and his work may also take a form that is the very antithesis of the preceding one. This is the abandonment of the idea of a virtually many-sided personality and the acceptance of the sanctity of one's station and its duties. The sign of such a response to the problem of worker and work is the sentiment of resignation to role previously described as a pervasive characteristic of the moral life in modern society. Stoicism is the natural religion of the bureaucracy; to play his part is the pride that is left to the Stoic after he has abandoned all other hopes, including the hope of becoming a full personality.

The ideal of immanence

The principle of common meaning that ties together the features of the emergent consciousness is a religious conception of the world and of society. But when one tries to define this conception, one discovers that it has two distinct sides, and that its ambivalence carries over to each of its particular manifestations in the culture of the welfare-corporate state. It would be foolhardy to expect from a mode of social consciousness the clarity and precision of a philosophical doctrine. But there is more than unclarity and imprecision here; there is a fundamental rift that repeats itself in many different forms. The discussion of the dominant type of consciousness in the liberal state concluded with the suggestion that the secularization of transcendence prepares the way for an equally secular version of the religion of immanence. The study of the emergent mentality bears out the thesis.

A secular version of the ideal of immanence would bear the same relationship to pantheism that the dominant consciousness in the liberal state bears to the theology of transcendence. It would repudiate the contrast of the universal and the particular elements in personality and, together with that contrast, the dichotomies of culture and nature, state and society, reason and desire. This is precisely what, on one extreme interpretation, the emergent consciousness in the welfare-corporate state tends to do.

Through the attack on instrumentalism, and particularly on the manipulative relationship to the natural world, it denies the discontinuity of nature and culture. Nature is to be conceived and treated as the totality of which social relations are a part rather than as a category of external objects whose value lies in their capacity to satisfy human desires.

Along similar lines, one might interpret the anti-individualism of the emergent consciousness as a radical rejection of the idea or ideal of a separation between self and others. According to this mode of consciousness, the view that there is an individual element in personality, distinguishable from its social nature, is simply an illusion bred by liberal society. It will disappear once communities of shared ends have been achieved. For the same reason, the separation of state and society will be abolished. In political reality as in belief the state is, after all, just the set of artificial institutions required to hold conflicting individuals together. The greater the coherence and authority of the sharing of ends, the less need is there for an imposed order.

Together with its rejection of instrumentalism and individualism, the mentality I describe changes the view of the relation between personality and social place. Despite their apparent antagonism, both the frontal attack on the division of labor and the Stoicism of resignation to role want to abolish the distinction between what a man is and what he does. They agree that personality as a heavenly or an abstract unity of the individual's latent capacities and dispositions and personality as an earthly or a concrete unity of one's places and jobs in society must become the same. The enemies of the division of labor propose to bridge the gap by so arranging social life that the works one undertakes in society will somehow reflect the many-sidedness of personality. The Stoics, on the contrary, wish to sanctify the division of labor and to take role as the basis for the definition of personality.

The union of immanence and transcendence

According to the preceding account, the religious ideal of immanence, transposed to a secular form, lends a unity of meaning to the emergent consciousness in the welfare-corporate state. Yet there is another equally plausible view of the general significance of this mentality. One may see in it the beginnings of a synthesis of transcendence and immanence rather than a reassertion of the latter over the former.

Thus, what is involved in the consciousness of the welfare-corporate state might be an attempt to develop a vision of the world and a corresponding social order in which man's relationship to nature, to others, and to his own acts, works, or positions, is somehow one of both separation and of union. Perhaps the acknowledgment of the continuity between nature and culture can and will develop in a way that respects the relative autonomy of each. Perhaps the supersession of the conflict between the individual and the social element of personality need not be carried out through the sacrifice of the first to the second. Perhaps the division of labor can be conceived and organized so as to overcome the conflict between personality as the unity of an abstract set of dispositions and personality as the unity of a concrete set of acts and works, without the surrender of one to the other. There are a number of points to be made about this alternative conception of the emergent mentality.

First, it is part of my thesis about the consciousness of the welfare-corporate state that both interpretations are equally plausible. Either one may eventually turn out to be true, because we do not know in which of the two directions the mentality whose manifestations they each describe will move. The hesitation lies in the historical circumstance itself rather than in the uncertainties of the theory.

Second, neither side of the emergent consciousness provides us with a clear and precise statement of a nonliberal system of thought. They are not theories, and we cannot expect from them the distinctness of a philosophic doctrine. Moreover, the study of the history of social consciousness fails to supply a standard by which to judge the merits of the contending views and ideals. To develop and to criticize in the language of speculative thought what the emergent consciousness foreshadows will be the aim of the next chapter.

A final remark goes to the issue of a possible reconciliation of transcendence and immanence. The transcendent ideal cannot long survive the disappearance of belief in a God who stands above the world, for a secularized transcendence is inherently unstable. But the religion of immanence is utterly hostile to the conception of a personal, otherworldly God. Thus, the problem of the nature of God is involved in the evaluation of the issues raised by the emergent consciousness, and especially in the idea of a union of immanence and transcendence.

SOCIAL ORDER IN THE WELFARE-CORPORATE STATE

The conflicts of bureaucratic organization

When institutional life stops being simply the manifestation of the struggle between role and class, between the ideal of impersonal rules and the experience of personal dependence, but becomes instead a response to these conflicts, a new type of social order arises. If one wants to discover whether there are signs in the contemporary state of a truly distinctive mode of social organization, the question to ask will be: Are there developments that transform the conflicts of liberal society or make it possible to overcome them? Regardless of how far reaching social changes may seem, they will leave the fundamental character of the social order unchanged unless they modify those underlying conflicts. No matter how subtle or fragile changes may be, they will indicate the presence of a different type of social order whenever they intrude upon the principles at work in the bureaucracies of liberal society.

Both the social policy activities of government and the proliferation of corporate bodies seem to reinforce and to enlarge, rather than to undermine or to restrict, the importance of bureaucratic organization in society. Far from suggesting a break with the social organization characteristic of the liberal state, they appear to represent its final triumph. The critical issues therefore become those that have to do with the internal organization of the bureaucracies and with the relationship between the way power is distributed within them and the control of government power outside them.

So it is important to keep clearly in mind the main problems of social order under liberalism. First, there is the continuing importance of class and the contrast between the requirements of class and those of role. Second, there is the issue of the justification for the distribution of power within the institution on the basis of merit, and particularly of natural talents. Third, there are the destructive implications of the victorious principle of role for community and personality, as those implications are revealed in the life of the moral sentiments.

The first two problems pose, in different ways, the question of the conflict between the ideal of impersonal power under rules and the experience of dependence on the will of another person. They both deal with matters of power. The third problem, however, goes to the general character of social relationships. Though the topics are connected, it may be wiser to begin by considering them separately.

There are, then, two prerequisites for the resolution of the conflict between the ideal of organization according to impersonal rules and the experience of personal dependence. One is the weakening and finally the elimination of the principle of class in its traditional sense. The other condition is the disappearance of the new type of domination and of class to which the principle of role and the ideal of merit give rise.

The resolution of the conflicts

The welfare activity of government and the institutionalization of the principle of role may or may not succeed in liquidating the importance of the principle of class. But at least one can see how such a development might follow and how sometimes and to some extent it has followed from the internal dynamics of the liberal state. It is much harder to visualize what would be meant by the overcoming of the new form of domination ushered in by the principle of role, and what sorts of events might evidence that trend.

Suppose a social order in which the principle of role were victorious on all fronts. In such a situation, a decisive place would be given to merit in the assignment of jobs and therefore in the distribution of power within the bureaucratic institutions. If we also assume, in accordance with the implications of the principle of role, that opportunities for the learning of skills were equalized, the weight accorded to natural talents would become the main point of contention.

One can imagine a condition under which the distribution of power within the bureaucracy would not involve personal dependence and domination. It might be called the condition of democracy. The exercise of power based on merit must be subordinated to the democratically established common purposes of those working in the institution. For this subordination to be effective, a number of requirements have to be satisfied. The chief of these is the availability of an independent mechanism through which all members of the institution participate equally and continuously in the formulation of the common ends. An ever broader scope is given to these common ends in determining the aims and the internal structure of the institution. For the purposes of participation, the distribution of talents is disregarded. This mechanism would be the internal democracy of the institution; its more complete description is one of the objectives of the theory of organic groups. Note that one's final view of the claims and character of democracy in the internal organization of institutions depends on one's conception of the worth of the meritocratic division of labor and power and on one's understanding of the place of natural talents within the ideal of merit.

We are now in a position to reexamine the final problem of bureaucracy, the consequences of role organization for personality and for the state of moral sentiments. It is the sentiment of isolation that describes most immediately the character of social life within the bureaucracy. Men know and interact with one another as role occupants. In each of their disparate roles, they are recognized as representatives of a different type of skill and talent. At no point do they acknowledge each other as entire persons. If recognition is one of the bases of personality, the system of roles fails to provide support for a unitary definition of personality.

The prerequisite for such a definition is community. Community, in the most general sense, is the situation in which social relations are based on shared purposes whose moral authority is recognized and in which men view and treat one another as concrete and complete beings, that is, as individuals. There is a tension, though not a necessary contrast or logical contradiction, between the two elements of community, the sharing of values and the recognition of concrete individuality. It is by participating in one another's ends that men come to understand and to respect what beyond the boundaries of their shared purposes makes each person unique. The metaphysical justification of this point will be given in the theory of the self, and its institutional implications developed in the theory of organic groups. For the moment, it is enough to see that, whereas institutional democracy may require simply a limitation on the principle of role, the condition of community seems to demand a frontal assault on bureaucratic organization. It puts the group of concrete individuals with shared purposes in place of the association of abstract role occupants, assigned to their jobs by merit and held together by rules.

Such is the general character of the ideal solutions to the main problems of bureaucracy: the weakening of the principle of class, internal institutional democracy, and community. The first represents the final triumph of the bureaucratic system of roles; the second its confinement; and the third its transformation or dissolution. Viewed as a whole, the solutions raise once again the interrelated issues of domination and of value. The subversion of class and the internal democracy of the institution respond to the problem of domination. Each is required by the other; so both must be achieved together.

The welfare-corporate state is the society whose politics are marked by the relationship I have described among the problems of class, internal institutional democracy, and community. More particularly, it is the order whose characteristic antagonism has ceased to be that of class against role, or even of the ideal of impersonal rules against the experience of personal dependence. Instead, it has become the conflict between the continuing forms of domination by class or merit and the claims of the ideal of community. The issue of value lies at the core of the conflict. Both the moral authority of shared purposes in community and the judgment of what constitutes domination depend on the availability of an alternative to the principle of subjective value.

Signs of change

As a possible outgrowth of bureaucracy, the distinctive predicament of the welfare-corporate state comes to our attention in many ambiguous ways. My examples will be drawn from two areas, the organization of labor in bureaucratic corporate bodies and the law. Some of the developments have been institutionalized; others remain programs. This should be a reminder that the welfare-corporate state, like the type of social consciousness with which it is closely associated, is a nascent rather than an established form of social life.

Take first the situation of the working classes. One familiar issue is the transformation of the traditional class system itself through the importance technical skill and knowledge assume for the economic success of corporate activity. The ideal of merit increasingly becomes the official program of the bureaucratic institutions, and the gradual opening up of educational opportunities gives it a real, though limited, significance.

Still another characteristic development is worker struggle for participation, first in the profits and then in the management of enterprises. To the extent the attention of manual workers or technicians focuses on the distribution of power within the enterprise rather than just on the achievement of immediate economic advantages, the issue of internal democracy presents itself. And then there is the tendency of the enterprise or of the corporation to overflow the mold of a unit of production and to become a community of life as well, a community that embraces many aspects of labor and leisure. The corporation and the factory itself increasingly turn into states in their own right, with internal systems of rules and institutional mechanisms that efface the clarity of the distinction between public and private organization.

These developments have a two-faced character. On the one hand, they are the armaments of a sophisticated and relentless manipulation of labor. They reinforce the stability of the bureaucratic institution and increase the control exercised over workers by the managers and by the elites to which the managers belong. In this sense, they are simply a perpetuation of the liberal state. But they may also help create the objective circumstances within which the characteristic conflicts of liberal society can be replaced by those of the welfare-corporate state. The meritocratic institution is confronted with the need to justify and to limit the distribution of power through internal democracy and then to counteract through the establishment of community the disintegrating effects of role organization. Thus, in the same indirect, unintended, ambiguous sense in which the cartels, according to Lenin, create socialism under capitalism, the bureaucracy establishes community under liberalism.[32]

The development of conceptions of justice in public and private law provides another indication of the passage from liberal society to the welfare-corporate state. In the history of modern liberal thinking about justice, one may distinguish two distinct though overlapping stages. These stages can be traced in the evolution of standards governing private exchange (commutative justice) and in those regulating the distribution of advantages by government (distributive justice).

The first stage is that of formal justice. Its central characteristic is the almost complete acceptance of the principle of subjective value. Given the individuality and subjectivity of values, there are no criteria for the distribution of social benefits. From this, two consequences follow, one for the justice of exchange, the other for the justice of government activity. The enforceability of contracts must be determined by rules that can be formulated and applied independently of any judgment of the equivalence of the performances. Commutative justice comes out from under the heel of distributive justice and becomes autonomous. The government, in turn, is to feign distributive neutrality and to entrust distributive decisions to the seemingly automatic devices of the price system. In both the private and the public sphere, subjective value means exchange value, and its hegemony is the hegemony of the market.

The second stage is that of procedural justice. No longer is it assumed that the outcomes of market transactions are by definition just. The process of bargaining among private parties and institutions must increasingly satisfy certain requirements. The chief of these is a relative equality of bargaining power, in the absence of which corrective measures have to be carried out. In contract law, the stage of procedural justice is illustrated by the development of already existing standards governing the bargaining process and the uses of economic duress.[33] In public law, the focus of procedural justice shifts from individuals to institutions and from separate transactions to permanent power relationships. Government action tries to make up for the 'deficiencies' of the market rather than to redistribute directly power, wealth, and access to knowledge. It accomplishes this objective by encouraging the growth of some institutions (labor law) and limiting the size or power of others (antitrust law).

The stage of procedural justice has contradictory implications. In one sense, it is an attempt to establish all the more securely the conditions for the operation of the market and of the system of formal justice. But in another sense, it leads beyond formal justice into a third stage, of substantive justice. In the private area, procedural justice fails to provide a clear alternative to subjective value or a standard for the limitation of private autonomy. In the public sector, it leaves the bureaucratic ideal of distribution according to merit unrealized.

The stage of substantive justice is one in which both private transactions and the welfare activity of government are measured against criteria of equivalence in exchange or of merit in distribution.[34] The interest in the control of unjust enrichment, in the justification of a policy of income distribution, and in the definition of the criterion of 'public interest' for the control of administrative agencies all push in the same direction. Standards of substantive justice have always had a place in the liberal state. But the more they are relied upon, the greater the urgency of the break with the principle of subjective value.

The requirements of the subversion of class and of the institutionalization of role and merit make it necessary to develop a jurisprudence of substantive justice. But such a jurisprudence presupposes a solution to the problem of value, and therefore also, if my previous argument is correct, the development of communities of shared purpose. Thus, the fundamental issues of the law become those of the welfare-corporate state.

Significance of the emergent social order

The concept of an emergent social order provides a framework within which to understand the tendencies in the corporate and legal organization of society to which the preceding section refers. But what is the general significance of these tendencies, and of the types of social organization they exemplify? Suppose the conflict between the principles of role and community were indeed resolved by the subordination of the former to the latter. There are two different ways in which this subordination might occur, because there are two distinct interpretations that can be given to the ideal of community.

One is the idea of a hierarchical or closed community. In such an association, men occupy fixed social places; the relations of power are sanctified by a particular set of shared values; and these values carry weight just because they are the ends of the particular groups who entertain them. This is the ideal of conservative corporativism, which resembles the hierarchical community established by the principle of estates.[35] The alternative is an egalitarian or open community in which the exercise of power is subordinated to the condition of internal democracy. The shared values of any one group are treated as indications of the good only insofar as the universality and the stability with which they are held in other groups and the democratic circumstances in which they are fashioned allow us to take them for expressions of human nature at a certain moment of its development. A large part of the next two chapters of the book is devoted to establishing the metaphysical foundations and the institutional characteristics of the second conception of community.

The social order of the welfare-corporate state does not represent either of these two types of the communitarian ideal. Both are contained within it as possible responses to the conflicts it generates. Therein lies its most general significance and the tie of common meaning that connects it with the emergent social consciousness.

The choice between hierarchical and egalitarian community, or between the two corresponding conceptions of shared values, is the counterpart to the duality in the emergent consciousness: immanence or the synthesis of immanence and transcendence. Hierarchic community, with its sanctification of established power relations and of the ascendancy of corporate values, actualizes the view of social relations implicit in a purely immanent religiosity. We should therefore expect to find that wherever such an ideal of community takes hold, it will be associated with the conceptions of nature and of social place that distinguish the religion of immanence. The ideal of egalitarian or open community describes a crucial part of what would be involved in an alliance of the immanent and the transcendent form of the religious consciousness. To the extent that the welfare-corporate state establishes objective conditions for the realization of such an ideal, it prepares the way for making the union of immanence and transcendence a form of social life.

THE SOCIALIST STATE

How different are socialist societies from the welfare-corporate state? Do they represent a distinct alternative to liberalism? Without answering these questions directly or offering a theory of socialism, it is possible to grasp certain relationships between the problems of the welfare-corporate state and those of socialist society.

One of the sources of socialist doctrine was the deviant, Romantic consciousness that developed under liberalism and foreshadowed the emergent consciousness of the welfare-corporate state. Socialist theory, and particularly Marxist theory, is replete with the themes of attack on instrumentalism, individualism, and the liberal view of social place. Moreover, it has always had the same basic duality of meaning identified in my study of the emergent consciousness. Thus, to the extent the theoretical tradition of socialism describes a mentality present or even dominant in socialist societies, its fundamental problems are those raised by the nature of consciousness in the welfare-corporate state.

The consequences of socialism for institutional organization are of a similar kind. The socialization of the economy may drastically hasten the subordination of class to role. With this, the problems of internal democracy and community become all the more acute.

The politics of socialism are characterized by two fundamental conflicts: one is the contrast between the political and the economic needs of the society; the other is the still more basic struggle between the claims of role organization and those of community. Both conflicts are endemic to the welfare-corporate state, but under socialism they acquire a greater urgency. The subversion of the class system establishes the prevalence of the principle of role and of the bureaucratic institution at the same time that official doctrine lends unprecedented authority to the ideal of community.

Institutional democracy requires a significant degree of institutional autonomy, and this implies limits on the pretensions of central planning. Without internal democratic procedures for deciding the character and objectives of work, the experience of personal dependence will be pervasive. The institutionalization of standards of merit can only add another form of dominance; it cannot abolish domination itself.

Beyond the problem of institutional democracy, there looms the broader issue of community. The alternative is clear: either the socialist institution becomes a community for the democratic formulation of shared purposes, or it remains a bureaucracy governed by the meritocratic division of labor. Until the former is achieved, there is no true basis for the legitimation of power. Rules will be used to limit the exercise of power, and the socialist society will be forced to choose at every point between despotism and legalism. Moreover, unless the communitarian reconstruction of socialist bureaucracies is accompanied by the continuous improvement of their internal democracy, the community that is created will be a closed and hierarchical one. The shared values on which it is based will be the prejudices of a faction or of a moment.

Thus, the importance of socialism to my argument lies in the intensity with which it presents the problems discussed in the preceding two sections. In socialist society, we can see clearly and fully what is still partial and obscure in the welfare-corporate state.

TOWARD A CONCLUSION

Now that the historical inquiry is over, reconsider for a moment its double objective: to understand the form of social life of which liberal thought is a theoretical representation and to find in experience itself a basis for the revision of theory.

Liberal thought states, as if in code, the truth of a social situation. Its antinomies carry the conflicts of society onto the grounds of philosophy. The unity of its doctrine must ultimately be seen as part of a more general unity of meaning in everyday reflection and existence, for which no metaphysical criticism, logical analysis, or causal explanation can fully account. When this form of life becomes transparent, it is already in dissolution.

The theory of the welfare-corporate state suggests a possible reorientation. Liberal thought is the philosophical counterpart to a secularized ideal of transcendence. A doctrine antithetical to liberalism would stand for the ideal of immanence. Might it be the mark of a true philosophy to provide an interpretation of the union of immanence and transcendence and of the achievement of egalitarian community? To this most important question history gives no answer. It can neither define the content of the ideals at stake, nor establish their worth. One must therefore continue to philosophize.

5

THE THEORY OF THE SELF

INTRODUCTION

In this chapter, I state a metaphysical theory of the self. It is the aim of this theory to describe the relationship among certain aspects of human nature and to lay the groundwork for the definition of a social ideal.

A theory of the self is needed to resolve the main problems posed by the argument of this book. Such a doctrine establishes the vantage point from which one can begin to piece together an alternative to the liberal theory and a resolution of its antinomies. It also clarifies the two-edged significance of the welfare-corporate state. Finally, the study of the political conditions for the achievement of the social ideal pulls together the metaphysical and the historical parts of my argument. The way will then open to study in the next chapter the connection between the social ideal and the circumstances of the modern state.

The argument begins with a conception of the scope and method of a theory of human nature. It then discusses certain familiar attributes of humanity that occupy a central place in our ideas about personality and society. A more general view of the relation between the self and the world is inferred from these attributes.

Silence your scorn, reader, if at times in this as in other parts of the essay I abandon the heavy-handed though frivolous sobriety we have come to expect in philosophic argument. Remember that all men, no matter how modest their contributions, are entitled to the answer Rousseau gave to the detractors of his enthusiasm: When Archimedes ran naked through the streets of Syracuse to announce his findings, what he said was no less true because of the way it was communicated.[1]

THE CONCEPTION OF A THEORY OF THE SELF

The idea of the self

The liberal doctrine fails to provide a coherent view of knowledge, personality, and society, a failure evidenced by its antinomies. We cannot resolve these antinomies by simply standing the liberal metaphysic on its head. That procedure would lead to absurd conclusions and misrepresent the relation between theory and history. Where then can one find solid ground upon which to establish an alternative set of principles and to fulfill the task of total criticism?

The study of forms of social life has suggested a second puzzle. Whether viewed from the standpoint of order or of consciousness, both the welfare-corporate and the socialist state seem to have a double nature. What are we to make of this duality, and what would it mean to resolve it favorably?

At first these two questions seem unconnected. One has to do with the defeats and triumphs of speculative reason; the other with the understanding and the judgment of a political circumstance. Despite this, the issues are the twin heads of a single sphinx. The possible synthesis of immanence and transcendence and the actualization of an ideal of nonhierarchic community in social life suggest a perspective from which to reconstruct liberal thought. But the belief that these possibilities represent an advance in experience and an occasion for progress in thought presupposes a certain ideal of personality and society; it cannot itself be made the foundation of such an ideal. Just as we fled from metaphysics into history, so we are driven across the border back into metaphysics again.

The criticism of liberal thought already implies an idea of personality and of community. The conception of being a person always includes an account of relations among persons. The view of society always relies on an interpretation of the nature of individuals. Because the ideas of personality and of society contain each other, it is impossible to arrive at a coherent and complete understanding of either by referring to the other. To try that would be like standing between two hazy mirrors, each of which threw the same image back into the other innumerable times without improving the onlooker's ability to discern the contours of the image.

The common origin of the ideas of personality and society is a certain notion of what men are in their relationship to nature, to others, and to themselves. When we think of this notion as a quality, we call it human nature or humanity. When we speak of it as a substance or subject of which qualities are predicated, we might call it the self. The self is the individual person. But to the extent individuals share common attributes, including a similar relation to the species, the self is the personification of mankind. This personification of the whole race in the individual will turn out to mean both more and less than a basic, unchanging similarity among men.

Decisive issues

In the tradition of our culture, three topics have dominated the study of human nature. The first is the problem of the connection between human nature and history. The second is the choice between the essentialist and the relational view of humanity. The third is the question of the place the individual occupies in the species. A theory of the self can be defined by the position it takes on these three issues.

One of the fundamental doctrines of ancient political philosophy was the belief in a single human nature all men have in common regardless of the society to which they belong or the age during which they live. Mankind is forever condemned to move within the iron circle of its virtues and vices. Some political regimes, however, may be preferable to others because they are better able to suppress the evil side of human nature and to make use of its beneficial capacities. In our day, this classical theory has undergone a kind of revival with the search for hidden, universal 'structures' of the mind.

On the whole, however, modern social theory moved in the opposite direction. It often embraced the view that there are as many human natures as societies or even as individuals. Each way of being human is inseparable from a particular form of social life so that the very notion of a unitary human nature dissolves at the touch of history's magic wand.

Neither the suprahistorical nor the historicist conception seems satisfactory.[2] The former flies in the face of our knowledge of the varieties of human existence. What is constant and universal in men may often be what is least important about them. The claim that human nature is independent of history has striking political implications: the limits of man's nature restrict the power of his striving to transform his experience. Thus, no matter what its proponents' intentions, the suprahistorical doctrine invariably tends to become a tool of the sanctification of actuality.

On the other hand, the historicist view, taken to the extreme, deprives us of criteria with which to compare forms of social life and to answer the kinds of questions discussed in this essay. Insofar as it is associated with a relativistic belief in the equal worth of all cultures, it takes us back to the principle of subjective value and to the system of thought of which that principle is a part. To the extent it trusts in the progressive character of history, it makes the individual the servant of a future ideal he is unable to realize in his own life.

The conflict between the unhistorical and the historicist position is loosely associated with the dilemma of essentialist and relational views of human nature. Essentialism is the thesis that, at least at any given moment, each individual and mankind as a whole have a core of being identifying them as what they are. Attributes can be added or taken away around the core without destroying the basis of species or individual identity. Relationalism, by contrast, affirms that man consists in a set of relations to beings or situations in the world. Essentialism is usually allied with the suprahistorical outlook, and relationalism with the historicist. But this need not be the case: the kernel of humanity can be conceived to evolve in history, and the relations that define the individual or the species may be regarded as timeless.

The essentialist theory forces one to accept the classical doctrine of intelligible essences and all the untenable ideas about mind and society that doctrine implies. The relational view threatens our ability to identify individuals or mankind. Because everything is ultimately connected with everything else, there would be no place to set the boundaries of individual or species nature. Relationalism is especially dangerous as a philosophical expression of the primacy of role in modern society; each person becomes the dimensionless and shifting intersection of his role relationships. Thus, he is denied the tranquil possession of self.

The third dilemma opposes a view that makes the individual a mere example of the species to one that reduces the species to the status of a category of classification. The former asserts the primacy of the species nature; the latter that of individual natures. The species-oriented view usually accompanies the essentialist and suprahistorical doctrines because of its need to give the species concept a core that can survive the variations among individuals and societies. The individualist conception fits more easily with the relational and the historicist theories because of its commitment to look for the quality of humanity in the unique and fleeting experiences of individuals.

The exclusive reliance on the species idea leaves the subjective sense of individuality unexplained, and dissolves the parts within the whole. The individualist thesis fails to account for the significance of similarities among individuals, and makes the whole a mere sum of its parts.

An adequate theory of the self would have to be one that somehow avoided the defects of the suprahistorical and the historicist, the essentialist and the relational, the species-oriented and the individualist approach. The device with which to accomplish this is the doctrine of universals and particulars suggested by the criticism of liberal thought. If one takes human nature as the universal and its manifestations in forms of social life and individual personalities as particulars, one may say that human nature is neither an ideal entity that subsists in its own right nor a mere collection of persons and cultures. Instead, it is a universal that exists through its particular embodiments, always moves beyond any one of them, and changes through their sequence. Each person and each form of social life represents a novel interpretation of humanity, and each new interpretation transforms what humanity is.

The consequence of this view for the problem of human nature and history is to allow us to affirm the existence of a unitary human nature though we deny that this nature stands above history. Its reality and its unity are consistent with its ability to change and with the distinctiveness of its manifestations.

The implication of the thesis for the choice between essentialism and relationalism is to provide us with a language in which we can both acknowledge that a person is his relations and affirm that he has a distinct identity. Universal human nature consists in a certain set of puzzles men confront in their relations to nature, to others, and to themselves. It is the universality of a predicament rather than that of a substance. But each particular representation of this predicament in an individual life has an organic wholeness and weight of its own, the weight and wholeness of the particular in the face of the universal it embodies.

The doctrine of universals and particulars also shows a way to look at the relationship between the species and the individual without reducing human nature to either a monolithic species character or an aggregate of individual personalities. The species nature as a universal achieves a different existence in each person. The capacities of mankind are dispersed among individuals, but each participates in the many-sideness of the race. Thus, knowledge of the individual presupposes knowledge of his place in the species. To talk about the self is to speak of both mankind and individual men.

Method of exposition and proof

The three theaters of life are a man's relationship to nature, to other persons, and to his own work and station. In each of these theaters, an individual faces certain recurring problems, which arise from the conflicts among his most basic demands upon nature, others, or himself. What makes the demands basic is that they are presupposed by all other tendencies of human conduct; they define the meaning of humanity. They are the characteristics or attributes of the self. There may be variations in the degree to which they are asserted or satisfied, but none can be forgotten for long.

One can identify the fundamental demands through reflection on some commonplace ideas we have about human nature. The difficulty is to see what these ideas amount to when put together rather than to recognize them one by one. When their implications are worked out and their connections understood, they produce a vision foreign to the liberal doctrine and capable of replacing it.

The characteristics of the self are both facts and values, and the doctrine that describes them is simultaneously descriptive and evaluative. Evaluation and description meet at the point at which one defines human nature. There is perhaps nothing to say to a man who would like to be a centaur. Moral discourse always presupposes the acceptance of humanity and the authority of the striving to be and to become ever more fully human. One who has seen how completely the division of fact and value depends on liberal premises will expect this result as the consummation of the critique and embrace it as the reward of his patience.

The doctrine of the self answers two questions, one historical, the other metaphysical. For each of the two sorts of questions there is a corresponding type of justification.

Thus, one criterion for the choice of a theory of the self is historical: Does the theory allow us to clarify the sense of the antagonistic trends we have discovered within the welfare-corporate and the socialist state? More particularly, can it explain the alternation of immanence and transcendence in the dominant modes of social consciousness and in the equivalent types of social order? Because the antinomy of theory and fact remains unresolved, we have to acknowledge both that our theory shapes our interpretation of history and that the subject matter can be examined independently of the theory so as to establish the truth or falsehood of the ideas.

The second standard of preference for a theory of the self is a metaphysical and moral one. It is an appeal to our everyday judgments, tacit and explicit, about what men are and what they ought to be. In fact, our present ways of acting and speaking include a picture of humanity more complete than the one allowed by liberal premises. But we rarely hold this picture before our eyes at once, either because our attention is drawn to its details or because its design is obscured by the influence of liberal principles.

There is a difficulty in the use of moral intuitions that is the exact counterpart to the problem one faces in using history as a justification. The difficulty lies in the contrast between the willingness to reject some judgments about the character of humanity as wrong and the wish to use others as evidence in favor of the view I propose. Where is the line between the correct intuitions and the false ones to be drawn except by reference to the very theory the intuitions are supposed to support?

Speculative thought works through the criticism of present ideas and practices. Nevertheless, in the absence of revealed moral truth or objective value, the only ultimate basis for the definition of an ideal is experience itself. Normative theory must in the end stand or fall by its ability to gain our reflective assent as we come to understand the implications of moral insights we already hold and to refine or to revise the insights in the light of this understanding.

The theoretical criticism of established ideals and the theoretical statement of new ones consists in the appeal from one level of experience to another, more basic one. This appeal is the provisional solution to the dilemma of proof. We call judgments basic the more their abandonment would have consequences we would recognize as absurd, and the less they could be suppressed by hostile doctrines and modes of consciousness. No system of thought, however powerful, can subjugate entirely the minds of its adepts. Because we are men as well as liberals, we have a knowledge of our humanity that the liberal doctrine cannot exhaust. Look then into yourself, and measure by your own experience the truth and falsehood of my claims.

It is likely that the appeals to history and to critical self-understanding will turn out to be insufficient to demonstrate the truth of any one view of the self. Historical experience will be open to different readings; intuitions will speak with discordant voices. Two other aspects of the situation are likely to help us deal with the quandary. First, it may turn out that the number of alternative plausible accounts of human nature and of its relationship to history is in fact severely limited. Second, when our ability to determine which of these accounts is true runs out, the failure may be a sign to us of more than the transitory limitations of our knowledge. It may suggest that human nature as it now exists contains different possibilities within itself and is capable of progressing in diverse directions.

In this circumstance, one of the criteria for choice among doctrines of human nature becomes our moral interest. We are not indifferent to which of the competing views will in fact turn out to be more true. Our choice of one view and our commitment to act according to its dictates will affect the circumstances for which the view accounts. This is the sense in which any metaphysical or social doctrine has something of the character of a self-fulfilling prophecy and becomes part of the story it tries to tell. The overt acknowledgment of moral interest poses an additional problem of circularity for a theory of the self: the moral interest that helps justify the doctrine must in the end be justified by the doctrine itself. The only escape from this circle lies in accepting the notion that the theory of human nature must build on a moral vision that partly precedes it but that is constantly refined, transformed, and vindicated through the development of the theory.

I am sure there is nothing new in the doctrine I shall sketch. It is ancient, and its elements are familiar, though they may seem strange when put together. One might call it the classic theory of human nature. All the great thinkers of Europe have contributed to its development, for it is the theoretical expression of that more basic insight into humanity no theory has managed to destroy. The sway of its teachings has been so unbroken that even the friends of the liberal metaphysic have further-ed this view of human nature despite their own principles. We have only to grasp the implications of what is already known.[3]

I despair of formulating the doctrine in a fashion worthy of the statements we possess, but perhaps my version will make up in simplicity for what it lacks in richness and depth.

SELF AND NATURE

Man differs from all other animals in this: for him his place in the world is a riddle as well as a fate. He is separated from the world in an objective sense because his conduct is indeterminate and in a subjective sense because it is conscious. Indeterminacy and consciousness are the first two attributes of the self.

By indeterminacy I mean simply the limited hold the instincts have over human activity. The concept of instinct is a shorthand way to describe those uniform orientations shared by all members of a species and transmitted genetically rather than culturally. The instincts work uniformly and unreflectively, with the same blind and irresistible neces-sity with which the waves of the sea beat against the rocks of the shore.

In the human species, however, there is a gap between what the instincts require and the possible forms of social organization. Many features of conduct are either not universal or not genetically transmit-ted; indeed, most may be neither one nor the other. Because of this, man's relationship to the natural world is not foreordained. Therefore, he is not wholly a natural being.

The idea of the indeterminacy of the self presupposes no judgment about the limits of causal explanation of human conduct. It simply restricts the influence of a specific category of causal determinants. It thereby forces us to describe what fills the gap left by the limitation of instinct.

The subjective aspect of the separation of the self from the world is the reverse side of indeterminacy. Because man's relationship to nature is not given at once and forever, it is always a problem to be solved. The capacity to be puzzled by any feature of one's state in the world, to represent that state to one's self, and to be guided by such representations is called consciousness. Consciousness, the ability to reflect on existence, is the second attribute of the self. So fundamental is consciousness to all aspects of human action that it creates a realm of being, the realm of mind discussed in Chapter Three, that requires a distinctive method of study. To understand an act in its peculiarly social sense, we have to grasp the beliefs and ideals of the agents.

Assuredly, the distinction between the conscious and the instinctual is far from absolute. On the one hand, consciousness invades the realm of nature. Every feature of existence, even when it holds universally and perpetuates itself genetically, must be mediated through the mind. Thus, the instincts themselves become in a sense indeterminate and must be given a definite form of expression and satisfaction by the social order. On the other hand, there may be universal features of conduct which, though social rather than instinctual, are not products of reflection. They are the content of the unconscious.

The concepts of the unconscious and of the social determination of instinct throw light on the relation of culture to nature, but they do not change the fundamental character of consciousness. To be conscious is to have the experience of being cut off from that about which one reflects: it is to be a subject that stands over against its objects.[4] A prerequisite of the distinction between subject and object is that the subject be capable of defining its relationship to the object as a question to which different answers might be given.

The subjective awareness of separation, which defines consciousness, should not be mistaken for an objective difference of identity. If a man is influenced by forces or persons of whose influence he has no reflective understanding, he is not conscious of his relationship to them, even though they are objectively separated from him. The link between object and subject can never be reduced to one of causal determination. Conversely, the object may be distinct from the subject, although they are objectively identical. This is what happens in self-reflection. A man takes his own person as an object of his thought. The premise of self-reflection is that one is able to divide oneself into a subject and an object whose relation to each other is puzzling despite the fact that for a third person the subject and the object may be the same. The capacity to stand apart from one's own being is the basis of what I shall later describe as the distinction between the abstract and the concrete self.

The ancient view of philosophy as the most exalted of human activities was an interpretation of the importance of consciousness among the attributes of humanity. The philosopher, according to this view, asserts clearly the power to change fate into a riddle by transforming all relations of force into relations of subject and object. In this way, he makes complete and explicit what is only haltingly present in the lives of his fellows. His exemplary worth consists in his ability to free the quality of consciousness, which he shares with all other men, from the cares and preconceptions that narrow its range in ordinary human lives.[5]

Consciousness, then, is the sign of the self's distance from the world. If one could imagine this separateness from nature in its pure form, before it was counterbalanced by the effects of human activity, its sign would be the experience of terror before the strangeness of the world. Because this terror is the mark of that very separation between self and nature upon which consciousness itself is based, it has never been driven completely out of conscious life. On the contrary, the strength of the social bond, the willingness to accept almost every form of degradation and enslavement at the hands of society, owes much to the need men have of belonging to a social world in which the foreignness of a pre-human nature does not prevail.

The terror of separation corresponds exactly to the predicament of knowledge described by the antinomy of theory and fact and by its underlying contrast of the formal universal and the substantive particular. In the sciences of nature knowledge advances by becoming steadily more formal. The substance of things, the rich and concrete appearance with which they strike the senses, is left to prescientific perception. Thus, the greater the perfection of science, the stricter its partiality.

Knowledge is perfect when it achieves the full development of what its method makes possible, and complete when it leaves no aspect of the phenomena it studies unexplained. The natural sciences can never ally perfection with concreteness or completeness in the understanding of nature. There will always be a more concrete knowledge of nature left over to art and to common-sense impression. Hence, the progress of science increases rather than diminishes the strangeness of the natural world. It does this by abstracting from the particulars of experience only what is capable of an increasingly more universal explanation and by abandoning the rest to the domain of the contingent and the inscrutable. It parades before the mind a vast apparatus of forms in which the particularity of experience is wiped out.[6]

There is a second type of knowledge in which we know not only perfectly but completely because the object of knowledge is pure form and this object is constructed by the subject himself. Such is the nature of our knowledge of geometrical, or mathematical, or logical truths. I remarked before that each particular example of a circle is fully defined by the geometrical idea of a circle. There is therefore nothing to be known about any given circle, except for the dimension of its radius, that is not part of the theorem of its construction. The geometer's knowledge is complete as well as perfect, but only because, unlike the phenomena of nature, the subject matter of geometry is without particularity or substance.

As ideas and relations among ideas, the objects of geometry, mathematics, and logic can always be imagined as if they were constructed by the theoretical mind, even when one thinks of them as preexisting truths the mind has discovered. The reason for this is that they lack the feature of substance that distinguishes natural phenomena. The problem of the universal and the particular does not present itself in this field because in it there are no particulars. Therefore, we do not treat the objects of geometry as parts of nature, and the completeness with which we understand them does nothing to lessen the strangeness of the natural world.

Indeterminate because it is conscious and conscious because it is indeterminate, the self is separated from the world and, above all, from the natural world around it. The moral sign of this separation is disconcertment in the face of everything in nature that is alien to human concerns and immeasurable by human proportions. The cognitive sign of the separation is the necessary and radical incompleteness of our knowledge of nature.

Because man has no predetermined place in nature, he must make a place for himself in it. In doing this, he is not satisfied with treating the natural world as a source of means to the achievement of his ends. He wants to recognize himself as one who belongs to the natural order from which he has been thrown out by the gift of consciousness. The sentiment of being part of the whole of nature is as deeply rooted in the self as the experience of its separation from nature. This participation in the whole is not given; it must be conquered.

Thus, all human activities have a twofold aspect. On the one hand, they acknowledge and perpetuate the barrier between the conscious self and the natural world that is the condition of subjectivity. On the other hand, they seek to bridge the gap. The characteristics of the self that exemplify this struggle to become a part of the greater whole are as basic and as universal as those that contribute to the autonomy of the part within the whole.

When the attempt to reconcile self and nature is viewed subjectively, from the standpoint of the acting self, it takes the form of the tendency of all conduct to change the world in conformity with human ends. This tendency may be called the practical character of the self. When the same reconciliation with nature is viewed objectively, from the perspective of its effects on the world, it appears as the tendency of work to create objects that survive the worker and become part of the world.[7] This is the objective quality of the self. Practicality and objectivity, like consciousness and indeterminacy, are the reverse sides of each other.

All human action is meant to transform the world, and transforms it in fact, even when the change accomplished has little in common with the change intended. Because of the indeterminacy and consciousness of the self, the world for man is not already completely formed, and every one of his acts carries its formation a step further.

To test the claim that all conduct is practical, one should consider the issue of the practicality of knowledge, for knowledge would seem almost by definition a counterexample to the thesis. That even knowledge is practical by its very nature has already been implied by the discussion of consciousness. Because of the impossibility of drawing a clear line between the objective situation of the self and its own comprehension of that situation, every understanding changes the world it represents.

The practical character of knowledge is more than an empirical matter. It is part of the meaning of the relation between subject and object. To achieve the separation from the object consciousness requires, the subject must be able to treat the object as something subordinate to its will. In the measure in which it is known, the object surrenders its secrets to the subject. It can no longer be just a force acting upon the subject; it must also become something that can be held at a distance and submitted to an inquiry that will reveal its possibilities and its limitations, and establish its relation to the subject.

The subject's capacity to establish its relation to the object is ambiguous. On the one hand, it means the discovery of something already there. But, on the other hand, the discovery itself changes what was discovered, as is shown by the following two-staged argument. First, unless we are willing to accept the doctrine of intelligible essences and all its consequences, we must define each thing by its relations with everything else. Second, for the subject there can be no clear distinction between the objective character of these relations and their meaning to him. The idea of describing a relationship 'in itself,' independently of the sense it has for the subject, is meaningless, for that idea presupposes the possibility of escaping from the condition of subjective existence. A being whose knowledge of the world penetrated into what things were 'in themselves' would be God.[8]

It follows from my argument that knowledge changes the object by placing it in the state of subordination that being an object implies. When, therefore, the object is another man, every claim by the subject to know him involves a struggle for power. There is no situation of life in which individuals do not have and show the desire to be hidden, alongside the wish to be known. Men want to resemble the God who is seen through a glass darkly, never face to face.

A being for whom knowledge was merely contemplative and did not include the attempt to change and subordinate the thing known could suffer in the world, and be enchanted by it, but he could not be said to know it. Knowledge implies consciousness; consciousness, separation from the object; and separation from the object, the need to define and to construct a relationship toward it that is not fully given. For this reason, all theories that deny the practical character of conscious conduct and treat knowledge as passive contemplation end in mysticism, the denial of the independence of the knower from the known and of the individual self from the whole of which it is a part.

The same arguments show that action transforms the agent as well as the world; knowledge changes both the subject and the object. This reactive quality of conduct is another implication of its practicality. Like everything else, the self is defined by its relations with the world. Every act changes these relations and therefore changes the self. Because the relations 'in themselves' cannot be distinguished from the sense they have for the subject, they are modified by each new piece of knowledge. An important consequence of this process of self-definition is that all choices imply a decision about the kind of person one wants to be.

Thus, when it inquires, the self is engaged in the reconstruction of the world and of its own being. It is practical for the same reasons that it is conscious. Nevertheless, practicality and consciousness work toward opposite ends. Because conduct is indeterminate and conscious, men are separated from the world. But because it is practical, they are capable of uniting themselves with it.

Indeterminacy, consciousness, practicality, and objectivity are fundamental qualities of the self, and each is connected with the others. They describe a certain relationship between self and nature. This relationship is both a reality and an ideal, for it constitutes a perennial as well as a proper aim of human striving. The self experiences a separation from the natural world, an experience manifested in the sentiment of the strangeness of nature and in the incompleteness of what the person can learn about natural facts. At the same time, the self labors to overcome its separation from nature.

The problem to be solved is that of reconciling two primitive human demands. One is the need to preserve independence from the outside world. The other demand is the equally basic need of the self to live in a world transparent to its mind and responsive to its concerns, a world with which it can therefore be at one. The situation in which man is at one with nature though separate from it, in which he has overcome his moral and cognitive estrangement without losing his independence, is natural harmony.

To understand how natural harmony can be achieved, one must be attentive to an ambiguity in the concept of nature. Nature may mean simply the nonhuman world. But it may also refer to what is given in contrast to what men make or subject to their wills. In the former sense, the antithesis of nature is culture; in the latter, it is the artificial. The mark of the given is its universality; it follows universal laws. The sign of the artificial is its particularity; it embodies the particular intentions of particular individuals or groups. From the very start of Greek philosophy, the two conceptions of nature have been repeatedly confused because of the tendency to identify the notions of culture and artificiality. Were it to turn out, however, that there is an aspect of culture no less universal and prior to the will than the phenomena studied by the physical sciences, the distinction between the two concepts of nature would become crucial.

If we take nature for the nonhuman world, natural harmony will be the experience of belonging to that world while also standing apart from it. This is what Marx seems to have in mind when he speaks of the condition in which nature is humanized and man naturalized. When one views nature as the opposite to the willed, natural harmony means the capacity to reconcile the experience of rising above the circumstances of one's existence and recreating them through will with the experience of participation in an order of things that is universal and precedes human design.

In what sense and to what extent can each of these types of natural harmony be achieved by man? Take first the problem of reconciliation to the nonhuman world. The moral, artistic, and religious traditions of many cultures emphasize the persistence of men's desire to see themselves as members of a community of natural and, above all, of living things.

Because of its sexual aspect, love helps man overcome the distinction between self and nature within his own person. As a conscious and indeterminate being, he is distinguished by his relative freedom from the instincts or natural inclinations. These inclinations are the natural element within him. Insofar as he undergoes them, he is a natural being and, insofar as he is free from them, he is more than a natural being. The natural inclinations, like the drives for food and sex, appear as a tyrannical fate; they impose limits and demands on what consciousness can accomplish.

But in love, the union of persons, which represents an ideal of the relation between self and others, is consummated through the natural inclination of sex. It is not the case in love that the more a man is a natural being, the less is he distinctively human. On the contrary, the gap between mind and natural disposition is bridged. By satisfying the ideal of his relation with others and thereby becoming more human, he also becomes more completely natural. This naturalization of man without loss to his humanity is confirmed when sexual union produces children, for procreation allows the individual to serve as a link in the evolution of the species.

The ideal of natural harmony is often exemplified in art. This occurs most obviously in the artistic representation of the simultaneous unity and relative autonomy of different parts of nature outside man and within him, as in Leonardo's marvelous analogies of animals, humans, and angels. In a deeper sense, the ideal of natural harmony inheres in the very character of aesthetic contemplation, which confounds, as does love, the sensuous and the intellectual or moral aspect of our relationship to the external world.[9]

The most general expression of natural harmony is the religious idea of God's plan for the creation: man occupies a place in the order of created things, and shares their creatureliness, but has a distinct and unique relation to God. By accepting the creation, growing to understand it, and contributing to its development, he can grasp the sense both of his unity with created nature and of his separation from it.

Love, art, and religious worship, as we ordinarily know and practice them, are more or less discrete spheres of experience, distinct from everyday life and even opposed to it. Insofar as they fail to transform the commonplace world of social relations but remain private sentiments, they cannot represent the ideal of natural harmony adequately.

Work is the chief device for the achievement of natural harmony in day-to-day existence. The concept of work describes both practical human activity and its results. Material objects, services, theories, and forms of social organization are, in this sense, all works.

The accumulation of works progressively transforms the character of the world by making it a place full of things forever marked by the humanity of their origins. The more man labors, the more he superimposes on the original relation of self and nature a second kind of relation between the self and its own works. In this second, more perfect relation, the work as object is separated from the worker as subject. Yet the subject can also view the object as an expression or extension of his own being, and thus divest it of that terror of strangeness that surrounds the natural things his hands have not touched.

The tie between the worker and his work participates in the nature of the relation between self and nature; for worker and work are separate, and the latter can be viewed as an object by the former. At the same time, however, it differs from the original relationship between self and nature because the work is never just an object for the worker; it is also an external expression of his own subjectivity. As nature is transformed by work, and the human mark is set upon every facet of the world, the relationship between self and nature is itself recast in the image of the link between the human agent and the organizations, ideas, and things he makes. Once again, the general idea can be made more concrete in both a moral and a cognitive way.

The peculiar moral distinction of the relationship I am describing is the ability of the agent to recognize himself in his own acts and in their products. Instead of terror at strangeness, he experiences before them the reassuring confirmation of his own being. The products of human activity have an external form; they belong to the realms of social relations and of natural events. At the same time, however, they are the realized capacities of their makers, and therefore continuations of their creators into the external world.

It is possible to give a much higher degree of precision to our understanding of the distinctive emotion that may attach to the subject's relation with his works by considering the type of knowledge to which it corresponds. In my discussion of indeterminacy and consciousness, I distinguished two kinds of knowledge. The sciences deal with what is given in nature, and the knowledge they provide is at once perfect and incomplete because it relegates substance in favor of form. The objects of geometry, on the other hand, can be viewed as constructions of the mind. The knowledge we have of them is both perfect and complete just because they lack the substance of natural things.

Can there be a third type of knowledge, one that penetrates both the form and the substance of its subject matter? The objects of such knowledge would somehow have to combine the characteristics of natural phenomena and geometrical figures. Like the former, they would have to possess substance or particularity, the sign of which is the variation among individual members of a class of things. Like geometrical constructs, however, they would have to be objects the subject himself had made. By virtue of being their maker, he would be capable in principle of a complete understanding of them, for every particularity of theirs could be traced back to his efforts and intentions.

There is only one category of things that allies the features of natural and geometrical objects, and this is the category of works. Because the work occupies a place in the external world, it always appears as an individual entity, distinct from all other entities of similar kind. Each act committed, or object made, or relation established is unique. At the same time, however, the work has a meaning, originally given to it by the intention of its maker. The maker's intention is not the last or only determinant of the sense the object has in the social world, but it is its first and most simple one.[10] Aristotle and the schoolmen made the point when they said that the final cause precedes the efficient one; the stool exists in the carpenter's mind before it exists in the external world.

We make many different tables, each unique in its substantive particularities, yet all united by our conception of what a table is good for and by the end for which we are making it. Some of the singularities that distinguish any one table from the others can be traced back to the characteristics of the material and to features of our efforts of which we were not aware. But the less work uses natural things and the greater one's degree of conscious mastery in carrying it out, the more will it be true that every last detail of the individual product is intended. Thus, an artistic creation or the statement of a philosophy may contain little that the artist or the author did not mean to be there.

Man can understand the social world, as Vico pointed out, because he made it. Vico's remark describes both the basis and the subject matter of that third kind of knowledge which the objectivity of the self makes possible. Its basis is the peculiar relationship to one's work most perfectly expressed in the idea of God's knowledge of the creation. There is nothing in the world that was not first part of His plan, and everything in the world derives its meaning from the place it occupies in that design. When we transpose the same idea to the level of humanity, it means that the worker who intended the particulars of his work can understand them. Moreover, if he has made the work for some general use, that use too falls within the scope of his knowledge. His table can serve a standard purpose, or his work of art can describe a recurring aspect of existence, despite or rather because of its peculiarities. As soon as this conception of practical and objective character knowledge is developed, one discovers that it is the very mode of understanding described before as the one required by the phenomena of consciousness.

The more conscious and independent from natural contingency the work, the less is it possible to distinguish what it is from what it is intended to be. This restates the idea that reflection and existence are inseparable in the realm of consciousness.

The notion of what a work is for is rarely just a prediction; it usually involves a view of what it ought to be for, and this becomes truer as the element of conscious design in labor increases. Here we have the second characteristic of the method of study of social objects. The reflection from which existence is inseparable overrides the contrast of fact and value.

Finally, though intention may be the first, it is not the last arbiter of the work's meaning. Once made, it begins to exist, as it were, in its own right, and the intentions of the maker may be forgotten or dismissed. The work then acquires a new meaning, determined by the interests and intentions of those who use or observe it. For these third persons, however, the practical and objective knowledge of the work is possible only if they are somehow able to put themselves in the place of the worker and to grasp the relationship between his conscious reflection and the product of his labor. From this results the problem discussed previously as the ambiguity of meaning.

To the extent that the observer disregards the intentionality of the worker, or that the worker himself has not produced something that reflects his intentions, the kind of knowledge I describe is impossible. The object must then be treated simply as a natural thing, and it can be known only in the incomplete manner of scientific explanation. This establishes an important limit to the validity of Vico's claim. It is only potentially true that man can understand the whole social world with the intimate knowledge a creator has of his creation. It is true in the measure in which two conditions are satisfied; first, that the ideas, social arrangements, and material things respond to the conscious purposes of their makers; and, second, that men be able to enter into one another's intentions by belonging to communities or traditions of common purpose. When both requirements are fulfilled, we say that the purposes of work are not separate from the work itself, but, on the contrary, embodied in it.

The knowledge the worker can have of his work is a partial resolution of the antinomy of theory and fact. In the realm of practical, objective conduct, one rejects from the start the notion of a theoretical knowledge independent of its objects, and the idea of facts separate from reflection. Yet this rejection does not lead to the absurd consequences it would produce if we took it as the sole basis for our ideas about science. There is no necessity here for a pretheoretical experience of facts as the Archimedean point from which to choose among competing theories. The difficulty does not lie in the need to choose among alternative explanations. Instead, the problem is one of the worker's power to recognize the extent to which the work reflects its 'final causes,' his intentions. Just as the intentions only partially preexist labor, but more often develop in the course of its execution, so the recognition of the correspondence between the work and the intent is part of the very process of working. It is not a bond of contemplative interest in which one holds the object before one's eyes and asks, Is it this or is it that? There is a relation of immediate power in which the subject chooses what the object will become.

In the antinomy of theory and fact, the premise that all facts are theory-dependent is a consequence of the abandonment of the doctrine of intelligible essences. The postulate that one must be able to see facts plainly in order to judge theories arises from the abstraction or incompleteness of scientific knowledge. The natural sciences classify particulars under abstract general categories. The issue presented by the antinomy is that we are not entitled to assume that anything in the world corresponds to these categories. Certain individual facts or events can be classified under the same categories because they share specific characteristics; their other features are disregarded. In the worker's knowledge of his work, however, there is no such problem of classification. He views the work not as an example of some universal category, but as an individual entity all of whose features can in principle become present to his mind. The need to choose among possible abstract categories of classification simply does not arise for him.

The same reasons that seem to make the knowledge of one's work a solution to the antinomy of theory and fact also explain how, as a practical and objective being, man can cope with the terror of strangeness that marks his separation from nature. That emotion is just the moral counterpart to the subject's inability to know the entire substance of its objects.

Thus, insofar as the person can join together the human and the nonhuman world in his everyday life, he must do so through the experience of work. There are, however, certain obstacles to the use of work as a realization of natural harmony. Some of these obstacles depend on the form of social consciousness and the organization of society; others are universal and insuperable.

The first contingent limitation is the tendency to think of the subject as an individual, whose participation in groups is a secondary feature of his existence, according to the liberal principle of individualism. Clearly, though, the most striking and pervasive features of social life cannot be accounted for as the creations of particular individuals. As long as we insist on viewing the subject as an isolated individual, the fundamental arrangements of society, its ways of organizing life, the language its members speak, and the moral or political beliefs they adapt, will all appear to belong to the natural order of things. They will be known only as the phenomena of nature are known, and the understanding of the universal will continue to be separated from the perception of the particular. To reach a different result, it would be necessary to acknowledge the existence of collective subjects, in violation of the principle of individualism. The self might be able to view all social arrangements as its own handiwork or as the handiwork of others if it could see itself and others as members of the collective subjects or groups who have authored the arrangements.

The theoretical insistence on the individuality of the subject corresponds to the historical situation represented by the principle of individualism, a situation in which every group relationship not governed by rules is experienced, to a greater or lesser degree, as a coercive one. It is the circumstance portrayed in the theory of the welfare-corporate state as one governed by the principles of class and of role and propelled forward by the dialectic of the ideology of impersonal rules and the experience of personal dependence.

The second unnecessary impediment to the achievement of natural harmony through work is variously described by the Marxist theories of reification and alienation, by Weber's concept of rationalization, and by

Simmel's idea of the "tragedy of culture."[11] The products of human effort, once created, acquire a life of their own. They stand over against the conscious self that brought them into being. Thus, there is an unending struggle between their status as extensions of the subject and their nature as objects independent of the subject and capable of resisting him. In this struggle, the independence of the object may triumph utterly over the extension of the subject.

One can describe this process in theoretical terms as the failure to recognize the distinctive features of the realm of consciousness and of the kind of knowledge for which it calls. In the vision of social life produced by this theoretical failure, everything appears upside down. Political and legal theories are mistaken for actual situations. The arrangements of social life are separated from their source in the practical activity of individuals and groups and viewed as automatons that run on their own motion. This conceptual illusion has the same root as the inability to recognize the existence of collective subjects. That root is the social condition in which men are unable either to produce works that embody individual intentions or to participate in each other's purposes.

Imagine now a form of social life in which neither of the problems just mentioned would hold good. In that circumstance there would still be two restrictions on the achievement of natural harmony through work.

In the first place, work would extend only to society and to nature as transformed by society, but it would not change our relationship to whatever in nature remained untouched by human effort. Even in our creations we make use of natural objects that we did not create, and whose relationship to ourselves we cannot freely determine. Thus, though culture adds a layer of being to nature, it can never wholly erase the brute facticity of natural things. The peculiar significance of the work to the worker only serves to emphasize the distance between the realms of nature and culture.

Second, there would always be in labor, to a greater or lesser degree, an element of the narcissism of the subject. The worker desires to reproduce himself in his works, and when he feels at home with them it may be himself that he embraces. The object is known completely and deprived of its strangeness only insofar as it serves as a continuation of the subject. The task set by the ideal of natural harmony, however, is to establish a reconciliation with natural things that are truly separate from the subject rather than his own individual or collective image in a mirror.

Perhaps the main vice in the Hegelian-Marxist theory of work was its uncritical acceptance of the narcissism of the subject as an adequate solution to the problem of self and nature. There is a close link between this acceptance and the deification of mankind in the Hegelian-Marxist religion of immanence. One does for the individual what the other accomplishes for the species.[12]

There can be no full solution in history to the problem of reconciling man's need to be at one with nature and his need to stand apart from it. Because he is conscious, he must experience his humanity outside himself and within himself as something opposed to his naturalness. Love, art, and religious devotion may release men episodically from this antagonism, and work may diminish its force in everyday life, but nothing can undo it.

In its alternative sense, natural harmony means the alliance of the experience of participation in an order given to man according to universal laws with that of living in a world he can remake according to his particular ideas and desires. Such an alliance would have to be based on something that combined the features of givenness and artificiality.

This thing might be human nature itself, made present to the individual in a certain form of social life. Imagine the idea of a universal community, whose practices revealed the species nature of man so transparently that each person could understand both how the existing order represented everything humanity had become up to that point and how every change in that order would transform what humanity might become in the future. The structure of society would then be both given and made, and, though it would have the universality of natural phenomena, it would be open to criticism and revision. But should such a community be desired, could it be realized, and what would its impossibility imply for the interpretation of human nature?

SELF AND OTHERS

Consciousness is an experience of separation and limitation. A conscious being is a subject who is able to stand over against objects, and therefore to be aware of himself as something different from them.

There is a special class of objects from which the conscious self must also be separate, the class of objects who are also subjects, namely other selves. The attribute of the self by virtue of which it must always be a particular self, distinct from other selves, is called individuality. The nature of individuality is defined by its bases, which are the following.

First, unless the conscious self were distinct from other selves, it would have no fixed limits. Would the self be the species as a whole at any given time, or throughout its history, or some group within the species? Deprived of boundaries, consciousness would never be able to distinguish objects from itself; it would lose the experience of separate identity. The need for limits, however, is not enough to elucidate individuality, for we must know where exactly to place those limits.

The second basis of individual being is the bodily character of conscious life. Not only do we believe the conscious self to require boundaries, but we treat the body as its natural frontier. The significance of this practice is to acknowledge that, though consciousness implies separation from nature, it is also part of the natural order, and it constantly seeks the reconciliation with nature described by the ideal of natural harmony. The embodiment of the person is the sign that he is in nature, just as the possession of consciousness means that he is not wholly of it. Thus, the relationship between self and body repeats in miniature what is more generally true of the relationship between self and nature and between the universal and the particular.

The self can exist only in a particular body, and that body is part of the self, yet the characteristics of the body do not exhaust what the self is or may become. Because it is embodied, the self must be individual. Another way to make the same point is to recall that every aspect of existence has a correlate in reflection. From this it follows that if the self has a certain body the content of its consciousness must be distinct from that of men with different bodies.

The third basis of individuality is the peculiar relationship that exists in mankind between the members of the species and the species as a whole. In all other species, what any one member can do, and in fact does, is more or less what any other member of the species does. The indeterminate, conscious, practical, and objective qualities of the self collaborate to produce an altogether different relationship between the human species and its members. On the one hand, only a tiny part of the total fund of capacities of mankind can be brought to fruition in the life of any one of its members. On the other hand, each of the members draws on this common fund in a distinct manner. Every person is a unique, particular expression of the universal that is the species, a universal that cannot exist except in one of these particulars but that none of them completely describes. Individuality is an implication of the way universal and particular are linked in the constitution of humanity.[13]

The very manner in which the person is individual also makes him social. The problem of understanding the relationship between self and others, and of determining its ideal form, can be rephrased as the elucidation of the link between individuality and sociability as attributes of the self. This link may be considered from both a cognitive and a moral point of view.

Consciousness displays a peculiar paradox that poses the preliminary issue with which a theory of mind must deal. Consciousness implies autonomous identity, the experience of division from other objects and from other selves. But the medium through which consciousness expresses itself is made up of the symbols of culture, and these, according to the principle of totality, are irreducibly social. When you speak of language or make a gesture, you perceive and communicate meaning in categories that are the common patrimony of many men. By what power can you and they speak to one another? It must be possible for each to view the other's statements and acts as the signs of certain intentions. These intentions can in turn be understood because they are intentions you too might have. It follows that consciousness always presupposes the possibility of viewing other persons as selves that could, under favorable enough circumstances, see what one sees and believe what one believes. That is the cognitive aspect of sociability.

The paradox of sociability lies in this. The more precarious the bonds of common existence and belief among men as minds, the less are they able to express their consciousness through the social medium of symbols, and therefore the less are they secure in the experience of individuality that arises from consciousness. Nevertheless, the more intimate the similarity of experience and reflection among individuals, the less of a basis does individual identity seem to have.

As a theoretical matter, this proposition may be unfamiliar and hard to grasp, but the concrete experience it describes has never been far from modern eyes. It is the experience of the conflict between the hope that one might think for oneself and the need to be understood or, to rephrase it in a stronger and negative form, between the fear of enslavement and the fear of madness. The more one believes what the others believe, and lives as the others live, the easier will it be for them to understand what one means when one speaks. The greater the distance between self and others, in the things one says and in the way one lives, the heavier the strain put on the ties of common discourse. At last, the speaker becomes mad first to his hearers and then to himself, for he can only be certain he knows through the confirmation of his views by his fellows. In the measure of its conscious distance from others, the self both needs and fears assent. To look upon its desperate struggle to satisfy this need and quiet this fear is one of the ways one learns about the paradox of sociability.[14]

Consider now the moral aspect of sociability. It is one of the requirements of personality that one be recognized by others as a person. To be human, one must be treated as a human, or remember or imagine, by analogy to past experience, what it would be like to be treated as a human. The need for an acknowledgment of one's selfhood has the same character as the need for assent to one's ideas. The elucidation of this need can be approached from several complementary standpoints: the weakness of self-reflection, the relational character of identity, and the place of the individual in the species.[15]

Precisely because consciousness is always individual and embodied, it has only a limited power of self-reflection. It can never achieve enough distance from its own particular circumstances to view itself as a pure object. One might say that when he attempts to see his own personality through self-reflection the individual is like a man who looks at himself in a mirror and can never see all of his own body at once. As individuals, we must develop and complete our self-image by drawing inferences about what we are from what others suppose us to be. Our view of ourselves has to be mediated through the views of others.

Again, like everything else the self is defined by the totality of its relations with other beings and, particularly, with other selves. Insofar as these relations are social, they fall under the principle, applicable to all social phenomena, that what something is thought to be is part of what it is. More precisely, we are our relations; the way in which others conceive of those relations is one of their determinants, and therefore one of the determinants of our own selfhood. If one could imagine a situation in which no one treated a person or had ever treated him as a human being with a self, then in that situation he would have no self.

Finally, the need for recognition is based on the posture of the individual toward the species. Because each individual can develop only a minute fraction of the talents of mankind, the way in which he belongs to the species is never obvious. The universal quality of humanity is hidden as well as revealed in its particular manifestations. To find that universal quality in himself, a man must live in a community of persons who acknowledge one another's humanity by regarding each other's talents as complementary powers of the species.

The need for recognition involves a dilemma that is another form of the paradox implied in the need for assent. To be an individual one must win the recognition of others. But the greater the conformity to their expectations, the less is one a distinctive individual. The paradox of sociability is the problem posed by the relation between self and others. The self is individual and it is social. But the requirements of individuality are in conflict with the demands of sociability in a way that does not seem immediately capable of solution. Looked at from another angle, it is just the issue of what makes community possible, the puzzle that underlies the antinomy of rules and values. Liberal political thought phrases the problem of the link between the individual and the social character of the self as one of values and rules. The question put by the antinomy of rules and values as to how men who believe values to be subjective can be governed by impersonal rules is a version of the paradox of sociability.

What would it mean for the self to reconcile its individual and its social nature and to escape from the paradox of sociability? The person would have to be able to satisfy his needs for assent and recognition without surrendering his distinctiveness. He would have to find a way in which union with the others would foster rather than diminish the sense of his own individual being. This union could be described as a circumstance in which others are complementary rather than opposing wills in the sense that to join with them in a community of understandings and purposes increases rather than diminishes one's own individuality. An alternative statement would be that the union consists in the reciprocal acknowledgment of the universal attribute of humanity possessed by each in the particular mode of his being.

This hypothetical condition in which the greatest individuality is allied with the greatest sociability, and realized through it, is the ideal of sympathy. The ideal of sympathy is to the relation between self and others what the ideal of natural harmony is to the relation between self and nature. It is the dreamt-of circumstance in which one is both 'at one' with other selves and 'separate' from them. My argument about self and others has been designed to show that the struggle for sympathy is a necessary implication of the self's attempt to retain its individuality.

To make the notion of the ideal of sympathy more precise, let us consider certain vivid though limited ways in which we learn and speak about the sympathetic relation between self and others.

Take first the conception of God's relation to men and of their relationship to one another in the Near Eastern monotheistic religions and especially in Christianity. The universal brotherhood of man is a consequence of the universal fatherhood of God. The elements of individuality and sociability are joined in the conception of the soul. By its nature, the soul is unique, yet all souls are called to the same supernatural vocation, and have a common worth. The way in which they are related to each other is part of their relation to God. To the religious man, every other person is a particular manifestation of the universal substance in which the soul, including his own soul, consists, and this universal substance is inseparable from its particular embodiments. Such a man cannot prize God or himself without prizing others as the individuals they are. This is the meaning of the religious precept that men should love one another.

Personal love, particularly the love between a man and a woman, is the clearest example of the ideal of sympathy. Its distinguishing attributes are the complementarity of wills and the acknowledgment of the other as a concrete and unique individual.

The loved one is viewed and accepted as a separate person. And yet we say that in personal love individuality is not only preserved, but made more secure, because the will of the loved person is experienced as complementary rather than antagonistic to one's own will. The sense of the complementarity lies in the fact that one is able to feel that one's own existence is reaffirmed instead of endangered by the other. (In heterosexual love, this complementarity has a biological correlate.) Thus love flourishes because of the difference of persons rather than despite it. In this respect, it is useful to compare human love to altruism in other animal species. By altruism I mean the sacrifice of the individual's interests to the interests of another member of the same species. The higher one goes on the evolutionary scale, the less does altruism partake of the character of narcissism, the devotion of like to like. The more does it bind together what is different.

The passage from narcissism to this higher love presupposes the acceptance of the other as a whole person. Love is not given in exchange for the mastery of a particular skill or for the performance of a role. It is an acknowledgment of the entire being and of the particular features through which the other person's universal humanity is expressed. It attacks the separation of the universal and the particular in personality.

Nevertheless, personal love is an imperfect realization of the ideal of sympathy. Its first imperfection lies in its tendency to fall victim to the paradox of sociability it seems to resolve. This can be seen in the related experiences of romantic and perverse love, elements of which may never be entirely absent from any love relationship.

In romantic love the self alternates between the attempt to dominate the other (idealization is a form of domination) and the surrender of its own identity. It is forced to choose between the mystical sentiment of oneness with the other and the destruction of individuality brought about by its very isolation from the person it seeks to enslave. Thus, romantic love resembles the life situation of the schizophrenic, who feels both cut off from others and merged into them, whereas authentic love is the moral antithesis of schizophrenia.

Romantic love seems most likely to flourish in the political conditions of an artificial society in which every sharing of common purpose appears to be a diminishment of individuality. Consequently, it turns against the social order, whence its frequent hostility to the family and to child rearing. At the same time, romantic love perpetuates the sharp distinction between the individual and the social element in personality. Thus, it has a political counterpart: the romantic, revolutionary ideas of extreme individualism and extreme collectivism go hand in hand.

Perverse love is the condition toward which romantic love tends or the affect from which it arises. If romantic love represents a denial of sympathy, perverse love strikes at the root of sympathy. In perverse love, the other person is hated as well as loved; he is treated more as an antagonistic than as a complementary will. The individual who is an object of perverse love is admired for the possession of certain physical or moral attributes and denied recognition as a person.

Even if one sets aside the tendency of personal love to fall victim to the paradox of sociability by becoming romantic and perverse, there still remains in personal love a flaw that keeps it from being a perfect solution to the problem of sympathy. This flaw is its particularity, its incapacity to embrace many individuals at once. The relationship between lovers cannot be repeated an indefinite number of times in an individual life; it will be overwhelmed by the strangeness of persons to each other. The particularity of human love is brought out by contrast to a traditional conception of divine love. What makes divine love superior and miraculous is just that it can be both personal and universal; that it can reach out to everyone without losing the character of a unique relationship to each person if not to each thing in the world. Viewed in this light, personal love has an irremediable defect. It can resolve the problem of sympathy with regard to a few but not with respect to all or even to many other persons.

The limitation of scope that inheres in the particularity of love may be drastically accentuated by social organization. The social order cannot be governed by a principle of love as long as it continues to rest upon the antagonism of private interests and the system of private property as the device for working out this antagonism. Everything that pertains to love will melt away as soon as it is put in touch with the arrangements of social life. The struggle between the principle of love and the principle of private interest will be carried on within the very structure of the family, for the family will be both the social manifestation of love and a group marked by the contrariety of private wills and property interests.[16]

Because of the imperfections of personal love, it is necessary to cast about for some alternative way to achieve the ideal of sympathy, something that will do in the ordinary life of society what love does in limited encounters of two persons. This alternative, the political analogue to personal love, is the idea of community. The elements of the idea of community are the same as those of love: the complementarity of wills and the capacity to give to others and receive from them the acknowledgment of concrete individuality. The sentiment that animates community and pushes beyond the borders of love is called by Aristotle *philia* or fellow-feeling, by Aquinas charity (though with both a supernatural and a profane meaning), by Hume sympathy, and by Comte and Durkheim altruism.[17] Thus, sympathy names both the ideal and the affect that contributes to its realization.

The sentiment of sympathy differs from love in its conditions as well as in its context. Love is so strong that it may allow the lover to acknowledge the concrete individuality of the loved one and to perceive him as a complementary will despite an opposition of values between the lover and the loved. Sympathy is weaker. As the association becomes less intimate and total, it depends increasingly on shared ends to achieve the recognition of concrete individuality and the complementarity of wills.

Community is held together by an allegiance to common purposes. The more these shared ends express the nature of humanity rather than simply the preferences of particular individuals and groups, the more would one's acceptance of them become an affirmation of one's own nature; the less would it have to represent the abandonment of individuality in favor of assent and recognition. Thus, it would be possible to view others as complementary rather than opposing wills; furtherance of their ends would mean the advancement of one's own. The conflict between the demands of individuality and of sociability would disappear. Each person, secure in his individuality, would be able to recognize his own humanity in other persons. Moreover, in this community individuals would have to live together in a situation sufficiently varied, intimate, and stable to allow them to know and treat each other as concrete persons rather than as role occupants. To the extent that a community acquired these features, it would become a political realization of the ideal of sympathy.

Such a view of community makes a number of crucial assumptions, to all of which I shall return at greater length. The first assumption is that there is a unitary human nature, though one that changes and develops in history. The second premise is that this human nature constitutes the final basis of moral judgment in the absence of objective values and in the silence of revelation. The third assumption is that there might be certain political conditions under which an ever more inclusive sharing of ends in space and time would carry weight as an indication of the nature of man.

Let us suppose for a moment that these assumptions are true and that the ideal of community based upon them can be coherently formulated and politically achieved. There still remains a deep-seated tension in that ideal that limits its power to serve as a complete solution to the problem of self and others. This tension is the exact counterpart to the imperfection of particularity in personal love.

To become or to stay a community, the association may have to remain a particular group, limited in the size of its membership. Close, even face-to-face coexistence may be important to create the common experience that encourages the development of shared purposes. And this same closeness may be indispensable to the ability of the members of the community to treat each other as concrete individuals.

Nonetheless, the community also needs to become a universal association that ultimately embraces all mankind. Until it has been universalized there will always be some other persons in relation to whom the members of the community have not yet solved the problem of self and others. Moreover, on the view I have outlined and shall later develop, the moral authority of the shared values of a communal group depends on the degree of their faithfulness to human nature, and one of the necessary though insufficient measures of that fidelity is the universality of their acceptance.

It therefore seems that neither love nor community can fully resolve the conflict between the individual and the social element of personality. This conflict is an indestructible part of the experience of selfhood. No man can share in joint undertakings with his fellows without imposing limits on the degree to which he differs from them, for these endeavors presuppose common values and beliefs. But to become fully transparent to others and to lose all sense of them as antagonistic wills, his understandings and ends would have to coincide with theirs. Thus, he would cease to be an individual. But the sacrifice of either the individual or the social aspect of the self makes it impossible to speak or to be spoken to as a person.

THE ABSTRACT AND THE CONCRETE SELF

Every man is both a particular individual, with a definite place in the system of social relations, and an exemplar of universal humanity. He exists only as a person who takes certain courses of action and shuns others; who develops some of his capacities and leaves some dormant; who meets with only a few of the experiences it would be possible for a being of his kind to undergo. At the same time, no man is satisfied until he can connect the particular position he occupies and the particular work he produces with his universal humanity. He wants his life, in its limitations and in its brevity, to be an expression rather than a sacrifice of the many-sidedness he shares with mankind.

As a being who participates potentially in the many-sidedness of the species, the person is an abstract self. As a being whose life is always finite and determinate and who is never in fact more than a small part of what he might be, the person is a concrete self. The relationship between the abstract and the concrete self is the psychological counterpart to the relationship between self and others. It is the problem of individuality and sociability reexamined from the perspective of the internal organization of personality. Indeed, the issue of the connection between the elements of personality is just the question of the relation of self to others. The abstract and the concrete self correspond to two attributes of human nature, partiality and universality. Because man is partial, he has a concrete self, and because he is universal, he has an abstract one.[18]

The self is partial in the sense that its actual experience is always infinitesimal in comparison to the possible experience of human beings. Partiality is a consequence of what I have said about the self with respect to its relation to nature and to others. Its most immediate basis is the place of the individual in the species. Set against the background of the wealth of talents of which the species disposes and which it is forever increasing in history, every individual is fated to indigence, no matter how great his exertions or favored his circumstances.

Consciousness, which begins in the experience of indeterminacy, becomes more determinate with every choice it makes. Moreover, because identity is relational, we cannot imagine a man without a concrete place in society and in history, any more than we could a person without a body. The person is this particular being. But he is also something more.

An animal is particular, but it is not partial. Men can only be partial because they have the feature of universality. Universality is both a fact and an ideal. As a fact, it is the degree to which the self participates potentially in the richness of forms of life manifest in the history of the species. It has access, though not unlimited access, to the fund of talents of mankind, and it has the quality of humanity, the characteristics of selfhood all members of the race share. This is its abstract self. Universality is also an ideal. The self strives to find a way to express its universal humanity, the latent abundance of its modes of being. More precisely, it wants to reconcile the universal and the partial side of its personality so that the former will be expressed through the latter.

The issue presented by universality as an ideal is an aspect of the riddle that lies at the center of the antinomy of reason and desire, and thus of liberal psychology as a whole. For the liberal psychologist, reason is the universal element in man; desire the particular one. The liberal doctrine of human nature fails in its attempt to account for the unity of personality precisely because it cannot reconcile either the two elements of the person or the moralities based on them. Just as the problem about self and nature goes to the antinomy of theory and fact, and the problem of self and others to the antinomy of rules and values, so the resolution of the problem of the abstract and the concrete self would solve the antinomy of reason and desire.

There are two false and destructive ways to deal with the problem of the abstract and the concrete self. Each is exemplified in common experience, associated with a particular social situation, and productive of a characteristic moral sentiment. They both consist in refusals to take seriously either the universality or the partiality of the self.

One of these tactics is acquiescence in pure partiality and the abandonment of the universal part of the self as a hopeless dream. The person is completely absorbed in his concrete social position and identified with it. The use of the principle of role and of the division of labor as a foundation for the unity of the person constitutes such a response. But the role already represents a less complete identification of the self with its social place than the earlier principles of estate and of class. The acceptance of the pure partiality of the self as an inescapable fate appears in the moral life as the sentiment of resignation.

The other evasion of the need to reconcile the abstract and the concrete self is the vain attempt to approach in individual life the many-sidedness of the species.[19] This evasion marks the existence of those who as vestiges of a social order that has died or as forerunners of one yet unborn attempt to stand outside the division of labor. It is the typical posture of both decadent aristocracies and of critical intelligentsias in the history of the modern state. And it is also the recurring outlook of the adolescent, who is a natural aristocrat. Those who adopt this view, which one might call abstract universality, imagine themselves as occupants of the greatest possible variety of life situations and practice the cult of the fullness of 'experience.' The tragic character of abstract universality lies in its inability to escape from the realm of dreams into the world of social relations. Because it represents a rebellion against the irrevocable decree of partiality, it is condemned from the outset to failure. Lost in the multitude of its disparate exertions, the self cannot bring any of them to a successful conclusion, or bind its life to the progress of the species as a whole. The moral counterpart to abstract universality is the sentiment of disintegration.

A satisfactory relationship of the abstract and the concrete self would have to be one in which universality was achieved through partiality rather than through the attempt to evade it. This situation might be called the ideal of concrete universality. Concrete universality represents the kind of connection between the species nature and the individual suggested by the doctrine of universals and particulars. Since the person is an abstract as well as a concrete self, this connection must be established within him rather than between him and something else.

The most striking illustration of concrete universality is single-minded work in the service of an ideal whose universal significance the worker recognizes; his exertions have become a gift to the entire species. The power to infuse a universal significance into one's finite life is recognized and admired by all men as the quality of inspiration. He who is so inspired cannot rest, or play, or even dream in peace until he has awakened his fellows from their slumber as he was awakened by others. All his efforts are driven forward by the same passion, and the task he has set himself is before his eyes at every moment and in every circumstance. For such a man, partiality is a way to partake of the universal. At the same time, the capacity to put one's particular work in the service of a universal ideal presupposes that one is able to distinguish between the ideal itself and the particular form it takes in one's life, and thus to criticize and guide the latter from the standpoint of the former.

The love of the ideal, from which inspiration draws its being, has something of the character of personal love. Other persons, however, enter into one's love for the ideal solely as the unknown beings one hopes can participate in the same love or benefit from its works.

As a solution to the problem of the abstract and the concrete self, the love of the ideal has a defect similar to that which art, religion, and personal love have as responses to the problems of self and nature, and self and others. It is an exception to daily life rather than a transformation of it. The experience of inspired work is restricted to a tiny few, and even these few are oppressed by their isolation. They are thrown into a circumstance in which the union of universality and partiality can be accomplished only by sacrificing the reconciliation between self and others. Moreover, men are usually unable to discover universal ideals to which to devote their lives. On the contrary, that is a power which in retrospect is recognized as genius. Thus, genius acts as surrogate for the perception of objective values, which is why the moderns can never forgive themselves the lack of it. What then would it mean to generalize the experience of inspiration and genius by putting it within the power of everyone to live a life in which his particular work was bound to ideals he was entitled to recognize as universal?

The division of labor is in principle the political counterpart to inspired activity just as community is the political analogue of personal love. But we are blinded to this because of the type of social organization and social consciousness with which the division of labor has been and remains associated. So intimately is it connected with domination by class and role or merit that we find it hard even to begin to imagine how it might be disentangled from those kinds of dominance and what it would then become.

Suppose, however, the existence of communities of shared purpose. Imagine further that these common ends increasingly express the species of nature of man because they develop in conditions of diminishing domination and are ever more widely held. The more the community approaches this scheme, the stronger the chance that its evolving common ends may represent the ideals service to which satisfies the need for universality. At the same time, the particular way one's work furthers those values accommodates the element of partiality in the self. Thus, concrete universality is actualized through the division of labor within the group. Each man sees the general significance of his work. And through participation in the making and remaking of the common purposes, he transcends his particular place in the organization of the community.

The division of labor fosters concrete universality only to the extent it satisfies a number of stringent requirements that will be the subject of study at a later stage of the argument. The chief of these requirements is the overcoming of domination, a premise of our entitlement to take moral agreement as a sign of human nature rather than of the subjection of some wills to others. A subsidiary principle is that the specialization of tasks or forms of personal life must never to be so extreme or rigid that it smothers the individual's capacity to stand apart from his social place by grasping the common purposes and helping develop and criticize them.

Whether or not the division of labor can be transformed into a political expression of the ideal of concrete universality, there remains a deeper drawback to concrete universality as a solution to the problem of the abstract and the concrete self. It is not a solution that allows one to express the potential many-sidedness of one's nature directly in one's own lifetime. Indeed, its premise is that any attempt to do this misconceives the necessary and proper relationship between the individual and the species and leads to delusion and degradation. What is offered instead is the possibility of advancing the species nature or of being guided by it. Thus there is the danger that one will come to treat one's own life as a mere means to an end that lies beyond it. And there is the threatening fact that the gap between the universal and the partial aspect of personality is never directly or completely bridged.

THE SELF AND THE WORLD

The theory of the self can be taken to a higher level of generality and abstraction. From this vantage point it will be possible to gain fresh insight into the matters discussed in the preceding chapters of the book.

The self is indeterminant, conscious, practical, objective, social, individual, universalist, and partial. Together these characteristics define certain relationships between the self and nature, the self and others, the abstract and the concrete self. These relationships are both facts and ideals. They are facts in the sense that they describe strivings implied in the very nature of personality. They are ideals because, outside revelation or objective value, the strivings that inhere in the nature of humanity seem to be the sole basis of moral judgment. To achieve the good is to become ever more perfectly what, as a human being, one is.

When the relationships of the self in the different theaters of its life are placed side by side, one can see that they share a common character, and are particular forms of a more general condition. The ideal of natural harmony states that the self must be separate from nature though at one with it. The ideal of sympathy means that the self must be independent from others, yet reconciled with them. According to the ideal of concrete universality, the abstract self must be able to transcend its own situation and retain the sense of universal humanity while satisfying universalism through partial work.

In each of the ideals, the conscious self is opposed to and united with something external. In the first case, the external given is nature; in the second, other persons; in the third, one's own life situation insofar as it has assumed a concrete and determinate form. And, in each case, the ideal asserts that, as part of its interest in the development of its own being, the self must be both independent from an external reality and reconciled with it.

Nature, other persons, and the concrete self are the world, for they include everything given to the person at any moment of his life. The general problem is therefore one of the relationship between the self and the world, and the general form of the ideal is that the self must be separate from the world and reconciled with it. The self is in fact distinct from the world, and ought to become more and more independent from it, in awareness as well as in existence. It is in fact part of the world, and should increase progressively its union with the world.

Thus, the self has two complementary modes of being, neither of which ever appears in its hypothetical pure form, but each sometimes sacrificed to the other, to a greater or lesser degree. The first mode is one of separation between self and world. At best, separation means the assurance of one's distinctiveness from nature, others, and one's place in society. At worst, it implies the sense of being lost in a world alien to one's own concerns. The second mode of being is that of union with the world. At best, this union is the state in which the world is no longer experienced as a mere given that stands over against the conscious self, but as a confirmation of the self's own humanity. At worst, it signifies a fading of the distinction between the individual and his surroundings.

Each mode of being achieves its better form when it is joined together with the other mode, and falls into its worse one when it is separated from the other. Natural harmony, sympathy, and concrete universality describe the hypothetical ideal circumstance that combines the two ways of being and thereby perfects both. This circumstance is the ideal of the self, and its achievement is the good.

The two varieties of existence of the self represent alternative possibilities open to those who participate in social life. The problem they pose is therefore still another trait that distinguishes the sphere of consciousness from the realms of ideas and of events. From a broader perspective, however, it is simply the metaphysical issue of sameness and difference, or of the nature of identity. This issue arises at all three levels of being; it applies to the orders of ideas and of events as well as to that of culture.

The ideal of the self provides the most general standpoint from which to survey and to elaborate the results of both the critique of liberal thought and the theory of the welfare-corporate state. Each of the basic modes of being has a metaphysical counterpart in theories of mind and society and a historical one in forms of social life.

The metaphysical counterpart of the mode of separation is the liberal doctrine, the system in which the universal as theory, reason, and rules, stands opposed to the particular as fact, desire, and values. Indeed, liberal thought constitutes the philosophical representation of a circumstance in which consciousness is separated from nature, whence the antinomy of theory and fact; the self is separated from others, whence the antinomy of rules and values; and the universal, abstract, or rational part of the self is at war with its particular, concrete, or desiring part, whence the antinomy of reason and desire. The element of truth in the liberal doctrine, as description and as ideal, is the indispensability of the mode of separation between self and world. Everything false in the doctrine results from its disregard of the claims of the mode of union between self and world. Thus, one might say of liberalism what Leibniz said was true of every sect: that it tends to be right in what it affirms and wrong in what it denies.

The dominant social consciousness and institutions of the liberal state exemplify the mode of separation of self from world in a form of social life. The manipulative posture toward the natural world expresses a sharp division between self and nature. The conception of society as a battleground of wills describes the gap between self and others. The ambivalent view of work and social place corresponds to the contrast of an abstract and a concrete self. In the era of a secularized transcendence, the individual is opposed to nature, isolated from others, and condemned to view his own roles as a denigration of his implicit universality. The principles of class and role and the bureaucratic institution organize society around the same central experience. Thus, the separation between self and world is the tie that unites liberal theory, the dominant consciousness of the liberal state, and its characteristic type of organization. It is the approach to life they share, the principle of common meaning that joins them together, and the source of both their power and their weakness.

The mode of union between self and world is just as important to the philosophical antithesis of liberal thought, and to a form of social life based on a pure ideal of immanence and on a hierarchical, communitarian type of order. The identification of ideas and events, of rules and values, of reason and desire, and, thus, of the universal and the particular would represent in metaphysics the denial of the estrangement of the self from the world. To the extent that social consciousness in the welfare-corporate and the socialist state vindicates the ideal of immanence, emphasizing the sanctity of nature, of community, and of one's station, it affirms the union between self and nature, others, and concrete life. The hierarchical communitarian order, based on the principles of kinship and estates, and perceived as a mirror of nature's harmony, corresponds to the oneness of self and world at the level of social organization.

The theory of the self solves at a single blow the two main problems with which this essay has been concerned, and it clarifies their relationship to one another. It offers the beginnings of an alternative to both the liberal doctrine and its hypothetical antithesis. It is the passage of escape from the metaphysical prison-house, for it shows what a resolution of the antinomies of liberal thought would require.

At the same time, the doctrine of the self indicates an approach to a critical understanding of the situation of modern society. Insofar as the welfare-corporate and the socialist state move toward a reassertion of an earlier ideal of immanence and of previous forms of hierarchic community, they substitute one inadequacy for another. The mode of union replaces that of separation, and the ideal remains unrealized in history.

To the extent contemporary society contains the elements of a possible synthesis of transcendence and immanence in consciousness, and of autonomy and community in organization, it holds the promise of political solution to the problem of the self. Therein lies the peculiar significance of our age to mankind.

Hence, the critique of liberal thought and the study of modern society bring us to the same conclusion: the point at which philosophy and politics join hands. To develop the theory of human nature as an alternative to liberal thought and to carry through its resolution of the antinomies of liberalism, one must turn to politics. Only politics can make the ideal concrete, concrete in everyday life and therefore also concrete for theory, which anticipates, criticizes, and contributes to politics, but cannot replace it.

The theory of human nature also allows us to grasp the sense of the history of the modern state by revealing its significance for the development of personality. The different modes of being of the self are represented in the historical types of social order and social consciousness. Moreover, the ability of the self to achieve the ideal inherent in its being depends on the capacity of particular societies and of the species as a whole to satisfy the political requirements of the ideal. Our present historical condition makes possible a more complete resolution of the problem of the self for the species as a whole and for each of its members. Thus, the criticism of the welfare-corporate state, like the critique of liberal doctrine, invites us to examine by what means and in what way natural harmony, sympathy, and concrete universality might be achieved in society. For all these reasons, one may say that the self is realized in history, and that history is the story of its development.

This view is teleological insofar as it recognizes that history is made by men who have purposes and above all the purpose of affirming their humanity. In their other endeavors, they may oppose one another, and defeat each other's ambitions. Yet there is at least one ambition all persons have in common simply because they are human. They long for that ideal mode of being whose lack makes them restless and distraught. So it would not be surprising, though also not inevitable, if above the storm of conflicting beliefs and hopes, in which men are tossed to and fro among the different claims of personality, the interest they share in a complete self gradually came to prevail over the interests that divide them. And this higher purpose would then set its mark upon the ways in which they conceive society and organize it. In retrospect, it may appear that history developed as if it had worked toward an end, though properly speaking only the individuals and groups who make history have purposes.

The sense in which my account is not teleological should now be clear. It does not attribute designs to history itself, nor does it view as foreordained the actualization of the ideal or any of the past stages toward its possible accomplishment. The failure to reach the ideal in history, or even to progress toward it, may be complete and irremediable.

THE EVERYDAY AND THE EXTRAORDINARY

When we speak of the meaning of life, we often seem to have in mind the satisfaction of an ideal of the self. A doctrine of human nature that claims to guide conduct as well as to portray reality should include a view of the conditions under which the good to which it is committed can be realized and thereby give meaning to life.

Nevertheless, in every case the solutions offered by religious worship, art, and personal love, as these experiences are known to us, turn out to be incomplete and therefore imperfect. They need to be completed by a transformation of society that extends to the whole of life what they achieve in a limited sphere of existence. The moral significance of work, community, and the division of labor derives from this need.

Like the personal solutions, the political ones suffer from incurable defects. The gaps between humanity and nature, individuality and sociability, partiality and universality, are never fully overcome; the separation of the self from the world is never entirely reconciled with the union of self and world.

Let us, however, set aside for the moment the ultimate issue of the impossibility of a full realization of the ideal in history and focus instead on the relationship between the personal and the political form of the good. Politics is indispensable to a more complete though still imperfect realization of the ideal in history. Nevertheless, there is an important sense in which the personal encounters with the ideal do resolve the problem of the self and provide a basis for the sense of meaning in life. Can these two claims, the possibility of an individual solution to the problem of the self and the indispensability of a political one, both be true? If so, what are the limits and the significance of their coexistence?

If we consider some forms of art, religion, and personal love as isolated experiences, they appear to represent actualizations of the ideal of the self. Because they exemplify natural harmony, sympathy, and concrete universality, we may be inclined to see them as a heavenly kingdom in which the rifts and the incompleteness of the self are overcome. However, as soon as one reexamines them from the perspective of their place in experience as a whole, one is forced to a very different conclusion. Everyday life is given over to the profane, the prosaic, and the rule of self-interest. The sacred, art, and love appear as extraordinary deviations. Thus, the realization of the ideal is governed by an iron logic of the everyday and the extraordinary. Because the commonplace world is the denial rather than the confirmation of the ideal, the relationship of the self to it must be the mode of separation from nature, from others, and from its own station. For the self to be reconciled to the everyday world, it would have to recognize the ideal within the world, not above it.

The self reunited with actuality in the sphere of an isolated ideal nevertheless remains separated from it in the ordinary experience of life which that ideal can neither transform nor abolish. What from one standpoint represents a synthesis of immanence and transcendence, appears from another as the sacrifice of the former to the latter.

The extraordinary representation of the ideal in art, religion, and love has a two-faced significance for everyday life. On the one hand, it can offer the self temporary refuge. In this sense, the extraordinary is a mystification, the aroma that sweetens the air of the established order. Its very availability makes the absence of the ideal from everyday life seem tolerable and even necessary. Because the sacred, art, and love are separated out from banal events, everything in the ordinary world can become all the more relentlessly profane, prosaic, and self-regarding.

Nonetheless, the extraordinary also makes it possible to grasp the ideal, and to contrast it with one's ordinary experience of the world. In this sense, the extraordinary is the starting point for the critique and transformation of social life. It poses for men the task of actualizing in the world of commonplace things and situations what they have already encountered as a divine liberation from the everyday. Thus, the tools of mystification and of defiance are drawn from the same source.

The logic of the everyday and the extraordinary explains the sense in which art, religion, and love are able to serve as representations of the ideal. But it also shows the need for a political actualization of the good. In the course of this actualization both the extraordinary and the everyday must be changed. The final and most important change would be the disappearance of the distinction between them. If, as I shall later argue, the ideal can never be fully achieved in history, the conflict between the everyday and the extraordinary can also never be wholly overcome. But only through the attempt to destroy that conflict do we approach the ideal.

This attempt is the moving force behind much of what is most distinctive in the culture of our time. Its theological form is the reassertion of the claims of immanence and the corresponding rejection of the view of religion as a relatively autonomous sphere of life; the idea of the sacred as something with fixed boundaries is undermined. The same struggle reappears as the attempt to destroy the barrier between art as ornament and the objects of ordinary life; the expansion of the aesthetic into areas traditionally reserved to the prosaic implies an abandonment of the distinctive identity of art.[20]

To destroy the logic of the everyday and the extraordinary in the realms of religion and art, the features of commonplace life that make it profane and prosaic must be changed. The necessity of changing the actual condition of society becomes even clearer when one considers what it would mean to avoid the oscillation between love in the settings of family or friendship and calculating self-interest in one's work. The political counterpart to love is sympathy; sympathy flourishes in community; and community arises through the reconstruction of society.

What light, then, does the logic of the everyday and the extraordinary throw on the issue set out at the beginning of this section: the coexistence of the thesis that there is an individual solution to the problem of the self with the claim that a political solution is indispensable? In the understanding of the self's relation to history, there are two opposite mistakes of equal seriousness. They should be rejected not because they can be disproved head on, but because there is a third view that seems both richer in its descriptive uses and less likely to lead to paradox in moral judgment.

One mistake is to disregard the link between the development of the individual self and the situation of society. Such a view is characteristic of suprahistorical conceptions of human nature. As a basis for descriptive theory, this doctrine fails to do justice to the connection between the individual's moral sentiments and his political experience. As a foundation for moral judgments, it leads to conservatism and utopianism. No sooner is the tie between consciousness and politics cut than the ideal of the self takes on the appearance of something that must be realized in the private life, and whose attainment is independent of society. Religious

worship, art, and love become havens of comfort and illusion that perpetuate the character of the everyday world.

There is a second way to conceive the self's dealings with history.
It takes off from a historicist notion of human nature, and it asserts
that if the ideal of the self can be realized at all it must be realized
politically and in history. As a framework for descriptive social theory,
this position fails to account for those phenomena of individual consciousness that do not seem peculiar to any one historical situation. Its
moral implication is to deny that private and extraordinary experience
can ever, to any extent, actualize the ideal of the self. There is no private
resolution to the problem of the self, because the state of human nature
and the condition of society are at any given time one and the same
thing. Does it not follow that all those who live before the hypothetical
political achievement of the good are forbidden to achieve it altogether,
so that their lives are condemned to meaninglessness? Why, then, should
the individual work toward the political actualization of an end that,
whether it comes or not, will surely come too late for him? What duty
could commit him to participate in the cruel and capricious machinations
by which history makes the predecessors the witless instruments of the
latecomers? Thus, if the first view of the relation between the self and
history leads to mystification, the second produces absurdity.

The theory of the self developed in this chapter represents a position
that should not be mistaken for either of the two preceding theses. It
recognizes the existence of a unitary human nature, but it views this
nature as coming to be in history. Man cannot yet be fully known, because, in a sense, he does not yet fully exist. Human nature shows itself
only through the historical forms of social organization and social consciousness. It is not, however, exhausted or completely determined by any
of them. The relation of the self to history is like that of a musical theme
to any of the sequences of notes in which the theme can be expressed.
Hence, the idea of the repetition of phylogeny by ontogeny is a half-truth.
Each individual person must solve the problem of the self, but within the
limits of his place in the history of the species.

The moral intention of this doctrine is to show how one can admit
the possibility of an individual solution to the problem of the self in a
way that does not sanctify the logic of the everyday and the extraordinary. Religion, art, and personal love offer the self an experience of
the ideal that is available to it now and regardless of the ultimate
political fate of the species. They provide this solution precisely because

they foreshadow in the life of the individual, abstractly and therefore imperfectly, what can only be more fully accomplished in the history of mankind.

To anticipate the ideal, the individual must be able to see and to build in his own life a connection between the personal and the historical resolution of the problem of the self. The link is established by the action, political in the most ample sense, through which he strives to make the ideal actual and thus to move beyond the logic of the everyday and the extraordinary. In this way the theory of the self responds to the question of meaning in individual life in a manner consistent with the true claims of politics. That is its aim.

Faced with the everyday, we are incomplete; open to the extraordinary, we are capable of delighting in being. And this delight in being, which begins in the animal attachment to life and ends in the divine love for the world, was ours from the beginning. It is the foundation of both the moral significance of history and of our ability to accept the fact of incompleteness.

When religion views the good as rooted in reality, when in art the world is perceived under the species of a beauty beyond the claims of right and wrong, when in personal love we complement and by complementing reassert one another's existence, this delight in being takes an external form. It becomes something we can possess now and not at the end of history, as individuals and not as instruments of the species. The fact that we have this gift in a partial way, under the guise of the extraordinary, reveals our dependence on mankind. The fact that we possess it, nevertheless, and can love this part for the whole it foreshadows establishes the measure of our autonomy from the moral progress of the race.

When God speaks to Job out of the whirlwind, he asks his despairing servant to look upon the horse who in battle says, "ha, ha," among the trumpets. "Ha, ha," among the trumpets say all those who are able first to anticipate, then to recognize, but finally to embrace perfect being in imperfect, and fugitive, and earthly form.

6

THE THEORY OF
ORGANIC GROUPS

INTRODUCTION

How can the ideal be realized in everyday life? To answer this question is the objective of the doctrine of organic groups. In the view of the relationship between the ideal and society, there are two opposing dangers, whose false and nefarious character the theory of organic groups seeks to expose. One of the dangers is idolatry; the other, utopianism.

Idolatry consists in mistaking the present situation of the state for the accomplishment of the ideal. It would be idolatry, for example, to accept the welfare-corporate or the socialist state as representative of the complete reconciliation of immanence and transcendence and of community and autonomy. But what if some future society brought about a complete and final actualization of the ideal in history? If the good is defined as the union of immanence and transcendence, the idea of its being perfectly accomplished in the historical world is self-contradictory, hence false. By the very fact of that perfection, transcendence would have lost its basis, for no truth or ideal would remain beyond actuality. Nature, society, and one's allotted social tasks would themselves become the sacred idols from which there was no appeal. Thus, the foundation of individual autonomy would be destroyed together with that of transcendence. The belief in the power of politics to wipe away the failings of life favors the deification of the social order.

But there is also danger in utopianism, the tendency to define the good in such a manner that it cannot be related to the historical situation in which one finds oneself. Utopianism fails to give men either insight into their circumstance or guidance to move beyond it. Awakened from its dreams by the call of politics, utopian reason has no choice but to worship established power as a mystery it cannot grasp and as a fact it cannot change.

Just as idolatry is the form taken by a political imagination surrendered to pure immanence, utopianism is the political style of a consciousness contented with transcendence. In fact, the two modes run into each other. Immanence without transcendence turns into simple resignation; transcendence without immanence into the disintegration undergone by a self that cannot bring its ideals to bear on its experience. Undeniably, however, there may be situations so distant from the good that utopianism becomes in them the only alternative to the acceptance of evil.

The doctrine of organic groups shows how the ideal of the self can be accomplished in society through a transformation of the welfare-corporate and the socialist state. In this way, it avoids utopia. At the same time, however, it acknowledges the gap that separates these states from the ideal, and the sense in which even the political order it describes and justifies must continue to be an imperfect realization of the good. Thus, it shuns idolatry. Through its attack on idolatry and utopia, the theory of organic groups vindicates hope against both resignation and disintegration. Thus, it carries out the moral program for which the criticism of liberal thought was begun.

The chapter starts with the statement of a view of the good, drawn from the theory of human nature. The doctrine of the good implies an ideal of community, whose relationship to two major types of political thought is explored. I then contrast the abstract knowledge of theory to the concrete knowledge of prudence and suggest the inherent limitations of the former as a guide to conduct. Against this background, the argument goes on to describe the institutional principles of a kind of community that might both do justice to the claims of human nature and respond to the problems of postliberal society. In conclusion, I discuss the relations between groups and their members, the association of groups among themselves, the dilemmas of communitarian politics, and the meaning of the imperfections of theory and practice.

THE GOOD

Throughout this essay the problem of value or of the good has kept reappearing in a variety of forms. We encountered it first in the criticism of liberal thought. In liberal psychology, the moralities of reason and desire fail precisely because they either treat the good as something unknowable or define it in a way that leaves us at a loss about what we ought to do. In liberal political theory, the absence of a view of the good makes it impossible to justify any exercise of power at all, an impossibility underlined by the incoherence of all doctrines of legislation and adjudication in that system of thought. Our blindness to the nature of the good becomes an everyday experience and an actual historical force in modern society.

The despair of finding a source of value other than individual desire encourages the vain search for impersonal power through systems of rules and roles. The struggle to escape from the insoluble dilemmas that plague this search helps turn attention to the politics of community. The problem of the good appears once again in the theory of human nature. As long as we lack a criterion of value that goes beyond individual will, we cannot reconcile the experiences of immanent order and transcendence according to the ideal of natural harmony; we cannot deal with the paradox of sociability according to the ideal of sympathy; and we cannot give universal meaning to particular work according to the ideal of concrete universality.

All these difficulties result from the nonexistence of a conception of the good, from the acceptance of a subjective idea of value. Whatever its deficiencies, however, the idea of subjective value has one virtue in which the opposing principle of objective value is notably lacking. It recognizes that there is a relation between the good and individual choice.

The doctrine of subjective value has the merit of calling attention to the fact that, at least in the absence of revealed moral truth, the good is relative to the being of man. It is the realization of his being, and it can have no existence apart from him. If the doctrine of subjective value transforms life into a question without an answer, the doctrine of objective value is equally untenable and perverse. We must reject it not only because it relies on a mistaken view of mind and language and because it degenerates into either meaningless abstraction or unwarranted parochialism, but also because it falsely teaches us to forget the connection between what is good for us and what we are.

Our highest interest is therefore to discover an account of the good that might be free of the defects of the subjective and the objective conception. Such an account is the view presented in the theory of the self. Its core is the idea that the good consists in the manifestation and development of individual and universal human nature.

One may replace the subjective and the objective idea of value with a more adequate conception of the good by making use of a doctrine with two basic elements. The first element is the concern of the theory of the self: it is the notion that the good consists in the development of the species nature in the lives of particular persons. The second element is the thesis, soon to be elaborated, that both human nature and our understanding of it can progress through a spiral of increasing community and diminishing domination. After briefly reexamining the former idea, we shall be in a position to focus on the latter.

The previous course of the argument has justified the conclusion that the good is properly viewed as an actualization of human nature and that, when so interpreted, it can be pictured in two complementary ways. If we consider the good as the ideal to which human striving is addressed and from which it receives its meaning, it can be characterized as the relationship to nature, to others, and to oneself described by the concepts of natural harmony, sympathy, and concrete universality. When we think of the good primarily as a source of more concrete standards of right conduct, it may be useful to distinguish a universal and a particular good.

Personality has two aspects: one universal, represented by sociability and the abstract self; the other particular, expressed by individuality and the concrete self. Therefore, everyone must have both a universal and a particular good. The universal good is the perfection of the species nature in which he participates by virtue of his sociability and of his abstract selfhood. The particular good is the development of the unique set of talents and capacities through which the species nature of mankind takes a concrete form in him.

It is important to understand what this view does not claim. It does not rely on the notion that mankind as a whole and each of its members has an essence or an unchanging core that can somehow permeate history and biography. Instead, it starts out from the idea that the distinctive experience of personality is that of confronting a certain set of intelligible, interrelated problems that arise in one's dealings with nature, with others, and with oneself. Insofar as both the problems and the ideal ways of responding to them are continuous in space and time, one may speak of a human nature and of a universal good. But continuity does not mean permanence.

If the universal good is defined as the realization of human nature, it might seem that no room is left for the notion of a particular good, unique to each individual; goodness will in all important respects be the same for everyone. Nevertheless, to disregard the particular good would be deeply to misunderstand the character of personality. The problems of life never present themselves in the abstract, but always in the form of a concrete personal situation that calls for a concrete personal response. Moreover, the indeterminate fund of potentialities in which the individual as an abstract self participates is never just a mirror image of the species nature. The separateness of persons would be shallow were it not the case that each person represents in a limited and distinctive fashion the possibilities open to the entire species. Finally, the idea of a particular good may help remind us that no one can display the species nature fully in his own life and that the personal forms of the ideal in art, religious worship, and love only achieve their full significance through their bearing on the historical progress of mankind.

The connection between the two goods and the significance of this connection for the chief concerns of my essay are best understood in terms of the characteristic relationship of universals to particulars. The species nature advances through the development of the capacities of individuals. But no definable set of realized individual talents exhausts human nature, which is continuously changing in history. The universal good exists solely in particular goods, yet it is always capable of transcending them. The two aspects of the good are inseparable.

This view differs from the doctrine of subjective value in claiming that the good is more than the satisfaction of individual desires. But it also diverges from theories of objective value in its denial of the existence of eternal moral laws that inhere in the nature of things.

Having defined the good, we may now ask how knowledge of it can be gained. This question is especially pressing with respect to the universal aspect of the good, for a human nature that transcends any individual personality or form of social life must always keep some of the marks of a mystery.

A person shows what he is through what he says and does, though he can never reveal himself wholly in the choices he makes, because he is an abstract as well as a concrete self. By analogy, moral agreement may give insight into the species nature. To the extent moral beliefs prevalent in different ages and societies converge, the convergence can teach us something about what men have in common.

Nevertheless, all the many attempts to build a moral and political doctrine upon the conception of a universal human nature have failed. They are repeatedly trapped in a dilemma. Either the allegedly universal ends are too few and abstract to give content to the idea of the good, or they are too numerous and concrete to be truly universal. One has to choose between triviality and implausibility.

For example, one may acknowledge a universal and permanent interest in the goods of survival and health, but it is difficult to extend the list much further. If we come up with a detailed enumeration of values, it will always be possible to point out instances in which they have been rejected by some societies or periods. There will then be the need to judge the worth of the conflicting claims of different cultures and ages, and therefore to find some independent standard of the good. Were such a standard available to us, however, there would have been no need to look for shared human purposes in the first place.[1]

An erroneous conception of the problem of value lies at the root of these unsuccessful proposals for its solution. They treat moral beliefs entertained at different times and in different societies as if those beliefs were of equal weight. The basis of such a view is that a commitment to certain ends is an immediate and transparent representation of its author's nature. Hence, if many different individuals in widely diverse circumstances make similar choices, these choices must manifest a common humanity. The premise of the belief in a direct connection between convergent values and human nature is the still more basic assumption that this nature is not only unitary, but also similarly actualized in all individuals, whatever the society or age to which they belong.

Our inquiry into the relationship of human nature to history has already suggested that these views are mistaken and that the hunt for a list of universally shared ideals can therefore offer no real escape from the dilemma of objective and subjective value.

If human nature changes in history, choices made under varying social circumstances cannot be equally representative of the quality of humanity. Indeed, if the ideal of the self can never be fully realized, it must follow that no choice with which we are familiar can perfectly represent the good. To define the good by cataloguing the standard preferences of a past or present era is to risk sanctifying a partial and hence perverse moral vision.

A second, related objection to the traditional manner of listing common ends is that it pays no heed to the way values are determined by society. More particularly, it disregards the corrupting effects of domination on the capacity of shared purposes to show human nature and therefore to measure the good. We can only learn what men are by observing what they say and do; the study of choice is an unavoidable gateway to the understanding of the self. But it is not enough.

The values shared by the members of a group may be mere outcomes of social determinants that affect the individuals concerned more or less uniformly. This is especially significant if the wills and understanding of some men are captive to those of others. For insofar as dominance exists, shared values may express the concrete nature of particular persons within the group or outside it, namely the dominators, but they cannot pretend to stand for something universal about humanity. So it will not be surprising to find that, whatever the degree of moral union within particular associations, groups differ at the most basic levels in the ideals to which they give their allegiance. The identification of any of these sets of shared values with the good would again lend authority to the prejudices and interests of an existing order of dominance. This would be the ultimate prostitution of philosophy.

To avoid the recurring failure of the search for universal ends without falling back into the dilemma of objective and subjective value, a shift of focus is needed. Instead of asking what people want, we should ask first under what conditions their choices might inform us more fully about what is distinctive to each of them and to mankind as a whole. Our first concern should be to determine the circumstances in which we are entitled to give greater or lesser weight to consensus, taking agreed-upon values as better or worse indications of our common humanity. It may be that such an inquiry will show that one cannot hope to discover universal and permanent moral laws, and that the very striving for such laws betrays a misconception of what man and his good are like.

The idea of a spiral of domination and community elucidates the relationship between moral agreement and human nature. Let us first be clear about what is meant by shared values or moral union. The sharing of values in a group may be measured with respect to the number of persons who subscribe to the same ends or standards (extension); the degree to which the common purposes are concrete enough to guide practical decisions (concreteness); the importance people attach to the shared values (intensity); and the fidelity with which those values are followed or displayed in the behavior of the individuals who acknowledge them (adherence). For my present purposes, it is best to avoid any hard and fast distinction between value as reflective belief and as actual conduct.

The more shared values emerge from a process in which what some men want is predetermined by what others have desired, the less may we rely on the resulting convergence to infer something universal about mankind. Because of the fact of domination, moral agreement is often little more than a testimonial to the allocation of power in the group. For moral union to be representative of the species nature, it must arise from conditions of autonomy. In a slave-owning society, the slaves themselves may well be convinced of the goodness of slavery. So too in liberal society the discovery that accepted conventions are inseparable from the personal dominion of some over others leads to a desperate effort to render power impersonal through law.

Once the corrupting influence of domination on the authority of shared values is recognized, we run up against the vicious circle encountered often before. Shared values carry weight only in the measure to which they are not simply products of dominance. Yet domination and autonomy have no self-evident meaning. To be dominated by another is to be subject to his unjustified power. Thus, to define domination one must be able to distinguish the justified and the unjustified forms of power, and to trace the true limits of autonomy. This requires judgments that have to rely to a greater or lesser extent on our established moral intuitions and practices.

The chief difficulty lies in the disproportion between the seriousness of the problem and our capacity to resolve it. The more extreme the system of domination, the greater the need to overcome it in order to understand, to develop, and to manifest human nature. But, for the same reasons, the less confidence shall we be entitled to have in our moral judgments and therefore in our ability to define domination.

Politics, however, may change the vicious circle into a spiral. The solution to the quandary of dominance and community lies in a progressive approach to the ideal in which each step toward equalizing the way men participate in the formulation of common values adds to the authority of the latter, and each increase in the moral weight of shared purposes increases the precision with which domination can be defined.

A number of questions must be answered before the idea of the spiral can be accepted as an account of the relationship between moral agreement and human nature. How can such a process begin? What kinds of groups are supposed to serve as its settings? What can be said about the content of the values that emerge at each step along the way? And how could we know when the spiral had come to an end?

The types of dominance are placed on a scale, from the gross to the subtle, from those that take an extreme and outward form, like legally sanctioned enslavement, to the impalpable stratagems by which one mind becomes master of another. At the outset, when the burdens of domination are heaviest and the authority of widely shared moral beliefs correspondingly weakest, the difference between permissible and impermissible exercises of power must rest on the external signs of subjection. Still, the classical arguments in favor of slavery show that even the harshest forms of oppression may appear justified. Thus, one must acknowledge both the difficulty of defining the contours of legitimate power during the first steps of the process and the fact that those steps nevertheless take place. But whatever the mechanism of the initial choices, the bases of judgment become more secure as one advances.

Another issue presented by the idea of the spiral of domination and community is that of the range of social life that should be taken into account in determining the worth of shared ends as signs of man's species nature. Is one to consider a single group, an entire society with many different collectivities, or all of mankind? Here again a satisfactory answer must do justice to the progressive possibilities of the spiral.

The fact that certain ends are commonly held in a single group may be of only modest significance in suggesting characteristics of universal human nature. But the broader the foundation of agreement in different groups and societies and the greater its stability over time, the more are we justified in drawing from it inferences about the self and the good. The ultimate appeal must be to mankind as a whole, but comparison on so vast a scale is made difficult by the diversity in the circumstances of choice and in the degree to which domination has been expunged. Thus, in assessing the accuracy with which shared values express human nature there are two master criteria to observe. The first is the measure of success achieved in disentangling our ethical or political views from inequalities of power. The second is the continuity of those views over space and time. The former criterion is empty without the latter. The latter is dangerous without the former, for it threatens to enshrine the interests of the powerful and to deny the chance of moral progress.

We may still press forward and ask what is to come of the process described in the preceding pages and by what signs we may know whether it is proceeding in the right direction. It misconceives the character of the spiral to suppose that one can determine beforehand its final outcome, if indeed it has one. The attempt to do so would mean a slide back into the misguided quest for the immediate definition of universal ends. It would be to forget that both our knowledge of human nature and human nature itself can always move beyond their present state.

We cannot describe what men who lived under better conditions of community might know and want, because we are not such men. No trick in the world allows us to jump outside ourselves and pretend to the higher wisdom that belongs to a more perfect mode of being. It therefore follows that philosophy cannot hope to establish as universal and permanent truths the content of the values that ought to be shared or the meaning of domination. It can only aspire to determine the ways community and autonomy may be achieved and human nature more fully developed and known, though these overarching ideas must themselves evolve in accordance with the dialectic of theory and politics.

Yet choices must be made about what to do and how to characterize the uses and limits of justifiable power. If theoretical reason is an inadequate guide, another method must be found to continue where philosophy stops. I shall have something to say later of this alternative method, prudential reasoning, and of its relation to philosophy.

The view presented here rests on three major assumptions: there is a human nature; the development and manifestation of this nature is the good; and moral agreement may be a better or worse indication of what human nature is and demands.

The critic might begin by attacking the idea of a human nature. Does not that idea depend on the conception of an essence of humanity despite my claim to reject talk about essences in this book? Does it not disavow the ties between human conduct and the historical forms of social life? Is it not in any event made trivial by the fact that the deepest facts about men are the qualities that distinguish them rather than those they have in common?

These questions lose much of their force when one understands that my purpose is not to return to the classical idea of an essential human nature impervious to the course of history. The effort is to retain the conception of a unitary human nature while acknowledging that man makes himself through the different forms of social life he establishes. Humanity consists in a continuous predicament and in the kinds of relations to nature, to others, and themselves with which persons respond to that predicament rather than in a hard core that remains unchanged in the midst of a changing periphery. The suprahistorical and the historicist, the essentialist and the relational, the species-oriented and the individualist view of human nature are combined through the central doctrine of universals and particulars. From the perspective of this doctrine it is not surprising that we should be struck above all by the differences among individuals and societies. The universal human nature is always embodied in particular personalities and forms of social life, just as the light cast on humanity by a great work of art is inseparable from the particular characters or situations the work describes and is therefore irreducible to a formula.

The critic who accepts this version of the idea of a unitary human nature might still object to the second premise of the argument, the identification of human nature with the good. Is not evil as much a part of human nature as goodness? Indeed, must we not concede that the very passion to dominate constitutes a permanent spring of human conduct? And if we do grant this, should we then not admit that the idea of discovering humanity by taming domination hides a paradox?

The defect of this criticism is its willingness to do the very thing that the previous objection claimed to detect in my argument: to reify human nature as an eternal essence to which certain virtues and vices are forever attached. But the tendency to oppress is inseparable from the history of oppression; it can be modified as the quality of everyday experience is transformed. That at least is the hypothesis implicit in a doctrine that emphasizes the dialogue between what men are and the way their societies are ordered.

The theory need not be blind to evil. It sees evil as the deprivation that consists in a failure to move ahead in the spiral of domination and community. The mark of evil is the acceptance of a certain form of personal existence as complete in itself or of a particular kind of social life as the ultimate achievement of the race. It is the sacrifice of universality to particularity and the reduction of man to the animal state.

To be sure, this argument is inconsistent with the idea of evil as a positive, independent force at work in history and in individual hearts, but immune to human striving. And it is equally incompatible with the belief that human nature is morally indifferent, neither good nor bad in itself but requiring to be judged by some independent standard. The principle that animates the view is one of trust in the ultimate harmony of being and goodness in human nature as in the world as a whole. Of this I shall have more to say at the end of the present section.

Suppose the critic accepts the notion that there is a human nature with implications for conduct and that its better understanding and realization constitutes the good. He might still deny that we can ever infer anything about the content of that nature from moral agreement. An indefinite number of factors may cause individuals to agree in their moral beliefs. It is never possible to be sure whether a given convergence of beliefs reflects a shared community or simply indicates the effect of some other natural and social determinant of the choices men make. If this uncertainty were justified, human nature would be like the hidden God whose existence one can affirm but whose visage one cannot see.

This objection rests once again on a misguided essentialist idea of human nature. Its premise is that there exists a human nature and then, separately from it, a variety of social experiences that might be responsible for agreement. But once we conceive of human nature as something that resides in the totality of relations men have with nature, with others, and with themselves, this image becomes irrelevant. It has to be dismissed together with the notion of a static kernel of humanity that stands apart from thoughts, feelings, and behavior, or with the belief that all participation in social life involves a turning away from what one truly is. Whatever does not arise from domination is human nature; domination is the one form of social relations in which men's conduct fails to express their being.

If the critic were to accept all these responses to his arguments against my account of the good, he might still be left with a feeling of uneasiness about its tone and spirit. Does it not invite us to put an unjustifiable faith in the correspondence between history and the achievement of the ideal? Bemused by the idea of preestablished harmony, we may too easily surrender the safeguards against evil that liberalism so painfully built. For if it should turn out that there is no unitary human nature of the kind I describe, the lessening of domination might in fact lead to an exacerbation of moral conflict with the result that the premises of liberal thought would become all the more true and the political acceptance of the subjectivity of values all the more indispensable a guarantee of individual autonomy.

The idea of the good set forth in these pages rests upon the belief in a correspondence between being and goodness. This belief is neither arbitrary nor capable of conclusive proof. To accept it and to act upon it is to run a serious risk. Yet it is a risk a wise man might have reason to assume.

One justification of the postulate of correspondence between being and goodness is negative. In the absence of such a link, there would be no alternative to the subjective view of value, whose destructive consequences for moral and political striving we have examined. Indeed, the discovery that being and goodness are opposed or unrelated would condemn man to remain forever at odds with himself and his world, and would unmask his existence as a cruel and insoluble riddle. The darker the predicament seems to us, the more desperately will we try to escape from it even though we must concede that the attempted breakout may fail and leave us worse off than we were to start with.

Another basis of the idea of the association of being and good is an appeal to the insights of forms of discourse that lie beyond the boundaries of philosophy, but from which speculative thought can hope to learn without sacrificing its independence. Even when it portrays evil as an independent force at work in the cosmos, religion starts with the notion that the realm of values is somehow grounded in the reality of things; that truth and goodness are partners. This frequent religious perception has a counterpart in the primitive sense that it is better to exist than not to exist. Thus, when philosophy chooses the tie between being and goodness as a first principle, it does no more than embrace an intimation that runs through much of human experience.

This intimation could, however, be disappointed. Short of relying on revelation, speculative thought cannot deny that there may be some ultimate antagonism between the ideal and actuality, or between the inclinations of consciousness and the objective reality of the world. Nevertheless, to the extent we recognize hope as a virtue inseparable from love and love as something we cannot do without, we may still be willing to risk a commitment to the idea that being and good are joined.

DOMINATION AND COMMUNITY

The view that the formulation of an ideal of community is the highest calling of political theory has a long history. Before we embark on our project, we might draw from that history some warning and advice.

In modern politics, the politics of the liberal and the postliberal state, one can distinguish an inner and an outer circle. Within the inner circle, the main subjects of struggle have been the search for wealth and power by the nation and the distribution of private wealth and power within the nation. The issues of imperialism and nationalism, capitalism and socialism, are the central ones. The focus of concern is external or internal domination; the divisions between Right and Left come down to the different ways in which domination is viewed. The politics of the inner circle is the politics of reality in the liberal state, for it deals with the class organization of society and with the conflicting claims of class and role.

But in the history of modern political thought and action, there has always been an outer circle of reaction or utopia. The characteristic of this outer circle has been to subordinate the interest in class and role to an overriding concern with community. The division between Right and Left has consisted in different ways of defining the ideal of community and therefore of relating it to the present order of society. But both the Right and the Left of the outer circle have been condemned to marginality by their failure to accept the actual conditions of the modern state as the starting point of political action.

There are two main, loosely defined traditions within the outer circle of modern politics. Each offers a distinct solution to the problem of community. Together they bring out the two-faced character of the communitarian idea. One is the conservative corporativist doctrine of hierarchical community; the other the utopian socialist or anarchist conception of egalitarian community.

Conservative corporativism seeks to resolve the conflicts of the liberal state and of the bureaucratic institution by restoring an idealized version of the principle of estates. It looks to the corporate bodies of preliberal society as models for the ideal community. The social order is to consist of a hierarchy of groups, each represented in higher level associations and ultimately in a central government. The conservative corporativist must rely on two standards of corporate membership. He has to employ the criterion of membership in a particular institution because ranks are too large and abstract to serve as adequate bases for communities of shared purpose. But he also has to take rank position into account because the members of a given institution will ordinarily have conflicting beliefs and values according to their class or role (e.g., workers and managers in an industrial enterprise). Conservative corporativism is internally inconsistent, incapable of realization, and mistaken in its aims.[2]

First, though participation in an institution and participation in a rank are both indispensable criteria of membership in a communitarian body that respects the structure of modern society, they are on the whole irreconcilable because most institutions consist of individuals who differ in class or role. This irreconcilability strengthens the belief that only the transformation of society can establish the conditions of community. And it suggests that community is likely to emerge most rapidly in groups whose members both belong to the same class and perform similar roles.

Second, the corporativist doctrine shows a fatal misunderstanding of the circumstances of the liberal state. Forgetful of history, it proposes to resolve the problems of bureaucracy by reviving the very forms of social order whose dissolution created those problems in the first place. The awareness of personal dependence, once awakened, can no longer be completely stifled. If the fact of domination persists, as it must in a hierarchical society, every sharing of ends will in the end be recognized and rejected as coercive, a product of elite manipulation or factional interest.

Third, because it sanctifies an existing order of domination or proposes to put another one in its place, conservative corporativism fails to satisfy the ideal of the self. The individual and the social element of personality must remain at war with one another and sympathy unachieved as long as men are unable to enter into relations in which the sharing of purposes does not imply the permanent subjection of the wills of some to the wills of others.

The second major position in the outer circle of modern politics is the utopian socialist or revolutionary doctrine of egalitarian community. Despite the abundance of strands within this doctrine, some common themes persist. The objective is to establish a form of association that goes beyond class and role without restoring the estates and corporations of preliberal society. Sympathy is to be ensured through the creation of communities of shared purpose based on the greatest possible equality of conditions of power and participation in the making of the common ends. Abstract rather than concrete universality will be attained by the progressive confinement of the division of labor within the group and among groups. Each group must approach the condition of a self-sufficient society, and each individual that of a complete exemplar of the species. Thus, the development of the person has to be accomplished through the decentralization of society. And the social order will strive for natural harmony by giving freer play to instinctual needs within personality and by so simplifying the conditions of social life that man's life-giving relationship to nature can reassert itself at every turn.[3]

Seductive though the utopian socialist ideal of community may be, it suffers from defects almost as serious as those of conservative corporativism and analogous to them. First, the doctrine is saved from incoherence by a vagueness that allows it to mean everything and nothing. As soon as one attempts to make it concrete one has to deal with issues of power and freedom. But at that point, the utopian view comes up against a dilemma it is powerless either to escape or to solve. On one side, it imagines that the conflict between individuality and sociability, autonomy and community, can be resolved within the ideal association. On the other hand, it recognizes that the cohesion of the group may require the subordination of the individual element in personality to the social one.

A second objection to the utopian socialist doctrine of community is the failure it shares with conservative corporativism to take bureaucracy seriously. Instead of making use of the internal conflicts of the welfare-corporate state and working out their possible implications, it proposes to graft a new social order onto the existing one as an appendage or to transform society by a single revolutionary act of will. Thus, the Leftist conception of community typically appears in either of two forms. One is the utopian commune, a would-be island of harmony in the bureaucratic order, coexisting precariously with it rather than changing it from within. The other form is the revolutionary commune, which appears as a transitory body during the ardor of revolution, only to be sacrificed, after the revolution, to the needs of bureaucratic organization and centralized power, or to be itself made into a new bureaucracy.

The source of the preceding arguments against the utopian doctrine of community is a third, more basic difficulty. Until the problems of domination created by the hegemony of class and role are solved in the society at large, no alternative to the principle of subjective value can be found. The coercive and contingent character of every sharing of values will inevitably force men into the search for impersonal rules and into the attempt to institutionalize standards of merit. The result will be to perpetuate the experience of dependence and to institute still another form of domination in which the dictatorship of class is increasingly replaced by that of talent. The utopian commune itself will be at the mercy of the larger society: always in danger of being suppressed by it; always subject to the moral sentiments that life in that society has already inculcated in the members of the communal group. Only the simultaneous struggle for power in government as well as' within each of the bureaucratic institutions can overcome these obstacles.

The utopian commune provides an alternative image to the dominant social order and thus an inspiration to change it. But at the same time, by failing to subvert and destroy that order, it must in the end be subverted or destroyed by it. In its simultaneous hostility and submission to the state, it resembles both the family, the institution whose virtues it attempts to imitate in a purer and more universal way, and the abstract forms of the ideal in art, religion, and personal love.

Conservative corporativism and utopian socialism bring out the hierarchical and the egalitarian side of the idea of community. More generally, they exemplify the false alternative of idolatry and utopia in the understanding of the relationship between ideal and actuality. One embraces the corporations of past or present society as embodiments of the ideal. The other paints a picture of the ideal so vague and distant that it can serve as a reinforcement, even though also as a defiance, of the state.

We are now in a position to understand the relation between the inner and the outer circle in modern politics. Until the central problem of the inner circle, the problem of domination, is resolved, the search for community is condemned to be idolatrous, or utopian, or both at once. The lessening of domination depends on the victory of the Left over the Right within the inner circle, on the triumph of the program to which it has been devoted, with uneven clarity of insight and fidelity of purpose, since the French Revolution: the attack on imperialism in international relations, the subversion of the principle of class within the nation-state, and the confinement of the principle of role or merit through democracy internal to the bureaucratic institutions.

There are two important qualifications to the priority of the politics of domination over the politics of community. The first is that the overcoming of one kind of dominance must not become the occasion for the triumph of another. This will happen whenever the transitional character of the bureaucratic order is forgotten, its ideal of merit glorified, and the demands of institutional and government democracy sacrificed as antiquated, futuristic, or secondary.

A second, more fundamental qualification recalls the spiral of dominance and community. The progressive diminishment of domination makes community possible; the advance of community helps us understand and thereby erase domination. At different moments, the two aspects of this process demand varying degrees of attention. At first, the obstacles of domination are paramount, and community appears as the indeterminate ideal that guides political practice from afar. In time, this relation must invert itself if the ideal of the self is to be realized in society. As the harsher forms of domination are abolished, the issues of community gain the upper hand, and the problems of dominance remain as questions about the relations of groups to each other and to their members. Only the further universalization of community and thus the more precise definition of the good can respond to these questions.

All men should work toward the day when the priority of the fight against domination to the development of community will be reversed. Then at last will the calling of modern politics have been answered. The inner circle will be broken, and we shall escape into the outer circle, no longer to waver between utopia and idolatry, but to achieve the part of the good that can be realized in history.

THEORY AND PRUDENCE

Now that I have described the general idea of a view of the good and indicated its relationship to some traditional concerns of political thought, I am ready to put that idea to work. The theory of the good justifies a certain ideal of community. The study of the ideal and of its significance for modern society will occupy the latter sections of this chapter. As we turn to the implications of the doctrine of human nature for society, we should try to get clear about how much can be expected of philosophy as a political guide.

The vulgar attitude toward theory oscillates between the suspicion that philosophy can accomplish nothing and the demand that it do everything. Speculative thought is either dismissed as a mute goddess incapable of speaking to our practical concerns or worshipped as an idol whose lips can pronounce the secret of redemption. It seems always too simple to be true and too complicated to be helpful. Life is rich; therefore, comprehensive theories must be false. Life is short; therefore, they must be useless.

To understand correctly the importance of philosophy for practical choice one must acknowledge the difference between theory and prudence or practice and try to see wherein the difference lies. Prudence, as I mean it, is the knowledge of particulars or reasoning about particular choices. The concept of intuition has often been used to refer to the descriptive aspect of prudence, the direct apprehension of singular things, and the concepts of common sense or practical wisdom to its normative aspect, the capacity to judge rightly about concrete problems of choice. The term practice emphasizes conduct rather than the reflective understanding that may accompany it.

Throughout this essay, I have sought to throw off the shackles imposed by the liberal contrast of understanding and evaluation. But even when that contrast is swept aside, there remains the line between theory and prudence, a line with which the fact-value distinction is sometimes mistakenly confused. Theory and prudence each have both a descriptive and a normative side.

The chief difference between them is that one is abstract and the other concrete. Theory progresses by attaining an ever greater generality, which in turn implies a growing abstraction from the particularity of objects and events. We have examined before some consequences of this process of continuous abstraction for our ideas about knowledge. Let us now consider its moral and political significance.

If it is true that theory always involves generalization and abstraction, any political doctrine will be more or less remote from the particular contexts within which decisions must be made. There must come a point in its development at which it can no longer be made more concrete by the devices of theoretical reason. Different inferences may then be drawn from the doctrine to guide or justify decisions. There may still be reasons to prefer some of those inferences to others, but they will not be of the same kind as the reasons one has to prefer the doctrine in the first place.

Prudence, unlike theory, is inseparable from particular instances of choice or examples of conduct; it resists translation into general precepts; and it proceeds by analogizing particulars directly to each other without relying on abstract principles. Though our understanding of it remains in a primitive state, the practice of it is and has always been a pervasive feature of the moral life. I shall come back in a while to the issue of the nature of prudential judgment after putting the contrast of abstract and concrete knowledge in a historical perspective and indicating its bases.

Classic metaphysics was familiar with a distinction between speculative and practical reason, but it tended to phrase this distinction as a matter of the aim of each kind of thought—contemplation versus choice—rather than as a contrast of a logic of universals and a logic of particulars.[4] In the history of Western philosophy the idea that abstract and concrete knowledge are discontinuous though complementary has been attacked on two main scores. On the one side, there has been the tendency to claim possession of a theory or of a theoretical method that can also become concrete knowledge and teach people what to do in each situation. This belief is exemplified by certain kinds of Platonism, utilitarianism, and Marxism. On the other side, there has been the liberal view that choice is the province of arbitrary will.

The classic idea of theory as contemplation and of prudence as practical wisdom fails to appreciate that even a theory concerned with the rights and wrongs of conduct is unable to descend to the logic of particulars. The pretense of having a doctrine that overcomes the separation of abstract and concrete knowledge leads to a kind of charlatanism. By inflating the claims of philosophy and pretending to a certainty about practical affairs to which it is not entitled, it undermines both the usefulness of theory and the lucidity of practice. And the liberal belief that whatever is not abstract knowledge must be arbitrary choice throws us back into the dilemmas of subjective value from which we have been trying to extricate ourselves.

The reasons for the true distinction between abstract and concrete knowledge are methodological, metaphysical, and moral. The methodological reason is the dialectical relationship of theory and politics. Theory can never be fully concrete because at each moment its history depends on the condition of society. The progress of our theoretical ideas waits upon the transformation of experience and contributes to it. For theory to become concrete knowledge, experience would have to stand still long enough to allow one to work out all the practical implications of the premises it has made possible. This, however, never happens; each step in the development of a new way of looking at the world changes our experience of the world and forces us to go back to first principles.

The deeper metaphysical reason for the disjunction of theory and prudence is the impossibility of ever overcoming completely the gap between universals and particulars. The study of human nature has shown us that the universal and the particular aspect of personality, the demands of sociability and of individuality, of the abstract and the concrete self can never be fully harmonized. And in the course of criticizing liberal thought we have learned that a metaphysic which identifies universals and particulars is just as unsatisfactory as one which opposes them in the liberal manner. The search for a conception of universals and particulars that resolves the antinomies of liberal thought can temper the extremism of the antithesis and even change its character, but it cannot do away with the division itself. Thus, in morals we are still left with the conflict between the universalist ethics of principles or consequences and the particularist ethic of sympathy. And in politics, as later sections of this chapter will make clear, we confront the tension between the need each community has to become a universal association and its countervailing need to remain a particular one.

The contrast of theory and prudence is the cognitive counterpart to these moral and political disharmonies. It results from the confluence of a characteristic of the world and a feature of theory. Objects and events in the world have substance; they exist as particulars, each with its own identity. But theory presupposes a willingness to disregard some differences among particulars for certain purposes and to focus on others. Even as it succeeds in explaining the relations among things with an ever greater economy of means, it must forego any attempt to describe their particularity in a way that does justice to the richness of perception. So overwhelming has the influence of this mode of thought been that we have grown accustomed to identify it with reason itself. In so doing we have forgotten the existence of prudence, which thrives on the analogy of particulars rather than on the formulation of explanatory laws and on the appeal to concrete examples of right conduct rather than on the statement of moral principles. Generalizing explanation could not be the same as prudential perception unless we lived in another world.

There is, however, one form of knowledge that strides precariously across the gap between abstract and concrete knowledge. It is the knowledge of art. Aesthetic insight addresses particular situations, or it is inseparable from particular patterns, but these patterns and situations strike us as exemplary of widespread aspects of our experience. Yet in even the greatest art the logics of universals and of particulars push in opposite directions and constantly threaten to fall apart. The aesthetic synthesis never attains the transparency and the stability that would be needed to fashion a form of knowledge at once abstract and concrete, and capable of dictating a course of conduct as well as of providing a vision of the world.

The third reason for the distinction of theory and prudence is a moral one: it refers to the kinds of efforts that must be made by those who seek theoretical or prudential enlightenment. Theory is consummated in philosophy. Prudence as practical wisdom is the child of politics in the broad sense; it is won through the practice of leadership and association. But as theory and prudence reach their most powerful point in philosophy and politics, they make unlimited demands upon the time of their followers. Though philosophy and politics depend on each other, they resist combination in a single life. Those who mainly act must depend on those who chiefly theorize to help them understand the truth and the good. Those who theorize must rely on those who act to complete and to criticize their theoretical work in the realm of concrete judgment. But all such collaboration is cursed with the risks of misunderstanding and betrayal.

This obstacle, which has been the cause of so much rage since Plato, would be incomprehensible were it not the case that theory and prudence are in fact different enterprises and therefore require different gifts and exertions from those who take them up. Thus, the tragic difficulty in being a philosopher and a politician at the same time is ultimately tied to the disjunction of universals and particulars.

Viewed in the light of the distinction between philosophy and politics as forms of life, the discontinuity between theory and prudence turns out to be closely linked with the democratic ideal. If philosophy were a concrete knowledge, the best philosopher would indeed be the best ruler. But democratic doctrine must perhaps rely on the conviction that though men may vary greatly in their theoretical powers they all have or can easily hope to gain a measure of common sense roughly equal to that of their fellows. Hence, attempts to efface the boundary between speculative knowledge and practical wisdom carry the danger of elitism. When the thinker who claims to possess the charter of social order merges with the statesman who justifies his actions as a consequence of universal truth, where will ordinary people turn for support of their claims? They cannot wait for the hypothetical moment when theory will have become something that belongs to the masses, who would nurture it as an aspect of their political practice.

With the bases of the distinction of theory and prudence in mind, let us look more closely at prudential reasoning itself and at its place in the development of my argument. I have no worked-out account of prudence to offer, not because I believe such an account to be impossible or unimportant, but simply because I have not found one. The ideas that follow are merely tentative hypotheses, designed more to clarify the limits of theory than to portray what lies beyond them.

In every society, at each stage of the unfolding spiral of domination and community, we can find a core of more or less widely shared values, whose authority depends on the universality of their scope and duration as well as on the relative autonomy of individuals in the society. These values represent an interpretation of the species nature of man, and thus also of the legitimate uses of power, in the light of the society's own acquired conceptions of the good, the beliefs and experiences of other societies, and the available empirical ideas about human nature and social order.

Around this center of moral light lies the darkness of new problems or of old problems renewed by social circumstances. Between the light and darkness is the penumbra of debate, often extending far outward or reaching in toward the center, a twilight in which beliefs about the good are reexamined and changed. The master device of this penumbra is analogy. We compare the issues about which we have the greatest certainty with those that baffle us more. The decision to liken one instance to another, or to distinguish them, turns on a judgment of what differences and similarities are most significant to the moral beliefs at stake.

The procedure of analogical comparison presupposes that the issues one faces are linked as parts of a single moral universe. Nevertheless, their ties are not all simultaneously evident, nor does one's grasp of them remain static. Each new connection one makes in this network transforms his understanding of the connections he had already discovered.

Prudential reasoning of the sort described is needed to give content in each social situation to a number of key concepts in the doctrine of the good. Thus, it is by prudence rather than by theory that we choose which values to defend at a given moment, where to draw the limits of the concept of domination, and how to deal with the conflicting demands that inevitably face communitarian politics. Indeed, much of the issue of strategy, of the selection of means with which to realize the ideal in society, belongs to the domain of concrete knowledge. Hence, abstract knowledge can provide no general rule for the choice between persuasion and revolution.

Insofar as philosophy is universal theory, it can describe the framework within which, the process by which, and the ideals according to which practical judgments ought to be made. It can point out factors that practical choice should take into account, or preclude certain solutions as unacceptable. But it cannot sweep prudence aside. As a normative doctrine, its task is to act as a signpost for politics, not to replace it.

To many this will seem a disappointing result. They may object that it is precisely on the most urgent and important matters that speculative thought withdraws into silence. And they will in a sense be right. Our ordinary moral concerns are the problems of practical choice. We want to know what we ought to do here and now; whether we should permit a certain social practice or abolish it; whether we should disregard one kind of distinction among people and take another kind into account; whether we should commit our efforts to this objective or to that one. But whenever we try to speculate about such issues we characteristically make little headway. Because we cannot resolve the problems directly, we must take a detour and try to determine the theoretical premises upon which and the political conditions within which our moral judgments might become more secure. Only then will there be a hope of advance in the solution of the riddles of practical judgment.

That is why my argument is devoted to the revision of theory and to the description of a social ideal rather than to the study of concrete problems of choice. The need for the detour is a great misfortune. But it is a misfortune we must accept because it is the truth.

THE ORGANIC GROUP

General conception

The theory of organic groups has two aims. The first is to define the political implications of the view of the good I have sketched. The second is to suggest how the situation of modern society can be used to promote the good. If the doctrine were to content itself with the statement of an ideal, it would fall into utopianism. If it were to treat the study of the present or the prediction of the future as a surrogate for the elucidation of moral purpose, it would become idolatry.

The central conception of the theory is the idea of community. In discovering the inadequacy of the purely personal manifestations of the ideal of the self, we have also found their political complement in a certain experience of community life. The hypothetical image of a universal community whose practices reveal the species nature of man provides an interpretation of natural harmony. In such an association the sense of immanent order would be brought into harmony with the capacity of criticism or transcendence. A universal community would also resolve the paradox of sociability: as a kingdom of common ends, marked by each person's recognition of the concrete individuality of his fellows, it would dissolve the antagonism of the individual and the social aspect of personality. This community would make concrete universality possible for its members: each could develop his own talents through the division of labor in the assurance that his efforts participated in the advancement of human nature.

When we translate natural harmony, sympathy, and concrete universality into the concepts of the universal and the particular good, we find once again that they can only be realized fully by a universal community. The species nature is revealed and developed in history through the spiral of diminishing domination and increasing community. Thanks to that spiral individuals can hope to become more secure in the sense and in the expression of personality.

The ideal of universal community, like the ideal of the self from which it derives, is, however, incapable of being completely realized in history. The experiences of immanent order and of transcendence can never be wholly reconciled as long as man retains the gift of consciousness. No one can ever love everyone else as concrete individuals; nor can he lose all sense of his isolation from them without sacrificing individual identity. He is unable fully to represent his species nature in his own work and life.

We shall rediscover these imperfections at the very core of the problem of community: the different elements of the communitarian ideal ultimately conflict. Hence, the spiral of domination and community, always a risky venture, seeks an end it is forbidden to reach. Speculative thought must acknowledge a final, bitter, and unending struggle between what men can be and what they forever want to become. Whether there is some higher peace beyond history, but somehow perhaps prepared within it, philosophy is powerless by its own lights to say.

For these reasons, the notion of universal community is meant to serve as a regulative ideal rather than as the description of a future society. It is a limit never attained yet capable of providing guidance to those who try to approach it. To translate its message into the language of political possibilities, we need to distinguish different aspects of the communitarian ideal and then to determine in which way and to what extent each of those aspects can be represented in a form of social life. We must discover the institutional principles that might transform the general conception into a social order. These principles describe a kind of community I shall call the organic group.

The most obvious thing a doctrine of community tries to do is to determine what sympathetic social relations would look like and thus to describe the political equivalent of love. Two factors coalesce in sympathy: the communion of purposes by virtue of which each views the other as a complementary rather than as an antagonistic will, and the willingness to see and treat others as concrete individuals rather than as role occupants. The first institutional principle of the organic group will be concerned with the conditions under which these elements of sympathy might flourish.

The recognition of concrete individuality and the convergence of ends are not enough. Shared values help resolve the paradox of sociability to the extent they deserve to be taken as signs of the universal human nature in which the members of the group participate. And only then do they acquire the aspect of givenness that allows them to justify the experience of immanent order required by natural harmony and the authority to provide guidance for individual efforts in the spirit of concrete universality. So the second principle of the organic group must find an institutional counterpart to the spiral of domination and community by indicating the circumstances under which choice would become increasingly expressive of humanity.

The theory of organic groups would remain crucially incomplete if it did not go on to describe the overall form of work and of work relations. Natural harmony, sympathy, and concrete universality are particular as well as universal goods: their political expression must serve as a basis for the development of individuality as well as for the advancement of the species nature. The aim of the third principle of the organic group is to describe the kind of organization of labor that might make this possible.

I shall call these institutional principles the community of life, the democracy of ends, and the division of labor. They do not follow from the ideal of community with the same necessity with which the ideal of community follows from the doctrine of human nature: they call for a much broader range of empirical assumptions and a much looser set of inferences. Still, the principles can be stated in general form, and their generality keeps them within the realm of theory. With respect to each of them one should ask what precisely it implies for the ordering of social relations, which tendencies in modern society bear most directly on its realization, and what sorts of obstacles and objections to its achievement might be foreseen.

The argument should try to avoid the defects of the conservative corporativist and the utopian socialist view of community. And it should respect the prudential limits of theory. Unable to offer either a blueprint of social order or a prescription for social change, it has no choice but to accept the more modest job of pointing toward an image that lies beyond its field of vision. Alas, every man will find in the picture little to satisfy his desire to be told what to do and much to offend his wish to remain as he is.

The community of life

Definition. Community begins with sympathy. Sympathy means that people encounter each other in such a way that their sense of separateness from one another varies in direct rather than inverse proportion to their sense of social union. When individuality and sociability complement each other, others are viewed and treated as unique persons and as partners to whom one is bound by common purposes.

The acknowledgment of individuality and the communion of ends are unlikely to take hold unless two conditions are fulfilled. Each member of the group must have face-to-face dealings with all the other members. And each must live with them in so many different kinds of social situations that he can perceive them and act toward them as concrete individuals. Face-to-face coexistence requires that the size of the group be limited. Because of the importance of interaction among individuals in a broad range of life situations, the group must be the scene of many sorts of activities. An association characterized by face-to-face coexistence and by multipurpose organization is a community of life. The relationship of the institutional principle of the community of life to the initial conditions of sympathy, the recognition of individuality and the sharing of ends, is an empirical hypothesis rather than a logical inference.

Unless individuals deal with one another in a multiplicity of different ways, they cannot discover the organic unity of each other's personalities. When another is always seen as the performer of a particular role, he must tend to become that role, first in his fellows' eyes, then in his own. And unless the spectrum of interaction is broad, there will be no basis of common experience upon which common ends might develop. Or if they do develop, they will do so under the constraints of a particular specialized activity and of the outlook it imposes. The more rigid such outlooks become, the more will they hinder the growth of individual personality and the manifestation of the species nature in social practice.

In the bureaucratic institution, the bureaucrats labor together, but they do almost everything else separately. So they have a public language, based on shared experiences and conventions, to speak about work, but no common tongue in which to discuss their lives outside the group. When, however, the same individuals undergo together many different experiences, the insights and interests they acquire at work can no longer be kept apart from their views on the organization and aims of labor. Thus, the distinction between work and leisure, and between public and private existence, loses much of its force, and the oneness of personality is reaffirmed.

Multipurpose organization complements small-group interaction. Whereas the latter makes persons visible to each other, the former expands the variety of their encounters. In this way it both fosters the recognition of individuality and contributes to a shared experience from which shared ends might arise.

At first, the two defining elements of the community of life seem to fit together perfectly. The breadth of group life multiplies the number of ways in which men are drawn together. The intimacy of the small association makes multipurpose organization something that can add to the complexity of social encounters among the same persons without accentuating the division of labor. The larger the group, the less of a correspondence need there be between the number of activities practiced within it and the number each individual is expected to perform.

A conflict lurks beneath this symmetry, a conflict that becomes apparent when one thinks back to the ends the community of life is meant to express. The recognition of individuality is inseparable from the small group. In principle, others cannot be known and dealt with as real individuals unless they can be seen and touched in the flesh. Love may break through to the stranger or embrace a person whose ends contradict one's own, but only by an extraordinary and mysterious effort rather than by an ordinary exertion of sentiment. Unlike the acknowledgment of personality, the process of moral agreement becomes more perfect by becoming more universal. Thus, to accomplish one of its own essential aims, the community of life is forever tempted to destroy itself as a small group and to become a more universal association. But in so doing it sacrifices its other, equally important objective. This tragic conflict will reappear in a variety of forms and turn out to have portentous consequences for the entire endeavor of communitarian politics.

Possibilities. Now that the principle of life community and its inner dialectic have been defined, we can ask what sorts of institutions might serve as starting points for its realization and what kinds of problems one must reckon with in the effort to achieve it.

One of the institutions that comes closest to the community of life in our experience is the family. But there are several reasons why the family, as it exists in the modern state, constitutes an inadequate expression of community. It already exemplifies a rift between work and leisure, between the public and the private world. Established upon a cleavage in life, it fails as a sufficient basis for the affirmation of the unity and the completeness of personality. Because it is bound to the ties of blood and marriage, the family imposes a fixed limit to the free expression of sympathy. And there is no set of available mediating steps between the bureaucracy, based on role, and the family, founded on kinship. For all these reasons, the community of life must be a group distinct from the family.

The family nevertheless persists as both a primitive though profound expression of the values the community of life is meant to serve and as a limit to the universalizing tendencies of communitarian ideals. For the modern family forever draws men back into an association that competes with loyalties to all other groups and offers a measure of individual recognition through love, even in the absence of shared values. So communitarian politics must treat the family as both a source of inspiration and a foe to be contained and transformed. The conflict between family and community is just another aspect of the struggle between particularist and universalist tendencies that takes place within the communitarian ideal itself. Like that struggle, it can be moderated, but it cannot be brought to an end.

A more promising starting point for the realization of a community of life is the occupational group, exemplified by the bureaucratic institution. At first, the ordinary occupational group seems an even more implausible candidate than the family. A large factory, for example, to which workers come almost exclusively to produce a single commodity may provide few occasions for small-group encounters in diverse circumstances, and it may have no use for multipurpose organization. Nevertheless, the workplace is the point where the order of the public world comes into most sustained contact with the private longing to realize the ideal of the self. And because it provides so much of the scenario of daily life, its organization must be the foremost concern of an effort to break through the logic of the everyday and the extraordinary.

The welfare-corporate and the socialist state witness trends in the technical arrangement of labor that might be used to promote the transformation of occupational groups into communities of life. Everything depends on the kind of political action that directs their course. Decentralization may in fact be facilitated by technological developments that reduce the need for the concentration of large numbers of workers in a single enterprise or service. And similar tendencies may encourage the continuing expansion of the bureaucratic institution beyond the limits of single-purpose activity. On the one hand, the increase of 'leisure time' contributes to the possible diversity of community life even when specialization among groups increases. On the other hand, the effort to foster productivity may tend to bring the members of the occupational group more closely together by offering them joint facilities for housing, health care, education, or recreation.

In and of themselves, such tendencies are neither good nor bad. They can be mere devices for the control of labor that strengthen the bureaucratic character of institutions and the existing distribution of power in the society as a whole. Or they can be parts of a broader program of communitarian politics that wants to make it possible for men to encounter each other as concrete individuals outside the partial and private settings of family or friendship.

Problems. To each of the problems implicit in the effort to achieve the community of life there corresponds an important aspect of communitarian politics. The first set of issues has to do with centralization and specialization. Both decentralization and multipurpose activity may exact a high price in the production of goods and services. To some extent, this might be dealt with by policies of compromise. The community may be small and yet belong to a hierarchy of associations that provides many of the virtues of centralism without its burden of bureaucratic organization. The group may contribute to the larger society through one relatively specialized form of production and still provide a framework in which men may work and play together in a variety of situations. To this end, it is important for individuals to live in communities that foster shared interests and experiences extending far beyond the chief mode of productive labor in the group.

These measures, however, bring difficulties of their own, as the later study of the puzzles of communitarian politics will suggest. The deeper response lies in a kind of politics that refuses to reify the concept of efficiency, rejects the liberal belief in the separateness of means from ends, and proceeds on the assumption that the form taken by desires for consumption and power is never independent of the structure of social life. By undermining the barrier between productive labor for the larger society and other human activities, the organic group creates a brake to the aimless reproduction of needs and of means for their satisfaction. Questions about the forms and limits of material enjoyment become part of the broader issue of how life in the community should be lived, and it is as such that they are dealt with. Moreover, the greater the abundance of kinds of creative effort, the less need is there to escape from the boredom of work to the deadening hedonism of consumption. Thus, the same process by which the community of life is established can help moderate the impulses that stand in the way of its realization.

The second obstacle is the danger of utopian conservatism. To the extent class domination is not already destroyed in the society as a whole, the appearance of communities of life may make it even more difficult to deal with domination by leaving local groups all but impenetrable to the initiatives of centralized government. As a result, the community to emerge will be hierarchical rather than egalitarian, and its shared purposes will express little more than the convenience of the elites. For these reasons the effort to transform the workplace must establish an indissoluble alliance with the struggle for power at the national level, a particular aspect of the interplay between the politics of community and of domination.

The third difficulty is perhaps the most intractable and important, for its immediate source is the conflict between the individual and the social aspect of personality. The paradox of sociability reappears within the community of life as a paradox of group cohesion: insofar as sympathy in social life requires an allegiance to common ends, it threatens to destroy the individuality it wants to protect. By its very nature, community is always on the verge of becoming oppression. The existing consensus may be mistaken for the final expression of the good, and used as a justification for denying the humanity of individuals and rejecting the legitimacy of dissident groups.

A politics that responds to this threat must be one that emphasizes the transitory and limited character of all forms of group life as manifestations of human nature. Such a politics will be committed to the plurality and diversity of groups, and it will prize the conflictual process through which community is created and made universal above the preservation of any one collectivity. Each of these commitments, however, produces dilemmas to which we shall have to return after discussing the other principles of the organic group.

The democracy of ends

Definition. To serve as a basis for the realization of natural harmony, sympathy, and concrete universality, shared ends must be expressive of a human nature in which each individual participates in his unique way. Shared values begin to gain this authority as the spiral of domination and community is set in motion. The principle of the democracy of ends describes the features of group organization that can help do this.

Once the distribution of power according to class has been superseded in the institutions of the modern state, power may be allocated in a meritocratic or in a democratic manner. The meritocratic alternative relies on skill or talent to determine the place each should have in the division of labor and the degree of control over others' productive activities to which he is entitled. It is characteristically associated with the principle of role and with instrumental rationality. Its impulse is to define the internal affairs of the bureaucratic institution as technical rather than political because they deal more with means than with ends. The objectives of labor are taken for granted; somehow fixed from outside the institution; or established by a management that both belongs to the meritocratic division of labor and stands above it. The choice of means, however, is delegated to men whose skills and talents supposedly qualify them to make the best neutral judgments about the use of their own time or of the labor of others.

An organization is democratic to the extent it defines its problems as political issues and seeks to resolve them through a process of reciprocal persuasion and collective decision in which one view triumphs by winning more adherents than its rivals. As a basis for the arrangement of power, democracy shares what community represents as a general form of social relations: a deference to the individual founded on his concrete individuality alone instead of on his possession of particular attributes. Thus, the more perfect democracy becomes, the broader the range of personal concerns and capacities enlisted by its procedures of persuasion and decision.

The democratic principle can be found in varying degrees of purity. It is only dimly illustrated by a system of electoral representation in which the political activities of the citizen may be almost exclusively confined to the extraordinary episode of the vote, and the issues before him appear separated from the humdrum concerns of the institutions to which he belongs. Moreover, democratic and meritocratic ways of organizing power may and do coexist at many levels.

The democracy of ends in the organic group consists in the progressive replacement of meritocratic by democratic power in the ordinary institutions of society and, above all, in its occupational groups. Decisions about what to produce (whether the products be commodities, services, or knowledge), for which objectives to produce, and how to produce are increasingly defined as political and submitted to collective decision.

The principle of the democracy of ends provides the organic group with a method to formulate shared values and to ensure their preeminence over the life of the community. By expanding the range of political choice, it makes politics the master activity of day-to-day life, and everyman's pride and hope, the union of his love with his intelligence. At the same time that it fosters the development and elucidation of common purposes, it contributes to the overcoming of domination. It does this in an immediate sense by diminishing the importance of natural talents to the allocation of power. It does it in a more general way by helping create a circumstance in which all hierarchy appears more and more clearly as a political choice rather than as a technical given. Through this lessening of domination, the shared values may become ever more reliable signs of man's species nature.

There is, however, an apparent paradox in democracy. The democratic principle is hostile to the claims of meritocratic role organization and instrumental rationality because both of these distribute power in a nondemocratic manner. But as long as all shared values are acknowledged to be ultimately groundless, roles and means-ends judgments seem to be among the few assurances of impersonality in the exercise of power. They promise to limit, however imperfectly, personal despotism in everyday work relations. Thus, the paradox of democracy cannot be resolved without a solution to the problem of value, and this, according to the argument, depends on the change of bureaucracies into communities, which means in turn more democracy. Only the growth of institutional democracy can rob the democratic paradox of its force.

A deeper and more tragic tension within the democratic ideal is another aspect of that same conflict between particularism and universalism encountered before in the discussion of the community of life. Democracy means self-government; the connection it establishes between collective choice and individual participation must be a living experience. Yet the moral weight of the common purposes produced by the democratic process is ultimately inseparable from their universality. The former aim pushes toward the small group; the latter toward the worldwide republic. The issue of their reconciliation is just the general problem of how much and in which ways the demands of the universal and of the particular can be harmonized in social life as in human nature.

Standards of choice. The adoption of the democracy of ends describes a process of choice, but it does not establish the standards by which individuals engaged in that process ought to choose. Theory could not lay down universal principles of choice without trespassing upon the domain of prudence and lending a spurious authority to the beliefs and practices of a particular society or age. Nevertheless, there is the reverse danger that without some modest guidance democratic deliberation in the community may revert to an acceptance of the subjectivity of values. In fact, however, the theory of organic groups suggests two kinds of elements that should be considered in the practice of institutional democracy.

One set of factors has to do with the experience of other groups, involved in the same historical project. If it is true that common purposes indicate man's species nature only insofar as they become universally shared, the organic group must constantly look for inspiration to the experience and commitments of other groups as it develops its own ends and refines its own views of dominance. The perfection of each community is inescapably restricted by the progress toward the ideal made by the rest of national society and ultimately by all mankind.

The moral interdependence of associations means that the first basis of choice in the democracy of ends is circular. Like the circle of domination and community, however, it appears closed only when taken out of the dimension of time. Moral and political genius consists precisely in the capacity to transcend past visions of the good and to anticipate future ones. But whenever these revolutionary acts are looked at more closely, it will be found that they were made possible by an interpretation of what might be learned about human nature from the experience of their times.

The second category of considerations refers to what might be called the good of the community, the continual safeguarding and improvement of the institutional principles inferred from the theory of the good. Fidelity to those principles is the condition for the understanding and achievement of other values. Hence, in his democratic deliberations each person should have the good of the community permanently before his eyes. His foremost concern must be the effect a measure will have on the group as an institution characterized by the community of life, the democracy of ends, and the division of labor. The implication of these principles for particular practices are likely to vary with material circumstances and with each group's place along the spiral.

Distributive justice. There are, however, certain practices about which more can be said in a general way because they affect directly the basic pattern of relations in the community. These are the ways in which the divisible benefits of group life are distributed.

To work out the implications of a democracy of ends for distributive justice, it may be useful to set the issue of distribution against the background of a view of the history of ideas about equality. Inequality is always social, that is, recognized and established in society. Nevertheless, some of the infinite number of differences among individuals originate partly in nature, though it is society that establishes the significance of those differences for the allocation of power and wealth. Two of these natural distinctions are particularly salient: the inequality of physical force and the inequality of talents useful to other persons or admired by them.

The historical progression of ideas about equality lies in this. At first, the natural inequality of physical strength may be an important social concern so that the state's initial task is to compensate for it by becoming the monopolist of violence. Then the inequalities of a strictly social origin, exemplified by estates and classes, become major features of social life and subjects of political contention. But with the supersession of estates and classes natural inequality in the form of inherited differences of ability again comes to occupy the forefront of thinking about justice.[5]

Because of these differences in capacity, our political purposes are constantly in danger of defeat by the caprice of nature, which threatens us with a world of irremediable inequality and unquenchable envy. In our efforts to grapple with this predicament we might find the hint of a solution in Goethe's warning that "against the superior gifts of another person there is no defense but love."[6]

As long as men are rewarded according to their productive capacities, the distribution of goods will continue to reflect the same inadequate ideal that underlies meritocratic power and the association of roles. Hence, the main problem of distributive justice for the organic group is the discovery of a standard of distribution that might override the natural inequality of talents just as the democratic principle disregards this inequality in the assignment of fundamental powers of participation.

One way to approach this problem is to attempt to compensate the element of effort in work without rewarding the factor of natural capacity. Apart from the difficulty and dubiousness of any such distinction, there is a more basic reason a standard of productive effort should not become the final distributive criterion. It stops short of the ideal of sympathy, whose social implications the community of life and the democracy of ends spell out. Sympathy is most completely achieved when man's day-to-day labor is itself an expression of his reconciliation with others, both in the ends it serves and in the form it takes. But this cannot occur as long as man is treated as a producer whose work entitles him to acquire what his fellows are denied.

Whenever individuality and sociability are viewed as antagonistic principles, a person's dependence on others and on the products of their labor has to be seen as a mere constraint on the satisfaction of his desires. But the theory of the self teaches us that interdependence is an intrinsic part of individual personality; the form of our individuality is determined by the character of our sociability. A person manifests his own nature by the particular way he needs other human beings. Thus, there must be universal as well as particular needs in the same sense that there is a universal and a particular human nature. The distribution of benefits could therefore only respond fully to the sympathetic ideal by treating man as a being who has needs that reveal both his concrete individuality and his common humanity.[7]

There are two serious difficulties with the distributive criterion of need. It has no self-evident content; we lack standards by which to establish a hierarchy of needs. Moreover, a pure need principle might have ruinous economic effects when sympathy, though accepted as an aim, did not yet flourish as a sentiment. The community might find this an intolerable penalty to pay during a period in which the accumulation of goods remained necessary to the furtherance of its other ends.

For these reasons, the organic group must start by combining a standard of merit with one of need. And as it defines the basic needs that ought to be satisfied independently of capacity or effort, it should do what it does when it begins to define domination: to look for the most tangible and most widely recognized. Their satisfaction will then be treated as an absolute entitlement.

As the organic group progresses, its democratically chosen ends come closer to showing man's species nature, and individual capacities are realized more completely. The more we understand man's species nature, the better we are able to define the needs he has just because he is human and the relative priority of these needs in the order of his humanity. The more individuality develops, the easier it is to establish the particular needs of individual persons. Thus, one may hope to give an increasingly concrete and accurate content to the idea of need as it becomes the supreme distributive guideline of the organic group. The problem of distribution is resolved by the very same process through which meritocratic power changes into democratic power and the association of roles into a community of life.

Possibilities and problems. In Chapter Four I alluded to movements that might turn out to represent first steps toward institutional democracy. An example is the concern with worker sharing in the management of industry and, more generally, with participation by all bureaucrats in the institutions in which they work. Such initiatives in turn evoke the more basic departures from bureaucracy represented by socialist experiments with 'workers' councils' and other communitarian kinds of labor organizations. With respect to distributive justice, there are the welfare-state and socialist tendencies to recognize entitlements to the satisfaction of minimal needs, though on a national rather than on an institutional level.[8]

The task of politics is to carry such tendencies further; to place them in the broader context of the proliferation of organic groups throughout the society; and to avert the danger to individuality inherent in any tendency to make all life subject to public discourse and political choice. Unless they become part of such a broader program, trends toward institutional democracy may reinforce bureaucratic order instead of undermining it. Therefore, it is important to clarify the major difficulties raised by each element of the program.

First, one has to determine how far to carry the change from meritocratic to democratic procedures. In a sense, the answer is straightforward. The ultimate foundation of all power in the organic group must be democratic decision. The mere possession of skills can never in itself justify material advantages or the exercise of power. Nevertheless, a relentless insistence on deciding collectively all significant matters would make work flounder in a morass of political argument. It would strike at the group's capacity to produce anything but complaints, exhortations, and eloquence. And it would undermine the possibility of a division of labor in which the talents of each could be brought to fruition, for specialization allocates meritorious power.

The decision about which matters to subordinate directly to democratic choice and which to have decided by individuals selected for their special capacities cannot be settled in a permanent and general way. Like the issues of the size and specialization of the community, it must be resolved by prudential judgment.

Here too prudence has standards to go by, standards to which only the empirical understanding of changing circumstances can give particular content. The assignment of tasks should conform to the democratically determined common values both in the objectives it promotes and in the system of social relations it establishes. Moreover, differences of power among individuals must on no account become so pronounced that they subvert equal participation in the democracy of ends. Men whose everyday experience is one of submission or of predominance cannot be expected to think and to act as equals when they pass upon the affairs of the group. Finally, no notion of efficiency should be allowed to determine automatically the limits of democratic power. We must wait to see how the content and direction of desires will be reshaped by the group's new political experience.

A second set of problems has to do with the relationship between democracy in the institution and in the society. The struggle for institutional democratization makes sense only when accompanied by political action in the broader arena of national and supranational society. There are two reasons for this. Each group must seek instruction from others, and each depends on a certain concord among communities. Moreover, internal democracy moves forward as class domination is destroyed and the forces that support meritocratic power defeated. It is impossible as long as capital or an independent management, imposed from above or outside, controls the affairs of the group.

The third and deepest difficulty goes to the limits and dangers of politics. The principle of the democracy of ends recognizes that everything can be brought into the arena of public discourse. Nevertheless, though the boundary between public and private life is a shifting one, its effacement would corrupt the group. For a disregard of the limits of collective decision would mean either a denial of the gap between the demands of individuality and of sociability or a sacrifice of the former to the latter. In either case, it would spell the end of autonomy. At any given moment, some matters are properly beyond politics, but nothing is beyond it inherently or forever.

To affirm that the public world can never be absorbed completely into the private one because human nature is torn between its universality and its particularity is another way of saying that no set of democratically chosen practices can ever be either universal or particular enough to satisfy the full range of an individual's longings. The limits of politics are another side of the imperfection of all our efforts to achieve the good and to represent it in a form of social life. Thus, the appropriate political response to the limits is one that takes the imperfection seriously. Politics should keep away from those matters whose privacy at the time seems most important to strengthen the individual's capacity to transcend the experience of his age and his group and to initiate experiments in humanity.

The division of labor

Definition. The community of life and the democracy of ends describe the attributes of sympathetic associations whose practices manifest the species nature. But these institutional principles fail to define the significance to the group of the individual's particular good: the perfection of his talents and the affirmation of his sense of self. To do this is the aim of the principle of the division of labor.

The ideal of concrete universality establishes the general form of the achievement of the particular good. The principle of the division of labor is the political embodiment of that ideal. It holds that the allocation of tasks should allow each individual to develop his unique dispositions so as to serve and to express values or practices whose legitimacy as signs of the species nature he can recognize. But by what steps can the division of labor, the very heart of the bureaucratic order and the favored tool of domination, become instead the expression of concrete universality?

The first condition is the observance of the other institutional principles. Unless there were a community of life, the division of labor would make it impossible for men to know and treat each other as concrete individuals. Unless there were a democracy of ends, the powers conferred by the specialized work would be forms of dominance. A second requirement is that the division of labor should be arranged so as to allow the individual to understand and to experience the connection between his particular work and the more universal ends that give it meaning.

Both conditions imply a commitment to make the division of labor less rigid and to diminish its influence over individual existence. The community of life and the democracy of ends limit the extent to which an individual's time should be spent in specialized tasks. They presuppose a continuing set of social relations and political activities whose very nature is to dispense with any specialization, for one enters into them as a person rather than as a craftsman. Moreover, as the division of labor becomes extreme it produces its own hierarchy of power that undermines the communitarian and democratic character of the group.

Similar conclusions follow from the need to emphasize the tie between the species nature and the individual labors through which it is particularized and advanced. If the individual always views the ideals that justify his work from the perspective of a single job, he may fail to grasp their scope and to appreciate the contributions his fellows can make to them. And unless he can experiment continuously with different forms of life, he may lose the sense of his own ability to transcend his place in the social order and to make of his own work the voice of the universal as well as of the particular element in himself.

These demands suggest some practical objectives. The organic group should make use of a number of different criteria of ranking. Individuals who exercise power in one respect should be subject to power in another.[9] The rotation of tasks can be used as a moderating device. Lastly, there may be jobs in the group whose performance is indispensable, but are generally abhorred, have little value for the development of talents, or stand at too great a distance from the ideals they serve to satisfy the aspirations of the abstract self. The group must assume these tasks as a common burden until technical progress makes them unnecessary.

Though the principle of the division of labor requires that specialization be tempered, it does not prescribe that it be abolished. On the contrary, it embraces differentiation of life and work as an integral part of the good. Indeed, the more communitarian the group becomes, the less do differentiation and community operate as antagonistic forces. Looked at more closely, the texture of community consists in a series of bonds of friendship. The stronger the attachments these smaller associations have to each other, the less is each group threatened in its internal cohesion by differences among its members. Each becomes at once less important as a haven against the conflicts of social life and less dependent on the similarity of its members to hold them together against a hostile environment.[10]

Nevertheless, there is a crucial flaw in the principle of the division of labor that reflects the unresolved tension in the idea of concrete universality and parallels the defects of the democracy of ends and the community of life. To be perfect, the division of labor would have to express the universal ends of a universal community, for only then could it satisfy man's longing to overcome his finitude by living for the universal. But anything on earth that could be universal would also be remote from the concerns an individual has as a particular being. Only God, if He exists, would combine universality with immediate presence.

As the tension between the abstract and the concrete self stretches to the breaking point, the individual loses the capacity to see his own conduct as a representation of transcendent ideals. Instead those ideals seem taskmasters that enslave him. Thus, he is torn between the desire to belong to a division of labor whose setting is a universal community and the wish for one whose framework remains the small group. This opposition arises from his incapacity to manifest his species nature fully and directly in his own lifetime. Thus, it presents still another aspect of the irreconcilable conflict of universality and particularity.

Possibilities and problems. Attempts to diminish the division of labor have the same double-edged character as trends toward community or institutional democracy. They can become either superficial accommodations of human desires that leave the structure of power unchanged or occasions for a politics of the organic group.

Such a politics will take the claims of efficiency in the division of labor into account, but also constantly review and criticize them as the experience of community redirects human wants. It will acknowledge that only democracy within the institution and outside it can keep specialized work from being a form of oppression. And it will be sensitive to the inability of any allocation of tasks to satisfy the cravings of either the abstract or the concrete self. That is why it must resist all attempts to sanctify a particular division of labor. Instead, it should cherish those acts of defiance or genius, of art or play, by which the wholeness of human nature shines for a brief moment upon the world.

Conclusion

The institutional principles of the community of life, the democracy of ends, and the division of labor presuppose and reinforce each other. All of them suffer from the implications of the conflict between universalism and particularism in man's relation to the world. And all of them call for a communitarian politics whose distinguishing features are the critique of efficiency, the alliance between politics in the institution and politics in the society at large, and the acknowledgment of the limits to politics itself.

Some questions of great moment to the political achievement of the good remain open. What powers ought the groups to have over their members? This is the problem of freedom. How should the groups be ordered among themselves? This is the problem of the state. What is the relationship between intragroup solidarity and intergroup concord, and between the ideal structure of the group and the ideal process of its development? This is the problem of the dilemmas of communitarian politics. What is the significance of the imperfection of community? This leads to the problem of God.

FREEDOM

Many of the liberal thinkers were devoted to freedom, though their false metaphysical principles almost always kept them from grasping its true character. If for no other reason than for this devotion, they will rank forever as heroes and teachers of the human race, and all the sins of England will be forgiven because of her services to liberty.

Under the influence of liberal thought, common usage defines freedom as the nonexistence of external interference with one's ability to do what one wants. The term is often narrowed down to mean the absence of human or even only government compulsion. The antithesis of liberty is domination.

One objection to this concept of freedom is its fatal imprecision. The self cannot be imagined apart from social relations; it is a vain endeavor to extract the person and his strivings from the bonds of association with other men. Their conduct impedes, facilitates, and encourages his own in countless ways. The real issue of freedom is to distinguish legitimate and illegitimate power, for only the latter represents domination. To draw the distinction, however, one has to rely on a view of the good. If the good is the achievement of the ideal of the self, that ideal ought to be the criterion with which liberty is defined.

Another defect of the traditional usage is the apparent incongruity between its intention and its statement. The hostility to coercion seems to arise from an acknowledgment that what is good for the individual and what he chooses for himself are not entirely separable even though they may not be identical. Domination is hateful because it keeps a man from being himself. Once again, the doctrine of freedom makes sense only as part of a view of the self or the good.

Thus, we are led to redefine freedom as the measure of an individual's capacity to achieve the good. One is free according to the perfection of this power. Even the liberal might agree with this definition as long as the good were conceived as the development of the individual's particularity through his own choices. The antiliberal, for his part, would consider only the universal aspect of the good and define it as a set of objective or communal values. Hence, he might be forced to the seemingly paradoxical conclusion that any sort of imposed conformity to such a good constitutes freedom regardless of the means by which it is exacted.

Both interpretations are inconsistent with the view of the good advanced in this essay. The good for each individual has a universal as well as a particular aspect so that neither the affirmation of individuality nor the obedience to principles or practices suffices to characterize freedom. Instead, freedom lies in the relationship between the universal and the particular good, and between choice and value, portrayed by the theories of human nature and community. Individual choice is important both as a manifestation of individuality and as a sign of the species nature, a nature never fully represented by any set of shared values. But one may be mistaken about mankind or about oneself, choose wrongly, and thus become less rather than more free: value, though revealed by choice, always transcends it.

Therefore, the condition of freedom is the same spiral of domination and community through which one arrives at a better understanding of the good. So liberty is in a sense simply the reverse side of the institutional characteristics of the organic group; it is for the insight generated by the experience of community itself rather than for philosophy to make the doctrine of freedom more concrete.

Nevertheless, there are certain fixed outer limits to the entitlement of the group or of a democratic majority within it to impose measures that embody its shared ends on individuals who dissent from those measures. The argument for these independent limits is simple, and it follows directly from the general definition of freedom and from the doctrine of organic groups.

Freedom describes the individual's power to achieve the good. The good insofar as it is capable of social realization becomes available to the individual through the establishment of organic groups. Such groups are defined by the institutional principles of the community of life, the democracy of ends, and the division of labor.

These principles turn out to be meaningless or flawed unless certain all but unconditional defenses of the individual against the imposition of group power are respected. Thus, through the mediation of the doctrine of organic groups, freedom as the power to achieve the good requires more particular freedoms as entitlements to disregard group decisions and shared values. These liberties correspond to the three institutional principles of the organic group: a freedom of joining and leaving groups to the community of life; a freedom of expression to the democracy of ends; a freedom of choosing the character of one's work to the division of labor.

A forced membership in the community of life or a prohibition of departing from it violates the conditions on which its being is based. Suppose that there are many organic groups already established, each united by an initially distinct set of common experiences and shared purposes. The individual should be able to choose which of them to join or to leave in view of his own experiences and purposes. Otherwise, the distribution of individuals in the groups will be random with the result that the coalescence of beliefs and ideals in the communities may be rendered difficult or impossible. But this coalescence is indispensable to the group and the prerequisite to a later, more ample concord among groups.

Another foundation of the liberty of joining and leaving is the need of the community of life to work toward a form of social existence in which domination progressively disappears. But to be compelled to join the group or to remain in it against one's will is to be subject to a kind of second-order domination that corrupts social relations within the group. Sociability cannot satisfy the sympathetic ideal if it is established through an imposed restriction on individuality.

Lastly, if there is a relative specialization of labor among groups, the individual must be able to choose a community in which his peculiar capacities can be brought to fruition. Deprived of this freedom, the person will not be able to achieve his particular good, whose realization is one of the bases of the community of life. The same argument suggests, though it does not necessarily imply, that the individual ought to be entitled to be a member of various groups. The prudential problem will then be to reconcile the requirements of a community that embraces many aspects of life with the possibility of plural membership.

The second liberty the group may not violate is the freedom to express ideas. This freedom is required by the democracy of ends. The democratic principle establishes a procedure for the development of shared purposes. They carry weight insofar as they reveal both the individual natures of those who collaborated in making them and the species nature of man. Choice cannot show either the individual or the species nature unless there is freedom of expression in the group.

The discussion of self and others has shown how it is only through communication in society that individuality can be developed and revealed. Moreover, the species nature in which all individuals participate is hidden. To discover it and to express it in common purposes of social life, men must be able to compare their individual views and to discuss the grounds for those views.

The ultimate basis of freedom of expression is the relativity of the insight that any set of shared ends and beliefs can give into the character and ideal of a humanity. These ends are signs of the good, not the good itself, and so they must remain short of a completely universal concord and a final realization of the ideal in history. For this reason, there is always the possibility that the beliefs which have triumphed in the society of organic groups may differ from what they ought to be.

Indeed, there is the danger that the entire conception on which such a society is founded may be false and evil, as anyone must admit who has grasped how the antinomy of theory and fact makes knowledge imperfect. The interest in truth is supreme, for the first requirement of progress toward the good is to know the good. Therefore, an association that seeks to bring its common ends ever closer to the ideal must protect and encourage the freedom of expression in the awareness that a single proud and rebellious individual may show his fellows or his posterity that the truth about the ideal is utterly opposed to what they have imagined it to be.

The third freedom that follows directly from the institutional features of the organic group is the liberty of work. It is a requirement of the principle of division of labor. The freedom of work entitles the individual to choose which of his capacities to develop and whether to develop them within the established forms of the division of labor or outside them.

The division of labor is justified as an actualization of concrete universality. Thus, it is another way in which man's universal and his particular good may be realized more fully. For this realization to happen, the person's efforts within the group must be expressive of capacities in which he himself is able to recognize the mark of his individual being and aspirations. The fundamental guarantee of the possibility of such a recognition is the freedom to choose the kind of work one will do. It is through the liberty of work that the diversity of individual talents and of modes for their accomplishment may continually enlarge and improve the species nature.

The liberties of group membership, of expression, and of work represent a sort of constitutional charter of freedom. That charter is based on the very structure of the organic group and on the generic conception of liberty as the individual's power to achieve the good. To be sure, not even the doctrine of freedom can dispense with the need for prudential judgments that give concrete content to its abstract dictates or specify their meaning and establish their limits. The freedoms may always conflict with one another or with the survival of the institutional conditions that make them possible. Nevertheless, these liberties are so important to the organic group and to the ideal it represents that they ought never to be interpreted without reverence, nor restricted without trembling.

THE STATE

The organic group can come into existence only in the context of an emerging society of organic groups just as the bureaucracy is part of a whole form of social existence. The community of life, the democracy of ends, and the division of labor restrict the size of the collectivities in which men are to spend most of their day-to-day lives. Yet each of them also calls for a universal association capable of expressing a universal humanity. The task of the doctrine of the state is to examine the sense in which the conflict between the idea of the small group and the idea of the universal republic might be resolved. Its premise is the plurality of groups; its wish that the society of these groups might itself acquire the characteristics of community; its curse that this wish can at best be partially fulfilled.

Let us start with the fact of plurality. It is a good as well as a given: each group must rely on the experience and practice of the others to guide its own search for the ideal. But once plurality is granted, all the problems of liberal thought seem to spring up again with the difference that they apply to the relations among members of different communities rather than to every encounter among individuals. What is to keep the groups from destroying each other if they are separated by their places in the societal division of labor and consequently by the experience with which they provide their members? By what criteria can power be exercised over the groups? Must intergroup relations have all the features of liberal society?

If we conceive of society as a hierarchy of associations, leaving aside for the moment the question as to whether it is also a hierarchy of communities, the state is the highest-level association. Its first aim is to stand above the organic groups and to establish the peace among them. To accomplish this, it must have already helped subvert class and meritocratic dominance. As long as these persist, the spiral of domination and community cannot unfold with the result that there is no basis for an authoritative sharing of ends among groups.

The second aim of the state is individual freedom. The basic liberties of membership, expression, and work require protection by a body other than the very one whose powers they restrict. At the same time that the state guarantees the individual from the group, the group serves as a buffer between the individual and the state, protecting the former from the encroachments of the latter.[11]

The ends of peace and freedom, however, are insufficient either to distinguish such a state from the liberal state or to provide standards for the resolution of intergroup conflicts. There remains the risk that the relationship among associations may simply repeat the antagonism among individuals described by liberal political doctrine. The third aim of the state must therefore be to develop institutions that imitate in the relations among groups what the community of life, the democracy of ends, and the division of labor accomplish within the organic group.

There is the need for a type of association capable of replacing the community of life as a basis for the gradual development of common moral purposes among groups. For this reason, individuals should be allowed to belong to several groups insofar as this is consistent with the internal organization of each. Communities with similar places in the division of labor should be brought together in wider collectivities, and these in turn placed within still more inclusive associations. At each step in this ladder, the higher-order associations will be responsible for coordinating the activities of the lower-order ones and for carrying out tasks the latter are unable to perform alone. We shall see later that, though plural membership and associational hierarchy provide occasions for the elaboration of common purposes and the acknowledgment of concrete individuality, they exact a potentially intolerable price.

The achievement of a democracy of ends in the sphere of group relations builds upon the idea of a hierarchy of communities. Each higher step or organization must reflect the same preeminence of democratic over meritocratic power that prevails within the organic group. Otherwise, the activities of these overarching institutions themselves will represent a kind of dominance. To build the chain of groups that culminates in the state, the technique of occupational and territorial representation seems unavoidable, despite its vices.[12]

The foremost concern of the representative bodies should be the confinement of technical staffs to auxiliary functions and the subordination of instrumental rationality to political choice. The major problem is the need to reconcile a broad measure of autonomous power in the organic groups with the existence of larger associations culminating in the state. Without the former, the groups would lose an indispensable foundation of community, and their internal democracy would become meaningless. Without the latter, there would be no basis for peace and for a more perfect understanding and realization of the good.

The responsibility of the state for the division of labor is twofold. On the one hand, it must coordinate the activities of the organic groups so that there can be a division of labor among them. The specialization of group tasks seems necessary to broaden the spectrum of jobs in the society; if each group must be a microcosm of the entire social order, its internal differentiation has to remain severely limited. On the other hand, the state must be the setting in which ideals that transcend the experience of any one organic group can be expressed and developed. In this way, it fosters concrete universality by helping make the allocation of tasks within each community more expressive of the species nature. The quest for the universal imposes on the state a special obligation to propagate the works of genius, for the history of these works is the history of human nature itself, made explicit and permanent. It will not be surprising to discover that both the specialization of community tasks and the diffusion of universal culture threaten as well as strengthen the organic group.

With what entity can the state I have described coincide? As long as it continues to be the equivalent of the modern nation-state, it is still a partial association and to that extent an inadequate setting for the discovery of the species nature. Moreover, the task of modeling relationships among collectivities on relationships among individuals within the single organic group would remain unaccomplished in the international sphere. Consequently, there would be an insuperable obstacle to the better understanding of the ideal and to the further improvement of life within the organic group. Only when the state has become a world state and its peace a world peace can the good become as fully present to us as the limitations of politics allow.

THE DILEMMAS OF COMMUNITARIAN POLITICS

In developing a conception of the social ideal and of its relationship to the actual condition of society there is always the danger of glossing over the risks and difficulties that accompany the birth of a form of life. One passes all too easily from remorseless savagery in the criticism of the past to child-like innocence in the anticipation of the future. Thus, one encourages the mistaken belief that the ideal can be fully realized in history.

The opposite error would be to suppose that the hard choices faced by a society of organic groups are really the same as those of the society it seeks to displace. The dilemmas of communitarian politics may indeed resist solution. Yet they shift the focus of political struggle so as to draw out the ultimate conflicts among different aspects of the social ideal. These conflicts reveal and establish the outer limits of our ability to attain the end philosophy prescribes for us.

The first dilemma goes to the relations among groups. The second deals with the relationships between communal bodies and the higher-level organizations that coordinate them, or, more concretely, with the tie between community and state. The third dilemma has to do with disputes between established and emergent communities. The fourth is concerned with the reciprocal position of group values and universal culture and therefore with the place of philosophy in politics.

Two polar images might describe relations among organic groups. Each of those images has important attractions and fatal weaknesses. The first of them is the model of vertical integration. It sees each group as a relatively self-sufficient and closely-knit community, a commune very different from present occupational bodies. This means that there may be little division of labor among groups, but a great deal of it within them. The alternative pole is the model of horizontal integration according to which each association performs a narrowly limited range of activities, but interacts constantly with other communities. Consequently, there may be scant division of labor within groups, but much of it among them. The horizontal-integration model might focus on existing occupational groups as starting points of political action.

The policy of vertical integration seems hardly consistent with the commitment to an industrial civilization, for it imposes a strong barrier to the dimensions of collaborative work. Moreover, vertical integration represents a threat to individual autonomy: it seems that a system of vertically integrated communities could work only if there were significant restrictions on the freedom to join and leave them. At the same time, vertical integration keeps us from resolving the problem of self and others in our relationships to all but the persons who belong to the same group as we do. As a corollary, there will be no context for a universal moral experience upon which universally shared values might be based. And the extreme diversity of experience may encourage a destructive antagonism among the groups and deny them the criteria by which to choose among their competing ideals.

The dangers of horizontal integration seem just as serious. If there is a marked division of labor among groups, membership in each group will require the mastery of specialized skills or talents and the performance of particular tasks. Will not the group become an association of role players rather than a community of common purpose? And must not their specialization, like their isolation, produce moral conflicts favorable to war?

Another dilemma arises when we try to think of a hierarchy as well as of a plurality of associations. There are two extreme ways of conceiving the relationship between the groups and the state or, more generally, between the groups and higher-level institutions. On one view, the higher organizations are simply coordinating devices, with little reality of their own as communities; the state is just the constitutional order of the organic groups. On the opposite view, the superior institutions are real groups in their own right; the state is a community of communities.

An objection to the idea of the state as the constitutional order of the organic groups is that the weakness of the higher-order institutions would make it difficult to avoid the eruption of conflict among the baseline collectivities. This difficulty is merely the symptom of a deeper problem: unless the ideal of community is embodied in associations ever more extensive than the small group, the spiral may not only stop advancing but start to unwind. One of the conditions for the authority of communal beliefs and allocations of power is their progressive corroboration or revision in the light of the emerging consensus of a more universal community. Without such an appeal, the organic group turns into a solipsistic moral universe, caught in the trap of subjective value.

These difficulties may tempt us to grasp at the opposite idea of the state as a community in itself. But insofar as the higher-level agencies become more than instruments of coordination, they threaten to sap the vitality of the organic groups. A community makes demands upon the time of its members; it cannot survive unless they are constantly involved in its politics and thereby irresistably drawn away from the concerns of their original groups. The scarcity of time and the primacy of politics in communal life conspire against the division of loyalties that a hierarchy of communities implies. Still more disturbing is the possibility that the state may be incapable of becoming a true community even if one would want it to. Because it is by hypothesis an association of strangers, it cannot rely on the face-to-face coexistence and the common experience that might encourage shared purpose and the recognition of concrete individuality.

The third dilemma grows out of the competing demands made by old and new communities. Every community sets its seal upon the social world; it orders the activities of its members and their relations to the members of other groups. If all groups are free to move into the territory of an established association or to exert influence upon it in other ways, the disruption of communal experience may be so frequent and far-reaching as to be destructive of community existence. Each organic group may have the power to pass a death sentence upon the others by simply intruding upon their internal forms of life.

Nevertheless, the spiral of domination and community progresses through constant experiments in association. Unless emergent groups are free to develop and are not disadvantaged in relation to existing ones, there is the danger that a partial vision of the good will be petrified and the spiral arrested. Fundamental changes in moral vision may be more difficult to consummate within established communities than within new ones. Indeed, it seems likely that the threat to turn one's back on the community and join or create another one is a factor in making the group sensitive to criticism and capable of transformation.[13]

The fourth major tension opposes the demands of group cohesion to the ideal of a critical education that instructs in the past and present beliefs and creations of mankind in their richest and fullest variety. Community requires cohesion; it can survive only in an atmosphere of strongly felt, though relative and shifting, moral agreement. At the same time, however, individuals must have access to a culture that transcends what any one group can perceive or accomplish on its own. The different traditions of thought or work constitute the deposits of the species nature in history. For that reason, they represent, despite their distortion by the vices of dominance, parts of the good and indispensable aids to its further realization. Moreover, without a basis for the criticism of shared values, there will be the tendency to sacrifice autonomy to moral union, and transcendence to immanence.

Notwithstanding its indispensability, a critical education may have a permanently subversive effect on all group cohesion. With the diversity and the excellence of the ideals of culture forever before their eyes, the members of the group may find themselves repeatedly torn apart from each other and torn away from the politics of their community. Thus, despairing of a public good, each may seek the illusions of private enlightenment and salvation.

The four dilemmas I have described present similar problems for a politics of community. In each case, either of the polar views, carried to the extreme, would destroy the communitarian ideal. In none of the cases, however, does there seem to be a theoretical criterion for determining where and how to strike the balance. Nor indeed can we be sure that a balance can be struck; it may turn out that no possible mix of the two pairs is consistent with the characteristic features of the social ideal, because the ideal demands more than half of what each of the countervailing models provides. In that event, we would have to reject the idea of a society of organic groups as utopian, and revise our theoretical ideas in the light of our new experience. More probably, political practice would yield a changing blend, in which the temporary predominance of one side of the spectrum would give way periodically to the hegemony of the other side. We might even hope that this cycle would itself become a spiral, and that each oscillation would combine more perfectly the virtues of the contrasting trends.

Theory can define the tensions and suggest the factors that should be taken into account in dealing with them. But only prudence can teach us what to do about them at each moment. And only practice can yield the insights needed to correct the decisions we make.

The reason why the dilemmas create similar difficulties is that they arise from the same underlying conflict. The first two problems present the antagonism between the apparent ideal situation within a community and the desirable form of relations among communities. Vertical integration and the confinement of the state to a coordinative role may seem best for the organic group as an isolated entity. But they make satisfactory group relations impossible and thereby ultimately corrupt the internal life of the group, endangering its survival and robbing it of an indispensable source of moral guidance. On the other hand, horizontal integration and communal hierarchy may appear best suited to the foreign affairs of organic groups, but they tend to efface the communitarian character of the associations they are meant to join.

The second pair of dilemmas represents a conflict between what seems most important to the perpetuation of a society of organic groups and what appears indispensable to its progress. The protection of established communities and of group cohesion may seem requirements of the structure of a communitarian society. But they can constitute obstacles to the process by which communities are formed and improved. The emphasis on associational renewal and critical education may be basic to the development of communitarian politics, but it threatens to destroy with one hand what it has created with another.

The tensions between what is best for the group and what is best for the society of groups, and between the structure of that society and the process of its growth, express a still deeper and more general struggle between a politics of particularism and one of universalism. Vertical integration, decentralization, the emphasis on established groups, and the defense of consensus all point toward the maintenance of the particularity of each association. Horizontal integration, communal hierarchy, institutional inventiveness, and critical understanding all turn toward the ideal of the transcendence of existing collectivities by increasingly universal associations.

The study of the institutional principles of the organic group has already shown us that there is irreplaceable truth in both tendencies. The community needs to remain a particular group, yet it must also become a universal one. Thus, we rediscover on the larger screen of politics the same predicament of a universality at once desired and forbidden so characteristic of human love, the same irreconcilability of the universal and the particular that holds all human thought and life in its grip. It is this disharmony, diminished but never undone, that makes politics incapable of ever fully redressing the imperfections of existence and of reaching the ideal in history.

Theories of community have traditionally suffered from a blend of utopian flavor and totalitarian insinuation because of their failure to acknowledge the force of these dilemmas. By focusing on the static, isolated group, they have cast aside issues about the relations among groups and the political construction of community over time. But these issues stand in fact at the core of communitarian politics, and lend it depth and force by connecting it with the major concerns of human existence. (See Figure 2.)

FIGURE 2
The Dilemmas of Communitarian Politics

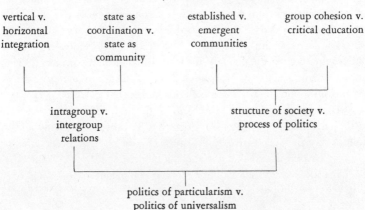

| vertical v. horizontal integration | state as coordination v. state as community | established v. emergent communities | group cohesion v. critical education |

intragroup v.
intergroup
relations

structure of society v.
process of politics

politics of particularism v.
politics of universalism

GOD

The virtue of politics is to make the ideal of the self into a form of social life. The doctrine of organic groups describes the construction of a society in which the ideal is no longer confined to the dreams and diversions of private life, but has penetrated instead into the everyday world of work and changed the character of social relations.

Nevertheless, there are limits to man's ability to achieve the good in history. Politics can push them back, but it cannot overcome them. Man's consciousness denies him the full experience of natural harmony. The gap between his individuality and his sociability deprives him of perfect sympathy. The opposition of his infinite longings to the finitude of his life cheats him of concrete universality. His private search for the good ends in a bitter awareness of the conflict between the reach of extraordinary vision and the quality of everyday life. His public struggle for community comes up against the need of the organic group to remain a particular association and its need to become a universal one. All his great endeavors on this earth are condemned to incompleteness.

As with conduct, so with understanding: man's insight into the world is torn between abstract and concrete knowledge. Theory never acquires the concreteness of prudence, nor prudence the transparency of theory.

The imperfections of politics and knowledge have a common source in the problem that is the central theme of this essay. Under its metaphysical aspect, it is the question of the universal and the particular: How can we conceive the universal and the particular as both united and distinct? Under its religious aspect, it is the puzzle of immanence and transcendence: In what does the union of immanence and transcendence consist and, if it is the good, how can we attain it?

The metaphysical and the religious issue are equivalent. What philosophy states as the union of the universal and the particular, religion knows as immanence. What philosophy describes as the separation of the universal and the particular, religion calls transcendence.

The elucidation of this problem is the indispensable prerequisite to the total criticism of the liberal doctrine. To solve it in theory and in politics, even though partially, is the necessary basis of every attempt to move beyond liberal thought and the modern state.

The ideal of the self could be realized completely in the world only if it were possible to bring about in history the conjunction of immanence and transcendence: the circumstance in which the self is at one with nature, with others, and with its own concrete being, yet separate from them. In the same way, the gap between abstract and concrete knowledge could not be bridged unless the universal and the particular stood in the relationship of simultaneous identity and separation that corresponds to the union of immanence and transcendence.

For men who had gained such knowledge, the world would have lost its secrets. They would see universals as transcending particulars and as fully immanent in them. Thus, they could hope that the species might acquire in the course of its history a complete and perfect understanding of reality.

It is the character of the world and of man's place within it, rather than some remediable defect of human powers, that makes the reconciliation of immanence and transcendence necessarily and permanently impossible. This impossibility is confirmed by the contradiction in the very idea of such a union. If it is true that the joining of immanence and transcendence constitutes the good, its complete realization in history would make the world the embodiment of goodness. But the basis of transcendence is the notion of a good that stands apart from the world. If the world and the ideal were the same, transcendence would become neither desirable nor possible. There would be nothing above or beyond the phenomena of nature, the society of others, and the concrete reality of one's life, station, and work. Thus, it is in the nature of the joining of immanence and transcendence to be incapable of complete manifestation in the world.

The same conclusion applies to the problem of the universal and the particular. Particulars have extension and duration. But everything that extends or lasts in the world has individuality; it differs from everything else. Hence, if a universal is instantiated by many particulars, each of these particulars must differ from the universals they represent. Otherwise, they could not differ among themselves.

The idea of a union of immanence and transcendence or of a universal being who knows and determines all particulars without destroying their particularity is the idea of God. Four main questions arise with respect to the idea of God: whether the same being is meant by the different senses given to the name of God; what attributes God would have if He existed; whether He exists; and how His perfection could respond to man's imperfection.

Men have not always conceived of God in the way suggested by my definition. In their religions they have often viewed Him as a sacred force that exists in the world or pervades it. And in their metaphysical theories they have sometimes defined God, in analogous fashion, as the whole of the world, though a whole that may be distinct from the sum of its parts according to the principle of totality.[14] In this doctrine, the individuality of things in the world must always lack a secure foundation, for they cannot be defined independently of the wholes of which they are parts.

At other times, however, religion has presented God as a transcendent person, contrasted to the world. Similarly, metaphysicians have depicted God as a universal being who, through the ultimate cause of all particular things, is nonetheless distinct from them, so that they can be perceived as separate from Him.

The argument of my essay suggests that these two sorts of metaphysical and religious beliefs are equally inadequate, but that they are views of the same thing from different perspectives. They are conceptions of the ideal of the self, the supreme good, or the perfection of being, which is the only sense *philosophy* can give to the idea of God. Their unity of reference is based upon the unity of man's predicament in the world. His imperfections determine what perfect being can mean for him. But because human nature is constructed in history, this higher being must be seen in different lights as historical experience changes.

Speculative thought establishes what such an ideal, or good, or perfection is like by reflecting on man. Man alone, because he is conscious, can ask himself about the nature of perfect being, and it is with respect to his existence and within the limits imposed by his mind that he must answer the question. One can infer the character of the ideal from the qualities of the self and from the manifestation of those qualities in forms of social life. Indeed, to make sense of either the former or the latter one has to rely on the conception of this ideal.

But why should philosophy talk about God at all instead of contenting itself with the notions of the ideal, the good, or the perfect being? The reconciliation of immanence and transcendence is the religious statement of a view of the self just as the synthesis of the two doctrines of universals and particulars is the metaphysical expression of that view. It is the notion of the self as a being both at one with nature, with others, and with his own life, and independent from them. A being with these qualities has the attributes of personality. Therefore,

God, who is the perfection of such a being, must also be a person, if He exists. It is the virtue of the philosophic concept of God to emphasize that only a person could fully realize the ideal and that this person cannot be man in history.

Thus, God has been defined as the person who is both revealed in nature and apart from natural things, as the maker of the world and the origin of its glory. Those who say God is love intimate that the problem of self and others is resolved in His personality. He holds all men in His universal love without destroying their separateness from Him. When the philosophers say that God's essence is identical to His existence, they mean that His possible or ideal being, unlike man's, is fully accomplished in His concrete works. So completely does He solve the problem of the abstract and the concrete self that He is eternally everything He might or should be.

By drawing analogies to ourselves, philosophy can name the attributes of the person who would be a perfect being. And it can show how the image of this person is implicit in human nature and history as a striving for that which we are unable to become. But there the power of speculative thought stops. It cannot show us either that God in fact exists or how His existence could remedy our own failings.

The existence of God and the salvation of men are ideas whose truth could only be shown, if they could be shown at all, by God through His direct revelation of Himself in history. As a person who stands above the world and apart from thought, He cannot be known except to the extent that He makes Himself present to us in the world; we must see His transcendence through His immanence. It is He who must reveal this immanent being, and we who must pray to Him for its showing. He alone could give us the signs of salvation. Revelation might tell us how through Him and in a world we can neither describe nor completely build, the opposition of nature and humanity could be overcome; how by seeking to imitate His universal love, according to the limited measure of our humanity, we can prefigure a circumstance in which the conflict of self and others would be resolved without the sacrifice of individuality; and how our participation in Him might give us the hope that we too might be able in another world to join together at last essence and existence, the abstract and the concrete self.

Philosophy is a territory bounded on one side by politics and on the other side by religion. As soon as it attempts to overstep its bounds and to take the place of political judgment or religious insight, it disintegrates. The practice of politics calls for prudence, the perception of particulars and the making of choices about particulars. But prudence can never be overtaken by a metaphysic that remains committed to the language of the universal.

A similar conclusion goes for the relationship between philosophy and religion. As a response to an immediate experience of truth, the response of faith to the event of revelation, religion is a kind of sight rather than a form of argument. Like prudence, though in a different way, it acknowledges an immediate given and therefore resists the philosopher's invitation to argue and to prove. Indeed, if my philosophical doctrine is correct, the more religion progresses toward its true aim, the less is it capable of being reproduced and replaced by philosophy. For the closer religion comes to this end, the more does it refer to a realm of being in which immanence and transcendence are united; universal and particular are both joined and separated. But the final union of immanence and transcendence is foreign to the earthly life of which philosophy speaks, and the idea of a simultaneous unity and diversity of the universal and the particular shatters the structure of the rational discourse on which philosophy depends.

The political and the religious passion have often been at undeclared or open war. Moreover, both of them have sought to vanquish and to enslave philosophy. And philosophy, most vulnerable and least loved of the three contenders, has sometimes struck back with a claim to be the master of politics or the successor to religion. Whenever one of these sorts of discourse and existence has trespassed on the domain of the others, it has corrupted both itself and its victims. For this reason, a peace must be concluded among the rivals whereby each might grant a measure of autonomy to the others and recognize their importance to its own concerns.

Within its province, philosophy is sovereign. But this province is limited, and the experience of running up against its limits is indispensable to our knowledge of it. When one thinks philosophical problems through, one comes at last to the outer frontiers, politics and religion, at which the philosopher's pride is cast down, and other kinds of striving come to the fore.

When philosophy has gained the truth of which it is capable, it passes into politics and prayer, politics through which the world is changed, prayer through which men ask God to complete the change of the world by carrying them into His presence and giving them what, left to themselves, they would always lack.

Desirous of faith, touched by hope, and moved by love, men look unceasingly for God. Their search for Him continues even where thinking must stop and action fail. And in their vision of Him they find the beginning and the end of their knowledge of the world and of their sympathy for others. So is man's meditation on God a final union of thought and love—love which is thought disembodied from language and restored to its source.

But our days pass, and still we do not know you fully. Why then do you remain silent? Speak, God.

NOTES

Introduction

See page 2.   1. Arthur Schopenhauer, *Die Welt als Wille und Vorstellung,* preface to 1st ed., *Sämtliche Werke,* ed. P. Deussen (Munich, Piper, 1911), vol. I, p. XXVII.

See page 8.   2. The term "deep structure" is taken from Noam Chomsky, in whose work, however, it has a different meaning from the one given to it here. See *Aspects of the Theory of Syntax* (Cambridge, M.I.T., 1969), pp. 16–18, 136.

See page 16.   3. Two advantages of the imitation of logical analysis are brought out by Descartes' critic in the *Secundae Objectiones:* "It would be worth your while to complete your proposals with definitions, postulates, and axioms that might serve as premises from which you might draw conclusions according to the geometrical method . . . Each reader would then be able to grasp the argument at a single glance and would be filled with an awareness of God." See *Oeuvres de Descartes,* eds. C. Adam and P. Tannery (Paris, Vrin, 1973), vol. VII, p. 128. Hegel points out the major vice of this method when, in criticism of Spinoza, he compares its formalism with the substantive character of philosophy's subject matter. See *Vorlesungen über die Geschichte der Philosophie,* vol. III, *Sämtliche Werke,* ed. H. Glockner (Stuttgart, Fromman, 1928), vol. XIX, pp. 374–375. On the significance of the dichotomy of form and substance, more will be said later.

See page 17.   4. Hegel, *Grundlinien der Philosophie des Rechts,* preface, *Sämtliche Werke,* vol. VII, p. 37.

See page 26.   5. See Diderot, *Le Neveu de Rameau.*

CHAPTER 1 *Liberal Psychology*

See page 32.   1. (A) For the authoritative statement of the doctrine of intelligible essences, a doctrine that may be understood as a revision of Plato's theory of ideas, see Aristotle, *Metaphysics,* bk. 7, ch. 4, §1030a. The essence is the form that by becoming embodied in matter lends each being its distinctive identity. For the development of the Aristotelian view, see Christian Wolff, *Philosophia Prima sive Ontologia,* §143, ed. J. Ecole, *Gesammelte Werke,* eds. J. Ecole and H. Arndt (Hildsheim, Olms, 1962), vol. III, pp. 120–121. In this tradition, essence is defined by contrast to accident, on the one hand, and to existence, on the other hand. It is both τὸ τί ἦν εἶναι and οὐσία. The two definitions are connected because existence is accidental (Aristotle, *Categories,* ch. 2, §1b, ll. 6–7), though later philosophy makes an exception for God. The classical doctrine of intelligible essences has been revived in the phenomenology of Brentano and Husserl.

(B) Modern metaphysics takes one of two approaches toward the problem of essences. The first is to reject the classical doctrine outright by developing a nominalist conception of essences. (See note 2.) The second is to attempt to accommodate some version of intelligible essences. There are in turn two main variants of this latter tendency. For some, the essence means whatever is needed to make something possible and intelligible; it describes nothing in the empirical world. See Kant, *Metaphysische Anfangsgründe der Naturwissenschaft,* preface, *Kants Werke,* ed. Prussian Academy (Berlin, Gruyter, 1968), vol. IV, p. 467. For the rationalists, however, the essence that makes understanding possible also makes existence necessary because the orders of ideas and of events are the same. See Spinoza, *Ethica,* pt. 2, def. 2, *Spinoza Opera,* ed. C. Gebhardt (Heidelberg, Winter, 1972), vol. II, p. 84.

(C) The acceptance and the rejection of the doctrine

of intelligible essences in modern thought correspond to the two characteristic ways of dealing with what I shall call the antinomy of theory and fact. If we accept the doctrine with the aim of guaranteeing or explaining the possibility of knowledge, we are forced to certain repugnant political and moral conclusions. (See the discussion in Chapter Two of the principle of rules and values.) Moreover, we fall into what Kant himself stigmatized as philosophical dogmatism because we assume a coincidence between the categories of mind and the relations among events in the world. If, on the contrary, we reject the doctrine entirely, knowledge is left hanging in the air. See the further argument of the present section.

(D) As we move ahead, it will turn out that there is a close link between the problem of essences and the issue of universals.

See page 32. 2. For the rejection of the doctrine of intelligible essences by liberal thought, see Hobbes, *Leviathan,* pt. 4, ch. 46 (Oxford, Clarendon Press, 1967), pp. 524–528. For a late stage in this tradition of thought about the problem of essences, see John Stuart Mill, *A System of Logic,* bk. 1, ch. 6, §2 (Toronto, Toronto, 1973), pp. 90–93. Mill views essences as simply the sum of the attributes connoted by a word; they do not inhere in the subjects of which they are predicated.

See page 32. 3. See W. V. Quine, *Two Dogmas of Empiricism,* in *From a Logical Point of View* (New York, Harper, 1963), p. 44.

See page 32. 4. A striking corollary of the claim that the mind participates in the construction of experience is Kant's distinction between things as they are in themselves and things as they appear. See Kant, *Kritik der reinen Vernunft,* 2nd ed., *Werke,* vol. III, pp. 69–71.

See page 33. 5. The antinomy of theory and fact is at the heart of current debates in the history of science. See Thomas Kuhn, *The Structure of Scientific Revolutions* (Chicago, Chicago, 1970), pp. 198–204; and Paul Feyerabend, *Consolations for the Specialist,* in *Criticism and the Growth of Knowledge,* eds. I. Lakatos and A. Musgrave (Cambridge, Cambridge, 1970), pp. 197–229.

See page 34. 6. See Kant, *Kritik der reinen Vernunft,* 2nd ed., *Werke,* vol. III, pp. 21–22.

See page 35.   7. For a discussion of the problem of form, substance, and accident in the conception of science I describe, see Emil Lask, *Fichtes Idealismus und die Geschichte, Gesammelte Schriften,* ed. E. Herrigel (Tübingen, Mohr, 1923), vol. I, pp. 38–44. See also Georg Lukács, *Die Verdinglichung und das Bewusstsein des Proletariats,* in *Geschichte und Klassenbewusstsein* (Neuwied, Luchterhand, 1970), pp. 199–200.

See page 35.   8. The example of the circle is taken from Lask, *Fichtes Idealismus, Gesammelte Schriften,* vol. I, p. 45.

See page 37.   9. For two variations on this conception of mind, the second of which departs from it in some important respects, see Hobbes, *Leviathan,* chs. 1–5, pp. 11–38, and Locke, *An Essay Concerning Human Understanding,* bk. 2, ch. 1, *The Works of John Locke,* 11th ed. (London, 1812), vol. I, pp. 77–128.

See page 37.   10. The first of these two points may be taken as a central theme of Kant's "transcendental aesthetic," and the second as the outcome of his "transcendental logic."

See page 38.   11. Hobbes, *Leviathan,* ch. 8, p. 57.

See page 39.   12. (A) Hobbes embraces the principle of reason and desire when he distinguishes reasoning from passion and argues the subordination of the former to the latter. *Leviathan,* ch. 5, p. 32. Locke states the principle as the distinction between the two "powers" of understanding and will. *Essay,* bk. 2, ch. 6, §2, and bk. 2, ch. 21, §§5–6, *Works,* vol. I, pp. 104–105, 223–224. See also Berkeley, *The Principles of Human Knowledge,* pt. 1, §27 (London, Tonson, 1734), pp. 57–58. The contrast of understanding and the passions presides over the plan of Hume's *Treatise.* Moreover, he asserts the impotence of reason in the face of the affections. *A Treatise on Human Nature,* bk. 2, pt. 3, §3, and bk. 3, pt. 1, §1, ed. Selby-Bigge (Oxford, Clarendon, 1968), pp. 413–418, 458 *supra.* Analogously, Spinoza differentiates the study of mind from that of the emotions, and holds that "desire (*cupiditas*) is the very essence of man," *Ethica,* pt. 3, definitions of the desires, no. 1, *Spinoza Opera,* vol. II, p. 190. Kant accepts the principle of reason and desire when he identifies desire with life itself and denies that the pleasure or displeasure with which desire is connected can represent any kind of knowledge, even self-knowledge. See

Einleitung in die Metaphysik der Sitten, Werke, vol. VI, pp. 211–212.

(B) The preceding views ought not to be identified with earlier distinctions between intellect and desire whose persistent influence can nevertheless be detected in the writings of the liberal thinkers. Thus, within the category of desire (ὄρεξις, *cupiditas*), Aristotle distinguishes will (βούλησις, *voluntas*) from concupiscence (ἐπιθυμία, *voluptas*). See *De Anima,* bk. 3, ch. 7, §431b, and bk. 3, ch. 9, §432b. Will is both the affirmation ·of truth by the speculative intellect and the affirmation of the good by the practical intellect, whereas concupiscence is the blind inclination to pleasure. The emphasis is on the contrast of rational and irrational desires rather than on the opposition of reason and desire. The classical conception of practical reason survives in the scholastic *prudentia.* Aquinas, *Summa Theologica,* pts. II–II, questions 47–51.

(C) The trend of the moderns is to abolish the notion of practical reason and, with it, the division of *voluntas* and *voluptas.* Both are absorbed into a more general *cupiditas.* Modern conceptions of practical reason, like Kant's, confirm the principle of reason and desire instead of overriding it, for this new practical reason has no relation to the content of the desires. See *Kritik der praktischen Vernunft, Werke,* vol. V, p. 21.

See page 39. 13. For a treatment of the link between the principle of reason and desire and the fact-value dichotomy, see Hume, *Treatise,* bk. 3, pt. 1, §1, pp. 459–463.

See page 40. 14. See again Hobbes, *Leviathan,* ch. 8, pp. 56–57.

See page 40. 15. See Locke, *Essay,* bk. 4, ch. 13, §2, *Works,* vol. III, pp. 84–85; Descartes, *Discours de la Méthode,* pt. 1.

See page 41. 16. See Aquinas, *De Ente et Essentia (L'Être et l'Essence),* ch. 3, ed. C. Capelle (Vrin, 1947), p. 39.

See page 41. 17. See, for example, Clifford Geertz, *Islam Observed* (New Haven, Yale, 1968), p. 97.

See page 42. 18. (A) Perhaps the most cogent statement of the principle of arbitrary desire is to be found in Hume, *Treatise,* bk. 3, pt. 1, §1, pp. 455–470. For a more recent formulation of the principle, accompanied by an attack on the doctrine of objective ends, see Moritz Schlick, *Fragen der Ethik* (Vienna, Springer, 1930), pp. 74–87.

(B) There is a recurring tendency in the history of liberal thought to attempt to escape from the principle of arbitrary desire by reverting to a doctrine of intelligible moral essences. Locke, *Essay,* bk. 3, ch. 11, §16, *Works,* vol. II, pp. 278–279. The advocates of the reversion characteristically try to perpetuate the doctrine without accepting its bases in more general ideas about thought and language. Moreover, they want to admit some of its consequences and to reject others. They therefore fall into an incoherent eclecticism.

(C) Several movements in modern philosophy have rejected more or less completely the principle of arbitrary desire and the fact-value contrast. Among these are: (1) phenomenological ethics, v.g.: Max Scheler, *Der Formalismus in der Ethik und die materiale Wertethik* (Berlin and Munich, Francke, 1966), pp. 270–275; and Nicolai Hartmann, *Ethik* (Berlin, Gruyter, 1962), pp. 183–185; (2) American pragmatism, v.g.: William James, *Pragmatism,* Lecture 2 (London, Longmans, 1922), pp. 75–77; John Dewey, *Experience and Nature* (La Salle, Open Court, 1971), pp. 341–354. These views represent partial criticisms of liberal thought from different perspectives.

See page 42. 19. Descartes' *Les Passions de l'Âme,* ch. 6 of Hobbes' *Leviathan,* and bk. 2 of Hume's *Treatise,* each represent attempts to establish a science of desire, whose offspring is modern empirical psychology.

See page 43. 20. See the remark in *Kritik der Praktischen Vernunft,* §1, *Werke,* vol. V, pp. 19–20.

See page 43. 21. On qualifications to the principle of subjective desire, which fall into one of the three categories I mention, see Hume, *Treatise,* bk. 3, pt. 1, §1, pp. 459–460, and J. D. Mabbot, "Reason and Desire," *Philosophy* (1953), vol. XXVIII, p. 113.

See page 45. 22. Aristotle defines substance as something that "can exist apart." *Metaphysics,* bk. 12, ch. 5, §1071a, l.1. This classical definition is transported into modern philosophy by Descartes when he describes substance in the *Principia Philosophiae,* pt. 1, §51, as "a thing which so exists that it needs no other thing to exist," *Oeuvres de Descartes,* eds. C. Adam and P. Tannery (Paris, Vrin, 1973), vol. VIII-I, p. 24. The concept of substance implies self-sufficient

individuality. We speak loosely of the substance of desires
or of that of (other) natural phenomena when we want
to emphasize the individuality of particulars, an individuality that formal reason must disregard in its effort to
generalize.

See page 46. 23. (A) The principle of analysis is stated by Hobbes, *Leviathan,* ch. 5, p. 32, and *Elementorum Philosophiae,* ch. 1,
§2, *Opera Philosophica* (London, Bohn, 1889), vol. I,
pp. 2–3; and by Locke, *Essay,* bk. 2, ch. 12, §8, *Works,*
vol. I, p. 146. Hume follows in the *Treatise,* bk. 1, pt. 1,
§6, pp. 16–17; bk. 1, pt. 4, §2, p. 207.

(B) A consequence of the principle of analysis is that
the infinite must be conceived as a never-ending series of
finite parts. See Hobbes, *Leviathan,* ch. 3, p. 23; Locke,
Essay, bk. 2, ch. 17, §§3–6, *Works,* vol. I, pp. 195–197.
Hence, both the theory of transfinite numbers and the
attempt to state metaphysically the attributes of an infinite, transcendent God presuppose the abandonment of
the principle.

See page 47. 24. Spinoza makes the principle of synthesis a cornerstone of
his philosophy. In this respect, he departs radically from
the liberal philosophers, though he fails to work out the
political implications of the departure. The nonanalytic
relation of parts and wholes is discussed in the dialogues
of the *Korte Verhandeling van God, Opera,* vol. I, pp.
28–34.

See page 47. 25. Thus, universality is only in names. Hobbes, *Leviathan,*
ch. 4, p. 26; Locke, *Essay,* bk. 3, ch. 3, §11, *Works,* vol.
II, pp. 159–160; Hume, *Treatise,* bk. 1, pt. 1, §6, p. 16.

See page 49. 26. For statements of the morality of desire, see Hobbes,
Leviathan, ch. 6, p. 48; Locke, *Essay,* bk. 2, ch. 20, §6,
Works, vol. I, p. 217; Jeremy Bentham, *An Introduction
to the Principles of Morals and Legislation,* ch. 1, §1, eds.
J. H. Burns and H. L. A. Hart (London, Athlone, 1970),
p. 1; Henry Sidgwick, *The Methods of Ethics* (London,
Macmillan, 1907), pp. 405–407.

See page 50. 27. See note 12.

See page 51. 28. The morality of reason is exemplified by the first formulation of the categorical imperative. Kant, *Grundlegung zur
Metaphysik der Sitten,* pt. 2, *Werke,* vol. IV, p. 421.

See page 53. 29. On the ceaseless character of desire, see Hobbes, *Levia-

than, ch. 11, p. 75; and Hegel, *Grundlinien der Philosophie des Rechts,* §§189–195, *Sämtliche Werke,* ed. H. Glockner (Stuttgart, Fromman, 1928), pp. 270–276.

See page 53. 30. This is Hegel's concept of the "bad infinity." See his *Wissenschaft der Logik, Sämtliche Werke,* vol. IV, pp. 160–161.

See page 53. 31. See F. H. Bradley, *Pleasure for Pleasure's Sake,* in *Ethical Studies,* 2nd ed. (London, Oxford, 1970), pp. 97–100.

See page 54. 32. For a critique of the morality of reason, see Max Scheler, *Der Formalismus in der Ethik,* pp. 65–126.

See page 54. 33. This point is brought out and developed in Hegel's remarks on the Sermon on the Mount. *Hegels Theologische Jugendschriften,* ed. H. Nohl (Tübingen, Mohr, 1907), pp. 264–266.

See page 57. 34. On the attempt to base personal identity on the continuity of the body, see Hume, *Treatise,* pt. 4, bk. 1, §2, pp. 187–192; and Sydney Shoemaker, *Self-Knowledge and Self-Identity* (Ithaca, Cornell, 1963), pp. 1–40.

See page 57. 35. (A) For a similar argument in the context of the critique of utilitarianism, see John Rawls, *A Theory of Justice* (Cambridge, Harvard, 1971), pp. 560–567.

(B) Because liberal thought cannot provide an account of personality, it must treat the concept of the person as a primitive one. See P. F. Strawson, *Individuals* (London, Methuen, 1959), pp. 87–116. For some of the ensuing difficulties, see A. J. Ayer, *The Concept of a Person* (New York, St. Martin, 1963), pp. 82–128; and Bernard Williams, *Strawson on Individuals* in *Problems of the Self* (Cambridge, Cambridge, 1973), pp. 101–126.

See page 58. 36. See the study of the disintegration of consciousness and of its relationship to the problem of personality in Eugen Bleuler, *Dementia Praecox* (Leipzig, Deuticke, 1911), pp. 289–297; and Silvano Arieti, *Interpretation of Schizophrenia* (New York, Brunner, 1955), especially pp. 314–318.

See page 58. 37. The distinction between universal and particular humanity is implied by Kant's contrast of a will obedient to reason, which is universal, and a will ruled by inclination, which is particular. *Grundlegung zur Metaphysik der Sitten,* pt. 2, *Werke,* vol. IV, p. 425.

See page 58. 38. See the distinction between the biological concept of man and the legal concept of personality in Hans Kelsen, *General Theory of Law and State,* trans. Anders Wedberg (New York, Russell, 1961), p. 94.

See page 60. 39. See Émile Durkheim, *Leçons de Sociologie: Physique des Moeurs et du Droit,* lessons 4 and 5 (Paris, Presses Universitaires, 1950), pp. 68–78.

CHAPTER 2 *Liberal Political Theory*

See page 64. 1. The view of society described in this section is stated in ways that for my purposes are fundamentally similar by Hobbes, *Leviathan* (Oxford, Clarendon, 1967), especially chs. 13 and 27, pp. 94–98, 128–132, and Locke, *Two Treatises of Government,* especially bk. 2, chs. 2 and 3, §§4–21, *The Works of John Locke* (London, 1823), vol. V, pp. 339–350. Montesquieu's discussion of monarchy presents a more partial though analogous account. *De l'Esprit des Lois,* pt. 1, bk. 3, chs. 5–7, *Oeuvres Complètes,* ed. R. Caillois (Pléiade, 1966), pp. 255–257, 288–292.

See page 68. 2. See Hobbes, *Leviathan,* ch. 6, p. 41.

See page 68. 3. For a modern development of this idea, see Mancur Olson, *The Logic of Collective Action* (Cambridge, Harvard, 1973), p. 11.

See page 68. 4. See Georg Henrik von Wright, *Norm and Action* (London, Routledge, 1963), pp. 6–16.

See page 69. 5. The conception of constitutive rules is developed in Ludwig Wittgenstein, *Philosophical Investigations* (New York, Macmillan, 1969), §§80–91, 197–241, pp. 38–42, 80–88.

See page 69. 6. On the conception of instrumental rules, see John Rawls, "Two Concepts of Rules," *Philosophical Review* (1956), vol. LXIV, pp. 18–29.

See page 69. 7. The constitutive conception of rules, made into the basis of a social theory of law, may serve as the tool of a communitarian critique of liberal political and legal theory. (See ch. 6, note 7.) The instrumental view of rules is the handmaiden of utilitarian jurisprudence.

See page 70. 8. See Hobbes, *Leviathan,* ch. 18, pp. 133–141; Hegel, *Grundlinien der Philosophie des Rechts,* §§205, 275–286, *Sämtliche Werke,* ed. H. Glockner (Stuttgart, Fromman, 1928), vol. VII, pp. 377–395.

See page 71. 9. Hobbes develops both the natural rights and the positivist strand in liberal political thought. From this flow many of the paradoxes as well as much of the greatness of his thought. See *Leviathan,* chs. 14–15, pp. 99–123. See also Locke, *Two Treatises,* especially bk. 2, ch. 11, §§134–142, vol. V, pp. 416–424.

See page 71. 10. Hobbes recognizes the problem in *Leviathan,* ch. 15, pp. 111–112.

See page 72. 11. Kant, *Metaphysische Anfangsgründe der Rechtslehre,* §44, *Kants Werke,* ed. Prussian Academy (Berlin, Gruyter, 1968), vol. VI, §44, pp. 312–313.

See page 74. 12. Franz Neumann, "Der Funktionswandel des Gesetzes im Recht der bürgerlichen Gesellschaft," *Zeitschrift für Sozialforschung* (1937), vol. VI, pp. 542–596.

See page 75. 13. The discovery of a connection between the appeal to terror and the artificial view of society has played an important part in the criticism of liberal thought. The decisive event in this respect was the French Revolution. Both the theme of an absence of community between the Republic and its enemies and that of the subordination of society to will are already implicit in the original justification of the "Reign of Terror." See Maximilien Robespierre, *Rapport sur les Principes du Governement Revolutionnaire,* in *Discours et Rapports de Robespierre,* ed. C. Vellay (Paris, Charpentier, 1908), pp. 332–333. The idea that the disintegration of community makes fear the supreme social bond recurs in the history of the conservative attack on liberalism. See Edmund Burke, *Reflections on the Revolution in France, Works of Edmund Burke* (London, Rivington, 1801), vol. V, p. 202. The relationship of voluntarism to terror is in turn brought out by Hegel's remarks on "absolute freedom and terror." See *Phänomenologie des Geistes, Sämtliche Werke,* ed. H. Glockner (Stuttgart, Fromman, 1927), vol. II, pp. 449–459. An analogous argument is developed by Marx and by some of his followers. See, for example, Marx's article in *Vorwärts* of August 7, 1844, *Marx-Engels Werke* (Berlin, Dietz, 1957), vol. I, p. 392; and Lenin, *The Proletarian Revolution and Kautsky the Renegade,* in *Collected Works* (Moscow, Progress, 1965), vol. XXVIII, pp. 227–325. Still another perspective on the matter is offered by the development in social theory of the view that in 'premodern' societies a clear line is drawn between what is immutable in the social order and what falls under the discretion of the rulers, whereas in modern states every aspect of social life becomes subject in principle to the political will. See Henry Maine, *Lectures on the Early History of Institutions* (London, Murray, 1897), pp. 373–386; and Max Weber, *Wirtschaft und Gesellschaft*, ed. J. Winckelmann (Tübingen, Mohr, 1972), ch. 3, §6, p. 130. In a very different context, the relationship of legalism to terrorism is highlighted by the doctrines of the Chinese 'Legalists.' See *The Complete Works of Han Fei Tzŭ*, 2 vols., trans. W. Liao (London, Probsthain, 1939); and *The Book of Lord Shang*, trans. J. Duyvendak (London, Probsthain, 1928).

See page 76. 14. See Hobbes, *Leviathan*, ch. 6 ("good and evil apparent"), p. 48. See note 18 to my ch. 1.

See page 80. 15. See Hobbes' fear that the doctrine of intelligible essences would imply a limitation on state power. *Leviathan*, ch. 46, pp. 526–527.

See page 80. 16. On the theory of naming and its political importance, see Hobbes, *Leviathan*, ch. 4, pp. 23–32.

See page 81. 17. (A) For a statement of the principle of individualism, see Jeremy Bentham, *An Introduction to the Principles of Morals and Legislation*, ch. 1, §4, eds. J. H. Burns and H. L. A. Hart (London, Athlone, 1970), p. 12. Nevertheless, there are thinkers, liberal in other respects, who ardently opposed the individualist principle. Rousseau, *Du Contract Social*, bk. 2, ch. 2, *Oeuvres Complètes de Jean-Jacques Rousseau*, eds. B. Gagnebin and M. Raymond (Paris, Pléiade, 1966), vol. III, p. 369.

(B) For a formal interpretation of the principle of individualism, see K. Arrow, *Social Choice and Individual Values* (New York, Wiley, 1963), pp. 61–62; and A. Sen, *Collective Choice and Social Welfare* (San Francisco, Holden-Day, 1970), pp. 87–88.

See page 82. 18. This is the spirit of J. S. Mill's remarks on the basic character of "the laws of mind" in the moral sciences. *A System of Logic*, bk. 6, ch. 4, §1 (Toronto, Toronto, 1974), p. 849. Even the alleged role of "ethology" in mediating between psychology and the "science of man in society" does not rob the former of its supremacy.

See page 83. 19. For a historical treatment of these conflicting theories of groups, see Otto von Gierke, *Das deutsche Genossenschafts-recht* (Berlin, Weidmann, 1913), vol. IV.

See page 85. 20. The formal theory of freedom is already implicit in Kant's statement of the "universal principle of right." See *Metaphysische Anfangsgründe der Rechtslehre, Kants Werke,* vol. VI, pp. 230–231.

See page 86. 21. The measurement of pleasures and pains is supposed to provide the legislator with such a method. See Bentham, *An Introduction to the Principles of Morals and Legislation,* ch. 4, pp. 38–41.

See page 86. 22. See Locke, *Two Treatises of Government,* bk. 2, chs. 7–9, *Works,* vol. V, pp. 383–415.

See page 86. 23. See John Rawls, *A Theory of Justice* (Cambridge, Harvard, 1971), especially ch. 3.

See page 87. 24. A formal demonstration of the insolubility of the problem of social choice, given individualism and certain related assumptions, is presented in K. Arrow, *Social Choice and Individual Values,* pp. 46–60; and discussed in A. Sen, *Collective Choice and Social Welfare,* pp. 37–40.

See page 88. 25. Durkheim's conception of the "conscience collective" refers precisely to the shared values and understandings at the basis of the social order. See *Les Formes Élémentaires de la Vie Religieuse* (Paris, Presses Universitaires, 1968), p. 605.

See page 88. 26. See Kant, *Grundlegung zur Metaphysik der Sitten, Werke,* vol. IV, pp. 422–433, and *Idee zu einer allgemeinen Geschichte, Werke,* vol. VIII, pp. 18–22; Wilhelm von Humboldt, *Über die Gesetze der Entwicklung der menschlichen Kräfte, Gesammelte Schriften,* ed. Prussian Academy (Berlin, Behr, 1903), vol. I, pp. 86–96, and *Ideen zu einem Versuch, die Gränzen der Wirksamkeit des Staats zu bestimmen, Gesammelte Schriften,* vol. I, pp. 106–111; John Stuart Mill, *On Liberty,* 2nd ed. (Boston, Ticknor, 1863), especially ch. 3, p. 114; T. H. Green, *Lecture on Liberal Legislation and Freedom of Contract, Works of Thomas Hill Green,* ed. R. Nettleship (London, Longmans, 1888), vol. III, pp. 370–372.

See page 89. 27. See Montesquieu, *De l'Esprit des Lois,* bk. 6, ch. 3, *Oeuvres Complètes,* vol. II, p. 311.

See page 91. 28. Weber's contrasts of logical and substantive rationality in law, and of formal and substantive justice, emphasize the degree of autonomy of legal rules from other kinds of rules rather than the distinction between the instrumental and the prescriptive. See *Wirtschaft und Gesellschaft,* ch. 7, §§1, 8, pp. 395, 506.

See page 92. 29. See Montesquieu, *De l'Esprit des Lois,* bk. 11, ch. 6, *Oeuvres Complètes,* pp. 396–407; Robespierre's intervention in *Archives Parlementaires,* 1st series (1790), vol. XX, p. 516.

See page 92. 30. See Augustine, *Confessions,* bk. 1, ch. 8 (Cambridge, Harvard, 1968), vol. I, pp. 24–26.

See page 92. 31. For the example of the surgeon see Nicolas Everard, *Topicorum seu de locis legalibus Liber, locus ab absurdo* (Louvain, Martin, 1516), pp. 21–22; and Samuel Puffendorf, *De Jure Naturae et Gentium,* bk. 5, ch. 12, §8 (London, Junghaus, 1672), pp. 717–718.

See page 94. 32. An alternative to formalism not discussed in the text is the one advanced by Hans Kelsen in *Reine Rechtslehre,* ch. 6, §36, (Leipzig, Deuticke, 1934), pp. 94–96. Kelsen's thesis is that the rule works as a "frame" within which different interpretations are possible. Legal science chooses the rule applicable to a case but is powerless to determine which of the permissible decisions under the rule ought to be preferred. This preference is controlled by "political," hence presumably "subjective," factors. One objection to the doctrine is that it is fallacious to distinguish between choosing a rule to apply and deciding how it ought to be interpreted in a particular case. The interpretation of rules consists precisely in the choice of instances in which they ought to be followed. Another criticism is that the contrast between the rational choice of the rule and the willful choice of interpretations under the rule presupposes the truth of formalism with respect to the former and the impossibility of limiting judicial power in the interest of freedom with regard to the latter.

See page 94. 33. For two versions of the purposive theory, see Ronald Dworkin, *The Model of Rules* in *Law, Reason, and Justice,* ed. Graham Hughes (New York, N.Y.U., 1969), pp. 3–43; and Josef Esser, *Vorverständis und Methodenwahl in der Rechtsfindung* (Frankfurt, Athenäeum, 1970), especially pp. 159–168.

See page 99. 34. For different views of the political significance of the antinomy of rules and values, see the debate on "planning and the rule of law": Friedrich Hayek, *The Road to*

Serfdom (Chicago, Chicago, 1944), pp. 72–87; Lon Fuller, *The Morality of Law* (New Haven, Yale, 1964), pp. 170–177; Charles Reich, "The Law of the Planned Society," *Yale Law Journal* (1966), vol. LXXV, pp. 1227–1270; O. S. Ioffe, "Plan and Contract under the Conditions of the Economic Reform," *Sovetskoe Gosudarstvo i Pravo* (1967), vol. VIII, p. 47, reprinted in *The Soviet Legal System,* ed. J. Hazard (Dobbs Ferry, Oceana, 1969), p. 267.

See page 100. 35. For the theoretical attack on legal justice in the name of socialist substantive justice, see E. B. Pashukanis, *The Soviet State and the Revolution in Law,* in *Soviet Legal Philosophy,* trans. H. Babb (Cambridge, Harvard, 1951), p. 279; and S. A. Golunskii, "On the Question of the Concept of Legal Norms in the Theory of Socialist Law," *Sovetskoe Gosudarstvo i Pravo* (1964), vol. IV, pp. 21–26, privately translated by H. Berman.

See page 101. 36. Cf. Wittgenstein's theory of rules and of their relation to forms of social life. See note 5.

CHAPTER 3 *The Unity of Liberal Thought*

See page 107. 1. Aristotle, *Nicomachean Ethics,* bk. 1, ch. 3, §1094G, ll. 12–14.

See page 108. 2. For other versions of this familiar point, see Max Weber, *Über einige Kategorien der verstehenden Soziologie,* in *Gesammelte Aufsätze zur Wissenschaftslehre,* ed. F. Winckelmann (Tübingen, Mohr, 1968), pp. 427–431; Willhem Dilthey, *Der Aufbau der Geschichtlichen Welt in den Geisteswissenschaften, Gesammelte Schriften* (Göttingen, Vandenhoek, 1965), vol. VII, pp. 225–227; Peter Winch, *The Idea of a Social Science* (London, Routledge, 1970), pp. 121–128. For a similar view in a more limited context, see H. L. A. Hart, *The Concept of Law* (Oxford, Clarendon, 1967), pp. 55–56.

See page 109. 3. On the problem of types, see Max Weber, *Roscher und Knies und die logischen Probleme der historischen Nationalökonomie,* in *Gesammelte Aufsätze zur Wissenschaftslehre,* pp. 190–212. Weber fails to grasp the relation of the methodological issue of types to the metaphysical problem of the orders of ideas and of events, and therefore lacks a clear account of the connection among the elements of the type.

See page 111.   4. Francis Bacon, *Novum Organum,* §58, ed. T. Fowler (Oxford, Clarendon, 1878), pp. 283–284.

See page 112.   5. The 'universal grammar' of the rationalists is, in this sense, linguistics.

See page 113.   6. For a classical statement of this thesis in its application to the study of society, see Émile Durkheim, *Les Règles de la Méthode Sociologique* (Paris, Presses Universitaires, 1968), pp. 3–14.

See page 114.   7. In his theory of types of social action, Weber adopts and clarifies this procedure. *Wirtschaft und Gesellschaft,* ch. 1, §11, ed. J. Winckelmann (Tübingen, Mohr, 1972), pp. 9–11.

See page 119.   8. Otto Neurath, "Protokollsätze," *Erkenntis* (1932), vol. III, p. 206.

See page 122.   9. See note 18.

See page 122. 10. See Gottfried Semper, *Entwicklung eines Systems der vergleichenden Stillehre,* in *Kleine Schriften* (Berlin, Premann, 1884), pp. 259–291; Alois Riegl, *Kunstgeschichte und Universalgeschichte, Gesammelte Aufsätze* (Augsburg, Filser, 1929), pp. 3–9; Heinrich Wölfflin, *Kunstgeschichtliche Grundbegriffe* (Munich, Bruckmann, 1923), pp. 1–19; Erwin Panofsky, *Über das Verhältnis der Kunstgeschichte zur Kunsttheorie,* "Zeitschrift für Aesthetik" (1920), vol. XIV, pp. 330–331; and *Studies in Iconology* (New York, Harper, 1967), pp. 3–31; Arnold Hauser, *The Philosophy of Art History* (Cleveland, World, 1969), pp. 119–276; Walter Böckelmann, *Die Grundbegriffe der Kunstbetrachtung bei Wölfflin und Dvořák* (Dresden, Baensch, 1938); Lorenz Dittmann, *Styl, Symbol, Struktur* (Munich, Fink, 1967), pp. 13–83.

See page 123. 11. On collective subjects, see Karl Marx, *Das Kapital, Marx-Engels Werke* (Berlin, Dietz, 1962), vol. XXIII, pp. 181–182.

See page 125. 12. The principle of totality is formulated by Spinoza. See note 24 to my ch. 1. Some of the best modern statements are to be found in the writings of Marx's disciples. See Georg Lukács, *Rosa Luxemburg als Marxist,* in *Geschichte und Klassenbewusstsein* (Neuwied, Luchterhand, 1968), pp. 94–97; Lucien Goldmann, *Introduction à la Philosophie de Kant* (Gallimard, 1967), pp. 60–70; Louis Althusser and Étienne Balibar, *Lire le Capital* (Paris, Maspero, 1970), vol. I, pp. 46–50; Karel Kosík, *Die Dialektik des Konkreten* (Suhrkamp, 1967), pp. 34–59; Oskar Lange, *Ganzheit und Entwicklung in kybernetischer Sicht* (Berlin, Akademie, 1967). See also Kant, *Reflexionen zur Metaphysik*, §3789, *Gesammelte Schriften,* ed. Prussian Academy (Berlin, Gruyter, 1926), vol. XVII, p. 293; Hegel, *Wissenschaft der Logik, Sämtliche Werke,* ed. H. Glockner (Stuttgart, Fromman, 1928), vol. IV, pp. 641–645; Schopenhauer, *Die Welt as Wille und Vorstellung, Sämtliche Werke,* ed. P. Deussen (Munich, Piper, 1911), vol. I, pp. 587–590.

See page 125. 13. See Wolfgang Köhler, *Gestalt Psychology* (New York, Liveright, 1947), pp. 173–205; Kurt Koffka, *Principles of Gestalt Psychology* (New York, Harcourt, 1935), pp. 26, 175–176.

See page 126. 14. Noam Chomsky, *Language and Mind* (New York, Harcourt Brace, 1972), pp. 155–160. For an example of detailed criticism of the analytical standpoint in linguistics, see Roman Jakobson, "Beitrag żur Allgemeinen Kasuslehre," *Travaux du Cercle Linguistique de Prague* (1936), vol. VI, pp. 240–288.

See page 126. 15. Claude Lévi-Strauss, *Les Structures Élémentaires de la Parenté* (Paris, Presses Universitaires, 1949), ch. 3, pp. 35–52.

See page 126. 16. For the discussion of difficulties in the definition of the principle of totality, see Moritz Schlick, *Über den Begriff der Ganzheit, Gesammelte Aufsätze* (Wien, Gerald, 1938), pp. 252–266; and Ernest Nagel, *Wholes, Sums, and Organic Unities,* in *Parts and Wholes,* ed. D. Lerner (New York, Free Press, 1963), pp. 135–152.

See page 127. 17. See Leibniz' letter to Remond de Montmort (1715): ". . . chaque Monade est un miroir vivant de l'Univers suivant son point de vue." Gottfried Wilhelm Leibniz, *Opera Philosophica,* ed. J. E. Erdmann (Berlin, Eichler, 1840), p. 725.

See page 128. 18. But for an awareness of this problem, see Jean Piaget, *Le Structuralisme* (Paris, Presses Universitaires, 1972), pp. 117–125.

See page 129. 19. For this reason, the structuralists deserve to be compared to those "charlatans of Japan" of whom Rousseau speaks bitterly in *Du Contract Social,* bk. 2, ch. 2, *Oeuvres Complètes,* eds. B. Gagnebin and M. Raymond (Paris, Pléiade, 1964), vol. III, p. 369.

See page 129. 20. On the marriage of skepticism and conservatism, see the note on Hume in John Stuart Mill, *Bentham,* in *Essays on Ethics, Religion and Society,* ed. J. M. Robson (Toronto, Toronto, 1969), p. 80.

See page 133. 21. For classical discussions of the reality of universals, see Plato, *Republic,* bk. 10, §596, *Parmenides,* §131; Aristotle, *Posterior Analytics,* bk. 2, ch. 19. For the development of the theory of nominal universals in liberal thought, see Hobbes, *Elementorum Philosophiae,* ch. 2, §11; *Leviathan,* ch. 4; Locke, *Essay Concerning Human Understanding,* bk. 2, ch. 11, bk. 3, ch. 3; Berkeley, *Principles of Human Knowledge,* Introduction, §§6–25; ch. 1, §§1–8; Hume, *Treatise on Human Nature,* bk. 1, pt. 1, §7; Thomas Reid, *Essays on the Intellectual Powers of Man,* bk. 5, ch. 6. For two attempts to escape from this tradition, see Bertrand Russell, "On the Relation of Universals and Particulars," *Proceedings of the Aristotelian Society* (1911–1912), vol. XII, pp. 1–24, developed in *The Problems of Philosophy,* chs. 9–10; Ludwig Wittgenstein, *Philosophical Investigations,* §§65–77.

See page 136. 22. See the discussion on the "Fallacy of Misplaced Concreteness" in Alfred North Whitehead, *Science and the Modern World* (New York, Macmillan, 1925), pp. 72–79.

See page 139. 23. On the conception of the "holy will," see Kant, *Die Religion innerhalb der Grenzen der blossen Vernunft, Kants Werke,* ed. Prussian Academy (Berlin, Gruyter, 1968), vol. VI, pp. 62–63.

See page 143. 24. I owe much to Hegel's discussion of the universal and the particular, which ranks as the single greatest achievement of his philosophy. See *Wissenschaft der Logik, Sämtliche Werke,* vol. V, pp. 35–65. The origin of the view of universals and particulars I outline is perhaps Aristotle's doctrine of the determination of matter by form, and the related idea of the change of potency into actuality. The particular being is form or essence embodied in matter. Though the form cannot exist apart from matter, it is capable of assuming different embodiments. See *Physics,* bk. 1, ch. 7, §189b, 1. 30–§191a, 1. 22; and bk. 2, ch. 2 §194b, ll. 10–15; *Metaphysics,* bk. 13, ch. 9, §1086a–ch. 10, §1087a.

CHAPTER 4 *The Theory of the Welfare-Corporate State*

See page 150.   1. On the homology between order and consciousness, see Émile Durkheim and Marcel Mauss, "De quelques formes primitives de classification," §5, *L'Année Sociologique* (1901–1902), vol. V, p. 67. Note that, unlike these authors, I reject the view that order determines consciousness. One cannot hold that view and maintain at the same time that the relation among the elements of a social order is one of common meaning. For a similar argument with different intentions, see Claude Lévi-Strauss, *Le Totémisme Aujourd'hui* (Paris, Presses Universitaires, 1962), pp. 131–139.

See page 151.   2. For the seventeenth century preparation of the liberal state, see E. J. Hobsbawn, *The Crisis of the Seventeenth Century,* in *Crisis in Europe, 1560–1660,* ed. T. Aston (Garden City, Anchor, 1967), pp. 5–62.

See page 152.   3. On the relationship between the dominant and antagonistic types of consciousness, particularly with regard to the working classes, see generally Raymond Williams, *Culture and Society, 1780–1950* (New York, Harper, 1966); E. P. Thompson, *The Making of the English Working Classes* (New York, Vintage, 1963), pp. 401–447; Perry Anderson, *Origins of the Present Crisis,* in *Towards Socialism,* eds. P. Anderson and R. Blackburn (Ithaca, Cornell, 1966), pp. 11–52; Louis Chevalier, *Classes Laborieuses et Classes Dangereuses à Paris pendant la première moitié du XIX Siècle* (Plon, 1958); W. C. McWilliams, *The Idea of Fraternity in America* (Berkeley, California, 1973).

See page 153.   4. For discussions of the relation between the beliefs in cosmic order and in social hierarchy in two different contexts, see Joseph Needham, *Science and Civilisation in China* (Cambridge, Cambridge, 1969), vol. II, pp. 530–543; Louis Dumont, *Homo Hierarchichus* (Gallimard, 1966). See also Samuel Eisenstadt, "Religious Organizations and Political Process in Centralized Empires," *Journal of Asian Studies* (1962), vol. XXI, pp. 271–294.

See page 153. 5. For a classic statement of the conception of instrumental rationality, see Max Weber, *Wirtschaft und Gesellschaft*, ch. 1, §2, ed. J. Winckelmann (Tübingen, Mohr, 1972), p. 13. See also Max Horkheimer, *Eclipse of Reason* (New York, Seabury, 1974), pp. 3–57

See page 155. 6. There is a close link between this conception of individualism and Durkheim's view of the "anomic division of labor." See *De la Division du Travail Social*, bk. 3, ch. 1 (Paris, Alcan, 1922), pp. 343–365.

See page 156. 7. See Schopenhauer, *Parerga und Paralipomena*, vol. II, §396, ed. P. Deussen, *Sämtliche Werke* (Munich, Piper, 1913), vol. V, p. 717.

See page 156. 8. For the narrower idea of the division of labor, see Adam Smith, *The Wealth of Nations*, bk. 1, ch. 1 (London, Strahan, 1784), pp. 6–19. For the broader view, see Émile Durkheim, *De la Division du Travail Social*, Introduction, p. 2.

See page 156. 9. See Karl Marx, *Ökonomisch-Philosophische Manuskripte*, no. 1, *Marx-Engels Werke* (Berlin, Dietz, 1968), *Ergänzungsband*, pt. 1, pp. 510–523.

See page 157. 10. On the conception of transcendence, see Martin Heidegger, *Sein und Zeit* (Tübingen, Niemeyer, 1953), p. 49; Paul Tillich, *Systematic Theology* (Chicago, Chicago, 1967), vol. I, p. 263; Gordon Kaufman, "Transcendence without Mythology," *Harvard Theological Review* (1966), vol. LIX, pp. 105–132.

See page 157. 11. See Émile Durkheim, preface to *L'Année Sociologique* (1899), vol. II, pp. iv–v.

See page 158. 12. See Werner Jaeger, *Die Theologie der frühen griechischen Denker* (Stuttgart, Kohlhammer, 1953).

See page 159. 13. On the polarity of immanence and transcendence as an axis in the history of religious philosophy, see Harry Wolfson, *Philo* (Cambridge, Harvard, 1968), vol. II, pp. 439–460, and *Spinoza and the Religion of the Past*, in *Religious Philosophy* (Cambridge, Harvard, 1961), pp. 246–269. On the importance of the polarity to the history of religion, see Robert Bellah, *Religious Evolution*, in *Beyond Belief* (New York, Harper, 1970), pp. 20–50. On the dialectical relation between immanence and transcendence, see Bernard Lonergan, *Method in Theology* (New York, Herder, 1972), pp. 110–112. See also Theodor

Adorno, *Negative Dialektik* (Frankfurt, Suhrkamp, 1970), pp. 102–112.

See page 159. 14. (A) On the conception of the sacred and the profane, see Émile Durkheim, *Les Formes Élémentaires de la Vie Religieuse,* ch. 1, §3 (Paris, Presses Universitaires, 1968), pp. 50–56. It is a major defect of Durkheim's theory of religion to reduce all religiosity to the immanent type, thus mistaking the religious consciousness for one of its parts and misunderstanding the part because of his failure to see its place in the whole.

(B) On the early manifestation of the problem of transcendence, see Godfrey Lienhardt, *Divinity and Experience. The Religion of the Dinka* (Oxford, Clarendon, 1970), pp. 28–55.

See page 159. 15. The relation between transcendence and instrumentalism is a major theme in Weber's *Die protestantische Ethik und der Geist des Kapitalismus.* See particularly *Gesammelte Aufsätze zur Religionssoziologie* (Tübingen, Mohr, 1963), vol. I, pp. 84–163.

See page 160. 16. For an alternative and more detailed account of the relation between individualism and transcendence, see Guy E. Swanson, *Religion and Regime* (Ann Arbor, Michigan, 1967).

See page 161. 17. See Karl Marx, *Zur Judenfrage, Werke,* vol. I, pp. 347–377, 487.

See page 161. 18. See Émile Durkheim, "Le dualisme de la nature humaine et ses conditions sociales," *Scientia* (1914), vol. XV, pp. 206–221.

See page 164. 19. For the conception of estates, see the discussion in Marc Bloch, *La Société Féodale* (Paris, 1939–1940), especially vol. IV, pt. 6; and Otto Hintze, *Feudalismus, Kapitalismus,* ed. A. Oestreich (Göttingen, Vandenhoek, 1970). Note that both the *Encyclopédie* and Hegel's *Grundlinien der Philosophie des Rechts,* §301, follow a settled tradition when they use the concept of estate solely to describe organized groups with political representation.

See page 165. 20. The conception of class with which I am working is similar to the one advanced by Weber in *Wirtschaft und Gesellschaft,* pt. 1, ch. 4, p. 177. It is therefore much narrower than the alternative view of class as a conflict group "generated by the differential distribution of authority" that Ralf Dahrendorf suggests in *Class and Class Conflict in Industrial Society* (Stanford, Stanford, 1969), p. 204. Its relation to Marxist class theory is more difficult to determine. The following points should be kept in mind.

(A) Membership in a class requires consciousness as well as an objective relationship to the distribution of wealth and power. For the development of this view, see the unfinished ch. 52 of *Das Kapital;* and *Der Achtzehnte Brumarire des Louis Bonaparte, Werke,* vol. VIII, p. 198; Antonio Gramsci, *Quaderni del Carcere,* pt. 1 (Rome, Riunti, 1971), vol. I, pp. 46–47. On the polemical character of the concept of class, see Asa Briggs, *The Language of 'Class' in Early Nineteenth-Century England,* in *Essays in Labor History,* eds. A. Briggs and J. Saville (London, Macmillan, 1967), pp. 43–73.

(B) I deny that the principle of class has always been the preeminent organizing principle of historical societies; that even its 'objective' aspects can be adequately defined by the relationship of individuals to the 'means of production'; and that its workings in liberal society can be understood without reference to a contrasting principle of role.

(C) As long as the critique of liberal thought is not carried through to its last conclusions, it will be impossible to clarify the tie between reflection and existence, consciousness and order, and this is just as true in the theory of class as in other fields of study. Hence, Marx is unable to dispel the ambiguity that plagues his view of class and reappears on a broader scale throughout his entire doctrine. Should the relation among elements of the social order, among classes, and among individuals within a class be conceived in a causal-deterministic or in some alternative ('dialectical,' 'structural') manner? And what is the connection between the two kinds of accounts? This issue, the methodological face of the metaphysical problem of the order of ideas and the order of events, runs through modern social thought. It reappears, for example, in Freud's work as a dualism between a causal-deterministic and a symbolic or 'hermeneutic' view of the way psychic events are linked together. See Paul Ricoeur, *De l'Interprétation. Essai sur Freud* (Paris, Seuil, 1965), pp. 79–119, and Jürgen Habermas, *Erkenntnis und Interesse*

(Frankfurt, Suhrkamp, 1971), pp. 332–364. Once again, the difficulty is twofold: to determine the relationship between a causal type of explanation and an alternative mode; and to define precisely what the alternative is. We have many metaphors to describe the latter, but no real account.

See page 165. 21. (A) It is basic to the principle of role that each individual be seen and treated as a 'bundle of qualities' that are pertinent to the performance of specific tasks. See S. F. Nadel, *The Theory of Social Structure* (London, Cohen, 1969), pp. 20–25; and Robert Merton, *Social Theory and Social Structure* (Glencoe, Free Press, 1959), pp. 368–380.

(B) There is an important connection between the classic liberal theory that the world has no structure except the one we give it by naming and the view that social relations and personality are both defined by the assignment of roles. The idea of the connection is implicit in Pareto's treatment of the use of symbolic designations by elites. See *Trattato di Sociologia Generale,* §§2035–2037 (Milan, Comunità, 1964), vol. II, pp. 531–533.

(C) The role is defined by the expectations of others, which both predict and demand conduct. It is therefore foreign to the distinction between factual regularities of conduct and rules that prescribe how one ought to behave. This distinction would mean a surrender to the liberal contrast of fact and value, and would fail to do justice to an important characteristic of the realm of mind.

See page 167. 22. (A) See Norman Birnbaum, *The Crisis of Industrial Society* (New York, Oxford, 1969), pp. 3–40; Peter Blau and Otis Duncan, *The American Occupational Structure* (New York, Wiley, 1967), pp. 401–441; Lucien Goldman, *Reflections on "History and Class Consciousness,"* in *Aspects of History and Class Consciousness,* ed. I. Mézáros (London, Routledge, 1971), pp. 79–84; Stanislaw Ossowski, *Class Structure in the Social Consciousness,* trans. S. Patterson (New York, Free Press, 1963), pp. 100–118; Anthony Giddens, *The Class Structure of the Advanced Societies* (New York, Harper, 1973), pp. 282–294.

(B) On the debate about the actual erosion of the principle of class in the United States, see Simon Kuznets, *Shares of Upper Income Groups in Income and Savings*

(New York, National Bureau of Economic Research, 1953); Gabriel Kolko, *Wealth and Power in America* (New York, Praeger, 1962).

(C) The idea of a class defined by the occupation of the same or similar roles has some analogies to Weber's conception of the "status group." See the appendix to John Goldthorpe and David Lockwood, "Affluence and the British Class Structure," *Sociological Review* (1963), vol. II, pp. 133–163.

See page 167. 23. See Karl Marx, *Grundrisse der Kritik der politischen Ökonomie* (Frankfurt, Europäische Verlagsanstalt), pp. 75–76.

See page 167. 24. For the classic conception of despotism as the denial of the impersonality of rules, see Montesquieu, *De l'Esprit des Lois,* bk. 3, ch. 9, *Oeuvres Complètes,* ed. R. Caillois (Pléiade, 1966), vol. II, pp. 258–259.

See page 169. 25. See Alvin W. Gouldner, *Patterns of Industrial Bureaucracy* (New York, Free Press, 1964), pp. 164–166.

See page 170. 26. See Max Weber, *Wirtschaft und Gesellschaft,* pt. 2, ch. 9, §2, especially pp. 551–556.

See page 171. 27. See Michel Crozier, *Le Phénomène Bureaucratique* (Paris, Seuil, 1963), pp. 247–250.

See page 171. 28. For an example of these developments, see Eckart Kehr, *Zur Genesis der preussischen Bürokratie und des Rechtstaats,* in *Moderne deutsche Sozialgeschichte,* ed. H.-U. Wehler (Cologne, Kiepenheuer, 1973), pp. 37–54; and Hans Rosenberg, *Bureaucracy, Aristocracy, and Autocracy* (Boston, Beacon, 1968).

See page 172. 29. See Robert Michels, *Zur Soziologie des Parteiwesens in der modernen Demokratie* (Leipzig, Klinkhardt, 1911), pp. 362–381.

See page 175. 30. The conception of a second stage of liberal capitalist society with features that call for the revision of classical social theory has been made current through the writings of two main categories of authors:

(A) The neoliberal students of 'postindustrial' or 'technological' society, more or less anxious to show that Marx has been overtaken by events (e.g., Aron, Bell, Boulding, Brzezinski, Ellul, Galbraith, Touraine, etc.).

(B) The neo-Marxist theoreticians, who seek to review Marx's doctrines in the light of alleged developments such as the increasing interpenetration of "superstructure" and "base," the place occupied in the modern state by the production of knowledge, and the appearance of new working, service, and professional classes (e.g., Horkheimer, Adorno, Habermas, Wellmer, etc.). Both groups tend toward a certain unity of perspective, which is closely linked to the ethos of bureaucratic service I describe later. They are indeed the theoreticians of Hegel's "universal class."

See page 177. 31. See Martin Sklar, "On the Proletarian Revolution and the End of Political-Economic Society," *Radical America* (1969), vol. III, pp. 1–41.

See page 186. 32. For a different though parallel line of argument, see Vittorio Foa, "I socialisti e il sindicato," *Problemi del Socialismo* (March 1963), vol. VI, pp. 718–730; and André Gorz, *Stratégie Ouvrière et Néocapitalisme* (Paris, Seuil, 1964), pp. 44–54.

See page 186. 33. See John Dawson, "Economic Duress," *Michigan Law Review* (1946–1947), vol. XLV, pp. 253–290.

See page 187. 34. On the conception and the political significance of substantive justice, see Max Weber, *Wirtschaft und Gesellschaft,* pt. 2, ch. 7, §8, pp. 505–509;' Émile Durkheim, *Leçons de Sociologie: Physique des Moeurs et du Droit,* lesson 18 (Paris, Presses Universitaires, 1950), pp. 244–259; Rudolph von Jhering, *Geist des römischen Rechts,* §29 (Basel, Schwabe, 1954), vol. II–1, pp. 88–97.

See page 188. 35. For fascism as an extreme example of the association of pure immanence with hierarchic community, see Ernst Nolte, *Der Faschismus in seiner Epoche* (Munich, Piper, 1963), pp. 515–521.

CHAPTER 5 *The Theory of the Self*

See page 192. 1. Jean-Jacques Rousseau, *Lettres Écrites de la Montagne,* preface, *Oeuvres Complètes,* eds. B. Gagnebin and M. Raymond (Gallimard, 1964), vol. III, p. 686.

See page 194. 2. For a modern version of the conflict between the suprahistorical and the historicist view of human nature, see Robert Redfield, "The Anthropological Understanding of Man," *Anthropological Quarterly,* vol. XXXII, no. 1 (1959), pp. 3–21; and Clifford Geertz, *The Impact of the Concept of Culture on the Concept of Man,* in *The*

Interpretation of Cultures (New York, Basic Books, 1973), pp. 33–54.

See page 199. 3. For the statement of the theory of the self, I have found special guidance in Plato's *Symposium,* Aristotle's *Ethics,* Aquinas' *Summa Theologica* (pt. 1, questions 75–102 and pt. I–II, questions 1–70), Descartes' *Les Passions de l'Âme,* Spinoza's *Ethica,* Hegel's early theological writings and his *Vorlesungen über die Philosophie der Religion,* and Marx's *Ökonomisch-Philosophische Manuskripte.*

See page 200. 4. See Friedrich Hölderlin, *Über Urtheil und Seyn, Sämtliche Werke,* ed. F. Beissner (Stuttgart, Kohlhammer, 1961), vol. IV, pp. 216–217.

See page 201. 5. See Maurice Merleau-Ponty, *Éloge de la Philosophie* (Gallimard, 1960), pp. 41–73.

See page 201. 6. Generalizing science may provide explanations for why we experience particulars as we do, but it still superimposes another knowledge upon the nonscientific understanding (i.e., perception, intuition, comprehension) of particulars.

See page 203. 7. See Henri Bergson, *L'Évolution Créatrice,* ch. 2, *Oeuvres,* ed. A. Robinet (Paris, Presses Universitaires, 1970), p. 613.

See page 204. 8. The very notion of an absolute and timeless knowledge presupposes the eye of a timeless and absolute being. Thinkers who claim mankind can reach such knowledge (e.g., Spinoza, Hegel) must, if they are coherent, deny the finitude of humanity and the separation of the self from the world. On the other hand, those who postulate that 'things-in-themselves' exist but are unknowable to us (e.g., Kant) suppose that we can affirm the existence of 'things-in-themselves' without being able to say anything else of them. But existence can be known only through its signs in experience. To talk about 'things-in-themselves' is to refer to a possible divine knowledge. The two kinds of error regarding the 'thing-in-itself' result from the attempt to treat a problem primarily about God in His transcendent, absolute, and timeless character as if it were a problem directly about man. When this attempt is made, either man must be taken for God or philosophy must dream up a reality hidden underneath the world of appearance. Thus, there is a close link between the rationalist claim to make the world transparent to the mind and the mystical denial of the self's separation from the world. This link is brought out in the philosophies of Spinoza and Hegel.

See page 206. 9. See Friedrich Schiller, *Über die Ästhetische Erziehung des Menschen,* letter 11, *Sämtliche Werke* (Munich, Winkler, 1968), vol. V, pp. 341–344.

See page 208. 10. On the conception of teleology in conduct, see Nicolai Hartmann, *Ethik* (Berlin, Gruyter, 1962), pp. 192–194. On teleology in work, see Georg Lukács, *Ontologie-Arbeit* (Neuwied, Luchterhand, 1973), pp. 11–60.

See page 212. 11. See Georg Simmel, *Der Begriff und die Tragödie der Kultur,* in *Das individuelle Gesetz* (Frankfurt, Suhrkamp, 1969), p. 116.

See page 213. 12. For a different view, see Alfred Schmidt, *Der Begriff der Natur in der Lehre von Marx* (Europäische Verlagsanstalt, 1962).

See page 214. 13. On the doctrine of man as a 'species being,' see Kant, *Idee zu einer allgemeinen Geschichte in weltbürgerlicher Absicht, Kants Werke,* ed. Prussian Academy (Berlin, Gruyter, 1968), vol. VIII, pp. 18–19; *Anthropologie in Pragmatischer Hinsicht,* 2E, *Werke,* vol. VII, pp. 321–333; Marx, *Ökonomisch-Philosophische Manuskripte,* no. 3, *Marx-Engels Werke* (Berlin, Dietz, 1968), *Ergänzungsband,* pt. I, pp. 535–536.

See page 216. 14. The cognitive aspect of the paradox of sociability recalls the 'other minds' debate in contemporary Anglo-American philosophy. This issue is intimately associated with the moral problem of recognition and with the way in which sanity and madness are defined. The relationship among the topics is brought out when they are placed in the setting of a more general theory of the self.

See page 216. 15. On the problems of recognition or honor, see Montesquieu, *De l'Esprit des Lois,* bk. 3, ch. 7, *Oeuvres Complètes,* ed. R. Caillois (Pléiade, 1966), p. 257; Jeremy Bentham, *An Introduction to the Principles of Morals and Legislation,* ch. 5, sec. 7, eds. J. H. Burns and H. L. A. Hart (London, Athlone, 1970), p. 44; Hegel on the dialectic of the master and the slave, *Phänomenologie des Geistes, Sämtliche Werke,* ed. H. Glockner (Stuttgart, Fromman, 1927), vol. II, pp. 148–158.

See page 220. 16. See Hegel's fragment on love in *Hegels Theologische Jugendschriften,* ed. H. Nohl (Tübingen, Mohr, 1907), pp. 378–382. For an opposite view, which brings out the paradox of sociability, see Sigmund Freud. *Massenpsychologie und Ich-Analyse,* ch. 4, *Gesammelte Schriften* (Leipzig, Internationaler Psychoanalytischer Verlag, 1925), vol. VI, pp. 286–288.

See page 220. 17. For a discussion of some of these doctrines of sympathy, see Max Scheler, *Wesen und Formen der Sympathie* (Frankfurt, Schulte-Bulmke, 1948).

See page 222. 18. For a distinction similar to that of the abstract and the concrete self, see Hegel, *Vorlesungen über die Philosophie der Religion, Sämtliche Werke,* vol. XVI, pp. 259–260.

See page 224. 19. See John Rawls, *A Theory of Justice* (Cambridge, Harvard, 1971), pp. 522–525 and his note 4, p. 523.

See page 233. 20. See Clement Greenberg, *Art and Culture* (Boston, Beacon, 1969), pp. 22–23.

CHAPTER 6 *The Theory of Organic Groups*

See page 241. 1. The idea of an existing universal consensus on basic values was a mainstay of the *ius publicum naturale* of the seventeenth and eighteenth centuries. For a contemporary counterpart, see H. Laswell and A. Kaplan, *Power and Society* (New Haven, Yale, 1950), pp. 55–73; and M. McDougal, "International Law, Power, and Policy: A Contemporary Conception," *Recueil des Cours, Académie de Droit International,* pt. 1 (1953), vol. LXXXII, pp. 188–191.

See page 250. 2. For a statement of the doctrine of conservative corporativism, see Louis de Bonald, *Oeuvres Complètes de M. de Bonald* (Paris, 1864), vol. I, especially p. 262. Institutionalist and fascist theories are latter-day variants of this doctrine, quite different from each other. For an example of the former, see Georges Renard, *La Théorie de l'Institution* (Paris, Sirey, 1930). For an example of the latter, see Alfredo Rocco, *La Transformazione dello Stato dallo Stato Liberale allo Stato Fascista* (Rome, La Voce, 1927), pp. 327–355.

See page 251. 3. Fourier is representative of the utopian theorists of community to whom I refer.

See page 255. 4. For the classical distinction among the lives of contemplation, political practice, and enjoyment, see Aristotle,

Magna Moralia, bk. 1, ch. 3, §1184b, l. 5; and *Nicomachean Ethics,* bk. 1, ch. 5, §1095b, l. 14–§1096, l. 10. For a view closer to my own, see the contrast of analysis and intuition in Henri Bergson, *Introduction à la Métaphysique, Oeuvres,* ed. A. Robinet (Paris, Presses Universitaires, 1970), pp. 1395–1396.

See page 270.   5. See Jean-Jacques Rousseau, *Discours sur l'Origine et les Fondements de l'Inégalité parmi les Hommes,* pt. 1, *Oeuvres Complètes,* eds. B. Gagnebin and M. Raymond (Pléiade, 1966), vol. III, p. 161.

See page 271.   6. Johann Wolfgang von Goethe, *Maximen und Reflexionen, Gedenksausgabe,* ed. E. Beutler (Zurich, Artemis, 1949), vol. IX, p. 503.

See page 271.   7. See Karl Marx, *Kritik des Gothaer Programms, Marx-Engels Werke* (Berlin, Dietz, 1962), vol. XIX, pp. 20–22.

See page 272.   8. (A) For the socialist theory of institutional democracy, see Antonio Gramsci, *L'Ordine Nuovo, 1919–1920, Opere di Antonio Gramsci* (Turin, Einaudi, 1954), vol. I; Karl Korsch, *Arbeitsrecht für Betriebsräte* (Berlin, Frankes, 1922); Svetozar Stojanović, *Between Ideals and Reality,* trans. G. Shei (New York, Oxford, 1973), pp. 115–134; Mihailo Marković, *From Affluence to Praxis* (Ann Arbor, Michigan, 1974), pp. 209–243.

(B) For an example of the concern with minimal needs in late liberal legal thought, see Frank Michelman, foreword, *Harvard Law Review* (1969–1970), vol. LXXXIII, pp. 9–19.

See page 275.   9. See Georg Simmel, *Soziologie* (Leipzig, Duncker, 1908), pp. 228–229.

See page 276.   10. For the related hypothesis that differences in the roles performed by husband and wife become less disruptive of the family insofar as the persons with whom husband and wife deal associate more closely with each other, see Elizabeth Bott, *Family and Social Network* (New York, Free Press, 1971), pp. 59–61.

See page 282.   11. See Émile Durkheim, *Leçons de Sociologie: Physique des Moeurs et du Droit,* lesson 5 (Paris, Presses Universitaires, 1950), pp. 76–78.

See page 283.   12. (A) For a view of the state as a community of communities, see Johannes Althusius, *Politica Methodice Digesta,* ch. 9, §§3–6, ed. C. Friedrich (Cambridge, Harvard, 1932), pp. 88–89.

(B) On the jurisprudential implications of the development of organic groups with respect to the breakdown of the sharp discontinuity between state and individual, see Georges Gurvitch, *L'Idée du Droit Social* (Paris, Sirey, 1932), pp. 15–46; Otto von Gierke, *Das deutsche Genossenschaftsrecht* (Berlin, Wiedmann, 1868–1913), 4 vols.; Eugen Ehrlich, *Grundlegung der Soziologie des Rechts* (Munich, Duncker, 1913), pp. 110–154.

See page 287. 13. See Albert Hirschman, *Exit, Voice, and Loyalty* (Cambridge, Harvard, 1970), p. 83.

See page 292. 14. See Spinoza, *Ethica,* pt. 1, propositions 14, 18, *Spinoza Opera,* ed. C. Gebhardt (Heidelberg, Winter, 1972), vol. II, pp. 56, 63–64, and letter to Oldenburg of November 20, 1665, letter 32, *Spinoza Opera,* vol. IV, pp. 169–176.

INDEX

There are no proper names in this index. The letter *n.,* following a page number, designates a note; *f.,* a figure.